Jeffrey Otto

Salutes for Books by Theodore Zeldin

The French

"More than just funny: it is intelligent, loving, caustic, learned, lively, serious, brilliant."—*Télérama*

"Buying Asterix in English isn't quite enough. Zeldin helps you more."—Paul Barker, *New Society*

"To read Zeldin's book is not to look complacently in the mirror but to discover the Zeldin method. A method that is both disconcerting and salutary, it invites us to see through our prejudices."
—*Elle*

"Zeldin's credentials as a cultural iconoclast are well established. . . . Because [he] believes that jokes and laughter are the most telling indications of the way people think, he includes rich studies of France's top comedians, as well as a wonderful selection of recent cartoons. As the evidence piles up, centuries of inaccurate assumptions melt away."—Scott Sullivan, *Newsweek*

A History of French Passions

"Truly a work of genius."—*The New Republic*

"A masterpiece."—*The New York Times*

"He is a modern Balzac."—*Boston Evening Globe*

An Intimate History of Humanity

"An intellectually dazzling view of our past and future."—*Time*

"No short review can do justice to the richness, humor, humanity, and range of this important book."—*Kirkus*

Theodore Zeldin

THE FRENCH

KODANSHA INTERNATIONAL
New York • Tokyo • London

The value of French and other currencies fluctuates so frequently, that the conversion of francs into pounds and dollars cannot be accurate, and is here done only very approximately, as a rough guide.

Kodansha America, Inc.
114 Fifth Avenue, New York, New York 10011, U.S.A.

Kodansha International Ltd.
17-14 Otowa 1-chome, Bunkyo-ku, Tokyo 112, Japan

Published in 1996 by Kodansha America, Inc. by arrangement with the author.

Originally published in Great Britain by William Collins Sons & Co. Ltd., London. First published in the United States by Pantheon Books, a division of Random House, Inc., New York, in 1982.

This is a Kodansha Globe book.

CARTOON COPYRIGHT ACKNOWLEDGMENTS
Dargaud Editeur Paris for cartoons from Lauzier's *Les Cadres* (1981) and from Fred's *Le Fond de l'air est frais* (1973); Editions André Balland for cartoons from Chenez, *Dessins du Monde* (1977), Gourmelin, *Pour tuer le temps* (1972) and Siné, *La Chienlit c'est moi* (1978); le Cherche Midi Editeur, for a cartoon from *Siné dans Charlie Hebdo* (1981); Editions Arthaud for cartoons from Piem, *A la petite semaine* (1975); Editions Jacques Glénat for cartoons from Serre, *Le Sport* (1980); *L'Automobile* (1978) and *Humour noir et hommes en blanc* (1980); *Le Nouvel Observateur*, for one cartoon from Bretécher's *Les Frustrés* (1975–80); *L'Etudiant* and the artists, for the cartoons of Plantu in *Les Lycéens* (1980) and Mathieu in *Les Grandes Ecoles* (1979); Alain Moreau, publisher of Plantu, *La Democratie? Parlons-en* (1979), for one cartoon; Intermonde Presse for Gad, *Y a plus d'enfants* (1974); Le Parisien-Libéré for Alain Saint-Ogan; Quipos, Milan, for Quino, *La Buena Mesa* (1981) (*A Table* in French); Mme Christiane Charillon, for Sempé, Faizant and Chaval's cartoons; M. Jean Dubout for his father's cartoons; and finally, but by no means least, all the individual cartoonists who gave permission to reproduce drawings of which they personally own the copyright.

Library of Congress Cataloging-in-Publication Data

Zeldin, Theodore, 1933–
    The French / Theodore Zeldin.
    p.   cm. — (Kodansha globe)
    Includes bibliographical references and index.
    ISBN 1-56836-157-2 (pb)
    1. National characteristics, French.   I. Title.   II. Series.
DC34.Z45   1996
305.8'41—dc20   96-34603

Printed in the United States of America

97 98 99 00 RRD/H 10 9 8 7 6 5 4 3 2

Contents

Part One

Why it is hard to meet an Average French Person

1

How to avoid Seeing the Sights

The 'average Frenchman' is often known today as Monsieur Dupont or Monsieur Durand. Durand means obstinate. John Bull, according to the Larousse Encyclopaedia, is 'the nickname given to the English people to indicate their obstinacy'. It may be more than a coincidence, for national stereotypes are concerned with obstinacy, and there are no opinions that survive more obstinately than those about national character. The first aim of this book is to show why people still believe they can sum up the French in a phrase or an epigram, and what absurdities follow.

The typical Frenchman is a joke, and jokes, to me, are an important part of life. Comedians and humorists are worth listening to at least as much as pundits and politicians, for it is nearly always the jester who blurts out the truth that no one likes to admit. I believe that nothing separates people more than their sense of humour. How people laugh, with whom they laugh and at whom, and when they stop laughing, reveals more about the real barriers and complexities among them than all the statistics in the world. You only understand a person when you know how far you can go without offending him: to understand foreigners, you need to be acquainted not only with their particular Holy Book, but also with their Dictionary of Insults. But French humour is not as well known outside France as is French cooking, wine or elegance. I wanted to know why that was so, which got me interested in French caricature.

The frontiers of laughter do not, in fact, coincide with national boundaries. The latter divide people according to some of their loyalties and customs, but not according to the ambitions they have, or what makes them happy, or angry, or how they treat their work mates, their friends, their children, their lovers, or how they resist the restrictions imposed on them by bureaucrats and employers, or what they believe and disbelieve. It is these sorts of questions that interest me. If only as much were known about human passions as is known about the production of grain or the sales of soap, world maps could be drawn showing the regional distribution of attitudes and temperaments, fears and hopes, and where one finds the people who

Grandville

can laugh at the same joke. I should like to know where the really impregnable frontiers between people are to be found.

To talk about a nation normally means identifying the way in which it differs from other nations. That begs the question of just how like one another people are within a nation; that to me is the necessary starting point. I am interested above all in the French as individuals, in discovering what they know about the art of life, what pleasures they extract from their existence. If they all gave one answer, there would not be much to say. But they do not. The French joke does not cease to be funny once it is explained, because it dissolves into an unending series of riddles. All human passions can be seen at play in France, which means that to recognize the French is to recognize something in oneself, also. The French probably have more interesting things to say about what it means to be human, than what it means to be French.

I am interested by international misunderstandings in their subtlest forms, by the inability of people to tune into each other's wavelength. French people often feel that they are misunderstood by foreigners, that they are insufficiently appreciated, unloved. They are quite right. Foreigners undoubtedly love France as a place, as a beautiful country, but they do not on the whole like the French as a people. This is particularly true of the English-speaking world. The British visit France more than they visit any other foreign country; over a third of them have been to France; but only 2% say they admire the French and very few indeed would like to live among them. Opinion polls regularly find that the British mistrust the French almost as much as they do the Russians, and this mistrust is not diminishing. It is not just that the British do not like foreigners; on the contrary, there are other nations we do admire, and that despite having fought wars against them. The Americans, who do not have the British handicap of having been traditional enemies of France for centuries, generally feel they have little in common with the country that once helped them in their War of Independence. They can seldom speak French. Whereas Germans and Italians, for example, have expressed great interest in France's new socialism, if not always enthusiasm for it, the vast majority of both Americans and Britons did not seem to have heard of President Mitterrand several months after his election, and could think of no opinion to express about him. Why is it that the French mystify or irritate so many people, and make such a superficial impression on the rest? They provide an interesting lesson in public relations, in the art of making friends and influencing people.

The French have devoted enormous efforts to explaining

themselves. No nation has tried harder to find and express its identity, none has looked in the mirror so hard, argued so much about what it sees in it, persisted in imagining wrinkles that are not there and worried as to whether the line of its mouth appears as a sneer or a smile. Their state publisher has just issued a large and learned volume entitled, *Frenchmen, Who Are You?* But it gives no clear answer. It may be that all these attempts to show how they are special defeat their purpose. The search for the essential Frenchman plays into the hands of the traditional foreign tourist, whose favourite game is to spot how typically French the French are.

The stereotype thus lives on inextinguishably, turning out to be a hoax that the French play on foreigners, so successfully that they are taken in by it themselves. If you are a foreigner, you will be quite rightly told that you can never know them properly; but if you are a Frenchman you can never understand yourself fully. Does this mean that agreement can never be reached as to the sort of people they are, and that there will always be this conflict between their self-image and the opinion of outsiders? I have tried to find out whether it is possible to steer between these two rocks. The fact that I have devoted my whole adult life to studying the French does not mean that I can claim to be qualified to do so. On the contrary, most admirers of France are so in love with the country that they are quite unfit to act as impartial judges of it; they are sometimes even more Francophile than the French. It needs a man from Mars to see both sides. Perhaps I have something of the Martian in me. Not that I have any illusions about being impartial: even a Martian has his prejudices, his tastes and his blind spots. But I am interested in discovering whether it is possible to question the assumptions of both the French and foreigners at the same time.

There is nothing unusual in a country being held in suspicion or dislike by foreigners, particularly when that country dreams of being powerful and influential. Discrimination on the grounds of race, sex and religion are all now discredited, but discrimination on the ground of nationality is written into the laws of every land. A new nation is born almost every year precisely because more and more people regard each other as foreigners. Technology has made it easy to cross national frontiers physically, but there has been no invention of new mental habits to enable people to cope with foreigners in a new way. For that to happen, the habits of tourists will have to alter. The hidden god of travel is still Karl Baedeker, even though he died in 1859. His guide books have set a permanent pattern, making travel essentially a matter of sightseeing, looking at places rather than at people. His achievement was to find sights that could be guaranteed to be there all the time, to be clearly identifiable, dated and classified according to the amount of admiration they deserved. He made visits to old monuments and to art museums the staple diet of the traveller, drawing attention away from the living inhabitants. To this day, tourism is a course in history, architecture, aesthetics, and the appreciation of hotels and food. The cult of 'sights' has grown so much that most foreign (organized) travel involves virtually no contact with the natives, beyond those who specialize in catering for tourists. The business traveller tends to meet mainly people in his own profession. How different from the itinerary of a modern package holiday is this programme, drawn up by an Englishman, Sir Francis Head, in 1852, before the guide books told tourists what to do. In Paris, he visited the municipal pawnshop, the asylum for blind youths, where Braille, still unknown in England, was being used, a prison, an orphanage for abandoned children, the Salpetrière old people's home, the morgue, the national printing works, the military academy, the national assembly, the public laundry, the dog market in the rue Poliveau and the horses at the Etoile, and finally he attended the lectures at the Conservatory for Arts and Crafts. The rise of bureaucratic officialdom soon stopped that kind of curiosity; but perhaps today a new openness will allow it to express itself again. In former times, the attraction of foreign travel was often that people did abroad what they dared not do at home, which is why foreign countries won reputations for sexual debauchery. (The French considered England as debauched as the English visitors to the Folies Bergères imagined the French to be.) But now that a visit to France is no longer a dangerous adventure, and that an international uniformity exists in so many of the goods and facilities the tourist encounters, where is the excitement, where the new discoveries?

It is to be found in the people. The foreignness in foreign travel today must come mainly from meeting individuals whom one would not normally meet at home. I say nothing about old monuments in this book; instead I have investigated living individuals; each, to me, is a monument. I have not tried to fit them all into a simple pattern of national character. Each individual is interesting because he has a different story to tell; in the experience of each there is a record of a way of life personally created, of choices made, of hopes triumphing over small obstacles as well as large disasters, and an exception to every rule. The Frenchman, says an old Fodor's *Guide to France*, is an iceberg nine-tenths of whose emotions are hidden under water: that may be an excuse for dismissing him as unfathomable, but those emotions are what I want to understand.

I have not sought to write a comprehensive survey of the French nation, even if such a thing were possible. I offer only my own particular vision or experience of it: anyone who claims he can offer more than that is deluding himself. I hope only to incite my readers to form their own independent vision, instead of repeating the hackneyed myths, and to reflect on precisely what they find attractive or repellent in the French (or perhaps in humans in general). I hope my selection is broad enough to enable the Francophile to recognize the limits of his admiration, and the Francophobe to find a hint of merit in at least some of the characters I present. But these characters are not to be taken as typical representatives of groups: I could have gone on endlessly adding other quite different examples, ideally 54 million of them. There are many occupations, relationships and states of mind which interest me but which I have deliberately not discussed. I could promise the reader many sequels to cover them, but I shall not, because I believe it would be more useful to treat them in the future more generally, not tied to a specific national context, but rather as part of an investigation of 'human nature', and of the assumption that it never changes. For me, this book represents an exploration of the value and limitations of discussing people in terms of their national allegiance.

One of the attractions for a historian of writing about the present is that he can create new sources. I have used the same kind of material here as in my previous work – all sorts of erudite monographs, journalism, magazines, memoirs, government publications, statistics (unbelievable, plausible or just amusing): the most valuable are listed in the bibliography. But in addition I sought out men, women and children who could tell me more. When I invited them to speak their autobiographies, I sometimes got the changeless patter that people offer strangers, like advertising handouts, which they may even believe through frequent repetition; but a surprising number were interested in exploring themselves, and responded to unexpected and personal questions with real efforts to work out what they felt more deeply. There is a new self consciousness which is giving rise to a new literary genre, the assisted autobiography, in which authors act as midwives to help those who want to tell their story. Every reflective person is a historian, in that he has a view of his own life; that may be truer than the more common saying that every imaginative person has at least one novel inside him.

I quickly discovered that the more famous a person is, the less he usually has to say that is interesting, because he has become

Chaval

something of a gramophone record on the topic of himself, and because he is surrounded by public relations officers whose task is to limit his relations with the public, and the time he gives to each task; but there are exceptions, and it takes some effort, or luck, to find them. On the other hand, doors which seem firmly locked turn out to be open if one knocks: the communists, for example, allowed me to attend their Central Party School, and see and hear what I wanted, within a few days of my asking. To get into an old people's home presented problems, because officials, worried by public criticism, have invented all sorts of obstructive regulations; but through the kindness of an ethnologist who put me in touch with a psychiatrist, who knew a hospital doctor, I was eventually offered a completely open choice as to whom I could talk to. A large charitable organization that helps the very poor was unwilling without lengthy negotiation to introduce me to some of its clients, whom it treated almost as private property — 'our poor'; by contrast, it took me only a minute to get a telephone call through to an archbishop, and receive an invitation to visit him. The characters in this book are thus not a 'scientifically selected sample', but people whom I happen to have got to know.

The world is divided into dog lovers and cat lovers: and each group is persuaded of the superiority of their favourite animal. I do not wish to persuade anyone that the French are more worthy of love than other species, because I do not think it is desirable for any nation to be considered more or less worthy, and besides no cat lover has ever been turned into a dog lover by reading a book. My argument is rather that the French are both cats and dogs, and many other things also, and that no one is wholly a stranger in France.

2

How to interpret their regional accents

'I never thought of myself as French, I thought I was human.'
Jean Estebe, a bearded professor at the University of Toulouse,
just turned fifty, local boy made good, has always been a
politically active socialist, and he believes in the brotherhood of
man. But then he visited the USA, and it was there that he
realized that he was French. He had not been affected by his
travels in Italy or Spain, where he had felt at ease, helped no
doubt by the fact that he could understand their languages
better than English. 'But in New York, I felt very French. I
would go into a shop, I would smile, people would not smile
back. I became very uncomfortable. I felt I was ridiculous: it
was as though I had held out my hand and they had not taken it.
I was frightened . . . I was shocked to have to pay to send my
children to school, to have to pay for a doctor. I had thought
before going to America that my being French was of no
importance, but there I discovered that there were many little
details that mattered to me.'

The examples he gives of these details show, however, that it
is not the differences between the two countries that really
bother him: American houses, he says, looked different, they
were not what he was used to, they made him uncomfortable.
But then he feels as though he is in a foreign country when he
visits new French suburbs. Still, in these at least he can find a
bar-tabac, which are virtually identical all over France, and they
make him feel at home again: he loves these *tabacs*, he
sometimes goes to one just for the pleasure, without wanting to
buy anything. He does not really believe that Americans are less
friendly than Frenchmen: on the contrary, he finds them more
generous with their time and their money. New York 'made me

realize that the French are mean, they always economize'; they might appear agreeable on the outside but they were morally inferior to Americans. 'As individuals, Americans are good people, but their institutions are bad.' Estebe accepts that his thoughts are confused, because he is expressing gut reactions he cannot fully explain. Would he have felt differently if he had known the English language better? What gloom made him imagine New Yorkers do not smile? Does he feel really more at ease in France? Not completely; his foreign travels have increasingly made him aware that there are 'aspects of my own country that I despise, that disgust me.' His own brother-in-law, for example. He has never been able to get on with his wife's family, who were of a higher social level than his own. His brother-in-law is a well-to-do notary, who worships success. Estebe laughs at successful people, who flaunt their success with smart cars and well-tailored suits; but his brother-in-law thinks it is right to dress up, 'it is a sign of respectability'. Even among his colleagues at the university, there are those who seem to him to be almost foreigners, the ones who are ambitious for success, who are always busy advancing their careers with new publications, hypocritically acquiring useful acquaintances. 'There is an abyss between them and those who do not like to make so much effort, who are quiet provincials. These two races do not understand each other.'

The paradox is that Estebe is not, deep inside him, a quiet provincial, content with his lot, or at least he reveals what emotions can boil beneath that amiable exterior. He is certainly all that he reproaches his countrymen for not being: he is generous, kind, thoughtful for the welfare of others, ever ready to be helpful. But he regards himself as a failure, eminent professor though he is. He is full of self-doubt beneath his easy-going manner. 'I need to be complimented.' Criticism not only hurts him, 'it confirms me in my poor opinion of myself.' Even friendship, for which he has a natural gift, does not satisfy him; 'I feel that my friends are not interesting, because if they come to see me, there must be something wrong with them. I used to think they came to see my wife. Now [that he is separated] they come to see me even more, but I cannot get over this feeling.' It may be, he speculates, that his doubts come from his mother, who has always been depressive and has ended up an alcoholic: he feels responsible for her decay; visiting her is painful, but he does it regularly and conscientiously, patiently sorting out the petty problems his mother brings on herself. His doubts have been reinforced by the collapse of his marriage. 'I feel my life is wasted, because for twenty-five years I tried to live a family life, and I have failed . . . I am proud that I can admit I am a failure, even if it hurts.' His wife, he says, was tougher than he, she had no idea of the suffering she could cause others. He could not bear her criticism. He easily felt insulted. They used to bicker all the time (though not in public: to outsiders theirs seemed a perfect marriage). Estebe shows that the self-

Grandville

The Café

confident and the doubters, the ambitious and those without hope, are aggressive, and chauvinistic, and French in different ways. But at least France was the one place where Estebe was accepted as he was.

Not quite. Estebe speaks with a marked Toulouse accent. 'I used to be laughed at for my accent; people would listen to the sound of my speech, not to what I said.' So he seized on the Occitan regionalist movement to 'give us our dignity', in the same way as the Women's Liberation Movement has given women a new dignity. Now he says not that he comes 'from the south', but that 'I am an Occitan: that gives me status.' He once hoped that the Occitan movement (which agitates for the recognition of the cultural distinctiveness of the South of France, *alias* Occitanie) would become as important politically as that in neighbouring Catalonia. But he no longer supports it: he admits 'it has not captured the masses.' So though he still has a grudge against those who despise southerners, he now regards himself as a Frenchman, though a Southern Frenchman.

Within those confines, he knows at any rate what the rules of the game are. He has only to go to England to see how important that knowledge is: 'I cannot understand the English at all. I never know what an Englishman will do. If I talk to an Englishman about a personal, intimate subject, I do not know what I am allowed to say, I do not know what is taboo.' To be French is to understand the taboos. But what the French do not know, is how different their taboos are from those of other people: they assume they are, which is odd, because so many of their own taboos are simply old wives' tales.

In Toulouse, Claude Sicre has the reputation of being one of the toughest advocates of Occitan regionalism. To visit him in his simple two-roomed apartment at the rear of a decaying old house in the city centre, to find him busy writing on the kitchen table, is to get a feeling of coming face to face with one of the dark, intrepid, isolated revolutionary theorists of the nineteenth century. Sicre's conversation is like a series of rapid explosions; one expects him to burst into flames from the sheer heat of his eloquence and exuberance; but everything he says is crystal clear and perfectly, logically ordered. He has confronted a whole series of walls of contempt in his life, or perhaps his lucidity has made him more conscious of the confrontation than others are. Born the son of a worker, he won his way into the best school in Toulouse, the Lycée Fermat, only to find that he did not fit; his classmates were largely middle-class; the French literature he was taught did not reflect the problems or feelings of his own background. He became a drop-out, intellectually, while still a boy: he became an addict of American detective novels, comics, films and rock music. He could identify more easily with the culture of the poor and the blacks in America than with the polite, conventional, middle-class French culture that was held up to him for admiration in his school.

As soon as he could, he went off to the United States hitch-hiking for a year in every direction. He did not become a hippy: he disdained that as an escape for middle-class children; he did not want to withdraw from the world. He hoped he might feel at home in America, but he was disappointed. He was immensely attracted by the American sense of being able to do new things, to create; he liked the way they built their own homes, bought a truck and travelled to make their own lives; there was much in common between that attitude and the way the poor workers of Toulouse did things for themselves without any money, their children playing in disused lots just like American blacks playing basketball. 'The self-made man fascinated me. I had a great desire to create, together with my family and friends. But I wanted to do all this at home. I wanted Toulouse to be the United States in France.' Back home he was impressed by the repatriated Algerian Jews who remade their careers so quickly, usually in commerce: 'I feel I had things in common with them too.' As a youth, he identified with almost every disadvantaged minority.

Academic success did not fundamentally alter that, for though he landed a plum job in Paris, as a reader in the prestigious publishing firm of Gallimard, he was quickly made to feel that he was not a real Parisian. One of his jobs was to arrange the translation of American detective stories, and find suitably French titles for them. It was amusing, but he discovered to his amazement that he did not speak the same language as his Parisian colleagues: when it came to slang,

Parisian French was incomprehensible to him, and there was a whole mythology surrounding the Parisian urchin that was meaningless to him. Paris was composed of networks of relationships to which he did not belong: he rejects the idea that a provincial can never succeed in Paris; 'that is a myth to console the mediocre'. But 'it was in Paris that I discovered my difference'. He was constantly reminded that he was an outsider by people who noticed his southern accent and who asked him futile questions about how sunny his homeland was and did he play *pétanque* (to make it worse, his father was indeed a champion in that game). 'I was not like an ordinary provincial worker who feels uncomfortable in Paris. I was among intellectuals. It was they who told me about Occitanie.' At home he had not been brought up to speak the Occitan language. His family had been workers in the city of Toulouse for three generations, they had no links with the peasants, they spoke 'Francitan', French with a sprinkling of 'occitanisms'. It was only in 1976 that he began investigating Oc, but he has refused to learn the language in a scholarly way: he does not like the idea of learning a language from books. He has picked up his knowledge mainly from talking to peasants who have inherited it, and he likes talking to them when he knows them well, but otherwise he avoids speaking it because he cannot speak it properly and above all because he still thinks in French.

Sicre has always wanted to be a writer. His first book was an American-style novel. In America he had been delighted to find self-taught writers who wrote crime stories without pretensions to literature; in France, he believed, a writer was usually a bourgeois. 'I could not become a bourgeois writer, because I was not a bourgeois. I could not deny that I played my guitar in the garage and football on the wasteland. I wish to prove that I have an authentic universal message to give, and I have one, because I can describe a condition that no one else has.' America provided him with his nearest model, but 'I decided not to publish my novel because I was not American.' He seemed to be torn, 'schizoid' between different civilizations. Then he discovered that there were Oc writers who were 'of my kind but they had written only on rural life.' Besides, he could not write in Oc.

'It is music that has made me Occitan. The youth of the world has found itself through American Rock.' Sicre is now trying to see whether the Occitans can discover themselves through their traditional music. 'There is a close similarity between Oc and American Black music': both are linked to dancing, both involve the participation of the public, the stamping of feet, the clicking of the fingers, the imitation of animal cries, both leave room for improvisation in the middle of songs, both seek to unify the community. But, of course, these are characteristics to be found in the popular music of many other countries. Sicre began studying these; he became interested in popular Italian, Greek, Berber, Mediterranean music and it is through these that he discovered the value of his own native music. He asked himself why he should like Oc music best. 'I realized that the reason why I found foreign music so rich was because I did not know how to look at my own music, and now I find it very rich.' There is no one Oc music. There are seven types of oboes used, while on the other hand the flute and tambour bourdon are found not just in Southern Occitanie, but also in Catalonia, Portugal and Spain. 'I do not want to invent a national Oc music. I do not want to be a great musician. I want to be a musician of the people playing according to local traditions. I prefer playing at dances. We give concerts, we perform in the streets, at marriages, in church for Christmas, at funerals, at ceremonies. The most popular music we play is dance music, and also comic carnival music; we have songs for every moment of life, satirical and political, for engagement parties and for cuckolds, for work and for bereavement.' But the words are not all that important. 'They do not say much to the present day.' It is the same with American music. 'We liked American music without understanding the words. There are people who sing American songs using English words they cannot understand. They pronounce the words perfectly; but do not know what they are saying.'

The important thing for Sicre is that he has escaped the sense of being imprisoned in provincialism: 'we are no longer on the dole.' In Oc music he feels 'everything is waiting to be invented.' Folk music involves the recreation, from a traditional repertoire, of music for a modern audience. It is not the revival of the troubadours whose music was not for ordinary people but for lords, and was more lyrical chanting than popular singing. 'I joined the Oc movement two years ago, because I did not want to be intellectually isolated. I have a great desire to create — a reaction to the lack of creativity in my background — but to create with others. I am fighting in the Oc movement in the hope of making it inventive. And I think that the traditional musicians of Oc are the most inventive. We cannot be recognized in France because we will always be provincials here, but we can hope for international recognition. I am trying to be scientific about this, and taking courses in linguistics and sociology at the university; but I have still to discover what is common to the different types of music in Occitanie. My aim is to contribute to ethnomusicology at a universal level, to show the world the musical inheritance of Occitanie.' What kind of nationalism will follow from this he does not know: that has still to be worked out. He recognizes there is no political Occitan consciousness outside a small minority; he does not really mind that. But he insists there is a cultural Occitan consciousness.

The congress of the Occitan movement gives little hint of what that consciousness is. The congress appears to be very much like any other political congress, rarely emerging from the routine of oratory and whispers, torn by factions, precariously dominated by its leader Robert Lafont, whom some find charismatic, while others argue bitterly against his tactics, or accuse him of behaving as though he were the 'Pope of the Midi'. They have not won enough power yet for it to be possible to foresee who among them will be corrupted by power. They talk as though victory is imminent. But the physics teacher (there are lots of teachers among them) selling pamphlets and badges outside admits he has no answer to the question of how they can stop foreigners buying up the land and the houses for summer residences (like the Jews buying Arab land in Israel, he says); and he sadly observes that his sons have refused to learn the Oc language.

The historian Rémy Pech presides over a session in a red polo-neck pullover. He has devoted his life to chronicling the economic decline of the Languedoc wine-growing peasantry from whom he originates. He dreams of recreating a rural civilization based on socialist co-operation. He was a Marxist in his youth, but he found Marx did not really suit his inclinations. The man Pech worships above all is his grandfather, a peasant wine-grower who founded one of the earliest co-operatives. 'I have always been a co-operative person, as a student, and as a rugby player.' But his father, an agricultural labourer, found he could no longer live off the land – 'as children we ate almost nothing but potatoes' – and he has gone into a factory; he is better off now, but he is not happier; his childhood friends are jealous because he has a regular wage; but he is jealous of them because they have managed to survive as wine producers; so there has been a breach between them, which is a serious matter for him, because he used to be the life and soul of the village, he loved organizing carnivals, he was the most sociable of men. Pech yearns for that old life, to the extent of going back to wine-growing, combining all its physical labours with his university job. His father mocks him as an amateur, saying he does not know how to tend vines properly; 'he is proud I am a professor and thinks it odd I should go to work on the vines. But I feel I need to. I have never found a common language with the bourgeois either in Toulouse or in Paris. Lafont is too intellectual for me, though he has made an analysis in which I recognize myself; I feel more at home among peasants. I think I would be a more balanced man if I had stayed on the land.'

Pech has more than a little of the nineteenth-century utopian in him. He respects the educational system; he feels he owes a great deal to his teachers; his early ambition was to be no more than a primary school teacher in his turn. Success in his career has not made him forget the grins of his examiners when they listened to his broad Narbonne accent trying to cope with a question about the North of France. He regrets that university research is so lacking in team spirit, so egoistic; he has tried to counter that by teaching in a pair with a colleague, calling their joint work 'share cropping'. He has always been a member of his trade union; he gives evening classes to the Dassault factory workers. The essence of the south, for him, is friendliness, sociability, people talk to each other. I told him that I had been to a popular restaurant in Toulouse the night before, where people sit at long tables to be served by a fat matron and her daughter, and that hardly anyone had uttered a word. Yes, he replied, perhaps this vision of universal friendliness existed only in his imagination. He himself really liked to be with other people only to do things, 'I am not in fact someone who opens himself out to everybody. For example, Estebe is one of my best friends, I have known him for seven years, and today is the first time I have spoken to him about personal matters. There is peasant modesty too. I have never seen my father naked.'

He says he wants to keep 'what is left of the civilization of the vine', but he in fact hopes to create something new. He is an unquenchable optimist, not a reactionary. 'There will be a society one day in which people will be better.' What needs to be destroyed, before that can happen, is the contempt that exists for the peasantry, and for the southerner. That is why he supports the Occitan movement, which will win recognition for him and his friends as a community, as worthy of respect as any other. The fact that southerners are divided among themselves, by dialect and by economic forces, is not an argument, he insists, against the existence of that community. He could have adopted Parisian manners, but he does not want to. He wants people to understand how he feels. The next day, he brought me a long essay he had written specially for me overnight, explaining his feelings, so that I should understand properly: it was written in the perfectly ordered logical style that French professors are so good at. In intellectual questions, he still thinks in French; even the movement's most uncompromising supporters slip back into French from Occitan when they want to argue about principles. But emotions he prefers to express in the tongue of his ancestors. And it is only when one has sensed that emotion, that one can appreciate the significance of the Occitan loyalty.

One reason why most southerners do not feel hard done by is that they are not competitors in the national rat race; unlike these professors, they are not rivals of the Parisian intellectuals, they are not interested in winning the top prizes. Georges Vaur, who left school at thirteen, and has just retired after forty-six years as a printer at the *Dépêche de Toulouse* newspaper, summarizes his outlook with the phrase: 'I do not like to give myself a headache (*Je n'aime pas me casser la tête*). I do not read the newspapers much, just the headlines. If I go to the theatre, I prefer musicals. I have only been once to the opera, four arias are about all I can take. But I would never show that I do not like it. I don't read books. I enjoy watching films on TV. I am content.'

He lives in a decrepit block of flats built by the municipality of Toulouse to house its staff; but as the buildings and the neighbourhood deteriorated, most of the first tenants moved out to be replaced by poor Algerians and Moroccans. He does not mind them at all, though some of his French neighbours never speak to them. He has furnished his flat in bright patterns, shining veneered 1960s department-store style, family photographs and reproductions of famous paintings on the wall, knickknacks everywhere, a varied supply of drinks, all spotlessly clean and cosy. He loves his home, and feels privileged to live in a city. He grew up in a neighbouring village, 'in d'Artagnan country'; his grandfather was the carpenter, and it was from his grandfather that he learned to sing, for the artisans used to sing all day as they worked, and as they drank together. His uncle was also an amateur comedian, and that perhaps was how Georges Vaur got his vocation in life. He loves clowning. Thirty years ago he went in for a singing and theatrical competition, in which he put on a humorous sketch, a monologue by a stuttering barrister. That started him off as an amateur showman. A radio producer spotted him and he was put on local radio. He created a Toulouse version of Laurel and Hardy. Then in 1957 he created a more native character, Piroulet, a scatterbrain, whom he has continued to portray ever since.

The essence of this character is that he has a strong Toulouse accent. 'I have kept my accent. People recognize that I am one of them because of my accent, that I am not someone who has made it. I'm not proud, I don't hold up my nose and tie my tie tightly.' He does not know any foreign languages, 'but I can imitate every accent.' I ask him to speak French with an English accent. He does it very amusingly, except that it is an American accent. He loves doing caricatures of the Japanese (though he has never met one), doing puns on famous brand names of their manufactured products. He does not claim to be original: 'I plagiarize,' he openly admits, but people enjoy the way he tells stories so much, they ask him to repeat them endlessly. Among his most famous is the story of the peasant who goes to a rugby match but his shoes are pinching him; his exclamations of pain, his confusion about the progress of the game, his always saying the wrong thing at the wrong time, and misunderstanding what is said to him, are in the classic music-hall tradition. 'I am a story teller.' There is never any venom in him. 'I don't like politics, which produces hate among work mates, just like women; it creates divisions among men, just like religion. I am an internationalist, a pacifist, a European. Occitanie is all very well, I like an Occitan evening, just for fun, but we have many foreigners here, I do not want to go back into the past, it is preferable for all nations to get to know each other better, not to cut themselves off from each other. I know there are stories about the Germans or the English doing harm in the past, but I don't care, that is all past – and so is Oc. I like everybody.' He seems to be without trace of racial prejudice, not a preacher of integration, but living among Arabs on friendly terms. He does not tell dirty jokes any more than racial jokes 'because that means children cannot speak to parents, and vice versa.' He performs his act both at Catholic and communist meetings: there is 'nothing naughty' in it.

His success has not turned his head. He has acted frequently on television, usually as a Toulouse simpleton, and in films also – one with Jane Birkin; four musical comedies were written for him by a journalist in his newspaper who became head of the local radio station. However, his clowning always remained a hobby and he continued to work as a printer, and to live in the same unpretentious way. Now that he has retired, 'I have forgotten everything about my job.' He seems to be always in a good humour, always ready with a quip. His greatest joy is to celebrate: 'I love Christmas and the fourteenth of July.' His alternative to protesting about discrimination is to make fun of the southerner's peculiarities, to turn them into a source of entertainment, since for him life is to be enjoyed, not worried over.

Many countries make a distinction between the mentality of their northern and southern inhabitants, one of which regions is usually poorer than the other. Occitanie covers one-third of the national territory, but that does not strengthen it politically. The leaders of its regionalist movement accept that it is almost as diverse as France itself. The Occitan language (*Oc* means yes) extends into Italy and Spain and is more comprehensible to Catalans, Italians, Spaniards and Portuguese than Frenchmen. The Romans gave birth to two languages in the territory that is now France: French and Provençal. In the twelfth century Provençal became an international language, whose songs were sung by its celebrated troubadours throughout Europe in roughly the same way as popular music is today everywhere sung in an American accent. But Occitanie never became a unified state and it developed at least three fairly distinct dialects: central (in Languedoc and Provence), northern (in the Limousin and Auvergne) and western (Gascon). In the nineteenth century Oc regionalists tried to unify these and produce a standard language, but that is now discredited, and today linguistic pluralism is accepted by the regionalists. They say it would be absurd to try and make the inhabitants of Marseille speak Provençal because Marseille is a cosmopolitan city and Arabic is almost as much its language as Provençal or French. Marseille in fact, because of its enormous size, has an independent sense of identity which leaves little room for sympathy for beleaguered peasants in the deserted countryside.

The football players of Olympique de Marseille, the city's professional team, for example, are all in their twenties, but their loyalties are concentrated on Marseille, not on Occitanie. Many have foreign names, but they were born here – they grew up to be passionate fans of the city team, and it is for their friends and family in the city that they do their best to win. Christian Caminiti, one of their stars, insists that only the O.M. has 'the real warm Latin, Mediterranean spirit': Nice and Menton are 'too snob'; he feels more in common with Rome and Barcelona; when his home crowd cheers him after a goal 'We feel as though we are in Argentina.' Monsieur Lopez, a small businessman who is one of the team's loyal fans, and is often to be seen watching them practise at their stadium, lays stress on the fact that 'we are a mixed race, Mediterraneans', with a spirit that is to be found in all the large ports, like Barcelona and Genoa; 'we are quite different from Béziers and Montpellier.'

Another of the players, José Anigo, says that when they play matches in other cities of France, they never speak to the other side. The enthusiasm of supporters and players has reached a new peak because the old team of ageing professionals has been sacked, having allowed the team to fall to the second division, and a new set of youngsters has been given the task of restoring the city's pride. The trainer, Roland Gransart, at twenty-eight the youngest of his kind in any major team, repeats that passion is the only word that can describe the link between the people of Marseille and their football team; schoolchildren spend the

Alain Saint-Ogan

They're growing fast, these little ones!

whole week preparing for the matches – he used to do that himself as a boy – and watching the match is a sort of festivity, a carnival, a pretext for having fun: 'when you look at the crowd before the match starts, the blood rises in you, you have a great feeling.' Another football fan, whose family has been in Marseille for 120 years, and who goes to the stadium every Sunday, says he is 'Marseillais first of all and French by necessity.' He adds that he does not accept the Algerians as citizens: their presence in Marseille 'cannot last, it will end in a gun fight:

there will be a great shoot-out. Let them go home, or live in their own separate parts of town, like the blacks in America.'

Altogether 21% of the French claim to be able to speak a regional language or dialect well and another 14% fairly well. But the minority is diminishing because it is people over fifty and country folk who speak most in dialect; the new generation will forget unless the school syllabuses are modified. The regionalists demand also 'the right to live in their own *pays*', not to be obliged to emigrate to other parts of France in search of work, protesting against the technocrats' ideal of a mobile society; but they also protest when work is brought to them by companies originating in the north or abroad, because though these bring low grade jobs, the top posts are largely filled by people from other parts of France. So they do a very delicate balancing act between seeking economic revitalization and developing their own brand of chauvinism. The only thing that it is possible to predict about this search for identity is that it is likely to manifest itself in an ever increasing variety of forms; almost each new recruit seems to have his own ideas; and as the programme and opportunities evolve, so too will the reactions to them.

The solution is not simply to think of the French as being composed of Bretons, Alsatians, Corsicans, Auvergnats, Normans, etc. and list all the old provinces. The man who has done more than any other to explain to the French what it means to be a Breton, Pierre-Jakez Helias, insists that the Bretons were never aware of belonging to an entity called Brittany, and call themselves Bretons only when they are outside Brittany. They think of themselves as coming from a particular town or district, as being Bigondens or Glazics or Bidars, and they behave as members of a clan or tribe. Their delight in the Breton language comes from the fact that almost every village speaks that language differently, so that it becomes the expression of their very local particularism. The differences are enough to make them use French when they meet Bretons from a different district: if Breton were standardized, 'it would no longer be their own private possession'.

To be a Breton in the past usually meant to be a poor peasant, made to feel inferior by the supposedly civilized Parisians. The attractions of prosperity and wider horizons have now turned most of those peasants into pseudo-Parisians, and most of the Breton nationalists are middle-class people educated in the towns. There has been a reversal of roles, and to be a Breton today in the aggressive or autonomist sense is to be dedicated to the creation of a new culture, as much as to the preservation of an old one.

Helias' memoirs of his Breton childhood have been a best-seller because he has shown that behind the shame Bretons were made to feel because of their poverty, and behind the facade of simplicity that townsmen imagined to be the essence of Breton life, there was an infinitely complex civilization, or rather civilizations. Typical Breton food did not necessarily involve lobsters, fish and oysters: there was a deep rift between the land folk and the fishermen, so that many ate fish only on Fridays, as a penance and with dislike. Traditional Breton clothes denoted the village from which one came, not membership of a nation; and within villages, loyalties were to particular parts of it, and to one's own profession. Pride came from a child's admission into adulthood, from a workman's ability to do a job properly, from membership of a small community, what they called a *coterie*, meaning something halfway between friendship and brotherhood. The sunny side of this was mutual help. The other side was fear, an obsession with death, a blind dedication to playing traditional roles. Helias' father would go and hide on the day his pig was slaughtered, to conceal his grief and for fear of the mysterious vengeance that might come if the killing was not performed in the proper ritual way; but on the other hand he accepted that rats should be caught and burnt alive, so that their terrible screaming should dissuade other rats from visiting his home. The occasional all-night feasting should not suggest that this was a society that knew how to enjoy itself better than its successors. It was a society that insisted on giving every one his due, so there was no conventional politeness, no good day or good evening, not even thank you, because a gift had to be repaid; there was virtually no kissing. Breton peasants were complaining of anxiety and nightmares long before they saw a motor car or other trappings of modern civilization. Today they still hold the world record for alcoholism, and one of the mixed blessings of progress that they have been found to value most is sleeping pills, of which they consume an unusually large amount, women in particular. But, to be more precise, it is a minority of Bretons that drinks and drugs itself. The Bretons, like the French, get their reputation from minority behaviour. They offer infinite permutations of the combination of satisfactions and terrors for which they are renowned, because, as one of their most famous sons, Ernest Renan, said, they are a people of heretics.

There is a tiny minority of Bretons who want to secede from France. There are some who point out that had the federalists not been defeated in 1789, France today might be a federal republic like the United States and Brittany might have preserved more of its uniqueness like Texas or California. There is no necessary reason why Brittany should be a part of France: propinquity, it is claimed, is not enough: Brittany is nearer Washington than is Hawaii or Alaska. Prosperity does not necessarily come from being a member of a large country, witness Switzerland, which is the model Breton autonomists hold out to France. They reject the Jacobin idea that every province must be treated the same. Italy has recently reversed its centralizing traditions and given different degrees of autonomy to different regions. The trend in Europe certainly is towards regional autonomy. Once Brussels has more power than Paris, French unity may collapse. But what is unclear is whether Brittany will not then be as artificial a unit as France is. The Swiss constitution allows parts of cantons to become independent, and Jura recently separated from Berne. There is nothing sacred about the units of two to five million people that the Breton autonomists see as the desirable shape of a Europe of Regions, to replace the Europe of States.

Bretons in process of assimilation used to have double lives, Breton at home and French in their contacts with the official world, rather in the way that the Japanese hover between their native and western civilization. The Alsatians used to have three lives. The older ones among them were usually raised to speak their own special dialect; they then had to learn both French and German as their province was ruled from Paris or Berlin. The result of their annexation and reannexation was that they developed a strong movement for autonomy: they felt that both

France and Germany did violence to their individuality. But anyone aged under forty has no memory of these old quarrels. Today 85% of Alsatians speak French as their main language. Autonomists get only 1% in elections. However the superficial assimilation conceals that a new kind of Alsatian particularism is growing. Alsace is certainly no longer what it once was: two-thirds of the population used to be peasants and only 4% are so now. It used to be one of the major centres of the textile industry, but that has lost its importance. Since the war, it has been transformed by a 33% increase in population, and most of the new jobs have been created by multinationals. Strasbourg has become one of the capitals of Europe. Alsatians can watch German and Swiss television. Germany is Alsace's main export market. Alsace is emerging as part of the Rhineland region, a bridge between several civilizations and the centre of Europe. English is making headway as the second language. Though obstructed by the teachers who persist in seeing themselves as emissaries of French proselytization, the desire to learn German is reviving and half of schoolchildren do learn it. There are young Alsatian poets who write in three languages – Alsatian, French and German – each expressing a different aspect of their thought. They see their traumatic experiences as qualifying them to create a new kind of France and of Europe, which rejects uniformity, which is open to outside influences in the world beyond, but which succeeds in giving them pride in their roots all the same. But that does not make Alsace a province that has found its identity. It is itself divided between north and south, the north having the largest concentration of Protestants in France. The presence of Eurocrats in Strasbourg once filled the inhabitants with pride, because it brought them out of isolation (it used to be easier to travel from the capitals of Europe to Reykjavik in Iceland than to Strasbourg, before the European parliament was set up here): but now there is disillusionment with the inconveniences of the European presence, high rents and sleazy nightclubs: 'Strasbourg has become a foreign city', an Alsatian nationalist has said: 'Strasbourg is no longer in Alsace.'

Are Corsicans Frenchmen? The island has been part of France for only two centuries. It is nearer Italy (83 km.) than France (170 km.); it used to belong to Genoa before that. In the eighteenth century it started a war of independence, proclaiming itself first a monarchy and then a republic, and finding a national leader in Pascal Paoli, who was applauded as one of the European heroes of modern times (James Boswell, Dr Johnson's biographer, wrote a biography of him too). Paoli believed that Corsica was too small to remain independent. So when France bought Corsica from Genoa (1768) and then gave Corsicans equal rights (1789), he accepted that, but when constitutional monarchy collapsed in France, he offered to make Corsica part of the British Empire, which it very briefly was. (Paoli was buried in Westminster Abbey.) Corsicans then sprang a surprise on the French, by taking them over. Napoleon was one of the first Corsicans to benefit from the scholarships and opportunities for advancement that the French offered its provincials. Corsicans had always had to go abroad to make their fortune (Paoli had served the King of Naples), and now all the careers of France were open to them. They have specialized in government service, particularly the police (15% of French policemen are Corsicans), the army and the colonies. They have a higher level of education than average, because that is the only way they can advance their careers on the continent. The effect of this is that Corsica has exported most of its talents and it has remained a very poor island. Recently large government grants were made available to develop its backward agriculture, but these have largely benefited farmers from Algeria, who moved to Corsica when Algeria became independent.

Corsica has always been a mobile society; it is only in the summer holidays that Corsicans can all be found in their island. If a Corsican is someone born in Corsica, or whose father was born there, there are 400,000 of them, but only one-third of these live in Corsica. Moreover, only 72% of people in the island are natives, the rest being either immigrants from Algeria and the former colonies, or foreign workers (and Corsica has the largest proportion of foreigners in France, 13%). The Corsicans are ceasing to be Corsicans, since 82% of them have intermarried with the mainland French. They have suffered no obstacle in making their careers in France in most walks in life: France's greatest modern poet Paul Valéry was the son of a Corsican customs official (and a Genoese mother). Tino Rossi was long France's most popular singer. Nevertheless, the Corsicans now have one of the most active and violent autonomist movements. About one in ten Corsicans are autonomists and 2% for total independence. They complain that Corsicans have had to go to the mainland to earn their living and that the island has been allowed to remain too poor to sustain its children. It has no significant industry; it imports four times as much as it exports, and relies on tourists to survive (a million a year, when the resident population is only 220,000). The autonomist movement still has to discover a workable alternative for economic prosperity: neighbouring Sardinia has had to rely on foreign investment for its development, so that it has become a sort of Third World island.

The opponents of autonomy say Corsica has no common culture to look back on: it was only in the middle of the nineteenth century that the first literary works began to be published in the Corsican language, and that language still has to be developed; it varies in spelling, pronunciation and vocabulary from district to district, and French is the most convenient way Corsicans have for making themselves understood outside their locality. In 1980 only 10% of schoolchildren were studying Corsican as a second language. The Corsicans have a long history of internal conflict. They accepted French rule partly, as one of them said, because 'Never will a Corsican do justice to another Corsican.' They have not been particularly interested by political ideologies, preferring personal and clan loyalties. In language, as in attachment, they have been as much Bastian, Cortean etc. as Corsicans. But the socialist government's policies for decentralization and a local island assembly will reshuffle the cards once again.

Local identity is not just a memory, it is a process of evolution and creation, and its shape is constantly altering. The nuances distinguishing Frenchmen from each other are thus multiplying all the time.

3

How to tell them apart

After General de Gaulle, Asterix is the best known Frenchman of modern times. The General was so unusual and so extraordinary that it is quite misleading to draw conclusions about his countrymen from his qualities and his eccentricities. However, he once conceded, in an unusual fit of modesty, that there might be just one other person who could rival him – the comic-strip hero Tintin. Tintin has now been outdistanced in popularity by Asterix, who is not quite the antithesis of de Gaulle, but rather the wink in the Frenchman's eye that enables him to cheer and mock the General at the same time; he is therefore in some ways a more complete Frenchman, even if he makes fun of all that Frenchmen are supposed to stand for and to worship. Asterix is short and ugly, but he is wily, brave and unsuppressible. He is not a cultured Parisian technocrat but an absurd backwoodsman; he has no ambitions to be a star (he is a mere asterisk). He is almost a Mickey Mouse, but at times he can be a superman too. He symbolizes France (Gaul) resisting the world almost singlehanded. He laughs at everything foreign, but he laughs also at his own silly stereotypes of foreigners. When the foreigners try to intimidate him with their giant glass and concrete skyscrapers, he repels them, but he does so by setting his country's most popular singer on them, who is so awful they run away.

Asterix parodies all that French children learn at school about the virtues of their ancestors, so that they can never be taken seriously again. He is proud of being logical and rational as a Frenchman should – 'what is so good about us,' he says, 'is that we are crammed full of ideas' – but his best friend, Obelix, is naive, dim, quarrelsome and interested mainly in food. So the

French are shown as having at least two sides to their character. And what they hate even more than foreigners are those of their own countrymen who are pompous hypocrites, bogus imitators of foreign fads, supposed great thinkers, popular heroes. The Frenchman's pride in his independence emerges as a form of extreme touchiness; this is raised into a virtue, but the conclusion is 'All humans are mad.' 'What shall we do?' they ask when in a quandary. 'Let's go and have a meal,' is the reply, and they get lost in arguments about what exactly they should eat.

Asterix is easily France's best selling book: as many as two million copies are printed of each of his exploits, of which over twenty have appeared. He shows that every supposedly French quality is either ridiculed by the French themselves or else balanced by a contrary quality. That helps to explain why Asterix has been translated into twenty-one languages. The country in which he is most popular is, by far, Germany, supposedly the incarnation of totally different qualities. Almost as many copies have been sold of Asterix in Germany as in France. The Germans laugh at French jokes very much more than do the English or the Americans. Not necessarily, by any means, all Germans, but there are clearly large numbers on either side of the Rhine who share a common sense of fun. It is no accident that in public opinion polls the French have picked out the Germans as the people for whom they feel most friendship. However much French and Germans have been political enemies, there is a love-hate relationship between them that draws them much closer than national stereotypes allow.

Asterix has become popular also because he fitted into a long tradition of writing about France; the ground had been prepared for him; he fitted perfectly into the world's prejudices about France, and there have long been French people who have liked to see themselves in the same way that Asterix does. In the eighteenth century, the *Encyclopaedia* laid it down that each nation has its character, and France's was that it was *léger*, meaning both lightweight and light-hearted, not taking oneself or anybody else too seriously. It contrasted the easy-going Frenchman with the jealous Italian, the proud Scotsman, the drunken German, the lazy Irishman and the dishonest Greek. A century later professors were still defining the essence of the

French as being the capacity to enjoy oneself in a particularly full way, both intellectually and sensually, to play with ideas, to converse brilliantly, politely and wittily, to dissipate sadness through art, to apply art to every aspect of life, from sex to gardens, for to be French was to be, above all, artificial. That made them, as they believed, the opposite of the puritan, snobbish English and the practical, insatiable Americans. But quarrelling amongst themselves, the French were far from agreeing that the qualities they attributed to themselves were to be found even among a majority of them; they had their full share of killjoys, bores and petty-minded money-makers. The definitions of their character were not descriptions of what they were like in real life, but what they (or some of them, the more witty ones) wanted to be. To be French was an ideal, an aspiration. It is inadequate to try to reconcile the varying opinions by concluding that the French are simply paradoxical and contradictory, sometimes serious and sometimes mocking, sometimes united and sometimes divided, and that if you mix up these qualities together you get a Frenchman. There have, in fact, been several distinct recipes for producing a Frenchman. But none of the recipes suffices any more.

In the beginning there were no French people. France is the creation of a monarchical dynasty, which gradually extended its dominions by force, diplomatic ruses and marriage alliances. It is not a natural geographical region: it is neither a continent nor an island. Its boundaries have frequently changed, and in today's form date only from 1919, or even from 1935 when the Saar voted not to become French. It includes regions which used to be independent states, like Brittany, Languedoc and Navarre; Aquitaine once belonged to England; Nice and Savoy were annexed only in 1860; the older generation of Alsatians, now French, were born German citizens. Belgium and Luxembourg have only narrowly escaped being swallowed up. There was nothing inevitable about the formation of the particular coalition of peoples that France came to consist of, and the idea that it is 'one and indivisible' is only two hundred years old. Strictly speaking, France meant only the Paris region, the Ile de France. It took several centuries to stamp out local independence beyond that, and to establish a centralized despotism.

When the kings who achieved this feat of diplomacy and politics were overthrown by the Revolution of 1789, the country was still not held together by mutual affection or consensus. Most of the king's subjects did not consider themselves to be more than that; loyalty to the French 'nation' was not widespread, because 'nations' for most people meant the regions and provinces. The students of the Sorbonne congregated in 'nations' according to the provinces from which they came.

But by the eighteenth century France was probably the richest country in the world. It was amazing not only for its military supremacy, but for its material luxury, its literature and its art. Its language replaced Latin as the universal language of educated men. France was virtually synonymous with civilization, the successor of the Roman Empire. Louis XIV was the Sun King. Napoleon *almost* succeeded in subjugating the whole of Europe, placing his family or marshals on the thrones of Italy, Spain, Sweden and the Netherlands. At this stage, to be French meant something far more profound than simply being born in a particular part of the world, and a French patriot was not just somebody attached to his native land. Patriotism meant rather devotion to the ideal of human happiness, to the rights of man. A patriot was, therefore, not a chauvinist, nor a blind follower of any government but a citizen of Utopia, a universal man. France's attraction in Europe resulted in part from this interpretation of its mission: it represented the liberation of mankind and it aspired to the creation of a new type of community, in which people would be ruled by reason, principle and altruism.

So France then held a place in the world which was not altogether different from that later assumed by America, the asylum of free men, the source of amazing new opportunities, new wealth, new ideas, until its image was tarnished by accusations of imperialism and of not practising what it preached. According to this recipe, a Frenchman was made by education, idealism, generosity; he was distinguished by a culture which all men could aspire to, and many educated people all over the world expounded French culture as they might a religion. Paris was their Mecca. But this recipe no longer works. France is no longer a universal civilization. Its old culture has proved too elitist for the democratic age, its language has failed to hold its own against English. To be a Frenchman in this old sense is thus like being a member of an old club with rather peculiar entrance requirements.

The alternative recipe, which is older in origin, stressed the qualities that distinguished French people from other human beings, rather than what humanity had in common; it meant moulding the French into a common type; it was based on an exclusive nationalism and an exclusive loyalty. Napoleon's dream of having every child study the same piece of Latin prose at the same time was an expression of the desire for a consensus that would be infallibly relied on. This gave rise to the stereotype of the French person as a clearly identifiable local phenomenon. But it took a surprisingly long time for the stereotype to be fully evolved, for the French never used to have the illusion that they could be synthesized into a single type. They originally had no real equivalent either of John Bull (who dates from 1712) or of Brother Jonathan (which is what Americans were known as in the nineteenth century; Uncle Sam dates only from the First World War). Jacques Bonhomme was a 'contemptuous nickname' that the nobility used for the common people and especially the peasantry before the Revolution; nobles did not imagine they had anything in common with him. Monsieur Prudhomme was a philistine bourgeois.

It was only in the early twentieth century that Monsieur Dupont or Monsieur Durand were invented. It was curious that these names should have been used to symbolize the average Frenchman; neither is a particularly common name, as the computers have recently revealed. Durands are rare in the north and east. The most common surname in France is Martin, with Bernard and Thomas second and third. Boys are most often called Jean, Pierre and Michel, girls Marie and Françoise; Patrick is surprisingly common. The most common French names are thus European ones, not exclusive to France; and none can claim to be typical, for when all the people with the hundred most common surnames have been added up, they account for only a tenth of the population. The 'average Frenchman' was probably born only on 19 April 1924, when the phrase *le français moyen* appears to have been first used in *Le Temps* newspaper: he was the creation of modern statisticians.

In 1980 Superdupont appeared. He was a comic strip hero designed to be the French equivalent of the American Super-man. The cartoonist Gotlib imagined him as waving a baguette of bread as a substitute for a gun, carrying a camembert cheese and a bottle of wine tucked into his belt, his feet in carpet slippers and on his head a beret. The beret dates the idea behind his caricature precisely. The beret never used to be the mark of a Frenchman; until 1923 it was Basque, and worn only in the Pyrenees region. Then suddenly it was adopted as a French fashion, becoming almost a national uniform by 1932, when twenty-three million were manufactured, virtually one for every Frenchman. But the fashion was almost as suddenly abandoned in the 1950s, and today less than a million are bought annually by men. The fad survives only in the army, which tries to look respectable and modest by clinging to outdated styles of cloth- ing (something quite new for it also, because when martial virtues were more admired, soldiers did their best to look conspicuous). Not the least glories of old France were its hat-shops, which once offered an almost infinite variety of styles in many different materials (a few such shops survive in the Sentier quarter of Paris). The man in the beret represents only a brief episode in French history, encapsulated in the films of the age of Renoir.

The snag with these kinds of stereotypes is that they are always out of date by the time they get fully established. Nowadays statistics can no longer create an average person who is at all real. The latest statistical version of the average French- man is said to spend half his time alone, without speaking; he buys a newspaper only once every three days; he travels by bus once every eleven days, by train once a month and by plane once every few years; he buys a pair of blue jeans every two years, and a plastic bag every day; he spends a day in hospital every six months; he goes to court once every four years; he resides in a town of 20,000 inhabitants and dies of heart trouble at sixty- nine. In practice, of course, the perfectly average Frenchman is a rarity, and a claim that one is average is a disguise or a subterfuge, since the average Frenchman has only a very hazy notion of what is average. It is as hard to know what is average in France as it is in America.

I have tried to discover what can be said uncontroversially about the French, in a practically observable way. It seems that what probably marks French people most definitely from foreigners, from the point of view of outside appearances, is the way they speak, not just that they speak a different language, but the facial movements that their language imposes on them. Their lips have to protrude when they speak because the French language has more sounds which require the rounding of the lips than other languages. Nine out of the sixteen French vowels involve strong lip-rounding, compared with only two out of the twenty English vowels. (Germans have five lip-rounding vowels.) The degree of lip-rounding in French is moreover greater because vowels following consonants often have to be prepared before the consonant is uttered. Vowels make more impression also, because French has fewer consonants in running speech than English does. And the French pronounce their consonants with their tongue in a more forward position than the English. So in French the mouth, tongue and lips have to be in a different position to when English is spoken.

In the Middle Ages, French and English sounded much more like each other, but now it is the rhythm of the two languages that is the most significant difference. The French emphasize every syllable, and are unique in not having a strong beat, so their words come out like a machine gun firing. That is why what is hardest of all for a French person learning English is to get the intonation right. (Aristocratic French comes much nearer English, because it involves some affectation of English accent and intonation.)

Finally, one can sense that a person is talking French without hearing what he is saying because the commonest sound in French is R (pronounced in several characteristic ways) and E acute next. English by contrast has the weak vowel A (as in another) most commonly, followed by N; English vowels have significantly weakened since the Middle Ages. Giscard d'Estaing used to be a perfect, exaggerated example of a Frenchman with protruding lips; Jacques Chirac, when making public speeches, is a colourful illustration of the way French speech

The First Lesson of the New School Term *by Cabu*

used to be made to sound like a song. French actors in the past studied 'diction', the art of reciting in public, and they used to speak their lines in a style quite different from ordinary conversation. There used to be much more to speaking French than knowing the words. Chateaubriand said that authors whose merit lay more particularly in the diction they made possible, could never be properly appreciated by a foreigner. 'An author can have good diction but no style.' But in the last decade diction has stopped being taught in drama schools: a more

natural acting style has been adopted, closer to that favoured in America.

However, the French reputation for gesticulating with their hands when they speak is probably no longer fully deserved. Gesticulation seems to increase in Europe as one moves south, but it diminishes as one moves up the social scale. It may be that it is, therefore, diminishing altogether as education spreads, or that only certain kinds of gestures are being preserved or developed by particular groups. The only detailed study of this subject, by a team of Oxford psychologists led by Desmond Morris, has

found very few gestures that are exclusive to any one country in Europe, contrary to received opinion which has imagined that there are typical national gestures. The gesture most commonly associated with France by foreigners, to the extent of being used by them when they wish to imitate Frenchmen, is that in which the fingertips are kissed and the hand then tossed forward as the fingers open out. This is indeed rare in Britain, and it is also rare in Italy, but it is found as frequently in Spain, Holland, Yugoslavia, Greece and Turkey as in France.

A native of Provence moving to Paris may have to change his gestures: for example, the ring gesture – the thumb and forefinger joined to form a circle – means O.K., good, in England, as it has done since the seventeenth century at least, and it meant the same in ancient Rome, as Quintilian reports. But in certain parts of France it can also mean zero, no good. Morris, finding two French anglers fishing by a stream side by side, asked them what the gesture meant: one said, 'C'est bon', the other said, 'Zéro'. They turned on each other in astonishment and broke out in argument. A Parisian recalls having to learn to use this gesture in a new way, to mean good, when he moved from the south, where he had been brought up to understand that it meant bad. The ring sign is gradually triumphing as an international sign for good, but it has not yet won in the south.

No one has yet discovered what happens to French gestures when they travel abroad, as has been done for Italian and Israeli immigrants in the United States. And no one has yet counted just how often the French do speak with their hands. Quinault said in the nineteenth century that 'no one looks at you if you do not gesticulate'. It is curious that when English people (who supposedly do not gesticulate much) are filmed for television, they sometimes wave their arms around. Gesticulation may have as much to do with nervousness as with national character. A reputation for gesticulating is often due as much to the peculiarity of the gesture as to the frequency with which it is performed: people may look more animated depending on the portion of their arms that they move. There are two gestures now considered typically French: kissing as a form of greeting, and frequent handshaking. Both were once typically English, and caused much wonder to French visitors. Kissing was the normal form of English greeting in the reign of Elizabeth I. In the nineteenth century 'le handshake' was imported from England by dandies; there even used to be professors who gave lessons in Paris on how to shake hands.

A Harvard professor, Lawrence Wylie, has studied the way the French move and hold themselves, by taking films of them, and he has concluded that they have distinct characteristics. The French, he says, seem to be in control of their muscles in a way the relaxed Americans are incapable of achieving: they hold their shoulders square; traditional French chairs are straight and uncomfortable, as though they are made for people who can hold themselves straight when they sit. Americans by contrast like to stretch their legs, put them up on a chair or desk, they often put their hands in their pockets, which the French, he says, rarely do. When Americans stand, they keep their feet apart and move their weight from one to the other. The French seem 'less troubled by the force of gravity': they keep their feet together, though placing one a few inches in front of the other; instead of swinging sideways, they move forward when they want to emphasize their point in conversation, and move back in reaction to a jibe or when they laugh. They walk with their heads slightly forward, holding themselves together as though they are moving along a narrow corridor: Jacques Tati's walk, claims Wylie, is a perfect exaggeration. But Tati's films have been far more popular outside than inside France; whether that signifies that the French do not recognize themselves in him, or that Wylie is wrong about Tati, is not clear. Tati is of course by origin a Russian, born Tatischeff.

Wylie's investigations have so far been confined to Paris and Boston, and he has made detailed films of Frenchmen only in Boston, who were presumably nervous, clever, ambitious academics. The relaxed Frenchman exists also; the contrast of French and American is not so easy to make. Wylie is himself a Mid-Westerner by origin, and he notes that Americans in New York smile much less than those in his home town. So it is not possible to deduce too much either from the discovery of another American professor, this time from the University of Florida, who observed couples taking meals in different countries, and counted the number of times they touched each other in the space of a single hour: the result for London was none, for Jacksonville (Florida) eight, for San Juan (Puerto Rico) twenty, for Paris 110. Far more sophisticated statistics will be needed to prove just who touches whom, when and where, and why.

The physical build of the French has, of course, always been highly diverse. A specialist in physiognomy wrote in 1830: 'It is very rare for Provençaux to be confused with Normans, or for Picards to be taken for Gascons'. Bretons used to be short (nearly three inches shorter than the average Cornishman across the Channel, around 1900); the inhabitants of the north and east the tallest; the people of the Dordogne used to be remarkable for their unusually large heads, those of the Auvergne and Burgundy for their unusually flat heads. Today social differences have a notable effect on height: the more well-to-do are on average taller; the children of the fifteenth arrondissement of Paris are taller than those of the twelfth arrondissement; farmers and employers in commerce and industry, as well as their wives, are the heaviest classes. Just how much diversity there is is best seen from the accompanying histograms, which were worked out for me on a computer at the Paris Faculty of Medicine, using measurements made on numerous French women by the Clothing Manufacturers (Cehti) Research Institute: these show how very difficult it is to attribute particular physical characteristics to them. But this is the first time that the figures have been analyzed in this way, or made public: the French do not have clear ideas about their shape.

The ideas commonly held about French girls are confirmed by their being, on average, at the age of seventeen, virtually the same height as their average English or American counterparts, but seven-and-a-half pounds lighter, and in adulthood the average French woman is about an inch shorter but still seven pounds lighter. Such international comparisons are, however, misleading, because national averages leave out too many peculiarities: the women of East Anglia, for example, are at the age of twenty to twenty-four, twelve-and-a-half pounds heavier than London women (as Berlei, the corset manufacturers, have established). There is enough variety in France to make it impossible to distinguish the French from other people. No one has been able to define a French nose: the average of all French

THE SHAPE OF FRENCH WOMEN

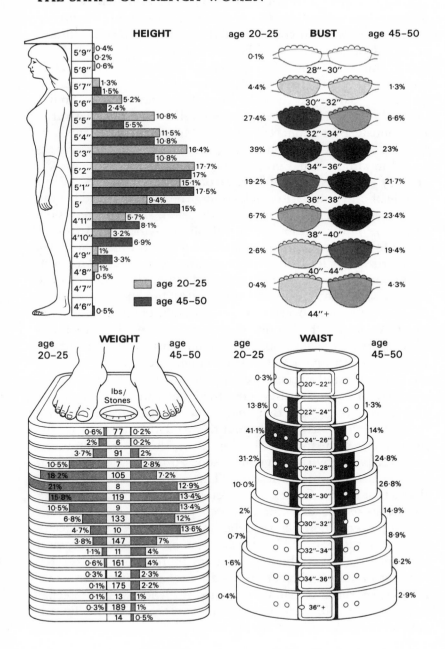

HEIGHT

Height	age 20–25	age 45–50
5'9"	0·4%	0·2%
5'8"	0·6%	
5'7"	1·3%	1·5%
5'6"	5·2%	2·4%
5'5"	10·8%	5·5%
5'4"	11·5%	10·8%
5'3"	16·4%	10·8%
5'2"	17·7%	17%
5'1"	15·1%	17·5%
5'	9·4%	15%
4'11"	5·7%	8·1%
4'10"	3·2%	6·9%
4'9"	1%	3·3%
4'8"	1%	0·5%
4'7"		
4'6"	0·5%	

age 20–25
age 45–50

BUST   age 20–25   age 45–50

	age 20–25	age 45–50
28"–30"	0·1%	
30"–32"	4·4%	1·3%
32"–34"	27·4%	6·6%
34"–36"	39%	23%
36"–38"	19·2%	21·7%
38"–40"	6·7%	23·4%
40"–44"	2·6%	19·4%
44"+	0·4%	4·3%

WEIGHT   age 20–25   age 45–50

lbs/ Stones

age 20–25	lbs/Stones	age 45–50
0·6%	77	0·2%
2%	6	0·2%
3·7%	91	2%
10·5%	7	2·8%
18·2%	105	7·2%
21%	8	12·9%
15·8%	119	13·4%
10·5%	9	13·4%
6·8%	133	12%
4·7%	10	13·6%
3·8%	147	7%
1·1%	11	4%
0·6%	161	4%
0·3%	12	2·3%
0·1%	175	2·2%
0·1%	13	1%
0·3%	189	1%
	14	0·5%

WAIST   age 20–25   age 45–50

	age 20–25	age 45–50
20"–22"	0·3%	
22"–24"	13·8%	1·3%
24"–26"	41·1%	14%
26"–28"	31·2%	24·8%
28"–30"	10·0%	26·8%
30"–32"	2%	14·9%
32"–34"	0·7%	8·9%
34"–36"	1·6%	6·2%
36"+	0·4%	2·9%

noses measured turns out to be exactly the same length as the average Slovak nose. It is impossible to distinguish the French from the Scots by the colour of their hair; the two have an almost identical proportion of red heads (4% in France, 5% in Scotland); and of blonds (12% in France, 11% in Scotland). Only 4% of the French have completely black hair. They are less frequently dark-eyed than the English (a quarter of the French are dark-eyed, while a third of the English are), but that varies enormously by region: 14% in the Morbihan, 42% in Gers, 57% in Bouches du Rhône. Blue, grey, hazel and dark eyes are found in almost equal proportions among them; over the past century there has been an increase of blue and dark eyes. When people of different nationalities doing the same job, and having the same kind of upbringing and education, are compared, such as airline pilots, almost identical physical measurements are found for France, Germany and Britain. NASA has done these comparisons in its search for the perfect astronaut. American pilots include some who are a little heavier than the rest, the Italians some who are lighter and shorter; but the vast majority of all these nations overlap. It is the exceptions, the occasional giant American, fat German or short Italian, who gives his country its reputation, but they are not normal. This is a truth that applies to much else besides appearance: it is minorities who have created national reputations.

It is an illusion to believe that the French are becoming more and more alike. Now that marriages are mixing up families from different parts of the country, and that a tenth of the French have some foreign blood in them, the genetic variations are multiplying with each generation. To say that one is French by blood has become misleading. The map of their blood groups shows that they are split up in several different ways, depending on the gene one examines. French people are very far from sharing a common physical heritage. 'My friend Lampa, a peasant of east Senegal,' the French geneticist Albert Jacquard has written, 'is very black, and I am more or less white, but some of his blood characteristics are probably more similar to mine than those of Monsieur Dupont, who lives in the flat opposite.' While national institutions try to make French people more like one another, physically the idea of the national 'melting pot' producing a uniform type is a myth: genes maintain their individuality and genetic variation increases with mixing. The French are becoming less and less alike. Individual differences between them are greater than the differences between the groups into which humanity is divided.

To look French is now partly a matter of choice: it has become more difficult to recognize the French because the range of choice available to them is wider than it used to be; Frenchness is not quite the same for everybody. It is no longer possible to conclude that French people are simply those who recognize themselves as such; that poses problems too. This can be illustrated by the case of Albert Jacquard. He is a member of the international scientific community. He has devoted himself to attacking racial prejudice. And yet he vehemently declares: 'I feel very French, very Parisian. I do not feel at home elsewhere. I need to speak French, because when I speak English, I feel stupid, or like a child, unable to express myself with nuance.' However, it is very much more than a question of language. Jacquard has spent nine months at Stanford University, taking his wife and children with him; he was paid more than he earned at home; he lived in ideal physical conditions; his work was intensely interesting to him. But when he was there 'we did nothing but dream of returning to France.' They all now look back on their visit as a marvellous experience, but Jacquard discovered that he 'needed to be a Frenchman'. He says he needs friends. The paradox is that he finds France appallingly competitive and unfriendly. American scientists, he says, are far more generous with their ideas than French ones, who are possessive and individualistic with their thoughts, like petty bourgeois: it was at Stanford that he really learnt how to do research, by which he means to work as a team. He had been educated at the Polytechnique, and so had the best mathematical training available in France, but he is scathing about the effects of that education, regarding it as encouraging conformity and an obstacle to original thinking: it only trains technocrats, capable of solving soluble problems, it seldom produces Nobel Prize winners. The intellectual life of Paris is brilliant only superficially, a kind of champagne, but one that leaves a bitter taste, because 'no one helps you'.

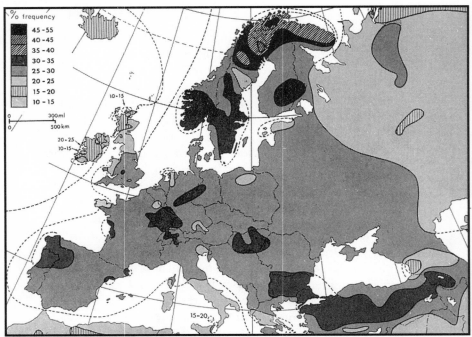

Map 1: ABO Blood Group System. Distribution of the A gene.

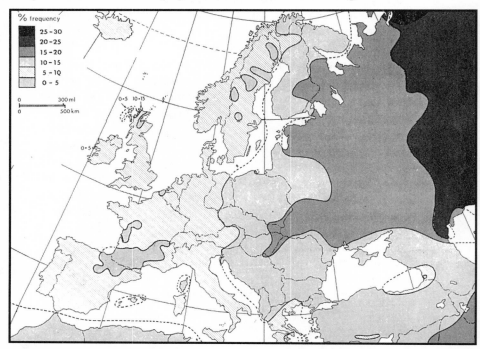

Map 2: ABO Blood Group System. Distribution of the B gene.

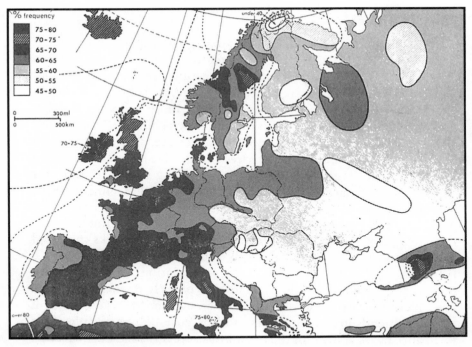

Map 3: ABO Blood Group System. Distribution of the O gene.

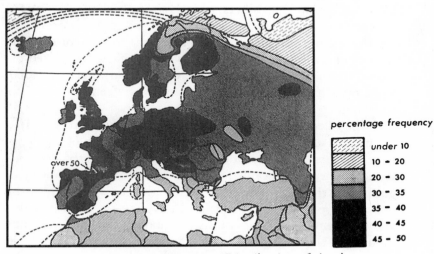

Map 4: Rhesus Blood Group System. Distribution of the d gene.

(based on A. E. Mourant, et al., *The Distribution of the Human Blood Groups and other Polymorphisms* (2nd ed., Oxford U.P. 1976)).

What kind of solidarity then does Jacquard find in France? It is not that the French are warmer as a people. He was ill in a Welsh hospital once, and speaks with amazed enthusiasm about the warmth of the care he received there, and of the friendliness of his fellow patients: there was far more solidarity in that hospital than he ever found in the Polytechnique. The old boy network that college is supposed to create is by comparison a cold elitism, and Jacquard hates elitism. He hates antisemitism and he believes antisemitism is very strong in France. A doctor friend was once asked by a perfectly average Frenchman with a *baccalauréat*, whether the child he was expecting would be 'marked' because five years previously, before getting married, he had once slept with a Jewish girl. Jacquard thinks that kind of attitude − a relic of myths about the breeding of dogs − common to at least half the French population: to them, the Jew is still a kind of devil. Jacquard also bitterly resents the French habit of putting a political label on everyone: because some of his friends are communists, and because he has written some anti-racist articles in the communist press, he has been labelled a 'submarine Communist'. He hates people who think they are more intelligent than others; he feels strongly about all forms of contempt (of which racism is the most savage form) because 'I am allergic to contempt'. He has a personal reason for that. At the age of ten he had an accident which slightly disfigured his face: the cruelty of his schoolmates taught him what it feels like to be made fun of. Tears come to his eyes when he recalls his suffering.

To be liked and appreciated matters very much to Jacquard. He has pursued several different courses in search of appreciation. At first he won academic honours and entered the civil service, where he became a deputy director at the ministry of public health. He would have preferred to be a doctor, but he did not have the courage to start all over again, until political disagreements with his minister, about how health funds should be spent, induced him to resign at thirty-nine. He became a student of genetics and graduated all over again at the age of forty-two. For ten years he found happiness doing research, writing learned monographs incomprehensible to the layman, and feeling that he was on the frontiers of knowledge in a new subject. But then, partly through conversations with his children, he discovered that he was not doing something really essential, that he was serving no useful purpose, that in the name of his beloved genetics people were being oppressed, that he was living in an unjust society. So he felt it his duty to become a popularizer, to tell people that science was a joy for those who studied it but a menace for those who did not participate in discovery. He has dedicated himself to dispelling the myths about inequality that bogus science encourages. He has written books 'on the danger of science' and 'in praise of being different'. Writing gives him a new joy, because he sees it, in personal terms, as a way of surviving. His boyhood accident very nearly killed him, and he has ever since looked on life as something very precious, a gift, very nearly lost, that he wants to taste and to preserve as long as possible. To see his name on the cover of a book gives him great pleasure: to win the affection of his readers is a great reward. But finally, when he looks back on his career, he considers that it was not as important to him as his family; his family life comes first, though his wife may say he has not given it enough of his time. He is proud of his children, and of his achievement in giving them a sense of identity. They are pursuing careers quite different from his: they will be different from their father, he says, with a strange kind of satisfaction.

What is French about all this? Jacquard's Frenchness is not attachment to the ideas or prejudices of the majority of his countrymen: he disapproves of a great many things in France, and not least the notion of conforming to a pattern. His life consists of participation in a minority crusade, in limited friendships, in family joys, in a personal adventure. He combines these activities in France, and that is why he avoids loneliness only there. Frenchness is therefore always a different combination of minority attachments. Jacquard shows that to recognize a French person, it is necessary to know not about one central loyalty, but many. That leads to the third recipe that produces a French person. The France of consensus has effectively been replaced by the France of minorities. Pluralism has been generally accepted as a national characteristic and by many as a goal. The rights of numerous minorities, ethnic, regional, generational and sexual, have been acknowledged as respectable. Politics are dominated today by the need to give satisfaction to these. That leaves France as just one of many countries that allow multicultural expression.

But I believe that this third recipe is already proving inadequate, because the minorities are composed of too many smaller minorities themselves, and above all because individuals are, and wish to be, members of several conflicting minorities. That produces an entirely new way of being French, which does not involve retreat into a particular sub-culture. That is why I give so much attention to individuals in this book: they are now shaping their own destinies more consciously and independently, selecting what they choose and reject from the many possibilities open to them, and mixing their selection in their own way. It has long been believed, following Tocqueville's critique of democracy, that people are becoming more and more alike; and the media are supposed to increase uniformity and conformity. I do not agree. I think Tocqueville was wrong, disproved – like so many prophets – by the obstinate unpredictability of individuals and by their wily capacity to resist the powers around them.

4

How to laugh at their jokes, and when to look solemn

What makes the French laugh? That is the best way of discovering what they take seriously. 'I represent the average Frenchman,' says Philippe Bouvard, one of the country's highest paid professional wits. 'My only educational qualification is a primary school certificate. I am short, I am not handsome. I do not like going abroad, and if I do, I stick to my favourite food of steak and chips. I speak no foreign language. I am chauvinistic towards foreigners, but at home I attack the army, the church and indeed I respect nothing and nobody. I hate paying taxes. I take no person or institution seriously.' He is just the sort of Frenchman whom most foreigners do not like.

Bouvard is a household name, but he is not quite content. He does not feel that he has got to the top yet. 'One of the obsessions of my life has been success.' He has founded a magazine called To Succeed (*Réussir*), because he believes this is an obsession the average Frenchman shares. He is proud of having started from nothing, as a messenger in a newspaper office, after having failed his *baccalauréat* because he was hopeless at mathematics. By his own unaided efforts he has risen to the point that he has been able to buy a Cadillac and a Rolls. He sees no limit to his ambition. He has five offices, in the radio, television and newspaper buildings to which he makes daily contributions, driving between them with one hand while he telephones with the other to his secretary, his family, his colleagues, talking non-stop. He has published a dozen books: it takes him three days to write one. He never puts pen to paper, but dictates endlessly. He never says no to a request for a magazine article: within ten minutes of receiving the request, he will ring back and dictate it. 'I am always ready to take on new assignments.'

He never feels he has had enough, because for him ambition can have no bounds, and because he feels he must constantly struggle to keep what he has won.

So Bouvard, the average man, is nervous and on the defensive, because he has discovered that he is outnumbered; he is not really the typical Frenchman after all. The average man, he says, paradoxically, can no longer live in France. An average Frenchman used to be one 'who was satisfied with a moderate fortune, and with a job that enabled him to improve it little by little'. But now if you make a good living you are frowned upon. Profit has become a dirty word. Bouvard regards this attack on hard work as undermining his whole life. He works ten hours a day every day, but he feels more and more a pariah in a society devoted to leisure. 'I regret having more and more difficulty getting those who are paid to help me to do any work, the young especially. Idleness is general, national, universal.' The election of a socialist government has put the nail in the coffin of what little respect for ambition was left. But Bouvard is still gnawed by a desire to 'win his self-esteem'. He has not done enough. 'All I have is money.' He dreams of writing a really great work. He will doubtless invent new goals when he has done that. He is dismayed that 'people no longer want to fight'. So it is with himself that he fights; there are always his own records that he can try to beat. 'The trouble with France is that the desire to succeed is now less strong than the desire to conceal one's success.' Bouvard is not one of those who changes the badge on his car, so as to make it appear to be a cheaper model, as some executives keen to avoid envy do. It is not greed for money that keeps him going; he has lived in the same street for thirty years, moving only once, to a house opposite the one where he started. He is driven rather by a sense of not being properly appreciated, not being taken sufficiently seriously himself.

How can he be a humorist if he is so tense, if he is so constantly rushing from appointment to appointment, with never a minute to waste, and if his fame rests on his being one of France's most aggressive, pitiless interviewers? 'I am paid to be aggressive.' He thinks now that he may have taken aggression too far. 'In my youth I was inhuman, I did not pay enough attention to people's feelings.' But his idea of humour is not one that requires him to be warm- hearted. 'Gaiety is an intellectual disposition that is slowly learnt,' he says. Life is not funny. You need to be a philosopher to extract joy from it. He loved cruel practical jokes as a young man; he used to telephone famous people in the middle of the night and tell them how much he admired them: they were so flattered they never complained about being woken up. A recent article in a woman's magazine asking the question: 'Have the French lost their sense of humour?' equated humour with practical jokes, and complained they were not as common as they used to be. For Bouvard a joke must contain an element of intelligence or cleverness. The average Frenchman for him is one who appreciates intelligence. (He regards the variety shows of Guy Lux — one of the country's most famous and most decried television presenters — as beneath him, because they appeal to people who refuse all intellectual effort in their entertainment, though he admits that Lux appeals to a 'large minority' none the less.) But the intelligence he likes must not be snobbish or exclusive: he hates intellectuals, who are 'too full of their own qualities', who wrongly imagine they have a monopoly of the country's brain-power. His own wit, he insists, is essentially masculine. 'Women have no wit.' He has a large female following all the same: what he means is that he continues a tradition of wit inherited from the male-dominated society of past centuries, involving verbal jousting, the ability to knock down your opponent with malicious darts of recondite knowledge and gossip. He organized, for example, a television game called 'Oil on the Fire', in which two people, known to have opposing views, are invited to attack each other, no holds barred, in the hope that the one who makes the other look ridiculous wins the prize awarded by the audience. Wit is a game: 'If I was really malicious, I would not be paid so much to be malicious.' Wit must involve subtlety: it mixes epigram and gossip to produce unpredictable explosions.

Bouvard's average man gets his self-respect from laughing at everything. Bouvard is famous, after recording at least 25,000 interviews, for his merciless mockery of all those who put on airs, for his provocative questions, for the pleasure he takes in getting his victims angry. 'Everyone is a hypocrite, except you

Claude Serre

and me,' he says. He is fascinated by top people, but he pulls them apart. He hates all those who claim to be experts. He has a special old-fashioned antipathy for priests, though he says they are a little less hypocritical than they used to be, for they nowadays 'do not hide their sexual peccadilloes'. Doctors are hypocrites because they promise more than they can do. Politicians are the greatest of all hypocrites; there are no sincere politicians; 'theirs may be a necessary profession, but it is certainly not an honest one'. The whole of society rests on a bogus politeness, on courtesies that no one practises except to mask their real thoughts. Hypocrisy in the arts means that no one dares to laugh at a blank white picture, and that Marguerite Duras is able to make a film in which she spends most of the time discussing with Gérard Depardieu the fact that she would like to make a film but cannot find a subject. No one is allowed to say that the architecture of Beaubourg is 'rubbish' and that the plays at the Chaillot theatre are 'nonsense'. Journalists are hypocrites who report only their own side of the question, and *Le Monde* is the most hypocritical of all, because it pretends to be objective. In face of a world that is going to the dogs, Bouvard makes cynicism the only virtue.

But not quite. He has very nearly lost hope, but never quite. He likes children; they deserve to be taken seriously, because they are defenceless. Family life he is more reticent about, because it can involve obligations to people he may not like, to cousins and aunts he never chose. Friendship is even rarer than love, and by friendship he understands a relationship outside work, of people 'who ask me nothing and of whom I ask nothing'; 'it is a luxury in a society based on self interest'. Disinterestedness is what surprises him most, and what therefore he admires most. The closest he gets to it is in his relations with children. The rest of life involves winning. For many years his recreation was gambling, and it was as obsessive as his search for success in his work; it was 'an inherited vice' from his family, who were always playing cards. He gambled more and more as he got richer. He has brought it under control now, though he is still fascinated by it. Like ambition, it is a game in which it is impossible to win the final prize.

Bouvard is not the average Frenchman, not the ideal Frenchman, for probably as many French people hate him as admire him. He despises so many things and people in his own country, he is so uncomfortable with modernity or change, he is such an exceptional firework of verbal ingenuity, that he is the very opposite of typical. He would be horrified to hear it, but (putting aside his animosity against clergymen) he has just a little in common with another mythical figure, the average American.

Why pay attention to a *mere* humorist? Because humour probes the limits of self-confidence, ambivalence and shame. Enough effort has been devoted to searching for the fundamental characteristics and beliefs of the French in the programmes of their four major political parties, whose leaders nevertheless somehow manage to remain enigmatic even to those who scrutinize their every word and action. I have preferred here to question four famous entertainers instead (and I shall meet others in later chapters). The comedian Coluche said that he would stop laughing at politicians if the politicians stopped making him laugh: to see what makes the French laugh with artists like him is to discover the reverse, hidden side of politics, the cynicism behind the idealism, and the fears behind the cynicism. Governments are based on institutions, but institutions are cushioned on humour, which makes them bearable. Humorists are the popular philosophers of our age, because they show how people put up with the pressures of institutions; and they help their audience to do so. Humorists do not prescribe panaceas, and they cannot be studied for their doctrines: it is their whole personality that counts. So what lies behind the act they put on for the world matters, however sordid or trivial it may appear to those who do not like to read the popular press. The private lives of entertainers have become the new mythology of this age, replacing the stories of military heroes that our ancestors loved repeating. Serious people may dismiss humorists as clowns, but clowns are probably the most serious people of all, because they cannot afford to fool themselves: they cease to be funny the moment they do. When Coluche stood as a candidate for the Presidency of the Republic, he revealed the absurd element in politics; when he was carried away by his fantasy, and came to believe that he might really be elected, he became absurd himself. His humiliation was not just personal; it represented the perpetual collapse of fantasies that takes place everywhere, every day.

Bouvard is worlds apart from Guy Bedos. Bedos is the comedian most frequently invited to perform at socialist festivals. He, far from seeing himself as a representative of the average Frenchman, positively dislikes the Average Frenchman. He was once walking around Rome seeing the sights when he came across a 'typical Frenchman' behaving like a caricature of a Frenchman abroad, complaining about everything that was not French, insulting the Italians for not being more like the French. Bedos got so angry he went up to him and said 'I do not like you'; and listed his disagreeable qualities. The Frenchman, recognizing him, overwhelmed him with compliments; Bedos would have none of it, and went on castigating him mercilessly. Bedos says that the first time he felt truly a Frenchman was when Mitterrand was elected President. At last France was going to become the sort of country he could be proud to belong to. Before that he considered himself a gypsy. This is only partly because he was born in Algeria, moving to the mainland at the age of fifteen; it did not mean that he felt at home anywhere: when performing in Rumania, he had the sensation that he was in a concentration camp, to such an extent that he spent all his earnings flying back to Paris for the weekend. He did not feel at home in the United States either, whose gigantic proportions terrified him, though he instantly sensed he was on the same wavelength when talking to individual American actors. He says his jokes go down well in Belgium and Switzerland because his criticisms of the average Frenchman appear as a kind of revenge for these countries, which are habitually regarded by the French as dull versions of true Frenchness.

At the beginning of his acting career Bedos worked for Jean Renoir, from whom he inherited the view that people are divided more by class than by nationality. But fraternity does not come quite so easily. Bedos is too independent to commit himself to any political party, even though he firmly considers himself a man of the left: the difference between East and West, for him, is that in the East they say, Shut Up, and in the West they say, Keep Talking. He has a great admiration for Mitterrand but no illusions about politicians; he quotes approvingly the words of Woody Allen, whom he also admires, to the effect that one should not expect any profound change in individual destiny or behaviour from political action. However, he is quite sure that there is a large portion of the French nation with whom he has nothing in common. One of the most famous incidents in his career was his public exchange of insults with

Guy Lux, the symbol of low-brow entertainment. Lux condemned Bedos as vulgar. Bedos not only says that he does not belong to 'the France of Guy Lux' but that 'everything I do, everything I have written since I began to write, has been to fight against what Guy Lux and his kind represent.' He said to Lux: 'You try to put people to sleep, to chloroform them. I on the contrary try to wake them up'. He links 'the Great Anaesthetist' Lux with Mireille Mathieu and her sentimental songs, and Giscard d'Estaing having hypocritically fraternal lunches with poor people. 'All of them have a nasty way of softening the public . . . as though they are tenderizing meat.'

Humour, he says, is a way of showing up falsehood and cheating. His kind of humour is a ferocious satire, quite different from that of the little pleasantries of the old fashioned bourgeosie, to while away the time after dinner, or the superficial, dry, mechanical witticisms beloved of Sacha Guitry. Bedos laughs 'to resist the majority'; his humour is a way of standing up to the pressures of those in power; 'laughter is our title of nobility'. So he will not laugh at everything. His humour has a moral side. 'I have an aristocratic idea of humour; there are things I cannot attack.' He will not make fun of justice or of racial equality; he will not pretend to be the friend of a social class he despises. The fight against racism 'is the centre of my public activity'. 'Only last week,' he says, 'I took three taxis in Marseille. Within a few minutes, each of the drivers was making racist complaints to me, as though they had been brainwashed to talk exactly the same.' He invites people who come to the theatre to hear him to 'change their ideas'. He wants his humour to 'change life'; to laugh is a way of doing just that: 'laugh, he says, even if, above all if, life is sad'. That does not exclude laughing at the most basic human functions: 'pipi-caca' jokes still throw him into fits, just as they did when he was a boy. (Two men are wandering through the corridors of a sanatorium at Chatelguyon, 'the Las Vegas of the constipated': Can you tell me where the toilets are? asks one. I do not know, the other replies, I have only been here a fortnight.) All these investigations of the drains Guy Lux considers vulgar.

Bedos admits that he would not have been a humorist if he had discovered happiness in his youth. Behind his humour there is panic. He has spent his life trying to understand himself. 'I look at myself a lot. If I am a sort of entomologist, then I am the insect I know best.' He thinks he is basically a wicked person in search of kindness. He comes from a broken home; he hardly knew his father; he does not like his mother; he despises the way his parents objected to his humorous vocation until he succeeded. He rebelled against his teachers; he is hostile to all who hold power, at school or in the family; he was expelled from the army as 'mentally deficient' and he hates all things military. He says he was a typical rebel of the 1968 variety, but long before 1968. He wants to be consoled. His stage performances give him indescribable joy, even if they are preceded by terrible nerves, because the applause and laughter of the crowds shows that he can be loved, and indeed that many more people love him than is given to most individuals. He will never turn himself just into an author, or a film actor, because the pleasure of the live applauding crowds cannot be surpassed. It is one of his methods of 'fraternizing', creating bonds with others. He is the comedian of fraternity, or as his enemies would say, of conspiracy. He first discovered friendship at the age of eighteen, when he, Jean-Paul Belmondo and a few others lived together in a sort of hippy community. When he makes a friend 'it is for life', even though they do not see much of each other now. The reward is that he has established that there are people with whom he can feel at ease. He cannot talk with those whom he regards as not his type. He keeps his friends in separate compartments: there are no friends on whom he regularly relies: he appeals to each one according to his special qualities: there are thus varieties of friendship.

Friendship with women has been hardest to achieve. As a young man he could never approach an attractive girl without a hidden hope of seducing her. It has taken him three marriages to sort out his relations with the opposite sex. One of his sketches recites the thoughts of a couple dancing a 'slow' in a nightclub. The woman has agreed to dance with the man so as not to remain a wallflower, but she is horrified by the way he holds her tight, by the foul smell of his after-shave, by his shortness and his dark looks, when she prefers tall blonds, but she dare not abandon the dance, or she would lose face in front of her jealous girlfriends who are watching. Interspersed with each of these thoughts are the man's thoughts: he is convinced he is attractive to her, she is not marvellous, but she is not bad, she has moist hands, but that must be because he is exciting her; he must keep up the attack. He bites her ear: she thinks he is a maniac. He sticks his nails into her back, he is sure girls love that, he read it in a male magazine. She is becoming hysterical and utters cries of protest. 'I've done it,' he says to himself. 'Women are not as complicated as all that. Need to know how to dominate them, that's all . . .'

This story of complete mutual incomprehension illustrates Bedos' skill at observing human weaknesses, but that does not mean he can escape his own. He is still friends with his first wife, and their daughter Lesley, even though the latter showed her independence by rejecting his political commitments. But his first marriage collapsed when he was carried off his feet by the beautiful Sophie Daumier. She was at that time a nightclub entertainer. Together they formed a famous duo, comparable to Maurice Chevalier and Mistinguett. But they were like cat and dog together. After about ten years, love, on her side, turned into hate. They separated with a public row: she published a book denouncing her marriage to him as a fraud, accusing him of being a Pygmalion who destroyed her independence. On the day of their wedding he said: 'From today, you entrust your future to me. I shall be the guardian of it.' She admired him, and was a little frightened by him: 'I protect you,' he said, 'allow yourself to follow.' But gradually she came to resent the idea that she could do nothing well without him: she complained that they composed their sketches jointly, but he never registered the copyright in their joint names, nor gave her any share of the royalties. He stopped her talking when they gave joint interviews, though she had things she wanted to say. She is proud of having been a feminist before the modern feminist movement got going; she became a friend of Gisèle Halimi, one of the earliest women's liberation leaders. She rebelled against the accepted canons of beauty and femininity. She refused to have children. She had had one illegitimate child (Philippe, now a rock musician) by an Italian she barely knew, when she was very young: she remembered the birth as a horrible experience, and had herself sterilized. She also had her two cats sterilized. She began to refuse to listen to Bedos telling her about his insomnia, and his troubles, when what she wanted was to 'discover her own truth'. She began preaching women's solidarity against male exploitation. The break-up was not coolly intellectual. She tried to commit suicide three times. He says they divorced because he hated to see the suffering he caused her, but he loved her still; he hopes to be less of a male chauvinist. She replies that is hypocrisy, he is simply admitting partial guilt in order to keep his popularity with his fans.

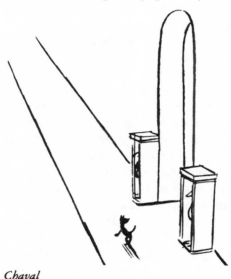

Chaval

Dog restraining itself from urinating in front
of a presidential palace

Bedos believes he has finally come to terms with himself in his third marriage, to a woman much younger than himself, by whom he has had a son on whom he dotes. The son is the centre of their life, the king of the household, he has made Bedos a sentimentalist. Bedos has discovered that happiness is to play with his naked baby, in bed with his wife. He sees that sentimentality is the opposite of humour; the combination has given him the sense of at last being complete. He does not think he can change much in the future. It has been so painful getting to know himself, 'making friends with himself' that he does not have the courage to 'assassinate himself', in an effort to create a better man. He has at last won his own kind of self-confidence. A humorist normally hides behind a mask, creates characters whom he allows to talk without committing himself. Bedos has taken the risk of speaking in his own name. He believes that has been his contribution to the development of humour in France. Others, like Coluche, have followed in his footsteps now; but it is the sense of being recognized as having a voice that comforts him. He is still dependent on having an audience to listen and applaud him; he is still dependent on his young boy needing him. He does not claim to have found the key to happiness that works all the time. His smile is a half-smile, and there is a suggestion of pain behind it.

It is Georges Wolinski, whose cartoons appear daily in the Communist paper *L'Humanité*, who has produced what is perhaps the most scathing contemporary portrait of the Average Frenchman. Flaubert, in the nineteenth century, wrote a *Dictionary of Clichés*, to ridicule the banalities of ordinary conversation, what people repeated to each other all the time. Wolinski's caricatures add up to a similar treasury of what old fogeys today in provincial France, *la France profonde*, regard as wisdom. He has created two characters, whom he calls the Two Dinosaurs or the Two Idiots. They are always seated at a café table, with a glass of wine in front of each. The large one is vigorous in his denunciation of the imbecilities of the age and florid in his nostalgia for the good old days. The small one meekly and readily agrees with him, for he is easily impressed by his friend's fine phrases and he wants to be respectable at all costs; his petty preoccupations, his efforts to please his wife, act as a kind of unanswered accompaniment, for the large one never listens to him.

The Two Idiots are stern believers in maintaining order. They approve of the Riot Police (the CRS): the large one says, 'You must be fair: the CRS are quite different from the SS'. 'They are only doing their job,' echoes the small one. 'Decent people,' says the large one, 'do not pay taxes so that the prison cells of bandits should be decorated like holiday resorts, with prison warders to serve them like waiters, a white napkin on their arm: A little more champagne Sir?' The small one timidly suggests that perhaps not everyone in prison deserves to be there: 'judicial errors do occur sometimes'. 'Perhaps,' his friend replies, 'but I would rather have the prisons full of innocent people than the streets full of criminals.'

The pair are agreed that the trouble with the country is that the old inhibitions have been destroyed, 'nothing is forbidden; the French have lost their sense of honour.' For example, one of the large man's cousins, who got engaged to a charming girl, happened to have syphilis. Everybody knew this, except the girl, because she was well brought up and did not know about such matters. So the marriage took place, no one said anything, and in due course they produced an idiot boy. But 'honour was saved'. 'Do you not think that is carrying the sense of honour a little far?' 'Monsieur,' the large man insists, 'that is how our families behaved in the past: there were no limits to the sense of honour.' That is the one thing where he is glad there are no limits. 'It's lucky they've invented penicillin all the same,' murmurs the small one.

But change is something both of them hate. They are appalled by the antics of the young. They protest at having to subsidize universities which are only schools for sexual orgies. They hate trade unionists, ecologists, Marxists, intellectuals, unmarried mothers and nude bathers, just as they cannot bear foreigners, Jews, the mini-skirt, abortion, lenient judges and divorced parents, sensuality and sociologists. They are suspicious of people who claim to have more talent than others: 'If God had wanted men to have talent, he would have given talent to everybody.' They look back to an imaginary age, when people were satisfied with their lot, when the unhappy man was content with his unhappiness, when even the leper was happier than the modern executive overworking so as to give the impression that he is rich. Like Voltaire's absurd Dr Pangloss, they say fear is needed because without it there would be no religion; hate is necessary, because without it there would be no need for an army. Without ignorance, there would be no distinguished people, *comme il faut*, who were superior to the ignorant. Without shame we would all go about with naked bottoms. 'As at St Tropez,' chirps in the small one. 'It is folly,' says the large one, 'to believe that one can make a society better than the people who live in it.' In the olden days, every village knew who slept with whom, who among the mayor, the chemist and the lawyer, were sexual perverts, cheats or Nazi collaborators; but they managed to live peacefully together all the same. What is the point of new-fangled interference, and technocratic computers? They are suspicious of modern inventions, and of all people who are not suspicious. The thought of having to bequeath France to the intolerable young generation appals them. But to whom else can they bequeath it? asks the little one.

Wolinski has spent his life attacking these kinds of average Frenchmen, who are Colonel Blimp in England and 'petty bourgeois' in France. He is the enemy of taboos and principles, of the assumption that the poor do not want to live like the rich, or that women should keep their eyes lowered, that children should not speak at table unless they are spoken to, that pornography and drugs should be available to the upper classes only, and that the best jobs should be reserved for those whose parents had the best jobs. He has not invented these conservatives; they have had a part in his own life. His father was a small employer who was killed by his communist workers during the Popular Front of 1936. His step-father was a 'typical Frenchman' who read the right-wing *Figaro* and the sporting daily *L'Equipe*. He was brought up by his grandfather, a pastry cook, in the European quarter of Tunis. (It is important to remember that to the previous generation, France was not just a corner of Europe, but an international empire of a hundred million inhabitants; that a proportion of Frenchmen are a Mediterranean, not northern people, and that both the Archbishop of Paris and the leader of the largest trade union are of Polish origin.) Old-fashioned ideals of respectable family life were piously preserved there: the colonial French, the Jews, the Mediterraneans each kept to themselves, but they shared similar attitudes. In Wolinski's childhood, women looked after the house, knitted, sewed and ironed, leaving the hard work to Arab servants; the men lived separately, going to the café to play cards and talk. Children were forbidden to swear and parents were careful to say nothing improper in front of them. The only rude jokes that were tolerated were about the bottom, excreting and farting, but not about sex. Wolinski discovered pornography by prising open a cupboard in which were kept the military decorations of an uncle killed in the war, and where he found the *Decameron* and *Lady Chatterley* secretly hidden. But he could barely understand them. He grew up chaste and prudish, and the chaste American films of those years, which he loved, suited him perfectly. It was only later on a motorcycling holiday in Italy that he discovered the joys of sex, in a Genoese brothel.

One of the great differences between that world and today's world, for him, is that it is now possible to mention such subjects publicly. Fifteen years ago the male magazine *Lui* was banned for a photograph that revealed too much breast. Now sex is a frequent subject of humour, and major cartoonists have produced what in other countries would be labelled pornographic humour. Wolinski has played a significant part in demolishing what he calls the France of Marshal Pétain, whom he remembers having had to honour as a schoolboy. He is proud of the battles he has had with the censorship in the course of establishing the satirical magazines *Harakiri* and *Charlie Hebdo*. French law punishes not the distributors of 'scurrilous' literature but the authors and editors. That meant that personal courage was enough, commercial restraints were absent. He won the battles because he had a more powerful weapon: humour. He made the nation laugh at its own principles. But not the whole country, by any means. 'Provincial France' looked upon him and his kind as 'intellectual terrorists' and he admits to the accuracy of that description. He has been terrorizing those in power with his mockery, like a naughty child who pulls faces at a teacher. He was initially inspired by the cartoons of the American Harvey Kurtzman and the magazine *Mad*, but he has been much more radically satirical. *Charlie Hebdo* has been able to attack in a way that would be impossible in the United States, where subjects like religion may not be touched; Charlie Chaplin's unpopularity in his later years, says Wolinski, shows that Americans refused to mock the very basis of their society.

But Wolinski does not represent the triumph of the new open-minded young France against the old France, which is an absurdly simplified contrast. Though he works for the official communist daily newspaper, he is not a member of the party. He feels most comfortable among the communists because he likes the warmth of their human relations, their unpretentiousness. Among socialists he meets too many well-educated people, who come from the same social background and the same schools as the Giscard technocrats, who are not his sort. The communists are more often self-taught like himself, rejected by their schools as hopeless failures; they have built up their own popular culture. Wolinski is not impregnated by the classics of French literature: as a boy, he liked American films and comics, English and American books, Edgar Allan Poe, Kipling, Jerome K. Jerome, Mark Twain, Fenimore Cooper. 'No French book made me laugh as a boy.' He believes he appeals to the same sort of 'uncultured' people, to the inhabitants of the working class suburbs, where dreary high-rise buildings have very little that is French about them. He produces three books of cartoons a year, and he sells 50,000 of each, easily outdoing more fashionable novelists and philosophers. Altogether he has published thirty books. His first film was seen by one-and-a-half million people. He admits that working for the communists means there are subjects that cannot be mentioned; he has learnt instinctively to recognize what the party line is; but he feels amply compensated by the friendliness of his readers, whom he meets at party festivals. He likes them because they are not snobbish, they are not ascetics either, they want to enjoy a good life like everyone else; he finds their company relaxing. If he worked for a large circulation paper, he would hate the fierce competitiveness, the life with daggers drawn; in L'Humanité the quarrels are ideological, but there is less struggle for money, for careers. He once aspired to be in charge of an important newspaper, but he has now decided that he does not like giving orders, or being a leader. He values his independence most of all, which means he values the right to be himself. He has achieved that right, because he feels that he is now at last in power, in the sense that his generation, who were teenagers in 1960, have now become successful pop stars of one sort or another. Now they are accepted as part of the middle-aged establishment; they have achieved their victory.

Humour for Wolinski today involves lucidity on the one hand and provocation on the other. He does not think there are specifically national forms of humour. Humour is the ability to see through the veils of convention. Humour is dangerous because it can reveal everything as absurd, which is why so many comics commit suicide. But it is also a kind of maturity. Though he is so scathing in his commentary on the world, he lives very calmly in it. He does not get excited. 'I have no complexes.' He is amazed at the way his wife gets worried by minor problems. Everything is a worrying problem, he thinks, but that means that perhaps nothing is a problem. There is no saying what is a real problem, and even if one knew, one would not know how to solve it. It is best not to try to understand too much. 'If you want to make mankind happy, start on yourself.' He thinks happiness is not achieved by a policy of self-sacrifice and loving others: it is made up of mere moments of pleasure, as when a hungry man gets a bowl of rice; it is a smile, and a note on a guitar, the promise that one will not be tortured today, a cool hand on a burning forehead, and of course reading the works of Wolinski while lying on a sofa, eating a bar of chocolate. However, it is never quite possible to believe what Wolinski says: he refuses to avoid contradicting himself, since he thinks now one thing and now the opposite. His challenge to accepted ideas means that he can challenge his own ideas too: a person who has definite ideas, he says, becomes either a fascist or a believer. That makes Wolinski one of the most terrifying of humorists because he makes a virtue of his contradictions. For example, he makes one of his characters say: 'If to be racist is not to like people who are different from one, well, then I am a racist.' His defence is that truth needs to be exaggerated, and pursued to its extremes; by this means he shows that everyone including himself has something of the racist in him. His is a humour that seeks to destroy all defences, and not to spare his own. It is different from Bouvard's cynicism, which is defensive; Wolinski is on the contrary a terrorist who blows up all certainties and himself in the process.

Behind his grenades, he is, of course, a quiet home-loving man, whose two main interests are his family and reading books. His little daughter trips into the room, saying she has a message for him; she kisses him and runs out. 'Is that your message?' The telephone rings all the time, but he knows it is for his wife, a journalist, who is *Le Monde*'s specialist on feminist affairs. He leaves it to her to answer. In his booklined study he seems cut off from the world, but he hates being alone. He and his wife, in nine years of marriage, have not spent more than three nights in separate beds. The one thing he has not succeeded in blowing up is the 'phallocrat' that resides deep inside him. He admits that when he married he treated his wife as a pretty toy; he says he cannot take women seriously because he always wants to touch them. He used to infuriate his wife by staring at other women: he tries to be more careful now, but he remains persuaded that if men have eyes, it is above all to look at women. He would give the sight of all the sunsets of Venice for that of a woman's bottom. If one could weigh men's staring at women, he says, how many kilos of stares would a woman count at the end of a day; and they would be stares weighing very different amounts, depending on whether they came from a Yugoslav window cleaner, an adolescent with complexes, a lorry driver whose cabin is full of pin-ups, or the woman hunter who is certain there is always one in a hundred who will respond to his advances. Wolinski is fascinated by all the traditional women's stratagems: 'I would be unhappy in a society that rejected flirting, high heels, transparent clothes, perfumes, and trousers that hug bottoms. I believe I am not the only one of my species.' He is quite unable to get used to the new feminist theories, which is inconvenient, because his wife, having refused to remain the housewife he would have preferred her to be, has become a leading activist in the feminist movement. He insists that he needs to feel loved, to imagine that she regards him as an idol, ridiculous though that may be. She treats him rather toughly. 'You really are the woman I need,' he retorts, 'because I have no will power; thanks to you, I appear to have it. Alone I would have spent my nights crawling round bars. I would have become fat, dirty and alcoholic. I believe that all that men do which is good, they do to try to impress their wives. What luck that there are wives.' But it is becoming more and more difficult to impress them. Men are becoming more like teachers whose pupils suddenly laugh at them. To laugh at his teachers was precisely what Wolinski did in his youth. So, ultimately, he is proud of his wife being what she is, and he is sorry for all those women who are not fortunate enough to have a husband as nice as himself. Having thrown grenades throughout his life, he is bemused by the fact that he has been standing on a feminist grenade all the time.

So perhaps the only thing all these various supposedly average Frenchmen have in common, is that they take defenceless little children seriously. But that is not a very helpful conclusion. The alternative is to abandon the whole notion of the average French person, which becomes quite inescapable when one meets yet another, totally dissimilar, character who also claims to be the Average Frenchman, a pretension that makes many shudder with horror. But it was the government's own statisticians who, only a few years ago, classified 44% of the nation as belonging to *La France de Guy Lux*. Guy Lux was for several decades one of the country's most popular radio and television 'personalities'. He explains his success by the fact that he is 'perfectly average'. 'I am Mr Everyman' (*Monsieur Tout-le-Monde*). He is the son of a chemist, whom he likewise sees as a representative of the old France. Lux senior was the caricature of a man of science of that generation: 'he covered our faces with glycerine in winter, and disinfected us with camphor, alcohol and iodine'; his hobby was talking: he was renowned as a story teller, and kept open house so that he could always have an audience. Guy Lux regards himself as continuing that tradition of the storyteller. His aim is not to ridicule people, like Bouvard, nor to moralize at them, like the news-reader Gicquel, nor to meddle in everything, like the agony columnist Menie Grégoire. 'I have not forced any message on you nor offered a miracle solution for your sexual problems or your financial difficulties. I have never told you how to vote.' He has no use for 'fuddy duddy pseudo culture, semi-thinkers and one-tenth-of-intellectuals' who want to use television to 'make everything sound complicated'. He remembers the sense of marvel with which he used to listen to the very first radio broadcasts: 'that made people happy'. He longs to restore that sense of the marvellous. 'I am nostalgic for that epoch which had not yet finally chosen progress', when you came home to a cooked meal and a family waiting to hear a story:

'families used to be buildings, sorts of cathedrals, created by words.' He grew up just when 'the vegetative, backward life was giving way to a mechanization that left the ordinary man in confusion.' He sees it as his mission to push aside people's worries by making them laugh and sing and talk. He admits one of the awful features of the good old days was Sundays – 'those long hours people spent yawning' – but it is his mission also to rescue the present generation from that boredom.

This is an example of Lux's many contradictions, which are one of the main reasons why he is significant. He is just not comfortable in the world, and he does not quite know why. 'I am by temperament rather melancholy and often pessimistic,' he says, with evident truth, but he describes himself as a 'jollifier' (*égayeur*). He hates silence – 'a world that shuts up is a dying world' – but because he has made people sit silently in front of the TV screen, he has also shut them up. 'Am I partly responsible for this emptiness, this collective decadence, lack of imagination and lassitude? I am horrified at the thought.' He is proud to have made people talk at least on his programmes. One of the most famous of his broadcast shows, *Intervilles*, was described as 'a national feast that is becoming a civil war': he was supposed to be spreading jollity, but he unleashed an extraordinary amount of aggression among the competitors, who took it all too seriously. He says he loves conversation, but explains he means by that not 'the exchange of bites' which the elite enjoys, but 'monologues'. He has been saddened by being called (he quotes the words himself) 'an imbecile, the gravedigger of the French language, the stupefier of the masses'. The laughter he encourages is that of escapism, which deliberately has no purpose other than to shut out the unpleasant realities of life. He believes that in each show he finds a new way of doing this: 'Ideas pour from me like water out of a tap,' he claims: 'everybody recognizes this: and I know how to apply my ideas.' His enemies say he always does the same thing. He pays lipservice to originality because that is fashionable, but he would be more accurate if he admitted that the popularity of the traditional storytellers came from the fact that they told the same stories over and over again: the stories were enjoyed because they were familiar, and the laughter came regularly at every point that was well established as laughable.

The quarrel about Guy Lux was between two worlds with totally different criteria. The socialists sacked him when they came to power, because they want to do away with what they consider to be an unacceptable mental vacuum: they believe the masses will appreciate more sophisticated jokes and music if only given a chance. That assumes that originality is, or can be, universally popular. They accuse Lux's variety shows (which were for years the high spot on television) of being veiled advertisements for third rate singers. Lele Milcic, who has been Lux's co-producer for twelve years, answers that. It is her that the impresarios constantly telephone to push their protégés. She is a Yugoslavian who was one of France's first women film directors — in the early 1970s. She knew nothing of French entertainment when she arrived in the country: 'I could not even understand Brassens.' Her personal taste is for the music she heard in her youth, jazz, the blues, the classics. But what she puts into the variety shows is different: 'a bit of everything to please everybody'. That is where the quarrel grows animated. How does she know what pleases? 'If a record sells, then it is popular: the public is the judge.' But does she give everyone a fair chance to be heard by the public? She has not set herself up as a judge of what the public like any more than any other broadcaster or publishers, who are always making that same decision for the public. 'Mireille Mathieu,' she claims, 'is liked by all generations, except the young, who do, in fact, like her but don't want to admit it: no one can dislike her, no one can reproach her.' Singers and comedians have become symbols of resistance and loyalty. Guy Lux is only the figurehead of the lowbrow, who rejects culture precisely because it is 'better', who resists it as 'boring' precisely because it is demanding, and who likes to laugh at what is meaningless, or sometimes even at what is cruel. The lowbrow cannot take the highbrow seriously.

So one of the answers to the question, 'What makes a Frenchman laugh?' is his fellow-countrymen. The French find themselves even more funny than foreigners do. But France is composed of a large number of small republics at war with each other, using laughter of different kinds as weaponry. The foreigner first begins to feel at home in France when he can identify with one of the temperaments that give these small republics their cohesion, and with one of the battles that they get so much fun out of waging. He can laugh with them when he can recognize that the object of their mirth is not really a local personality, unknown outside the country, but rather qualities, like snobbishness, or greed, or timidity, symbolized by a topical reference but which have universal meaning. Exactly the same applies to the French: they are at home only within their own small republics, whose obsessions and predicaments they share. To laugh is to belong to a conspiracy. And each member of a conspiracy has his own, not always obvious, reasons for joining.

The French do not, therefore, agree on what they ought to take seriously. These four comedians each have their own particular yearnings. Thrift, hard work, the right to make your way up the social ladder and to win respect for it, are the preoccupations of one. For another it is social justice, and the need to find emotional serenity. For a third, it is a horror of hypocrisy, a determination to accept your own faults and character, and to lay bare those of others. For a fourth, it is nostalgia for a less complicated world, a fear of boredom. The value of comedians is that instead of making general pronouncements to create an illusion of unity, they show up the tiny differences in emphasis that make particular individuals find their fellows intolerable, and the inconspicuous signs that attract warm feelings.

The belief that people in France have a basically different sense of humour to that of other nations, so that they are ultimately incomprehensible, is a relic of an eighteenth-century myth. A love of extravagant fantasy and of absurd exaggeration was a common feature of European literatures in the seventeenth century. Merrie England was not then divorced from Rabelais' Pantagruel, Cervantes' Quixote, Grimmelshausen's Simplicius Simplicissimus and the Italian Academies of Umoristi; Rabelais' most faithful readers were for long English clergymen. But then England, alone in Europe, raised humour to the status of a trait of national character, and dignified it with respectability. It therefore became platitudinous to repeat that the English sense of humour was something quite unique and special, to be contrasted with French wit (*esprit*) which was less spontaneous and more sophisticated. England became the symbol of the eccentric, and humour was defined as delight in eccentricity, an expression of individual originality, a sort of habeas corpus against the rigid rules of rational French taste. The French retaliated by accusing English humour of concealing an underlying sadness, a gloom that matched the grey English weather, and claimed that France was much more the home of jollity, 'gaiety', 'a light heart'.

But in the twentieth century, it became clear that these contrasts could no longer be sustained so dogmatically. Both English and American humour was increasingly read and appreciated in France, and undoubtedly influenced French humorists. The French also rediscovered neglected humorists of their own, and gave a new status to their caricaturists. Their experts began declaring that it was misleading to talk of national styles of humour: the unit of study could only be the individual humorist. It may be that certain types of humour are more frequently found in one country than another. I used to believe that at least understatement was peculiarly English, to be contrasted with the Rabelaisian tradition, which obtained the same result by gross exaggeration; but several late nineteenth-century studies of different French regional dialects claim that understatement is peculiar to each of them, or a particular characteristic of country-dwellers. What is intrinsic to any one country is no longer more obvious than that the French letter (known in France as *lettre anglaise*) is a sign of French debauchery. The reason why the humour of foreign countries is seen as odd is that one of the characteristics of humour is that it breaks the rules of reason, creating surprises by bringing together ideas that normally do not go together; and these juxtapositions seem more bizarre in foreign contexts. Thirty years ago a young Frenchman (now an eminent professor) got out of doing his military service by reciting the works of Lewis Carroll, which he knew almost by heart, to pretend lunacy. Today such ingenuity would hardly be successful, because English nonsense has been fully naturalized in France and produced beautiful and numerous offspring. In 1932 the French Academy finally admitted *humour* into its dictionary as a French word. The French sense of fun can now be seen to be broader and more varied than theorists about wit (*esprit*) used to claim. Histories of American humour argue that two of its peculiar features are the practical joke and the tall story. Histories of French humour say those are features of French humour. The failure to see these as universal is due to jokes being inevitably wrapped up in local detail and allusions which outsiders cannot easily recognize. So the affinities between the

Jean Effel

Too many pedestrians: I'll take the metro!

perky and irreverent Parisian *titi* and the English Cockney, or the wise-cracking *chtimi* of northern France and Paul Bunyan's loudmouthed American coal miners are not noticed, because people are normally immersed in only one culture: the 'big talk' of the American West is not seen as echoing the *galéjade* exaggerations of the Midi, and the Big Bear of Arkansas is not immediately recognized as being in the same tradition as Tartarin de Tarascon. The canny Scotsman and the mean Auvergnat are part of a universal joke, which distributes caricatured qualities to different regions.

The French now laugh at Chaplin and Laurel and Hardy and Woody Allen as much as anybody. That is not to say they will laugh at anyone, nor that they do not have jokes that are too esoteric to understand. One of the purposes of humour is to create a conspiracy in which only friends can decipher one's jokes, and the vocabulary of jokes therefore has to change fast, like fashion, to stop them becoming banal. Just as the class struggle created a bond across nations earlier in this century, so now there has developed a new set of international conspiracies: it is humour which enables the defenceless to hold out against the pompous. The pompous, who take themselves too seriously, are the real oppressors today.

Part Two
How to love them

5

How to appreciate a grandmother

The Bourrels have lived in the same house, in the sunny wine-growing plains of the Aude, for two and a half centuries. The family of Madame Bourrel, the Amiels, have lived in theirs, a few miles away, for 115 years. The Bourrel family are very conscious of the continuity that binds the generations together and of the ultimate similarity between young and old: heredity is the force they are most aware of. The oldest member of the family, Pierre Amiel, now ninety-five, remembers a great-grandfather who went to Moscow in Napoleon's army, and then walked all the way home. However, the pattern of inheritance has not reproduced itself quite perfectly. Pierre Amiel should have become a notary like his ancestors, but his life has been a series of disappointments. He was sent to boarding school very young: 'that was the worst thing that happened to me in my life: it was like a prison without bars. I was traumatized, to the extent that military service was a liberation for me.' He failed his school leaving examination. He became a broker in the wine trade, but his clients abandoned him; it was a job that allowed him to stay at home, but one in which there were vicious jealousies. Inflation hit the family savings; bit by bit their lands were sold, so that now only one-tenth of their property remains.

Pierre wanted to be a writer; he contributed articles to the local newspapers and had a novel published, but no one would print his second book. His brother made good in Paris, where he established himself as a prolific playwright of the second rank, but Pierre, though just as gifted intellectually, and capable of expressing himself with remarkable elegance and subtlety, probably lacked the will power. He therefore prided himself on being mediocre, except that since he was mediocre in so many things, he claimed that he had perfected mediocrity, so the total result was not mediocrity any more. He accepts life as it is: 'One must follow one's destiny. One must respect one's origins even if one does not believe in them.' What he likes above all else is peace, perhaps because his youth was often filled by sadness: 'my father was very hard on me.' He fought against depression by trying to find absorbing preoccupations – 'work is the chloroform of life' – by trying to be helpful to others, teaching his children, and avoiding confrontations: 'the danger points for family conflict are meal times.' The solution was not laughter, for laughter is 'a sin, though a minor one, against the spirit; one laughs to someone's detriment, and he emerges diminished as a result.' Pierre Amiel prefers to smile. Not that he feels there is much to smile about. People are becoming more dishonest, though only because they have more opportunities to be dishonest; progress means people need more money, which forces them to work ever harder – that is not progress. And children now scold their parents, instead of being submissive.

His daughter Colette, a very energetic sexagenarian, is the effective head of the family now. She has had her frustrations too. She would have liked to have studied, but her parents were against a girl being too educated: 'it was not done.' She wanted to go to the neighbouring city of Toulouse either to become a doctor, or else an actress but 'that was unthinkable.' She has always wanted to be 'someone else'. She loved dressing up, making up, play acting, assuming a role where she was not herself, best of all the role of a man; she would disguise herself as a beggar and go round the village asking for alms, or pretend to be a nun. She accepted the theatrical role of Judas; but she did not like playing the Virgin. She has fulfilled this side of her by encouraging her children to act and by becoming a domestic theatrical producer. Then during the war, she saw an opportunity to become a teacher, but again everybody was against her, she was forbidden. 'I have always been stopped from doing the things I wanted to do. But now, I do not allow them to stop me.' She married at eighteen. She learnt that her husband likes to have the impression that he is getting his own way: 'he always wants to be in the right: he was spoilt as a child. I let him feel he is getting his way, but I get what I want.' She has overcome her career frustrations ('I would have a pension now if I had worked') by creating a family world that revolves around her: her daughter lives across the road, her two sons within a few miles, all of them, and the grandchildren, are constantly coming for meals, or staying the night; and nearly every Sunday evening they all get together, as many as fifteen of them. 'I am not gentle by nature,' she says, 'but I try to be understanding.'

Her husband Pierre regards it as his main duty to set an example. 'I am a bourgeois; I was born a bourgeois; I have never

Grandville

The Happy Family

had contempt for those who are not bourgeois, but I have always tried to move around with other bourgeois, because there are fewer differences among us. A bourgeois is someone who is well brought up, with more duties than rights, who must set an example. To be a bourgeois confers no advantage on me: it involves dignity, loyalty, honesty, even sacrifice, nobility of mind. You do not have to be well off: I know old families who still live with dignity though poor, and I know very rich ones whose way of life I disapprove of. It is like cleanliness: you don't have to be rich to be clean. I am not infatuated by the title of bourgeois: I simply always try to be a decent person. And I think people in the village respect me. But I consider myself a bourgeois all the more because there is a tendency to level everything down, and this does not suit me. The government is destroying France, what France should be. It is deplorable. I admit the socialists are French (not the communists, they are Muscovites) but they do not see things the way I do. It's their right. I am a democrat, a republican. I never discuss politics.'

The world is not moving the way Pierre Bourrel would like it to. He has had an honourable career, but not quite the one he dreamt of. Having studied chemistry at Toulouse university, he established an agricultural laboratory, doing chemical analyses; he foresaw a marvellous future for himself. But the war put a stop to that. He became a chemist in the state agricultural service; he rose to be the local director, and he retired in 1975, at the age of sixty. He would have preferred to have had his independent business; he enjoyed his early years when he was doing real chemical analysis more than his later administrative duties: 'I did my work for the state conscientiously,' but there was a spark missing. He regrets that he does not receive a larger pension. Now that he is retired his main ambition is to enjoy good health, and to help his second son get a better job. His family life is the centre of his interests, what matters to him more than anything. His own parents died young, he was never able to exchange affection with them fully, so now he showers it on his own children without limits. 'He was indulgent to his children when they were young,' says his wife. 'He was weak,' says his elder son. He dotes on his grandchildren, kissing and playing with them with never-ending joy. With them, he is the opposite of what he is to the outside world. 'In trains,' says his wife 'he never speaks to anyone,' (which she does). He maintains a cold exterior. That is his armour against the world, as well as his way of letting others go their own way.

Between the outside world and his family, there is a kind of trench: his chosen friends, with whom he hunts in autumn and winter, and fishes in spring and summer. No one is allowed to discuss politics or religion while they hunt: as president of the hunting club, he immediately shuts up anyone who mentions the subject. The pleasures of hunting, for him, are essentially partnership with dogs who work well: it is the dogs who are the main topic of conversation. The pleasure of fishing is relaxation and patience in the quiet of natural surroundings.

At home he listens to classical music and reads history books, at least those books which do not try to make out that the past was all bad. He is content with the traditions he inherited; he does not like arguing about them; he begins to boil with indignation when those traditions are attacked, his measured prose becomes agitated, his accent becomes more regional, his speech less coherent when he senses that his basic values are no longer appreciated. He has to accept that his children do not think as he does, but their views make no impression on him. He considers it the duty of parents to win the respect of their offspring and make them want to imitate the parents. However, individual character upsets these plans, and he has not tried to fight against that, because he recognizes character as something hereditary also, each child inherits his quirks from some ancestor: there is inescapable variety and tension built into family life. He has been unable to hand down his own religious piety: perhaps that will happen later. He himself returned to the faith only because of two crises in his life: first, the bombings in the war, which made him pray as he had never done before: and then a serious operation which drew him not just to God but to the most traditionalist kind of religion. He thinks religion, too, is going downhill, priests are becoming vulgar, losing their dignity by abandoning their cassocks: 'A priest is not a man like everybody else.' He is appalled by the younger generation preferring an easy life and 'licence' to constraint. 'Faith is a constraint, though it is a liberation of the soul'. He likes constraint: 'it is an obligation that I accept, because it gives me dignity and pride.'

The decline in faith causes him as much pain as does the decline of his country. 'I am profoundly patriotic and nationalist. I feel myself to be French to the tip of my fingers.' Tears almost come to his eyes when he discusses the loss of French prestige. He cannot get over the defeat of 1940: 'France was dishonoured then, I still blush at the retreat of the French army.' He knows whose fault that is: the military spirit had been killed by the teachers (another socialist-communist disaster). His children say the changes in France's status are irresistible. That makes him all the more excited. 'For me, France will always be France.' His wife says he cannot even bear to see Japanese cars or motorcycles on the streets; and she admits to being a little racist herself. In vain does their son say that Spanish immigrants are often 'more French than the French' in their willingness to work hard. Foreigners worry Pierre Bourrel, 'I do not see why we should change our way of life just because of the Algerians.' 'One cannot congratulate oneself on what comes to us from the USA.' His son says America has brought a great deal that is good. He replies he thinks France must always welcome foreigners, but it should not change because of that. What he fears is the loss of France's old identity. He loves the Spaniards (who are less than a couple of hours drive away, and he often goes there for his holidays), or at least the Spaniards who live in Spain; those who come to France are 'hybrids'. But there are differences between them and the French: they eat at 2.30 and 10 p.m., their cooking is different. He wants people to remain faithful to themselves. He concedes that he is not just a Frenchman, but a Frenchman from the Midi, who is very different from the Frenchmen of the north: the latter are more reserved, less accommodating, less welcoming, though the friendship of southerners may be superficial. But that in no way alters his view that France is a unique entity, and 'the world cannot turn on its axis without the French.' Or without the English, either, he adds. The world consists of separate entities, like species of animals or trees, and he does not like confusion between them. He knows the role he wants to play as a Frenchman; he resents being told he must modify it.

His son Christian is a doctor, as several members of the family have been before him. Christian's son, aged eleven, already intends to be a doctor, and his daughter, aged eight, plans to be a pharmacist. Every six months Christian gives them check-ups, blood tests and X-rays. Christian loves his work, but his encouragement to his children that they should follow in his footsteps (he sometimes takes his son with him on his rounds) is instinctive rather than deliberate, for he believes that the kind of medicine he values, provided by private general practitioners on a fee-paying basis, is being killed. Christian is not quite as pessimistic as his father, but he tempers his lament about the decline in the love of work, and about people's 'refusal to dirty their hands, *je m'en foutisme*' (don't care attitude), with an acceptance of change as inevitable; though politically resigned, he is temperamentally vivacious, jovial, loving to please; 'he is a flatterer, a seducer,' says his mother. He is handsome and athletic, a tennis player and a regular gymnast. He is also an aesthete: he always carries his water colours with him in his car, pausing to sketch between his medical visits, and his paintings are much more than amateur daubs. He likes all kinds of music, and does not stop fifty years ago, as does his father; so as not to be woken up by patients late in the evening, he stays up to past midnight listening to records and playing the piano. His main hobby is cooking: he rolled up his sleeves like a surgeon preparing for an operation, and produced a grilled wild rabbit that he had shot himself with saupiquet. His parents are dazzled by his virtuosity, as his patients are by his efficiency. And yet, his family life has gone wrong. He was happily married, until he discovered his wife was deceiving him. He sees now he gave too much of himself to his work: with a rural practice, covering six villages and 4000 patients, with only one partner, he was busy all day, every day, and often half the night also, since visiting patients at home is the essence of the service he provides. It is only since his divorce that he has made arrangements to take a day off regularly to be with his children. The divorce he regards as 'a failure'; the bitterest part of it was that his wife 'fell from the pedestal' on which he had placed her. It was all the more painful because it brought a temporary breach with his mother, whom he accused of taking his wife's part. Amicable relations have been re-established both with his mother and his wife: and that is the most significant aspect. His parents, opposed on principle to divorce, have come to accept it. The close life of the whole family has not been disrupted. Christian and his wife live apart, but their boy has lunch with his father and supper with his mother; the children move without formality between their parents' and their grand-parents' homes.

Family life survives here because it has been made more supple; it has absorbed divorce, and it has adapted itself to

Alain Saint-Ogan

My children are having a party tonight.

accommodate individuality; the apparently conservative Bour-rels are, in practice, quite skilful at moulding themselves to the realities of life. Paule, Christian's sister, is unorthodox in another way, indeed in several other ways. She lives in the village, but her husband works in Paris, and comes home only for weekends. She hates Paris and has refused to move there. 'She is very strong minded,' says her mother, 'she never changes once she has decided what she wants to do. People say she is proud, but no, it is just that she is indifferent. She doesn't like to appear to want to please people, though she will do it. Marriage has changed her: she has become more closed in on herself, or rather, she has discovered her own personality. She will not talk to people in shops. She is not curious, and does not like the curiosity of others.' (How odd that is in the village was shown by a neighbour coming to visit the Bourrels within half an hour of my arriving, on the pretence of borrowing something, but with the purpose of discovering who the stranger was.) Madame Bourrel fully accepts that Paule will not tolerate criticism. 'One must not interfere in her private life. Even if I say to her: That's a nice pullover, where did you buy it? she will not tell me.'

Paule got married at eighteen and went off with her husband to Africa. He is completely different, a talkative computer salesman 'not as intelligent as his wife' says Madame Bourrel, but he loves his work: 'it is his main interest,' says Paule, 'probably more than his family, he loves doing it well.' He likes having lots of friends; he is a member of the Rotary Club. He is content with the arrangement that gives each of them their own kind of life. They get on well when he is at home: whether they would if they lived together all the time is uncertain, for she has got used to her independence. Paule probably dominates her husband; she certainly gets her own way with him; she has even refused to come home in time to meet him, on his weekend visit, because that would interfere with the Russian lessons she attends in nearby Carcassonne. (She has already learnt English and German.) She says she will go to the Sorbonne once her children are grown up. Her main interest is eastern religions and communion with the past. 'I am virtually a Hindu,' she says. She believes in reincarnation, without caring who she was in a previous life, or who she will be: 'the important thing is the journey of the soul to perfection.' She has been to India and loved it, because 'the idea of divinity influences everything, the Indians are very close to God, much more than us, they have an extraordinary faith, they are not beaten down by their poverty, they are not sad. I would not like to lose all my wealth (her home is luxurious, expensively furnished with antiques, a flowery garden and a swimming pool) but wealth is not the most important thing. We were happy in our young married days when we were poor. But it is nice to have your own books at home: that way you cannot be unhappy.' She does not like to buy clothes with famous brand names, to show off: 'I find nine-tenths of fashion ridiculous. I don't worry about it, except for its general lines; I wouldn't wear shorts if dresses were all down to the ground. I don't like exaggeration, but prefer classic clothes.' (I saw her three times in the course of one day: she wore a different outfit on each occasion, variations on the theme of elegant understatement; she is carefully made up, her hair artfully tinted.)

'When we were married, I forced my husband to go to church with me, but we have stopped.' She does not feel the need for church any more – she regrets it – the Catholic idea of paradise is 'puerile'. 'Catholicism gives me nothing, it is not what I am seeking, I don't feel satisfied by it, it has changed in the last fifteen years, so that there is nothing sacred left in it. Man needs mystery.' She finds her mystery in the past. She likes reading about the past, visiting and studying old ruins and castles, having old furniture around her: the single modern sofa in her sitting room is a concession to her husband's insistence on some comfort, and his horror of woodworm-holes. Her children mock her passion for 'broken furniture'. But 'my taste is for all things from the past.' So when she travelled to Egypt, what she liked there was the ancient monuments; but the decline of the modern Egyptians, in comparison to what they once were, pained her. Though she loves long journeys, she has no wish to visit America: modernity does not interest her.

She is not worried that people find her 'bizarre'. 'I do not care what people think.' Her idiosyncrasies are all the more apparent in a village 'where you must always worry about the opinion of others'. But she has only one friend in the village, with whom she talks about books. She does not talk much with her husband about her esoteric interests. She enjoys her solitude without being lonely. She visits her parents a lot, and knits while listening to conversation. 'I do not want to change.' She thinks her parents are horrified by her eccentricity. But in fact they accept it, because her mother recognizes in her wilfulness and independence something of her own character, and sees it as a hereditary trait, going back to her own mother. 'I tell people what I think,' says Madame Bourrel. She concedes Paule's character is 'not easy'. But that is the way they are.

The Bourrel's third child Philippe worries them more. His problem is that he has never had luck on his side. They cannot explain it. He took a degree in chemistry, like his father, but nothing has gone right since then. He would have liked to have started an agricultural laboratory, like his father, but that did not work. He is bitter that his education has, in fact, proved of such little value; most of his fellow students have been forced to seek a livelihood in every kind of work, unrelated to their university training, because there were no openings in the region for chemists. He started an agricultural machinery business which collapsed because his clients did not pay him. He has had a go at several other kinds of enterprise, without success. He is now working for a friend who owns a furniture factory, but he is not too optimistic about its prospects. He does not really like business: he does not like the competition, the feeling that 'there must always be a winner and a loser: it is not exactly a fight, but one must use weapons which I do not like using: it does not correspond with the idea I have of human relations.' It is in sport, in the home, in personal friendships that he finds the kind of relationships he enjoys. 'I am an individualist. I can work in a team, but I like taking my decisions alone, or to be left some independence in making decisions.' He feels human relations in industry must be changed, and he is reserving his judgement about the socialist government: not that he is for autogestion — whereby workers determine their company's policy, and elect managers at all levels. He believes there must always be one person to take the decisions, but there should be no more contempt towards subordinates. That is made all the worse because those in power in France are mediocrities: 'France has become a mediocre country.'

He would be happier, he thinks, as a farmer, with his own land, able to try out new ideas (he likes the technical side of business), avoiding the routine that is inevitable if you just concentrate on wine growing; landownership would give him a sense of 'solidity'. The nearest he can get to that is in his family life, which is what has enabled him to keep his equilibrium despite all the knocks he has received. 'We create our families ourselves, no one imposes a wife on you, we bring up our children the way we want.' He has a very close relationship with his wife, even if they have to live in a rented house and money is tight and the chimney smokes; perhaps because of that, and because she feels she is a bit of an outsider too. Her family moved to France from Algeria in 1968. 'We were more French than the French,' says she. 'We were surprised not to find the same patriotism here. It took me a year to get used to France. But people still call us *pieds noirs*. There is some contempt for us. So I feel at home only when I am at home.' The family spirit is strengthened by misfortune.

Philippe draws a very clear line between his work and his home. And he draws another line between himself and the Parisians. 'They are not our sort. If a man goes to Paris for ten years, he comes back knowing everything. He makes you feel that he has all the advantages, that he goes to the theatre every night.' Philippe does not, in fact, know any Parisians, except those he has seen on television. It is rather the sense of powerful forces beyond his control that makes him entrench himself as 'a man of the south', and as one who resents America's 'imposing its way of life on its allies'. He does not want autonomy for the south, though he prefers decisions to be made locally than by a Parisian minister who has never been to his town. He is a frustrated individualist, one who wishes to be master of his own destiny, and of his own family. He is firmly against parents being 'pals' of their children. He means to create his own kind of life in his own home. And that is yet another reason why the family survives so impregnably as an institution offering hope to so many different kinds of longings.

After all their experiment and searching, the French are marrying more than they have ever done in their history, and in the process they have also given new life to the family. They have modified this old institution in three ways: with regard to the role of money, of grandparents and of divorce; but the changes show how very much they still rely on the family.

The family in the past was often as much a business enterprise as anything else. Children were a source of income. Success in life meant augmenting the capital and reputation of one's family, to which individual whims had to be sacrificed, though of course, most families earned so little and had such feeble savings that this business side usually meant hovering on the verge of bankruptcy. Love, in this context, meant to enable one's child to be richer than oneself, to leave him an inheritance, it meant thrift and sacrifice. This financial affection is by no means dead. It is true that it is no longer taken for granted: the generations maintain their autonomy to a greater degree. Less than a third of young people know how much savings their parents have, and those who have a higher education know least of all, as though there is a deliberate attempt to reject this financial side of family life. Parents show their affection by trying to give their children the best possible education, rather than just endowing them with capital; and it is the pressure to do well at school which is felt most powerfully by children; that is the old pressure for social advancement. There are, however, parents (one-fifth in all) who still regard the transmission of property to children as their supreme duty. The majority now reject this old ideal because they want their savings to go to their spouse. The family has become a little less of a financial institution because children are no longer an insurance policy for old age. However, it is undoubtedly one of the most powerful forces for the maintenance and increase of inequality, because family subsidies remain a very important, and unequal, part in the budgets of roughly half the population. One-third of home owners have been helped to become so by their parents; the young husband is helped to buy a car by his father, and the young wife to buy kitchen equipment by her mother. Parents, of course, are very careful to avoid the suggestion that they buy affection; inevitably it is the richer ones who can afford to be generous; loans or gifts are rare in the working class.

To fall in love usually implies leaving one's parents to start an independent life with another person. Every generation feels it is breaking old traditions when it does this, imagining that the traditional family was a large one, with several generations cohabiting. In fact, the French abandoned the extended family centuries ago, but they have preserved the family as a clan all the same. The symbol of that used to be the Sunday lunch, presided over by a bossy grandmother, to which ten or even twenty descendants would come, as much from fear of her displeasure as from appreciation of her cooking. These lunches are still to be found, even if they have lost their formality. However, the shape of the family clan has been altered by people living longer and having fewer children. As a result, an increasing number of families have four generations co-existing; there are more grandparents and great grandparents but fewer brothers, sisters and cousins. The role of grandparents in family life has been strengthened: when grandparents are asked what it is they wish to devote their retirement to, the answer they give most frequently is 'to help the children'. Half of the population resent this as interference, believing that bringing up children is the business of parents, but the other half think that grandparents have a role to play, and even a duty to do so. It is not surprising, therefore, that though half of French people do not keep in touch with their parents, half live within twelve-and-a-half miles of their parents and visit regularly. One-third of infants are looked after by their grandparents in the role of babysitters or while the mother goes to work, and one-half of children spend their annual holidays with their grandparents. The larger the city (Paris excepted) the more frequent are the exchanges of visits, services and advice of married daughters and their mothers, as though to counteract the loneliness: urbanization has not killed the clan: the car, the telephone and early retirement have reinforced it. The balance of love is not perfect in these clans: parents seem to offer more than is reciprocated; grandparents have to compensate for their failures with their own children by lavishing affection on their grandchildren. Divorce has made them even busier: they often take care of grandchildren whose parents cannot cope. So love does not just join people up in twos, but also in twenty-threes, which is the average size of the effective family today. The shortage of brothers and sisters has been made up for by a new abundance of grandparents. It is natural that there is more talk of a conflict of generations, but that results from more contact between them.

The frustrations of the family ideal can be measured by the fact that no less than 7·7 million adults have chosen not to share their lives with another adult, or have been deprived of such company by the death of their partners. France has a million divorced people, nearly four million widows and widowers, and about 2·7 million bachelors and spinsters aged over thirty: together they add up to almost one-quarter of the population aged over thirty. That is the extent of the loneliness, or independence, that balances love.

6
How children deal with
their parents

Some would like to explain the difficulties that are upsetting family life by the experiences the French undergo in childhood. But there is no French way of loving babies or bringing them up. Each generation, each class, each family has inherited its own customs, and each has been searching for new approaches. The one constant factor has been the confident advice that doctors, psychiatrists and 'puericulturists' have ceaselessly offered, with a confidence that has never diminished, even though it regularly denounces the advice of previous experts. Child rearing in France takes place in a whirlwind of contradictory opinion and habit. A professor of the Sorbonne has entitled a book that sums up contemporary wisdom: *It is not easy to love one's children.*

Dr Spock is known in France, but he does not rule there. Until about 1960 the leading baby book was Mme Francisque Gay's *How I bring up my child* (1924). It was dethroned by Mme Laurence Pernoud who has now held the field for twenty years, but she has revised her advice almost every year and made several significant changes. Since 1970 numerous rivals have come on the scene, some translated from the American. The educated classes pay much more attention to this kind of advice than the workers, and foreign guides are appreciated only by a small unconformist minority, but the government ensures that every mother gets a jumble of these old and new ideas with a free copy of a booklet entitled *The Golden Book for Expectant Mamas*. The government wants parents to have more babies; it pays them handsomely to have more than three; it warns that an only child, brought up on its own, is in danger of growing up into a 'monster'. But government bribes have not had much effect on the decisions of parents as to whether to have children or not. There have been rapid changes in the fashionable size of family. The only child, quite frequent before the war, is now reappearing. After a period of large families in the 1950s and 1960s the French have as suddenly changed their behaviour and are now having only 1·8 children per couple.

Having a baby is still seen, except in the most 'advanced' manuals, as involving the father only in a minor capacity. Laurence Pernoud says firmly: 'The paternal instinct does not exist – at least before birth. When a man learns that he is to become a father, this news has no emotional effect on him and no reality.' The child needs a mother in its first year: 'it will not really suffer if it does not know its father.' The father is seen as useful to console and encourage the mother: 'Be the guardian of her nerves.' Changing nappies is something that men are instinctively nauseated by, and it is natural to leave that to the mothers, says Dr Cohen-Salal, the very latest expert on *Having a Child*. The man's main role starts at around seven or eight months when he begins playing with the baby for 'a few privileged moments': he is the sugar daddy. But many fathers are undoubtedly challenging this conventional wisdom. Grandmothers, too, are fighting back against the medical experts who used to regard them as representing outdated superstition: they help, but they also argue with their daughters.

There was a time when having babies was regarded as a natural activity which mothers knew instinctively how to cope with. The growth of the medical profession put an end to that, and the doctor became indispensable to the process, issuing rules on what was permissible and what was not. But since 1960 there has been a reaction, and now the country's leading child doctor, Professor Debré, has laid it down that 'the mother is always right.' Maternal instinct is now triumphant. The mother's whims during pregnancy, until recently denounced as superstitious 'cravings' have been given official blessing and must be satisfied. For long, breast feeding has been popular in France: if mothers did not want to do it themselves they sent their children out to wet nurses in the country. In 1966 Pernoud stated firmly: 'You must breast feed.' But now she has taken this back and says it is optional. Increasingly bottle feeding is

becoming fashionable and slowly working its way down the
social scale at the very time when a contrary movement is taking
place in Britain and America. The recommended period for
breast feeding, which before the war used to be six months, has
officially been reduced to only three months. In the space of a
generation there has been a complete change on the question of
when babies can start eating more or less anything. In the
nineteenth century, babies were rapidly turned into gourmets
and wine drinkers. Then came a reaction and special baby foods.
Now the tide is turning again. Thirty years ago, for example,
eggs were considered dangerous for babies of under ten months;
they are now thought acceptable at three-and-a-half months.
Today the French eat fewer eggs than any comparable nations,
but that will change.

There has been a complete switch in the attitude to rubber
dummies (Am. 'pacifiers'). In 1910 they passed a law forbidding the manufacture or sale of these: to use them became a sign
of backwardness. Today they have come back in fashion. It was
more than a matter of hygiene: sucking dummies was considered a sort of 'oral masturbation', a lapse in self-control. But
the witch hunt against masturbation is over too, and there is
even a psychiatrist (Philippe Nahoun) to say that 'to masturbate
signifies learning to love one's body in its totality'.

There used to be a distinction between French and English
ways of clothing a baby, and the previous generations used to be
worried about the dangers of the 'English' practice of allowing
the baby free movement of its legs. French babies were swaddled
to resemble a cocoon, not only by bandaging their legs together,
but also by putting special bandages round their belly, to keep
that warm. These practices have been abandoned, but Laurence
Pernoud was still recommending them in 1979 for use at night
and in winter. The difficulty this caused for changing nappies
may explain why the French gave their babies as little to drink as
possible; and why stones in the kidneys of infants are supposedly
more common there than, for example, in the United States.
Toilet training used to be attempted very early: but in the last
fifty years, the recommended date has moved gradually from
three months to two years.

Before the war, mothers were advised never to cuddle their

babies just for pleasure; crying was said to be a sign not of unhappiness, but a natural activity. That has changed. So too has the old instruction to feed the baby only at fixed times; now babies are individuals and no longer machines. So each generation has been subjected to new theories.

But different classes listen to this advice very unequally. A French sociologist reported in 1969 that only a third of working-class mothers thought a three-months-old baby should be bathed every day, while two-thirds of the upper class did, and the upper classes visited the doctor about their babies twice as often. The poor are more content to follow the ideas they inherit; they are more easy-going towards their babies, partly because they have less leisure to fuss, and partly because they see them as charming little animals on whom it would be both unfair and useless to try to impose discipline. The petty bourgeoisie have more principles and pretensions; they are keener on establishing order, regularity and routine. The upper class regard children as responsible individuals, who must be taught to distinguish themselves from others, and they are more likely to define each one with a single characteristic, because they prize individualism. These are large generalizations, and time has doubtless blurred whatever truth these distinctions may have had. But an American sociologist, in 1979, came to the conclusion that 'French parents are more like English, Italian, American or Japanese parents of the same social stratum than they are like French parents of a different social background.' What that meant was that the way parents expressed their love depended more on their ambitions, both for their children and themselves, than on any national customs or medical theories. On the basis of carefully marked, though rather simple tests, he ranked the French as average in the matter of leniency and discipline, compared to these other nations. But the French middle class were the most severe of all in their attitude to insolence, though they tolerated other forms of misbehaviour; they were most ready to comply with a child's bid for attention (as when it complains, Baby stepped on my hand), more even than Americans, but they were extremely negative towards its requests for help (e.g. Get me another puzzle) or for comfort (It hurts). The peculiarity of France compared to other nations is that its middle class is severe, while the workers are more lenient. The French working class resembles only the English working class in its kindness to children; it appears that everywhere else workers are less lenient than middle-class parents. The French resemble the Americans, however, in that fathers are less comforting than mothers, whereas the opposite is supposed to be the case in England. French fathers are harsher to their sons than their daughters, and do not show the egalitarianism Americans favour. Another study, comparing the French speakers of Belgium, France and Canada, showed the French to stand halfway between the Belgians and the Canadians, with the Belgians most severe and demanding; that suggests that some northern regions of France might well differ from other parts of the country.

There is probably a circular fashion in attitudes to children. As poor parents rise in the world and aspire to forms of behaviour that education and wealth suggest, so they make more demands on their children. But as these children rebel against the discipline they were subjected to by their pretentious parents and are disillusioned with the latter's ideals, so they rediscover the leniency of the poor. Particularly since 1968, the 'New Parents' are attempting to establish a different kind of relationship with their children from that which they themselves experienced. Father and mother, they believe, should share equally in all the tasks of child rearing; their goal should be purely hedonistic. They see children as a planned and desired investment that must yield the maximum happiness for all. The child has its rights, it is a person from the beginning and everything must be done to allow it to find its own tastes. So they have abandoned bribing children with sweets, forbidding them to watch television too much, they neither bargain nor punish, they allow them to eat what they please as they please. The family is a commune with no hierarchy, authority or formality. They do not aim to teach children what is right. They treat boys and girls alike. They argue as much with reference to American as to French child rearing theorists; they say they are rejecting the new more disciplinarian later Spock. No one can say how many French parents feel quite so militantly iconoclastic; the iconoclasts themselves admit they are a minority. It may be that they are already producing a reaction against themselves, and that discipline is becoming 'modern' again. With all these currents at work, France appears to be bathed in conflicting, ever changing solutions to the problem of raising children. That means that parents are increasingly making personal decisions about what path to take; it means also that when one meets a French person, one cannot make any assumptions about how he was brought up, about how much, how little or what kind of love he knew as a child.

What disastrous results follow from all these conflicting recipes for happiness? How do French parents continue to love their offspring as they grow into independent personalities and unpredictable adolescents? How do the children return their love? There is much discussion of these questions, but actual behaviour has probably changed less radically than people imagine. Love, once upon a time, meant first of all obedience and duty. At the end of the last war French schoolchildren, when asked which of the Ten Commandments was the most important, were still answering Honour Your Parents. That was the drill they were brought up on. The ideal family was modelled on a monarchy, in which the father was a benevolent but frightening king, who knew best what was good for his subjects; the home was the one place where the downtrodden, ill-paid clerk, the overworked factory hand was at last master. But that was only the ideal, and in reality the attempt to subjugate children, and wives, was only sometimes successful. When fathers today lament that they do not enjoy the respect that their fathers or their grandfathers received, they are wrong to conclude that the fundamental transformation in the family is the decline of paternal authority. The peasants who supposedly incarnated patriarchal tradition were notorious also for neglecting their children, and for being in return maltreated in their old age, despite the careful precautions they took to hold on to their property. The bourgeoisie were already complaining more than a century ago that they could not keep their children in order, that children answered back rudely, smoked, lorded it over the household, even in their early teens. Parental authority could not be sustained in the past in any case, because parents

Gad

The spirit of rebellion is spreading among the
young. Things will come to a bad end if you
don't give us more benches!

died younger; nearly half of adolescents, at the beginning of the
century, were orphans. The old ideal of love implied breaking
the will of children, eradicating their original sinfulness, preserving them from temptation. But the traditional family, in
practice, also represented the custom of the father ignoring his
children, either because he was at work all day, or because he
was drunk, or because he treated children as the responsibility of
the wife.

Authoritarianism and neglect are probably the two most
common complaints that children make about family life. They
would like to modify their relations with their parents, but they
are nevertheless not hostile to the family as an institution,
indeed they mostly wish to strengthen it; they often want more
not less family life, provided it gives them freedom as well as

security. One poll of sixteen to eighteen-year-olds found only 22% against the family (and only 10% of adults). Their opposition to authoritarianism is not revolutionary, because 60% of them accepted the principle that children could not be properly brought up without considerable punishment (and exactly the same proportion of adults took that view also). The majority of parents see more 'discipline' as the remedy for violence and chaos in the world; but they have trouble in imposing it themselves in their own homes because they are so dependent on their children for affection. There is so far no clear victory for either side in the innumerable battles being waged between parents and children, even though parents are always complaining that they are losing. The French *père de famille* may be on the defensive; he may have to argue to get his way, but he still gets his way surprisingly often. Nor is it necessarily only in traditional, Catholic homes that he survives.

A factory worker with five children at Vallourec (Nord), who considers himself politically 'advanced', is very much the boss in his family. His wife runs the house: he does nothing at home. When they first got married, it is true, he used to lay the table, because in those days she worked and came home an hour later than he; but now she finds it natural that when he gets home he should find all the housework done and his meal ready. 'Because the factory is a sort of a prison,' she explains. 'I've been there, I know what it is. I do not feel a slave, as he does in the factory. That is what I tell him. I feel privileged, compared to a factory worker. The only thing I regret about not working is that one can have friends in the factory.' Besides, her husband had an unhappy childhood: 'he does not come from the same background as myself.' When they first got married 'I tended to feather-pillow him too much, I realize I was wrong to, I got him comfortable in his slippers, and I think I made him selfish. So things are not at all egalitarian between us but it is entirely my fault, I got it wrong, but I wanted to give him a little happiness, I put him before me in everything. I got him comfortable.'

The husband takes little interest in the children's education: he might argue with them for five minutes, but once he gets himself in front of the television, no one is allowed to move. He takes them fishing, because he wants them to enjoy that as he does, but, 'to play with them, do things with them, all that, no.' From time to time he gives them a spanking. For example, a neighbour knocked at the door and complained that the children had let the tyres of her car down. He at once got out his belt. 'I do not want them to be vandals, to destroy other people's goods, one has enough trouble earning money to buy them.' You see, adds his wife, 'we are revolutionaries, but even so, we respect other people's property.' But that was the only hard beating they had given their children and they regretted it afterwards. One boy was in trouble with the police for stealing from the school canteen, but the parents did not worry; they do not believe in interfering much with what the children do at school. As for school homework, they do not have enough education themselves to follow it: 'It is beyond us.' They do not go to see the school much, because they find the teachers disagreeable, even the communist one is as unfair as the rest. The children are given pocket money only when they earn it by helping in the house.

The eldest boy is now married, and he behaves exactly like his father: when he gets home, he flops into his armchair, and leaves the housework to his wife. He regrets that he was never able to have any real communication with his father, and hopes to do better with his own child. Though his parents give the impression of having been lenient to their children, he thinks they were severe with him. This is a very frequent tale. The traditional father sets things up so that he is left in peace, which means things are done to suit him. He feels he is liberal because he does not bother with what does not affect him.

To judge just how authoritarian parents are, one must ask the children, and not just believe the liberal claims of the parents. Some thirteen-year-olds in a secondary school were made to write essays about their families. One girl wrote 'My relations with my parents are average. With my mother all goes well, but I don't feel the same about my father. He is not interested in us: he does not actually try to cause trouble; he shouts to frighten us. We must never speak when something interests him; but when we are interested, we have to shut up.' But she concludes, 'My children will respect their parents.' Sometimes it is the other way round. 'My father plays with us as though he were a child of our age. My mother is not like that, she forbids me to speak to boys, she does not like my going out and when she sees my father amusing himself with us, she shouts: "You are worse than your children!" She gets cross easily.' Even a father who obviously enjoys family life, who discusses every subject with his children freely, and who gives them almost complete independence, is accused of neglect: Gérard Barthélemy (described in a later chapter) is friends with his children, but they complain that he is friends with too many people, he has too many other interests, and is always bringing guests home for meals. They would like him to give them more time; they want to eat together as a family more often, without guests. But when children try to imagine how they would treat their own children when they grow up, their imaginations are limited: they hover between promising to give their children everything they ask for, and simply reproducing their parents' ideals, being strict but fair, teaching what is right and wrong, as though they knew.

One of the pressures which children are particularly conscious of is their parents' continuing obsession with their passing examinations and obtaining diplomas. Here is an essay by a fourteen-year-old attending a lycée in the suburbs of Paris. 'I like my family. My parents are always with me, they support all my wishes. They are always ready to help me, though they are of no use outside the family, i.e. at school. When it comes to school, they have their hobby horse. They want me to work hard, so that I achieve something in life. When I do not work, punishment! I am forbidden to go out on Sunday, I am no longer allowed to do what I like. They give me liberty provided I work at school. Since at the moment I am not working, I stay indoors and twiddle my thumbs. Now in class I am no longer saying a word, so that I can get better reports, and my parents will be satisfied and I shall once again be allowed to go out. At present, I am not on speaking terms either with my father or mother. They are angry, we have quarrelled about school, and so I live my own life. In the evening, it is supper with scowling faces. Order will have to be restored one day, I hope so profoundly. At home, life is impossible when it comes to school. My parents are doing their best to educate me as well as

Sempé

possible. I am not independent, I eat at the same time as them, I go to bed when they tell me to. I have to do what they want me to. Apart from that, I very much like family life and my parents, and their way of living. We are a united family, and on fairly good terms.'

A recent enquiry among managers and their children showed that 28% of these parents thought that their first duty as parents was to ensure that their children studied well; 29% of their sons took the same view, but only 13% of their daughters. What the girls wanted from their father was more affection (24%), but only 6% of fathers thought fulfilling their need for affection was their prime duty. (Only 8% of their sons took that view.) The most widely accepted aim of these managers was to allow their children 'to develop their personalities' (50%). And on the whole their children were satisfied. The subject on which they were most satisfied was the amount of pocket money they got (90%). Most parents have bought peace. The price is quite low; even the well-to-do managers most frequently pay less than fifty francs a month to their children under sixteen.

There certainly are children who feel the victims of their parents' confusions and private problems. Gaby, a welder in the naval dockyards of St Nazaire, is full of utopian plans to reform industry and society, but he philosophically accepts that the war his wife Michèle wages with their eleven-year-old son is inevitable. Michèle complains 'the boy maltreats me. He calls me a prostitute.' She tells the boy: 'You ought not to speak to me like that, we ought to be friends.' When she smacks him, he takes it very badly and complains: 'You bash me because you are stronger than me,' and she cannot bring herself to say 'I am sorry, I was carried away.' Gaby's political views prevent him from exercising any authority over the children, but he says he understands that Michèle cannot behave otherwise. If she has no power at home, then she would be nothing. She says: 'If the children do not want to obey me, what do I become? I am just reduced to cooking and making the beds.' They have stormy rows about television. He feels he has no right to force programmes on the children just because they are interesting to him. She insists: 'You must intervene. They must go to bed.' His friends' advice is: 'Give the children a smack and there'll be no more to say.' He is deeply distressed by his inability to apply his beautifully clear political ideas to his home, and to get his family out of the rut of rows and power struggles. She thinks she could solve her problems if she had a job, but she has no qualifications, and does not really want to work; she is rather frightened by the outside world.

Michèle always punishes her son, but not her daughter. Gaby says 'it is healthy' that she should do this, even though she is simply taking out on him her revolt against her husband and her father. 'For her,' he explains, 'men are swine. The boy is a little male, demanding his rights to behave as he wishes, and she cannot bear it; that is to be expected.' Many other families say that in the old days 'the son had the right to do as he pleased.' Michèle replies that has nothing to do with it. 'I would like my son to be nice to me, to accept everything I say, even if I am wrong. But he is not like that. So we row all the time. But my daughter Natacha always wants to be protected.' So mother and daughter get on very well.

On the other hand there are probably as many parents who feel that they just cannot understand their children. They believe they have done all the right things, made all sorts of concessions; talked with them and tried to see their point of view. A primary school headmistress in the Nord, Catholic by upbringing and by conviction, but cured of all dogma in the matter of bringing up children as a result of her own experience, says: 'We have no influence on the evolution of the relations between parents and children. Those relations are imposed on us by the children. We are always faced by *faits accomplis*.' She is a jovial and extrovert woman in her early forties, ready to talk freely. But she is baffled by her daughters' behaviour: 'Why do the girls not take us into their confidence? We always try to discuss with them . . . But on the essential things, they say nothing to us . . . Or we listen and we do not understand properly.' Her husband says he is sure their eldest daughter speaks more freely with her friends than with him, and that he himself (a gymnastics instructor) is more at ease with other girls than with his own daughter.

A professor at a southern university believes likewise that he has brought up his children sensibly; he would do exactly the same if he had to do it again; but at forty he suddenly finds that they no longer have any use for him. He got a letter from his son of seventeen to say that there was no point in their trying to communicate. He can no longer talk with his daughter of fifteen. And yet when they were younger he used to talk a lot with them, about everything. 'We were never pals,' he admits; 'I always rejected laxity, the idea of the child as king, just as I refused to give them too much protection. I disapprove of children being sat upon or knocked about by adults, but in return I refused to allow my children to oppress me . . . I tried to respect them and to make them worthy of respect, especially in their own eyes. And I always appreciated that their most violent anger against adults was produced by a feeling that they were treated like babies, despised . . . Now we have not quar-relled. I think we still love each other as much as before, but as for our "relations", they are finished — at least for the time being.' He concludes that parents cannot win. It is all very well to say they should try to understand: that is easier said than done.

The new factor in the relations of parents and children is that sex has ceased to be unmentionable. The degree to which freedom is now allowed is seen in the family of the St Nazaire welder. Michèle once found her children, at the age of six, playing at 'making love' with their friends — imitating their parents, kissing on the mouth, masturbating each other and lying on top of each other. She decided she had no right to interfere. That was partly because she had grown up in a tradition of active juvenile sex, except that in those days it was done secretly. A technician says that as a boy 'I would rather have chopped myself into slices of sausages than talk about masturbation. We never discussed it, even among friends.' Now he has a son of fourteen and a daughter of ten. He speaks freely to them about sex, telling them it is quite normal to have sexual impulses. When his son reached puberty at thirteen, he gave him a packet of contraceptives: he has since given him another, and 'I shall slip him a third when he goes to England. My daughter knows I shall give her some when she starts having periods.' Among themselves, at home, the family are not worried by nakedness. But this kind of behaviour is probably still that of a minority. *Pudeur* still rules. A forty-six-year-old chicken farmer confesses it took him ten years of marriage before he could talk freely about sex with his wife: she says the women in the village do not even talk about taking the pill; their daughter adds she would certainly be shocked to see her parents naked; at her school, she is sure at least half the girls feel uncomfortable just undressing with others present. Parents who claim they have told their children all there is to know about sex are often disconcerted to find their children denying it. [1]

Do the French succeed in palliating their family frictions by their physical warmth, their lack of inhibition about touching each other? That is probably something they have learnt quite recently. Once upon a time kissing as a form of casual greeting was not a peculiarity of the French, but of the English. 'To salute strangers with a kiss is considered but civility (in England) but with foreign nations immodesty,' wrote an Englishman in 1620; and the English kiss was upon the lips. French visitors used to marvel at this. There are people in Brittany who recall that among peasants in their own lifetime, 'love was not demonstrative'; parents and children kissed only on special occasions, once or twice a year, at Christmas or on family feasts. But whether the warm touching and hugging that French southerners delight in now, even among males, goes back to the Romans, or is much more recent, is not known. Nor has anybody found out how much influence the hygienists had when they forbade mothers to fondle their babies.

It is not necessarily in the direction of more warmth that the young generation is moving. Girls of between fourteen and eighteen are the first generation to have passed their whole lives in mixed schools. One observes that 'the boys play at being hard. It is out of date to court, to show one's feelings. Everything moves too fast: three compliments, a non-alcoholic mint drink, and immediately they get to the point.' The pill makes the girls feel they have become interchangeable; adolescent love

[1] Hélène d'Istria and J. J. Breton, *Les Relations parents-enfants* (Belfond, 1978), an excellent enquiry.

has not become any easier. Most want their men now to be companions. They nearly all (91%) aspire to being economically independent of their men. They want jobs, moreover, which give them plenty of 'human contact'. They are moving towards a society of pals, away from the ideal of passion.

7

How they get married

They met in Paris in 1967. Both were strangers in the city. Alain's family was bourgeois, southern, atheist. Monique was from Brittany, her parents were peasants and pious Catholics. 'We had nothing in common,' says Alain, 'we were not made to meet.' But they were lonely. They had a child after only a year together, when they still hardly knew each other. 'We are one of the few couples among our friends who are still together.' For long, their marriage was a constant war. Their wedding was 'horrible'. Monique had dreamed all her life of a beautiful traditional ceremony, but when the two families got together in the church, they did not conceal their mutual animosity. Monique had to make a deal with her atheist husband: she agreed the children should not be brought up in any religion, in return for which he agreed to a Catholic church wedding. But his father was of Jewish origin and his mother a renegade Protestant, a member of the Communist Party, who felt her son was 'lost' by the masquerade. Monique's parents also think they have lost a daughter. When they wrote to say they wanted to attend the baptism of the baby, she had to write back to say that there would be no baptism. That was a bitter blow: it has confirmed Monique's mother in the feeling that she has failed in her task as a parent. Monique was an only daughter with five brothers; she had always resented having to behave as a girl should, and to do the housework. They have never been able to make it up. The last time her mother visited – nearly three years ago – Monique hated being treated like a naughty adolescent: 'Why is your hair like that?' It was impossible for them to discuss anything. But Monique found no compensation in her husband's family for her rejection by her own; she felt out of place there also. 'She had different tastes,' says Alain. 'We used to fight,' says Monique. 'I often nearly left. We have learned now to have common interests, but it is always a struggle, the game is never won. I haven't got a submissive character. It is always one of us who is pushing. But there is an exchange between us, it is not always the same one who wins. I don't think there are couples who get on together – when they seem to, it is only a superficial veneer. We talk a lot. I provoke crises.' And it is out of these crises that Monique has worked out the way she wishes to live.

At first she was stunned by the move to Marseille, where Alain got a job. He insisted on going south, feeling that all the money to be made in Paris was an inadequate consolation; he did not and does not like Paris. For her it was a 'great crisis'. 'I came south without family, friends, work, and with a child I hardly wanted. I was twenty-two. I had never been away from home, my parents had had no friends. It was only very gradually that I got to know Marseille. I was a stranger there; that meant I had to explain myself: Who are you? So I had to invent myself. I started with an inferiority complex, and I still feel inferior towards people who are more cultured than I am.' She got a qualification as a chemical technician. Alain started a trade union among his workmates, and that made them new friends. She began writing for newspapers; she now earns her living as a journalist. But she has not said anything to her employers about her background. 'I want to prove what I am, then we'll discuss it.'

Two recent crises have made her realize more clearly what she wants out of life. They bought a dog – a Scottish collie – who became almost a third child in the family. They let it come and go as it pleased, refusing to be a slave to it. It was run over. That affected her as deeply as any death in the family might have done. Then her doctor told her she had cancer, or rather that she might have it: for six months she worried about death. It proved to be a false alarm. But these encounters with death have made her determined to live life to the full, to seize opportunities. She is clear, for example, that she is not going to sacrifice her own life for her children. 'My eldest daughter used to be hostile to my working. But there is no point in sacrificing myself to my children. My daughter will be gone in two years. My parents sacrificed themselves for us; they were of modest origins; their only aim was that we should succeed, that is, study and become middle-class, as my brothers have. But we treated our parents with contempt, we used them. If your parents are severe towards you, you react by leaving your own children alone. My parents did not really educate us, they did not teach us to respect them, because they were like servants to us. I won't allow this with my children.' Monique is not easily frightened. As a journalist, she produced by far the best reports on the murder of Judge Michel in Marseille, because she did not hesitate to report what she heard; while others wrote conventional paeans of praise for the judge, she made public what people said in private.

Monique and Alain are not a couple with firm ideas on marriage. They evolved their ideas on the family and children as they went along. Alain says he does not really believe in the couple as an institution, but more in the idea of the clan, that is to say the couple surrounded by friends with strong affective ties, 'a tissue of relationships which are regenerated all the time', held together by 'fidelity', confidence in each other. He sees the family as a sort of mafia. That may be just his way of theorizing, because he has abandoned his job in advertising to become a theorist or artist of Mediterranean life. His father had been a 'photographic artist'; his elder brother became a cinema cameraman; now his brother and he have formed a company, of which he is the business manager, to make films 'to show what the Mediterranean is'. 'The Mediterranean is a meeting place for many civilizations.' He organized a Festival of Mediterranean Music, which included Spanish and Moroccan contributions. There is now Algerian rock music being played in Marseille, on Algerian instruments. He has dropped out of the Occitan movement because he finds it too intellectual, too remote from ordinary life, too unwelcoming to strangers: Monique has lived in Marseille for fifteen years, but, as a Breton, she is still considered an outsider. Alain wants his films to be seen as much by Arab audiences as by French. Perhaps it is by such means that new civilizations are created, but meanwhile a Breton girl and a boy from the Cevennes can still find that they belong to separate civilizations even when they join to build a family of their own.

The most radical change concerning marriage has been not the growth of divorce but the increase in prenuptial cohabitation. Nearly four out of ten couples live together before getting married, for an average of one-and-a-half to two years. This is a fashion that has spread with remarkable rapidity, having doubled since 1968. The old ideal of a bride having to be a virgin is thus dead: only a tiny minority remain attached to it, and even those who are attracted by it admit it is an unrealistic ideal. Most young people under thirty believe that sexual experience before marriage is desirable, and that it can start at eighteen or even earlier. But it is quite wrong to deduce from this that the institution of marriage is threatened, or that promiscuity has increased. On the contrary: for in the first place, prenuptial cohabitation in France is contained within strict limits. In Sweden the marriage laws really are ignored: two-fifths of cohabitants under twenty-four have a child, and three-fifths of those aged twenty-five to twenty-nine. But in France only one in ten does. For the French, pregnancy is usually followed by marriage. Moreover, prenuptial sexual relations are not really an innovation: in the past a considerable proportion of children were conceived before marriage: the only real change was a temporary

Wolinski

Victorian puritanism which is played out. The Swedish attitude is a superficial change likewise, in that cohabitants behave pretty much like married couples: all that has been dropped has been the marriage ceremony, and that is, in fact, an old Swedish peasant custom. In the end between 70 and 80% of French people still get married in church, even though most of them never normally set foot in a church. Prenuptial cohabitation is thus, in effect, an alternative to the old 'engagement' – not that the latter has wholly vanished: engagement parties can still be found.

When a boy and a girl decide to live together, one-third of them have already decided that they are going to get married, one-third are uncertain and cohabitation is a form of trial for them; only a quarter have not discussed getting married, and a mere 7% are opposed to the idea of marriage itself. And in seven cases out of ten, a girl cohabits with only one person and in due course marries him. That is doubtless the reason why parents have come to accept this new institution, and only in quite rare cases disown it as immoral. Parents see it as a preparation for marriage. The young think it keeps their options open, it seems a mark of independence; and when they get married, the young are able to justify their relapse into conventionality by treating the ceremony as a mere formality and seeing it as a prolongation of their free cohabitation. Marriage has thus been saved. Promiscuity has without doubt been diminished by cohabitation, because it has reduced the period during which young men habitually sowed their wild oats. They now become faithful to one partner much earlier. The free sexual life of communes is theoretically approved of by two-thirds of young people as an idea, but very few have tried it and only a third of boys and a quarter of girls think they themselves might conceivably be attracted by an experience of it.

Prenuptial cohabitation is a fashion that the educated and managerial classes have set and that most other classes are following. It used, of course, to be a working-class fashion, condemned by the bourgeoisie, in the same way as jeans used to be a working man's garment. Today, more than 50% of young married couples in the most privileged classes have cohabited

Reiser

before marriage, but only a quarter of young workers have. It is among the working class, and also among the old-fashioned conservative bourgeoisie, that resistance to the practice remains strongest. Cohabitation is superficially a sign of a more general rejection of convention. Most people think that marriage is one of the institutions that has gone wrong worst; only a quarter of the couples of the previous generation, it is believed, stay together (for the forty-five years that marriages last on average nowadays) because their marriages are really successful; the young see their parents as bound by routine at best, oppressive or oppressed, angry or resigned. But what do they want for themselves? They certainly do not reject the idea of the couple, and on the contrary they want much more from it than their parents did. Young men are seeking a partner in the fullest sense of the word, a friend who shares as much as possible their tastes and ideas, who protects them from loneliness. Young women are increasingly moving towards the same conception of marriage, instead of being content just with security and a home; they stress their need of affection; but on top of that at least half of them say they wish also to be swept off their feet by a man; these are sometimes the very ones who want to keep a certain degree of independence at the same time. For the privileged class, there is a choice between pursuing their education further, establishing themselves in their professions, or having a family. With all these uncertainties before them, it is not surprising many are unable to find at once what they are looking for; they cannot know exactly what it is that they are looking for, their lives are changing too fast. Their partner must, therefore, have very remarkable qualities. In addition, since sex can now be enjoyed without marriage, a marriage partner must be a sexual athlete also, satisfying in more ways than the traditional virgin was expected to be.

The working class is sometimes demanding in different ways. When a worker gets married, he is more likely to break with his mates than are educated couples, who tend to keep their circle of friends. Workers keep their marriages more private, and publicly denigrate them. It is not done, among men, to speak romantically about one's wife; more common is the saying 'My old woman is a pain in the arse.' (*Ma bonne femme m'emmerde.*)

Working-class girls seldom have career prospects to tempt them, so marriage must inevitably mean above all a home and children.

There are still young people who think in very traditional ways. A man in his twenties of 'good family' says 'the physical side is important, both for the pleasure of the husband and so that the children look nice . . . As for character, I appreciate a certain gentleness, I will not say submission, but a certain kindness, and also liveliness, goodness, that is perhaps the essential. From the social point of view, I would like the girl I finally choose to have a social status equal to my own – which means either that she has a diploma sufficiently superior to be able to earn her own living, or that she has enough inherited wealth not to have to work.' There are still those who marry their childhood sweethearts, those who are content to say, 'I like him, *but* he likes me. He is nice, so I do not see why I should look elsewhere.' A cashier of twenty in a supermarket, the seventh of twelve children, whose brothers and sisters got married at eighteen, says her family expect her to marry soon, and she is quite keen to, adding that she considers herself lucky because her boyfriend is nice.

The French have gone on getting married despite much preaching to the contrary. Their philosophers and novelists have frequently been enemies of marriage. 'Those who love each other are man and wife.' said the revolutionary St Just. 'In the designs of Providence, the union of man and woman must have been meant to be temporary. Everything is opposed to their permanent association, and change is a necessary part of their nature,' wrote the feminist George Sand. Jean-Paul Sartre and Simone de Beauvoir symbolized, for the last generation, the implementation of these ideas: they practised *union libre*, unmarried bliss. They had a lot of influence on intellectuals with their other theories but in this matter of marriage very few followed their example. Free love has made no progress in France, and indeed there are probably fewer unmarried couples today than there were in the nineteenth century, when many industrial workers did not bother to marry. There are about half a million unmarried couples today, but most are very young and will marry within a couple of years. This is all the more surpising because the law has been amended to give virtually equal rights to the married and the unmarried. Since 1978 an unmarried couple have the legal status of a married couple if they simply sign a declaration 'on their honour' that they are living together 'totally and permanently'. The phrase 'living maritally' is legally accepted as meaning living together unmarried; in 1970 the [Supreme] Court of Cassation ruled that this was no longer 'contrary to today's morals'. Since 1972 illegitimate children have the same rights as legitimate ones. The unmarried mother even has an advantage over the wife in that she automatically gets custody of her children in the event of a break-up; she can obtain an allowance from her lover for her child just as though she had been married to him; she does not even have to prove he is the father only that they had sexual relations during the relevant period; if he cannot prove himself innocent by a blood test, his only defence is that she has led a life of debauchery, and to prove that it is not enough to show that she slept with many men: she has to be an actual prostitute. Since 1978 a 'concubine' can obtain social security benefits on the basis of her lover's insurance, just like a wife. There is even a tax inducement to keep people from marrying: a couple who both work and have two children would be considerably better off if they divorced. A women does not have to be a man's wife to be able to spend his money: if they register themselves as Monsieur and Madame at a hotel, and she goes off on a shopping spree, he will be liable to those debts if the purchases are intended for their common use. The only financial disadvantage in free love is that the partners do not inherit and get no pension when one of them dies.

Union libre was fashionable with the 'generation of 1968' but only briefly. The French as a whole seem to think that marriage is part of love, and that marriage bolsters it more than it hinders it.

8

Why it is becoming harder to find and keep a spouse

'Executive, top job, forty-nine, most attractive, five foot ten inches tall, sense of humour, would like to marry very beautiful young lady, under thirty-seven, at least five foot six, cultivated.' This small advertisement in a newspaper attracted eighty replies. The advertiser tore most of them up – because the respondents did not fit the specifications. Neither does he fit his own description of himself. He is not quite in a top job, he is in fact fifty-six, he has no sense of humour according to his wife, he is not free to marry and marriage is the last thing he wants; but at least he was honest about being attractive, he really believes that. Why the deception? Because old age terrifies him: 'getting old is the worst of all things in my life.' Because he has dreamed ever since his youth of finding a tall, very beautiful Scandinavian goddess to give him some kind of bliss that he cannot define. Because his life has been a bit of a disappointment to him, and he has not lost hope. Because he would like to sparkle always with witty, cultured conversation. Not that he is sorry for himself, but love has somehow eluded him, or at least he has been unable to recognize it.

He blames this on the religious education he received; his teachers told him that the greatest sin was to have anything to do with a woman until he got married; he had no girlfriend until he was twenty-two; as a student he had no idea what to say to a woman, even when his friends told him that someone was 'devouring him with her eyes'; it took him five years to make up his mind whom he should marry, and he was never certain that he made the right choice. His wife cannot understand why he chose her, since he loves tall girls and she is short; and he says he still, after thirty years, cannot understand his wife; he sees her as essentially a cunning actress, and he never knows what she is up to. She wanted the perpetual attention of a man, to be made to feel secure, to be recognized by him, to be given a sense of her worth; she was very conscious that she had little education and less brain, whereas he was a graduate of a *grande école*: 'I liked his bohemian character, I liked the way he talked of literature, music and theatre; he was the man of my life; I admired him.'

Jean Pierre Aldebert

Are you alone, Mr Chairman?

But marriage or not, he never gave up looking at other women, doing a complete round about turn when a pretty one passed them by. 'It is natural for a man to look at women,' says she, 'but to do it systematically, that was too much.' It was neglect, more than infidelity, that she reproached him for: he never noticed a new dress, even a change in the colour of her hair: 'as a married woman, I did not exist.' For the first six months of their marriage, he used to say to her every day: 'I married you, you ought to be happy'; it infuriated her. She accepts that he loves women; to her he is the typical Latin macho, not quite a Don Juan, for he is neither nasty nor lacking in virility, but a seducer, who needs to go out with women as he needs to drink water, who needs to see his own glory reflected in the eyes of every girl, but more particularly very beautiful girls. He told her not to be jealous, because there were many girls, not one, and she learnt to overcome jealousy. But he was, of course, not as macho as he tried to be. He has never been as decisive as she would have liked; she could seldom get a straight answer from him on how household problems should be solved; but to him, she appears too hard, authoritarian, ungenerous. She found a little consolation in treating him as a child, which she says he loved, but she did not find that a perfect arrangement.

He retorts that married life with her was 'paralysis for me'; she did not give him the confidence he needed. He found his work enervating, too competitive; he could not sleep for worry; he changed his job half a dozen times, and in the end, at the age of thirty-eight, he decided that he had had enough of the constant conflicts of business, he said goodbye to ambition; he got himself a job in the middle range of management of a highly technical nature, so that few people are anxious to displace him. That leaves him slightly dissatisfied, because he has, as he puts it, settled for being the equivalent of a major, and will never be a general; but the advantage is that he can lead a much more relaxed life, and give himself up to his more fundamental needs, the search for the 'woman of his life'.

When his wife was unfaithful to him, he was very deeply hurt, but that gave him his liberty. Since then, in the space of six years, he has seduced at least a hundred women. At present, he has eight mistresses simultaneously. One is eighteen, a friend of his daughter; one used to be mistress to the Shah; one is a divorced executive; most are blonde and blue eyed; all are under thirty-five – he never goes above forty. None is married, because he does not want complications. None is from his own office for the same reason. Women, he confusedly believes, seek security from him, they want to learn from him, but because of his experience with his wife he is mistrustful of all women.

With American women, he has to 'change my personality': all American women have Clark Gable's Butler, of *Gone With The Wind*, as their secret ideal, the man who knew how to dominate the American woman. But he is most attracted by women 'from the east', meaning Russians, Poles, Scandinavians, 'who have a sense of mystery', as though the mystery of women has not been the bane of his life. If a woman makes advances to him, he will not respond; he likes the excitement of the chase, he prefers a difficult challenge. If a girl turns out to be simply stupid, he sleeps with her once and that is an end of it.

It was a colleague who taught him the art of picking up girls: it is important not to be too serious; one should be light and gay like champagne, paying unexpected compliments; a pretty girl wants above all to be told that she is intelligent. He has so mastered the art, that he can now guarantee to get a phone number within five minutes. 'A beautiful woman stimulates my thoughts: she makes me say things she has never heard before. I go to the Louvre: no woman there can resist me with my Latin and Greek culture.' Normally he is nervous, but in this kind of chase, he is exhilarated. He planned to go the next evening to Orly airport with an unmarried colleague of forty-eight, an accountant who was 'mad about women'; normally when he is at Orly, he is exhausted and unable to do anything about all the pretty girls he sees there; so they would go with their attaché cases, pretending that they had just returned from an international conference, and see what they could find. By this means he is able to sleep with a woman once or twice a week; the rest of the time he is alone.

When he is not with women, or travelling abroad for his firm, he plays tennis, skis, swims; he is proud of his physique: 'I do not look over fifty, do I?' he says with a mixture of satisfaction and apprehension. He is proud of being an educated man; he would like to write a book: *The Hundred Ploys of a French Seducer* would be bound to sell well. But he will not be too outrageous. The literature he likes reading must be literature that has been confirmed as good by universal agreement, the classics; he does not read modern novels; he will not go to the cinema unless a film has been highly praised. He buys *Le Monde* every day, even though he finds it too left-wing, because it is well written. He needs public approval. That does not make him a blind conformist: he is a nationalist because he admires France's past glory, its literature, architecture, music, its glorious wars, but that is all in the past, France is now 'an old woman', and displeases him when he compares what it is to what it was; he hates 'its loaded dice' and 'its caste system': there is now a socialist caste in power, replacing Giscard's caste. If he was thirty years old again, he would go to America, not that he approves of 'Wall Street capitalism', but because America offers space and liberty, and, he fondly imagines, if you tell someone there that you have been fired from five jobs, they will still give you a chance, whereas the French never will. But since he is not thirty, he will go on as he is for five or ten years concentrating on physical pleasures: he consulted his doctor, who told him it was all right to do so. Perhaps then he may feel the need for a woman who is more intelligent than beautiful; perhaps then he will play more chess and bridge, 'which I am good at, but which I neglect'. He insists he is happy; he repeats it energetically, with a sad face, a face that he says is very photogenic, 'which helps me with women, but not in business'.

'My wife is jealous of me,' he claims, 'because she is losing her looks.' She is indeed even more terrified of old age than he. 'I am quite sick with the thought that I am fifty. After a certain age, a woman is not a woman any more. There is nothing worse than to feel oneself physically diminished. One is not born sinful; it is old age that is the real sin, the greatest punishment.' She had a grandmother who never worried about her looks, but 'I haven't the strength of character, I am an ordinary woman. I have never done anything remarkable.' She has in fact had a try. Her great ambition as a child was to be a dancer, but her prim parents thought that improper; so she never acquired any skills. But at the onset of middle age she met a judo instructor, and she went off with him to start a gymnastics club: that is what gave her the courage to leave her husband. She moved into a separate flat: the marital flat had been 'his flat and I never felt at home there'. Now that the children have grown up, she has found a new purpose in life, teaching dance to middle-aged women who want to express themselves physically. 'I felt I was not capable of brainwork. My husband thinks intelligence is all important [that is what he told her] and I have no brain. I felt left out when he talked to the children, who are very clever. I have only common sense.' Now through dance she gets the pleasure of helping others to feel good, and when she dances herself, she feels as though she is twenty again, for a couple of hours. But when she stops, 'the body grows cold, life resumes its course.' It is not a total answer.

So she has never quite broken with her husband. They live in separate flats; but he comes to visit once or twice a week; they go on having their Sunday family meal: she does not want a divorce. Some of her friends say that he will eventually come back to her, but she doubts it. Would she want him back in old age? Being alone frightens her, and she does not know whether she will be strong enough to bear loneliness. He still treats her as he always did, telephoning suddenly to say he is coming to dinner; at first she was pleased, but then she started saying no, she was sorry, she was going out herself, to stop him taking her for granted. But she tries hard to keep his friendship, even if love has weakened. When he comes to her flat and just sits down and reads the paper without saying anything, she knows he has had a good week; when he arrives bearing a bottle of champagne, she knows he has had no girls. There is still something between them, a cross between a flirtation and a war.

The war is fought mainly over the children. She has consoled herself for her loss of her husband by mothering the twenty-year-old son, whom she looks after like a baby, feeding and clothing him; he seems to like that; he is very withdrawn, very religious, reads the Bible a lot, apparently deeply hurt by his parents' separation. But she is at daggers drawn with her daughter, who is intellectually outstanding, lively, independent and who cannot stand being told what to do; the daughter has got herself an American boyfriend; she has been to school in the United States for six months and is planning to go back there to study international relations; she blames her mother for wasting her life, by not becoming a dancer as a girl and saying *Merde* to her parents; she is indulgent towards her father who she says simply needs affection, and if he likes girls, it is a false pleasure, they are only after his money, but they excite him, and it is his life, he needs them for his loneliness. This daughter, aged seventeen, far from suffering from the parents' quarrels, has developed a strange maturity; she is full of optimism 'because all is before me'; she does not take those in authority too seriously, and finds nothing more amusing than people who do take themselves seriously, 'confusing the fact that they are men and that they have a position, mistaking themselves for the clothes they wear'; she is suspicious of superficiality and hypocrisy, which she sees as a particularly American fault, as she sees coldness and egoism as the French vice. 'Inside of me, I am always laughing at people.' Her mother takes that laughter as a personal attack: 'my daughter is a praying mantis: she devours me'; but she does her best to keep up appearances. They spend all their money on a very smart flat, in a fashionable district, so that they have no money for a car, or holidays. So that they can keep up appearances, they have asked me not to reveal their name.

To the statisticians, these parents are a married couple, which is why statistics about divorce mean so little. To statisticians, divorce can be counted like cases of smallpox; and every year they horrify the public with revised figures showing that the divorce rate is going up, that even if it is still running at only half the level of America's (one-sixth of French marriages end in divorce, compared to one-third in the United States) it will sooner or later catch up. These divorces, however, are a sign of the continuing appeal of the traditional family more than of its collapse. People who divorce do differ slightly from the rest of the population. They are not just those who believe in freedom in marriage, but include an unusually large proportion of people who wish to make the family the principal social relationship in their lives, who say that they have no friends outside the family, and that all their attention is concentrated on the family. They break up because they have an elevated idea of family life which they cannot apply in practice. They more frequently take up extreme positions in favour of wives staying at home. Women who go to work divorce more often, though partly because those who do not cannot afford to so easily. They are unusual, also, in making joint decisions about the children's education only half as frequently as the population at large.

Divorce is not a luxury in which the rich indulge; on the

contrary it is found pretty uniformly in all classes, but slightly more frequently among people who have only a primary education, and among office workers. The details revealed by the divorce courts give no support to the view that the French are tiring of marriage. Divorcees believed in marriage for life (when they got married) as frequently as the rest of the population. It is failure for them not to have attained that ideal. Only a quarter of male divorcees and a third of female ones do not wish to remarry, and that is mainly because of the different way they interpret the interests of the children. In 1976, a minister referred to wife battering as 'the English vice'. That was because the English had recently protested against it, but since then the French have discovered they have the same vice also. At the moment it cannot be said whether husbands and wives quarrel and divorce differently in France and England, because English researchers have found it impossible to show up any clear patterns. The film *Kramer versus Kramer* was, however, immensely successful in France, and with the divorce rate going up 8% a year, the French believe they will soon be just like the Americans. The children of divorced parents are beginning to

Dubout

get over their sense of being abnormal, particularly in Paris, and are defending themselves against teasing by forming their own network of friendships. But divorce remains a tragedy; it is very far from being accepted as an experience that is part of living.

Increasing divorce must inevitably produce a different kind of French child, or at least a new minority (yet another) of children confronted with new problems. The children of divorced parents learn to fight special kinds of battles, at an early age. For example, those of the judge, who married a sculptress during the war. They did not get on. Increasingly their time together was spent either quarrelling or actually fighting. They did their best to hide this from their children, but their restraint towards each other meant only that they beat their children when they were not beating each other. They sent their children to boarding school from the age of six and left them there even for holidays. The grandparents and cousins pretended that nothing was wrong: outside appearances were kept up. But everybody really knew that the judge had a succession of mistresses, even though his absences from home were explained by the demands of his profession, and everyone knew the sculptress had her lovers. In a provincial town, such conduct brought not just whispered disapproval; other parents forbade their children to have anything to do with the family; the daughter said, 'I was considered the daughter of a slut, not to be visited.' Her schoolmates came to see her only on Saturdays, secretly, when their parents were out; she could not visit their homes. This social ostracism hurt her as much as her abandonment by her parents: right into adult life, she would cry in the night. The judge in due course went to live in a neighbouring town, to avoid the scandal. The sculptress spent a lot of time abroad. Their children were left to cope as best they could; often gas and electricity were cut off because the parents omitted to pay the bills. But such was the judge's view of his rights as a father, that he forbade his daughter to study music, saying that when she was twenty-one she could do what she pleased, but until then he would decide what was good for her. Music was her one love. He returned home to take away her harp and sold it. When she started living with a man he threatened to have her taken to court and sent to a remand home. She replied by having a child. He had to consent to marriage then, for the sake of appearances. He himself had just had a child by his mistress, and that had made him divorce the sculptress, so that he could be respectable too. It is a story that could have come from the nineteenth century, except for the ending. The daughter divorced soon after, and now lives alone with her child: as a single parent, with a job of her own, she has found peace.

A more 'modern' example is the case of Martin, well known ethnologist, journalist and author. He comes from a Protestant bourgeois family, from whom he has cut himself off. He fought with the communist resistance while still a boy. He was a student of brilliance and passion. He met Benoite at university, the daughter of a respectable civil servant. They lived together for two years until she got pregnant; they then married (in 1949). For them, life was conviviality and discussion. Their flat in the fifth arrondissement of Paris was always full of friends arguing about politics, sex and international affairs. Martin slept with the women who came to argue, and Benoite slept with the men. Amongst themselves, however, they argued most about how their boy and girl should be brought up. Benoite complained that Martin had ruined the boy, Stéphane; she devoted herself to spoiling the girl, Ariane; the children were, as it were, divided between them. Eventually she told Martin to clear out. He went to live in a separate house, and installed first a beautiful young Eurasian girlfriend there, and then a redhead Rumanian, whom he eventually married. The children now lived in two homes, though mainly with their mother, but their mother constantly complained to them about the misbehaviour of their father, who in turn accused the mother of forcing him to live apart from his children. In the end the children had to stop visiting the father, because Benoite had turned him into an ogre. Several years later, in the riots of 1968, Stéphane, now a student at the School of Political Sciences, was repulsing an attack of policemen, when a man emerged from the melee, his face covered in blood: it was Martin. Their emotional reunion on the barricades made Stéphane realize that there was no good reason why he should not see his father. He now heard Martin's side of the story of his parents' separation. He has freed himself from the need to choose between his father and his mother. He now sees that though Benoite is a vocal feminist, she is also a typical possessive mother. Stéphane has been through all sorts of nervous crises in coping with his parents, even to the extent of attempting suicide. Now aged thirty, married with two children, he is a senior civil servant full of promise, but his torn childhood has left its mark.

France has more alcoholics than it has divorcees. Too much drink may well have more effect on family life than divorce, less noticed because it has been going on for so many centuries. The kind of hate it can create is seen in Raymonde and Monique. Their father is the incarnation of the unsuccessful petit bourgeois. He was a greengrocer, with two shops. He used to work three days a week, and spend the rest of his time fishing or hunting with his dogs. But he was too fond of drinking, and a competitor denounced him to the police for drunken driving: he was arrested and had his licence withdrawn for three years. That put him permanently on the bottle, because he could no longer do his deliveries. He refused to find alternative work: he told his wife to work and she refused. He bitterly resented not being obeyed. He saw himself as the head of the family, and he expected to be served at table. His children had to ask permission to leave after a meal, but first enquiring whether there was anything else of which he was in need. He was a proud man, and he would not tolerate that his children should argue with him; hence there were constant arguments, which got even more dramatic when he started hitting his wife. He stopped sleeping with her, partly because he insisted on bringing his dogs to bed with him also. His wife had been his secretary before their marriage; he had soon become unfaithful to her. She also took to drink. The children have a deep hatred of their father; they feel powerless to stop their mother's slide towards alcoholic suicide . . . .

It is the debris of these battles whom one finds advertising for partners in the newspapers, as the handsome executive in search of a very beautiful wife did. Of course, one also meets people clinging to traditional attitudes, especially in *Le Chasseur Français* – a hunting paper in more ways than one – which since 1892 has carried marriage advertisements, which must clearly state the 'matrimonial intention' and be 'moral' and 'honourable'. It still contains advertisements like these: 'Elderly parents wish to arrange marriage for their son, age thirty-four, tall, thin, serious, Catholic, with comfortable home, property and stable job, primary education certificate, timid, traumatized in infancy, wishing to develop through marriage, seeks happiness in a deep sentimental union with young woman, thirty-three to thirty-five.' It even produces answers like these, in reply to an advertisement by a man of forty-seven: 'You will perhaps be surprised that at your age you should receive a letter from a girl of twenty-six. My reasons are . . . that I think that when a man is nearly fifty, he has, fortunately, fewer needs than at thirty, and that he is less likely to be unfaithful. I must warn you that I shall not tolerate the slightest faux pas!' The *Chasseur Français* forbids the offer to send a photograph. That, by contrast, is what most of the advertisers in the *Nouvel Observateur* want. This carries the 'modern' advertisements, in the style of the *New York Review of Books* or *Time Out*, with less emphasis on marriage, more on the fulfilment of fantasy, shielded by a banal humour. 'In the *Chasseur*, it is possible to seek pity for one's misfortunes; in the *Nouvel Obs* one is better off saying one has been psychoanalysed.'

Some of the pathetic correspondence and meetings to which these advertisements give rise have been meticulously recorded by a divorcee who, in her forties, tried this method of regaining happiness. The first reply she received was of six closely written pages in beautiful and ardent prose from an old gentleman who turned out to be seventy-four: he invited her to his flat in the sixteenth arrondissement of Paris where, surrounded by Ming vases and two pianos, he offered her camomile tea and told her of his dreams of a mistress who would console his loneliness. The next was from Ernest, a senior manager in a large company, whose wife had just died: he promised to fulfil all the desires and demands, intellectual, musical and social, that a new bride would have: he asked her how she would like him to dress for his first meeting, since he attached great importance to elegance and wished to do honour to his 'lady': he arrived in a bright check suit and bow tie, reeking of eau de Cologne; he laughed a lot, leered at her breasts, said his aim was above all to have fun; but he was uncultured, had small pig's eyes and, worst of all, was completely bald. (To such an extent is baldness an obstacle, that marriage counsellors advise bald men to buy wigs.) There was Guy, profuse in his apologies, tormented by his own inadequacy, who touched her hand accidentally and excused himself long-windedly for this unintentional indecency, who smelt powerfully of a mixture of tobacco and medicine, who could talk only about his own failures, his neighbours who hated him, his bad health, his poor sleep. Charles, by contrast, was forty-five, good looking, tall and upright with a nice smile, but he was incapable of conversing, refusing to do more than answer questions with monosyllables. Michel, young, with a full beard and a majestic body, captivated her by his brilliance and sensitivity: they had drinks, then dinner, then more drinks; he made her feel twenty again; but in the end she said goodbye because, though he spoke in praise of maturity, she took fright at being ten years older than he. Bernard was in the process of getting divorced after eleven years of marriage; he saw his two children at weekends, 'they are my sole emotional link with humanity.' He wrote poignantly of the loneliness he had experienced both during his marriage and since: the 'tragedy of his life' was that he needed both beauty and affection in women. When they met he confessed he was 'not very virile', but he decided he did not want to get involved with her because she offered only friendship whereas he needed love: he wrote to say he would wait: 'I deserve pity.'

Didier was a senior judge about to retire, who wanted someone to join him in his house in the Charente. He spoke authoritatively on the telephone. But he turned out to be physically small and unimpressive; and his house was less grand than he made out, dark and sad, with furnishings that appeared to have been inherited from his grandparents. For five hours he told her about his habits and quirks, his favourite foods, how he liked his salads seasoned, making her feel that he was engaging her as his housekeeper. He spoke only about himself and his troubles, without asking anything about her. As night fell, he recounted his adventures with his mistresses, assured her no woman had ever pleased him so much as she, and invited her to see what a man he was, straightaway, in his bed. The elegance and ornateness of some of the other letters she received is a reminder that classical habits of courtship have not vanished; but the even more numerous letters full of spelling and grammar mistakes, clumsy with the formulae of commercial correspondence, struggling to express simple hopes, show that wife-hunting is often undertaken in ways not all that different from job-hunting.

The multiplication of marriage bureaux is the result of specialization in catering for increasingly varied tastes. One bureau is designed to satisfy men as rapidly as possible: it places its male clients in a series of tiny rooms (six feet by four feet) with two armchairs, and seven women are introduced, one every fifteen minutes, for a rapid interview; 200 presentations take place in its dingy offices every day. The supermarket principle is carried to its extreme by what claims to be the largest marriage bureau in France: it offers seven different prices, depending on how choosy the client is: for women limiting their aspirations to a worker or a peasant, there is a specially low fee; this is the bureau favoured by the poor. At the other end of the scale there is the lady who receives her clients individually, introduces them personally, and gives the impression of being a friend bringing friends together; or the extremely expensive agency, situated near the Elysée Palace, which asks its clients not just whether they own a car, but what make it is, whether they have a yacht, what exactly their income and capital amount to, claiming to cater for 'the privileged, company directors, leading personalities of the world of business, the arts, diplomacy and the university'. One computerized firm appeals particularly to managers, balancing its pseudo-scientific methods (including graphology) with old fashioned advice that a man should present himself as being 'strong, elegant, hardworking, sober and distinguished', while a woman is urged to stress her qualities of submissiveness, generosity, gaiety, understanding, and above all avoid any hint of irony or sarcasm. A Christian bureau requires a promise to get married in church. But there are also clubs which simply bring people together by distributing their photographs and organizing parties, and one which offers 'anonymous psychosexual relations'. Some marriage bureaux claim a 30% success rate; investigating journalists have put the figure at 2%. That shows how much harder the bureaux' job is than the marriage-broking by the notary, the doctor, the tailor, and the village busybodies who in the past found partners for the less demanding ancestors of the present generation.

What increasing marital incompatibility shows is that people are finding it harder to meet their soul mates because they have a strong idea of their own individuality; they are becoming more different from each other, even if it is only in slight nuances, but they have not found new ways to replace the resignation, complacency or tolerance that marriage used to demand. The daughter of the seductive executive and his dancing wife has instinctively seen the ability not to take oneself too seriously as the way to avoid repeating her parents' confrontations, but she is bemused by the problem of what her friends are really like, behind their hypocrisy and the roles they play. That turns marriage into an exercise in metaphysics. As the options open to both partners increase, each being able to add a different element of education, travel and work experience to complicate his or her personality, living with another person the modern way is as different from marriage in the past, as car-driving is from horse-riding.

Contrast the way the more traditional Gaston Lucas, locksmith, found his second wife. His first one had died four years ago, after a long illness; he was tired of living on eggs and salads; he was lonely; he still felt young at forty-six: 'instinct and feeling are always there: one is made to live with a woman, that is the way nature wants it.' Travelling in the metro, he picked up a copy of *Ici-Paris* and read an advertisement of a marriage bureau. He wrote to say he wanted a wife with whom he could get on and who was capable of looking after the house properly; he did not demand a beauty and did not mind from what part of France she came. He wrote to several of the names he was sent; most replied but only two held his attention. The first was from a woman who turned out to be lame and to have a blind mother with whom she wanted to go on living in Villejuif. He replied he was sorry about her mother, but he had his own flat and did not want to move to the suburbs. He had sworn to himself that after his trials with his first wife who had been an invalid, he would not marry anyone unless she was in good health. The second woman whose letter he liked, from Lyon, had just lost her mother and so her flat, because this was on a life tenancy. They exchanged letters and photographs, and she visited him in Paris. She then revealed that during the war she had spent a long time in a sanatorium, had been badly treated and had not fully recovered. He was embarrassed. But then he took pity on her, he knew she had been rejected several times for this reason; he thought to himself that it was not a valid reason to refuse to marry someone simply because she was ill: 'she did not displease him, she seemed capable of running a home, she held herself well, she was clean. I could not ask more.' He had thought of living with her unmarried for six months to see how it worked, but she came from the provinces, where that sort of thing was not so easily tolerated. So they got married. No statistician has counted how many people there are left who confront human relationships with such unambitious philosophy.

9

What lovers want from each other

Brigitte Bardot believes that her fame is both understandable and the result of a misunderstanding. She appealed to her generation, all over the world, because she seemed to represent a new kind of girl, entirely natural, devoted to carefree enjoyment, undisguised by cosmetics, and breaking away from the traditional hypocritical role that women used to be expected to play. She does not consider herself beautiful, because her features are not perfect, but she represented simplicity and the absence of false shame. Jane Fonda proclaimed that Brigitte struck the first blow for Women's Lib., because 'she kicked out any man she was tired of and invited in any man she wanted, she lived like a man.' That is one of several misunderstandings. Even if she behaved like that, she would have been living like a very old-fashioned kind of man. Being natural was in fact very hard work. It made her profoundly lonely. She used to need constant company at the height of her fame: 'If I did not have fifteen people around me, I used to become very unhappy and say to myself: Good God, what is happening to me, I am all alone.' She used to want the full attention of her male admirers for twenty-four hours a day, and what was worse, she used to despise them when they gave it to her. She had great difficulty in coping with her natural impulses, or making sense of them.

Born in 1934 to a well-to-do manufacturer of liquid oxygen, brought up in genteel style, with traditional bourgeois strictness and spoiling, she was discovered by the cinema world when her photograph appeared, at the age of fifteen, on the cover of *Elle*. Brigitte instantly 'fell in love' with the young film-director's assistant who was sent to seek her out: Roger Vadim. She interpreted love as meaning instant attraction.

Marguerite Duras commented: 'When a man attracts her, Brigitte goes straight to him. Nothing stops her. It does not matter if she is in a café, at home, or staying with friends. She goes for him on the spot without a glance at the man she is leaving. In the evening, perhaps she will come back, or perhaps not.' Brigitte herself said: 'In love, I give myself completely.' But she was not quite the modern girl she thought she was, and more a nineteenth-century romantic than she realized. She was obsessed by the desire to be happy, she longed for admiration, but she did not know how to keep that admiration once it had passed the stage of outward appearances. Like a romantic heroine, she attempted suicide when her parents forbade her to marry Vadim. That made them relent, but with the proviso that he got himself a 'proper' job and was converted to Catholicism: it was only after the religious wedding, and not the civil ceremony, that they acknowledged his right to sleep with her.

Her search for carefree enjoyment meant that she liked the company of men who went out a lot, who had nice cars, who were fond of dancing and who told silly stories. She 'fell in love' with at least twenty other men after Vadim. But these relationships were such that her lovers would sometimes 'go off for three weeks without warning, leaving me without news like an imbecile, and then come back and express surprise when I say it's finished.' She may have wanted to 'give herself completely', but she adds, 'When I discover that I am not repaid, that gives me a shock.' Roger Vadim encouraged her to exaggerate or even misrepresent her tastes by presenting herself to the world as an unattainable erotic fantasy; he made her play down her intelligence like Marilyn Monroe, so that she might become a female version of James Dean. But that was because Vadim is a man who all his life has been tormented by the very old-fashioned desire to shape young women, only to protest, when they mature, that they demand their independence, as he protested, with his next creation Catherine Deneuve, that she grew up to become too bossy.

Brigitte appearing publicly in the nude was outrageous, but not really modern; it had been done before. She may have given the impression that she was a rebel against her parents' respectable sort of marriage, as basically an arrangement involving ritual and duty, because affection was not something that could be relied on; but she has come to a very similar conclusion after all her experiences: 'Now,' she said when she reached the age of forty-five, 'I know that one can never count on a man.' She believes she went wrong because 'I did not understand just how exceptional it is for a couple to succeed.' She has discovered that what she really likes best is looking after her house, making it nice, rather in the way her mother did. 'I prefer to succeed in my life more than in my career. I am not competitive. I am not against being obedient to a man, if the man is capable of making me obey – it would be a very good thing if he did.' She thinks she is ready now to settle down with a man; she is less demanding; she enjoys 'observing what is happening around her', and being alone sometimes, so as to be able to think, or to think about nothing at all. She is, therefore, far from being a 'liberated woman': She is indeed all for liberation, but not for the women's liberation movement. She says she has never wanted to be treated like a man because 'a woman must above all remain a woman.' It is all right for women to 'refuse to submit to the yoke of a man who will not give them enough money, or to be able to earn their livings without depending on others, but on the other hand I believe that women, in wanting to liberate themselves too much, are going to be increasingly unhappy. Because a woman is not made to live a man's life. A woman has her weaknesses, and is so very vulnerable . . . A woman is a gentle creature.'

She concedes that her upbringing has left an imprint on her. She is so far from worshipping youth that she is not at all worried about becoming old: a nice old lady can be admirable, and all the more so if she does not try to hide her white hair and wrinkles with cosmetics. Beauty, she insists, is very important for women (not for men), but every woman has some kind of beauty in her: it is simply a question of finding it, and looking after it. Perhaps the main point on which she has moved away from her parents is in her attitude to property: Property, she has discovered, involves too much responsibility, 'property is slavery.' So Brigitte resents the reputation that has been built up around her. She knows she has been unpopular with some people in France: 'they say I am egoistical and unsociable; they say I have no heart.' These are accusations that lost love has always produced: in fact she does social work with aged women, as the rich have always done, and she has devoted herself above all to the welfare of animals: that she says expresses the 'quixotic' side of her character.

The significance of Brigitte Bardot is not that she aroused male lust, but that she represented an attempt by a generation to find a new style of relationship in which sex and sensuality had a more central role. She quickly crashed against obstacles as perplexing as the restrictions of her parents' generation, but her personal failures and return to more conservative ideals do not mean that hers has simply been a youthful escapade. She must be seen in the total context of attitudes to sexuality. These cannot be discussed as a continuation and exacerbation of France's supposed tradition of debauchery. The studies of sexual behaviour which have appeared in the last decade do indeed show that much sexual activity fits into the traditional game or war of the sexes; the Frenchman's reputation as the Latin lover, fluent in his compliments, theatrical in his passions, needing a mistress as well as a wife to perpetuate his romantic excitements does still inspire some people; so too does the Frenchwoman's reputation as the incarnation of coquetry, in which charm is deliberately cultivated to conquer man, and hard work is involved in deploying wit, beauty and domestic skills to continue to earn for France the title that the Victorians gave it, 'a paradise for women'. But sexual relations are increasingly more than natural acts, they have become in addition a means of self discovery, the expression of an effort to make living a fuller experience, and above all a touchstone of the quality of human relationships.

If Gallic love is just the sign of physical vitality, why is it that half of French women say that their sex lives are unsatisfactory; and why is it that three-quarters of those who say they are now satisfied with them confess that they have attained this state only after years, sometimes many years, of frustration? French women complain first of all of their ignorance, of the way they were brought up, which means they, to a certain extent, blame themselves, or their mothers, for their difficulties with men. Even women in their thirties make complaints like these: 'As an adolescent my mother explained to me clearly that pleasure was reserved for men "who were all pigs" and that women had to go through that ordeal to have children and keep their husbands.' Another was told by her mother: 'If you want to be happy one day, you must make a generous gift of yourself to him, intact, otherwise he won't want you. He who loves you will lead you to the altar without touching you.' Says a third, 'Brought up in a very Catholic family, I tend to give no importance to my sexuality. I sometimes have the impression of being unable to separate pleasure from the act of procreation. This creates tensions with my husband who, for his part, likes pleasure for pleasure's sake.' The warnings of mothers, who themselves had a tough time with their husbands, have left many women feeling guilty and worried by men's caresses; that this has not happened more often is due to the fact that, as recently as ten years ago, only one-third of women had discussed sex with their mothers and only a tenth with their fathers. One, who is now thirty-four, says she postponed her sex life as long as possible, because she knew nothing about the subject and would not ask, for fear people would laugh at her; her husband was as ignorant as she was, and his brusqueness put her off sex even more. There are women in their forties who have only recently discovered the clitoris and masturbation. There is a sizeable minority who are

Gondot

Be careful! There's ice on the roads, dear . . .

so shy they prefer to make love only in the dark. On the other hand there is the woman of twenty-eight who owes her sexual education to *Lady Chatterley's Lover*, which she read at fifteen in defiance of her father and for whom sex has ever since been a series of disillusionments.

Men for their part complain, often uncomprehendingly, that their wives are frigid. It is an old complaint counterbalancing the myth that women are sexually insatiable. Twenty years ago, a priest claimed that frigidity was 'the most serious problem in marriage. Wives are amazed when they are told that, from the Church's point of view, it is a serious transgression to refuse their husbands . . . In most cases, not having seen marriage as a gift of the body, the wife was shocked and disgusted by sexual relations from the beginning.' It was not necessarily a greater source of enjoyment when the idea of marriage as a gift of the body was accepted. In the 1950s only a minority of women admitted they were satisfied by physical love in marriage. For long, frigidity was accepted either as a physical defect, or as the result of some psychological block. But recently women have started replying that it is their husband's fault that he does not know how to make them happy; that he makes love so quickly that they are barely aware of it; two men in five utter not a word throughout the proceedings and three women in five are equally silent. Women probably make more effort to please their partners than men do: and in order to stop intercourse ending with an angry interrogation, a large minority pretends, sometimes or often, to have had an orgasm.

A woman recalls how since her marriage at the age of twenty-five, when both she and her husband were virgins, she has never been happy making love. She has had five children; she is a practising Catholic. A year ago, a man started courting her; she resisted as best she could, but eventually she 'fell into his arms.' Despite her remorse, she has suddenly discovered the orgasm and found sex a pleasure. What, she asks, has happened to her frigidity? 'I do not regret this experience which showed me that I could be a woman'. Husbands have been slow to learn: 'I had been married for nine years,' says a woman of twenty-nine. 'I had never had an orgasm. Our sexual relations take place very, very fast, without much emotion or tenderness. For some years now, he has classified me as a frigid woman, which absolves him from all effort. Every discussion on this subject ends with insults and shouting.' 'Driven by despair,' as she says, she took a lover and now both enjoys intense pleasure in sex and suffers guilt at her infringement of her inherited morality. It has been the new generation of women who have urged men to show more delicacy and understanding. Ten years ago, only 13% of women said they would like more sex (as opposed to 30% of men). Today, at least among the more educated, half of women say they want more, and regret that children, or exhaustion, or the absence of their partners, and above all their own timidity, obstructs them. Sex, they say, has become more important to them in their thirties and forties, or even fifties, which may be another way of saying that people are becoming more concerned by the degree and nature of the pleasure they derive from it. The pill has not quite liberated them, because only about one-third of women use it; a tenth use the diaphragm; so the majority of French women still live with fear of pregnancy and depend on men to protect them from it.

Young wives may believe their husbands have imagination but they think so less and less as time goes by; and by middle age, about half of husbands are condemned as being unimaginative. There are husbands for their part, who argue that imagination has no place in marriage. A women who is only thirty-one years old makes this complaint: 'My husband was a hardened bachelor, a butterfly man who lived till the age of thirty with a diary filled with girls' addresses. When I got to know him, I was twenty-five, I had never slept with a man before. For three years I used to see him at weekends and once during the week. It took me a long time to realize that he saw other girls at the same time: I had the privileged role of the half-wife, surrounded by mistresses. Our sexual relations at the time gave me great satisfaction, because it was he who taught me all sorts of sexual games. We were constantly making discoveries; we gave great importance to different kinds of caresses and went through intense excitement. Then one day I saw him in the company of another girl. I broke our affair off brutally. For six months I tried to forget him . . . Then suddenly he reappeared, completely changed, offering me marriage and faithfulness. He has become the best of husbands, loving, thoughtful – and faithful. But for him marriage is incompatible with a rich sexual life. He makes love like a husband. There are no more long sexual games. He caresses me mechanically, always the same way, without any variety. It is a boring habit. And when I express other desires, he exclaims, 'But this is what marriage is.' In short, he said goodbye to excitement when he left his mistress. Now I am worthy of profound and committed love and as a result I lose the right to pleasure. How can I make him understand that one can be both husband and lover to the same woman and that after three years of marriage I am accumulating frustrations? Our feelings for each other are very strong, but I refuse to accept the luke-warmness of our sexual relations.' It works the other way too: a forty-five-year-old woman explains that she feels she has become 'a useful piece of furniture between a pair of sheets around ten o'clock every evening. Gradually, I have lost sexual desire, and I have rejected him more and more often, which does not help things . . . an abyss of silence has grown between us.' Or a girl of twenty-four complains that her mate is too expert, her orgasms have become routine and so boring.[1]

All these people are searching for something more than a physical act, but also something more than romantic love as a universal panacea. That kind of love has played a smaller part in French life than legend suggests. Even twenty years ago, when addiction to the romantic novel may have appeared to have reached its height, very few women said they would be willing to give all up for love; most said they were not romantic. Even among girls in their early twenties, there was a large minority that was not looking for a 'great love'. Only a little more than a quarter of all Frenchwomen said they had actually experienced a great love: those who did claim this experience were above all married women under thirty-five with higher education and successful husbands. The romantic tradition is essentially a literary one that exists in books. Today it is still the educated who talk about a great love most, and peasant and working-class women often say that love is something that takes place in youth, and that they do not expect to be swept off their feet by

Letters to F. Magazine, in *La Sexualité des Femmes*, ed. S. Horer (Grasset 1980).

some marvellous man. One-third of the population thinks that a good marriage need not necessarily be based on love. Another survey, mainly of middle-aged middle-class women, but including some workers and peasants, recently found as many as three-quarters claiming that they had not married for love, but mainly to get away from home.

Adultery seems to be less often a solution to the dissatisfactions of married life than France's reputation would suggest. Ten years ago 30% of married men and 10% of married women admitted to having committed adultery at some time. Most had done so only once or twice; only 5% of men and 3% of women had repeated it often. There was considerably more adultery among educated men (40%), but most of all among men over fifty living in medium-sized towns (42%) — the proverbial bored provincials with their hypocritical moral codes. For men adultery was most common in middle age, but for women in their twenties (13%). In 1980, however, another enquiry (loaded in favour of the more educated) found 12% of women saying that they were then actually having sexual relations with several men at the same time (and not just at some time in their lives); 22% were not firmly attached to the idea of having sex simply with their regular partners; 38% did not think that they had to be in love in order to have sexual relations; and 48% felt they were not having enough sexual relations. It is impossible to say whether in the last ten years Frenchwomen have become either more promiscuous, or more frank, or more demanding. These figures, for what they are worth, do not distinguish the French dramatically from other nations. Roughly half of American men claim never to have deceived their wives. The English are more reticent; one researcher could find only 8% of married couples who admitted to having been unfaithful to their spouses; another concluded there were about four million promiscuous people in England. But the significance of the 1980 enquiry is that it suggests more activity in the imagination than actual extra-marital adventure. And this is confirmed by yet another reply to a questionnaire by readers of a middle-brow woman's magazine, in which 13% said they had had a homosexual relationship, 58% said they definitely did not want one, but the rest thought they would be interested, or might be.

The French may write erotic books, but they are not quite satisfied by them. Foreigners are more excited by French naughtiness than are the French themselves. One of the best known erotic works of the post-war era, the *Story of O*, has sold over four million copies in the United States, but only 800,000 in France. The average sale of a pornographic book is only three or four thousand copies, and perhaps ten to fifteen thousand if it is put into paper-back, which is more or less what a fashionable philosopher or theologian would expect to sell. Anaïs Nin's novels used to sell only 1500 copies, but her *Venus Erotica* sold 100,000 in two months, because by then she had established a reputation as a serious novelist, and a much wider public was therefore willing to read that book as literature. Most pornography comes out in small, expensive editions; collecting it remains a hobby for an equally small fraternity: the largest collection is probably that of a successful politician who ended up as a minister of education. Three-quarters of the population say they have never read a pornographic magazine and two-thirds that they have never seen a pornographic film. That is partly because pornography follows very traditional lines and everyone knows what to expect. There is much more to be learnt about attitudes to sex from the lives of those who write or produce erotic books, than from the books themselves; the intentions, that is to say, have not been quite fulfilled in their writings, where the variation has more often been in literary style than in imaginate originality.

Jean-Jacques Pauvert, who is the country's leading publisher in this field (but who has also been adventurous and successful in several other branches of publishing), has championed Sade as France's answer to Freud, or rather as being Freud's precursor, a great investigator of the passions. Pauvert was prosecuted for publishing Sade thirty years ago, but now Sade is on the shelves of every university library, though still in the literature rather than the psychology section. When Pauvert gives public lectures, his audience is full of housewives who have come not for titillation, but apparently to improve their minds: they study his books as they study books on psychoanalysis or sociology. His aim is to end the segregation of erotic books into a separate category.

The author of the *Story of O* was for many years an editor on one of the country's most respected literary journals, though she has insisted on preserving her anonymity. She was brought up in an upper-middle-class family whose motto was 'Stand up straight, people are looking at you'. She began reading porno-graphic books at the age of fourteen, borrowed from her father's library, and beginning with Boccaccio. Her father said to her, you are starting early, you won't understand them, we had better explain; so a cousin was delegated to tell her all about sex; he took her to a brothel, which she found both frightening and comic. But no further mention was made of this subject in the family. The *Story of O* is almost a transcription of the fantasies its author had as a child and adolescent, which she told herself as she fell asleep and which persisted throughout her life. It owes a great deal to Ann Radcliffe and Sir Walter Scott for its atmos-phere and background, for the author is a passionate Anglo-phile, and very widely read in English literature: her favourite reading is the King James version of the Bible and Shakespeare, from whom she quotes freely, as well as Proust and Baudelaire. The elaborate description of clothing is explained by her having studied the history of costume; her obsession with wearing no underwear dates from her mother's telling her how scandalized she had been at her convent school to discover that the nuns wore nothing underneath their skirts. The violence in the book is, she says, like the violence in detective stories, not to be taken to heart. Her book is not meant as a manual for debauchery: she wrote it to please her lover when she feared he might leave her; she insists she did not publish it to make money: indeed it did not make much until critics began demanding that it should be banned. The paradox is that her fantasies were not shared by her lover, and that she did not want to be humiliated in the way the book describes. What is the point of it then?

First, that she thought it absurd that she should dislike humiliation. She wanted to imagine herself different from what she was. That is a constant refrain in her. She enjoys fantasy because 'one gets bored with oneself, don't you find? I am tired of being myself.' She reads books unceasingly because even though most of them are bad, she likes to discover the human being behind them: she admits reading is an alibi, another way of delivering herself from herself, trying to live through others. 'I would have made an excellent nun.' The trouble with real life is that it is never as perfect as you imagine it; people make promises they do not keep, they say they love you and even if that is true, it does not get you very far. So, secondly, she thinks there is no harm in sham love. The only sacred thing in the world, she says, is love, but it is so rare and difficult, that a sham version of it has its uses, in that at least it encourages people to try and make themselves more beautiful, pleasant and jolly. To love someone is dangerous and danger is exciting; secret danger even more so. She participated in the Resistance because she found secret societies and danger a masculine preserve that it was almost an erotic experience to enter. A husband, a job, children, the ordinary things of life are her idea not of life, but of slavery. She wishes to escape from that, but it is only 'in the head'. In her real existence, she has no sense of being inferior to men at all. She denies that her book can do any harm, saying 'it is not the readers of Sade who established the concentration camps, but those who had never read him.' What her book shows is that the fantasies she recounts are very much in a traditional mould; they are like fairy tales that are no use in resolving the problems of daily life. She defends pornography as a means of delivering people from fear, and therefore as a contribution to the love of liberty, if by liberty is understood 'sharing one's thoughts'. People discover that 'in the depths where Eros is hidden' strange sources of love exist, and that these are not necessarily evil. Love, she says, is 'a tour de force of the intelligence [sic] which needs to be perpetually reinvented.' The trouble is that though she praises imagination, that is precisely what is lacking in her work, stylishly written though it is.

The author of *Emmanuelle* (who is the wife of a French diplomat now at UNESCO) is more aggressively a reformer: she sees herself as leading 'a crusade for the upheaval of our amatory customs'. Eroticism, she argues, is 'the only modern rationale we can find through which to understand one another, whatever our race, the only way we can . . . revel in our differences and communicate our dreams'. However, love, as it is organized at present around monogamous marriage, has created too many problems; she thinks a new kind of love needs to be invented which will solve problems instead of creating them. Her programme includes ending the exclusiveness of love, as an unnecessary limitation on experience, the abolition of jealousy, the acceptance of a distinction between family and erotic love; she sings the praises of masturbation as 'the autonomy of pleasure', of homosexuality, of 'prostitution for pleasure'. Her ideal is to be like a mollusc: a creature born male, which turns hermaphrodite and finishes up female. Only such a certainty of occupying varied roles would end the battle of the sexes. That is looking very far into the future.

By contrast, Régine Deforges, the first woman to become a publisher of erotic books, has used the genre to discover what it was that she personally found erotic. She claims that she has the traditional ordinary peasant woman's attitude to sex, a physical delight in it; but as an adolescent she was prevented from expressing her feelings, and so eroticism always contains an element of transgression in it, which stimulates her just as much. She says publishing forbidden books was partly her way of saying *Merde* to the establishment; advertising her books with a photograph of herself in the nude was designed to provoke it even more. Her appearance remains even more striking than her photograph: she regards clothes as an incitement to men; she does not mind being called a fetishist; she likes, and is always aware of, the way men look at her and react to her appearance. 'Nothing is more exciting than to present oneself to another completely disarmed, transparent, naked.' 'I need the desire of men,' she says; she calls it a weakness, but one she cannot help; she missed being loved as a child; and literature plays its part also in encouraging girls to search for a hero. The search is always a bit of a game. She likes to please women as much as men; she likes pleasing, because she likes to be loved; that is what seduction is all about. If she meets a man who attracts her, accompanied by his wife, she will talk only to his wife, as a tactic; the friendship of the wife protects her. But what bores her stiff is theorists of love. And when she is in love, she loses interest in the problems of finding it. She has always needed a certain amount of solitude; even now, living happily with her man, she goes off occasionally to a nunnery for a week or two; love is not a game to play all the time. It happens to be her speciality, and she earns her living writing romantic historical

Roubille

I shall reveal to you all the beauty of love!

novels and film scenarios about young women in distress. But with her too there is a gap between what she likes in real life and her fantasies. She has no universal answers; she has 'searched for love and invented it' for herself. Each person has to do that.

The effort to get beyond traditional answers is seen also in attitudes to prostitution. The prostitute does not play as significant a role in men's lives as she used to. Paris could once claim to be the world's capital for organized debauchery and every little provincial town once had an array of brothels in the same way as it had cafés and later cinemas and pin-ball machines. But today France seems to have about as many (per head of population) as the United States, twice as many as Britain, but only half as many as Germany.[1] Prostitutes used to initiate schoolboys into the mysteries of sex. In the Simon report of 1972, only 45% of men definitely said they had never been to one. Increasingly, young people no longer pay for their early experiences, and the clients of prostitutes are men who are alone, or cannot get from their wives what they want. However, in the last two decades, there has been a growing demand for more than just a body, clients want 'the heart also'. A new type of prostitute has developed who offers to listen to the confessions of her client and to be sympathetic, to give love more than sex. This marks a change from the attitude that sex is dirty, which meant that the prostitute had to be punished by the very people who used her services. But there is a long way to go before she is regarded as no more a danger than masturbation and loss of virginity before marriage once were.

Sexual fantasy has become a modern mystery and how to make sense of it a challenge that many have tried to confront. When Nancy Friday published her account of American women's fantasies, a French feminist was amazed, and firmly convinced that French women were excited by totally different things. But when she proceeded to question them, she found a surprising number conniving at the traditional ploys of masculine pornography. A teacher of French literature in Le Havre, married to an industrialist, mother of a daughter of twenty, and secretly mistress to a married man, says she likes being beaten when she makes love, because it liberates her from the guilt that a religious education has permanently instilled into her. She gets her excitement also by spending a lot of money on cosmetics and clothes; she goes up to Paris regularly and often; after one of these trips, she longs for a quick anonymous seduction. Her charwoman adds that she shares her excitement in buying 'useless things' and nice underwear, but for her part, she hates

---

[1] France 100,000, USA between a quarter and half a million, West Germany 200,000, Britain 50,000.

being beaten; she enjoys pornographic films, when they show straightforward sex between a man and a woman, but not when there are lots of people around, nor when there are perversions; her taste is for traditional he-men; she loves actors like Luis Mariano and Jean Gabin, and above all men in uniform. She adores firemen. What is most marvellous for her, is that she is also excited by housework: the more she does it, the more it pleases her. 'When I use the vacuum cleaner, I feel funny. And as for dusting, it is unbelievable the effect it has on me.' A thirty-three-year-old Parisian journalist says her pleasure is to have a great deal of money spent on her, to have a lover accompany her to an expensive shop and buy her a ring or clothes, while she despises both him and herself, but relishes the sexual excitement. A dressmaker reveals that none of these things is a pleasure for her, she has never considered herself pretty, she is not herself interested in frilly underwear; her sole erotic pleasure has come from dancing, particularly the rumba, close together, in dimly-lit halls. Sexual relations have always disgusted her. Her husband, an office worker, goes to see a pornographic film every Saturday, to her severe disapproval. She is sixty-one now, and retired. Her only love has been for her son: 'I need something that belongs to me alone, and I have heaped all my love on him, all my eroticism.' There is a whole world separating her from the Parisian maid, married to a foreman, forty years old, who often goes to see pornographic films accompanied by her husband, and is shocked by nothing. 'I should like to see everything, to know everything about life.' She gets pleasure from hearing people groan when they make love; 'the other day, I heard my mistress doing that in the next room, she was shouting loudly, and I listened and I was pleased, very pleased. I am like her; I need to shout.' She goes with her husband to sit on the terrace of a Pigalle café on Saturday nights, to watch the prostitutes: it is fun watching. For her, sex is to be relished like food; it is nice to look at it as well as to enjoy it.

All this is, of course, in different degrees anathema to many feminists. They see brain-washing, exploitation and violence concealed beneath these traditional attitudes. They argue that female sexuality is aroused only by gentleness, by touch more than fantasy; and some conclude that if men cannot offer them what they want, they would rather do without them. There are men who have responded, saying such women have taught them an entirely new way of making love. A recent poll by *F. Magazine* revealed that the two qualities women disliked most in men were brutality and arrogance, the feeling that men knew best. In real life, they wish to be well treated. But what happens in love is more complicated; there is no unanimity as to what constitutes a good lover or an attractive suitor. Out of every ten women, nine believe that men should take as much care of their appearance as women, seven like men who use perfume — they love their men to be *soigné*. Three-quarters like men to court them, and they prefer men who place their private lives before their work. But it takes more than glamour or chivalry to please them. Only four out of ten are swept off their feet by beautiful men who are stupid. Life being what it is, another four out of ten end up by saying that looks are of secondary importance, and that they do not mind a man with a pot belly or shorter than themselves. And since men do not court enough, seven out of ten have in practice taken the initiative in courtship and most say they like doing that. If there is that much truth in the myth of the seductress, half of women on the other hand report that male colleagues at work have tried to seduce them. So it seems that the French are not quite the great artists in love that they are made out to be, but that they are students of the art and that perhaps is almost the same thing.

In 1961 an opinion poll asked American women to name their ideal man. The four they picked were John Kennedy, Gregory Peck, Cary Grant and Yves Montand. It was just after Montand had starred in *The Millionaire* with Marilyn Monroe, who declared that he was, after her husband, and equal with Marlon Brando, 'the most seductive man I have ever met'. Twenty years later French women, asked the same question, put Yves Montand at the top of their list. It does not follow that he is liked for the same reason by American and French women; neither perhaps know all that much about him; but it is no accident that the two countries should be capable of sharing a god. What is more, Montand has enjoyed great popularity in the USSR also, where he has been hailed as a fighter for 'the right to happiness', with an inextinguishable 'faith in man'. Montand's universal appeal has nothing to do with his nationality, but is the result of three universal qualities that he expresses.

He is first of all a self-made man in the fullest sense of the phrase; he is not only a poor boy who has made good, but a frightened, worried boy who has conquered his timidity and created a more or less efficient personality for himself, His real name is Ito Livi. His father was an Italian peasant and broom-maker, whose workshop was burnt down by the fascists, and who fled with his family to Marseille in the hope of emigrating to the United States, but could not get a visa. As a boy, Montand used to speak to his parents in French; they replied in Italian; he also learnt Armenian, because there is a large Armenian population in Marseille (about 100,000 today). He grew up among the disadvantaged; he left school early because his father went bankrupt; he worked as a hairdresser and then as a labourer in a metal factory. In his imagination, however, he lived in the United States; the American cinema was his passion: he dreamt of Harlem and the Far West, jazz and Fred Astaire and he learnt to imitate Donald Duck. He began his singing career dressed as a cowboy, singing imitation American songs; his first success was a song called The Plains of the Far West. But he was not willing to become one of the 'pretty boy' singers who were then fashionable. To cut himself off from them, he appeared on stage in an open-necked brown shirt and plain trousers: that has been his uniform ever since. He has worked extremely hard for success, but not at the expense of his self-respect. He has not tried to create a bogus image of himself that would be a trade mark with which he could sell himself at a high price. He has not hesitated to change constantly; he refuses to be called a 'professional' because that savours too much of routine; professionals are cold; for him professionalism means only punctuality and hard work. What he has wanted to avoid is the repetitiveness that is the sign of age. 'If one copies oneself, it's all over, that means one is already dead. And I know people who copy themselves from the age of thirty: they are to be found in every walk of life.' He gave up singing on the stage because he got worried that this was happening to him; 'Because people applauded me every evening, I came to take myself for Montand.' He wanted to make a break with the young man who no longer existed. He wanted people to say when he reappeared in a new role: 'Who is this new singer?' He wants to win afresh each time, which is why his favourite, passionate hobby is poker.

To seek victory all the time requires courage, and Montand has always been timid. Everyone who has known him agrees he is perpetually frightened. That timidity is the second of the characteristics that enables so many people to identify with him. He is not the successful man who makes the failures uncomfortable. 'I have always,' he says, 'been almost pathologically timid. I tried to cure myself by myself. For example when I took the tram in Marseille, I remained standing on the outside platform whether there were seats or not, whether I was tired or not. I dared not open the door in case people looked at me. One day I said to myself: That's enough. You are going to open that door. If people look at you, you will look at them straight in the eyes. I did not carry out my resolution straight away. But in the end I managed to open that damned door. People looked at me, automatically. I looked back, trembling. They lowered their eyes. I felt a great wave of pride. It was my first victory. I sat down like a pope on my seat.'

Montand has remained frightened but he has learned to overcome his fear without destroying it. On becoming forty, he underwent a particularly terrifying six months: 'I was afraid of everything, of death, of cancer.' He recovered, but fear haunts him still. He is worried about what people will think of him, about the choices he has made, about what he has said. That is why those colleagues who find him too dominating when they work in films together do not hold it against him, because they are conscious of his fragility, and they are disarmed by his quickness in admitting his mistakes; they see that he is absolutely determined to get every detail right. He hates people who judge him, and misjudge him; he wants to prove himself to them. The tragedy of his life, one condescending friend has said, is that he cannot get over his inferiority complex towards intellectuals. It is not certain that he has this complex, because, as Alain Resnais has pointed out, he is an intellectual, in the sense that 'he is the opposite of a man of instinct. He uses his intelligence enormously, he reasons a lot. He likes to reason about everything, about politics, about work, about the least detail of daily life.'

Some people admire him for the stands he has taken in politics; he has become one of the regular supporters of humanitarian and left-wing causes, to the extent of being excluded from the United States during the McCarthy period; but other people claim he is out of his depth in these discussions, that he has not remained loyal to his socialist principles: his brother, a communist, stopped talking to him for a decade because in 1968 Montand publicly insulted a communist leader. 'I have never joined any party,' Montand has said, 'because my reasonings lead me to contradictory conclusions, because I constantly doubt everything and because I do not tolerate intolerance.' When accused of hypocrisy for preaching social justice while driving a Rolls-Royce, he replies: 'Yes, I am contradictory: who is not? And it is better to be a communist in a Rolls than a fascist in a tank. I do not deny my origins, or my class; I intend to continue to defend the oppressed, as far as I can, and as I feel it, but I cannot be silent about what has, historically, happened when the oppressed get power. It is no longer possible to think that capitalism is the sole source of our ills, even if it is painful for me to admit it. There are bastards who do not drive Rolls-Royces. To say that all problems can be solved is to tell fairy tales.' He wants to keep his independence of all dogmas, even while attacking injustice. He regrets his scepticism, which makes him feel lonely and vulnerable. His favourite maxim he has borrowed from F. Scott Fitzgerald: One needs to understand that there is no hope and yet to be determined to change things. If he were English, that would be called pragmatism. It is just one facet of his acceptance of his own limitations.

He insists that there are ideals he believes in, things he wants to say, but he does not know how to express them himself to his own satisfaction. He has not written his own songs, and he has never made his own films, but he will only sing songs that express what he wants to say and act in films where he can play roles that he can identify with. In that, he says, he behaves like his audience, who come to the cinema with confused feelings, but then recognize themselves in the parts that actors play before them. There he touches on a crucial point: popular actors are as important as popular politicians in expressing public opinion, perhaps more important, because the public is willing to pay to see them suffering the dilemmas that confront everyone; the fact that the actors are merely adopting a role does not make them different from their public, which also adopts a role: to be the French male, whom Montand symbolizes, is to adopt a role, which is not necessarily one's only or truest role. Gossip about film stars is neither frivolous nor irrelevant to a people's view of themselves.

Montand's roles are universally significant because, thirdly, his basic philosophy which balances his anxiety, is his belief in 'human warmth'. 'I have known the warmth of family ties so characteristic of Italian and Mediterranean families, the complicity of boys' gangs in the Cabucelle quarter [of Marseille], the fervour of popular music halls, the political fraternity of workers.' 'What counts most for me is human warmth. I want to like my friends, to like the people I meet. I don't care whether they are right or left-wing or in the centre, Catholics, Protestants, Jews or anybody else, provided they are human, with qualities and defects, like me, but they must behave in good faith. Because what I hate most in the world is bad faith.'

To like people is of course easier said than done. Montand also wants to be liked in return, and the kind of affection he demands is not in everyone's power to give. As a young man he was haunted by the worry that he was ugly, as well as stupid and poor. He dreamt that the day would come when things would be different, and that he would only have to go into a bar for all the pretty barmaids to go crazy about him. The first woman in his life was a seventeen-year-old barmaid in Marseille, who fascinated him, but she was a girl who knew how to make every client feel that he was the one she preferred. The first great love of his life was Edith Piaf, much older than he, with whom he lived for three years: they spent most of the time laughing together; he rejuvenated her; she helped him to become a star, and to be himself in his singing, rather than to follow fashions, something he has never forgotten. But in the end she tired of the laughter and abandoned him.

It took him two years to get over the cruelty that lay behind her laughter. Since 1949 he has been married to Simone Signoret. 'Montand,' says she, 'is ten years younger than me, because we are the same age and he is a man.' He admires her as the most intelligent woman he has known, but also as one who does not cheat, who is not ashamed of her grey hairs or her wrinkles, who is never bothered with dieting, who loves eating and drinking and living. He is quite capable of having affairs with younger women. 'I do not seek them out, but I can be drawn into them simply because I am a man. Simone has the wisdom never to ask me questions about that. She is a real wife. To have a wife like her means that it is difficult to meet a girl who will make me question my marriage.' He used to be very jealous, but he conveniently believes men can temporarily deceive their wives without really betraying them; 'Women are more absolute when they love'; now each lives the life that suits them; they have no need to abandon each other. His wife is home. Younger women are explorations: 'to be sexy, a woman must be naked inside her, it is not the absence of clothes that matters.'

It is rare for him to find a true spiritual partner. His enthusiasm for Marilyn Monroe – which was not an affair – was based on the discovery that they had something in common. She said she was frightened. He replied: 'You may be frightened but I am shaking with terror.' But he has no women friends. Human warmth, in fact, he does not find easy to share. He is always jovial, laughing, making light of difficulties; he enjoys making people laugh. 'That', says his friend Costa-Gavras, 'is perhaps a form of generosity in him, a way of continuing to put on a show, and so a way of living. But he is not a happy man.' His humour is his most obvious trait of character, but it only superficially creates the bonds he seeks with others; on the contrary, by making his relationships into joking ones, he ensures that they get no further; in the end the jokes appear to be a form of coldness, or of self-protection. Even his best friends find that he is evasive about his private life. That is because he is constantly searching for it.

It is appropriate that the French woman's hero should not be that mythical seducer who knows all there is to know about women, and can play on them like a violin, but someone who does not know the answers and is searching for them. There is no established French attitude to love, and the search for one will doubtless multiply the variety of attitudes in the future. The search is being conducted within the framework of the family, but that, as has been seen, is constantly being readapted to make room for new forms of desire and behaviour.

Part Three

How to compete and negotiate with them

10

How to find the people with real power

It is now customary, when seeking to glimpse the real secret of bureaucratic power, to visit the National School of Administration, ENA, where many of the rulers of France have been trained. The atmosphere is cold and nervous. 'Most people here are always nervous,' says Roch-Olivier Maistre, a tall, powerfully built third-year student, very spruce in a blue blazer and grey flannels. 'Everybody is watching you all the time. You are under pressure from the first day to the last. They just want to rank us, not to teach us. And after the exams we will forget everything.' The anxiety is heightened by the fact that there are exams every two months and no one is told the result until the very last day, when the graduates are given a sealed envelope, which announces what rank they have reached among their fellows: that rank decides their future, whether they will direct the economy, or shuffle files in the ministry for veteran soldiers or pensions. But the prospect of real power seems worth all this stress for Maistre. He has no illusions. His father works for an American company and he has been out to work there too: he liked the United States – 'the American way of life is more exciting' – and he started studying for an MBA in a Mid-Western university. But he was ambitious for power, he openly says so, and business did not give him the chance 'to change the whole life of a people. In France I shall be able to.' That is why he moved back to France, when ENA gave him the opportunity. 'This school makes you ambitious: you realize power is held by only a very few people, and so you feel obliged to try to get the highest rank, in order to get power, difficult though you know it to be to enter the "charmed circle" that controls it.'

The actual course was not much use in itself: 'you do not learn anything, only techniques, how to use your knowledge quickly to solve a problem, how to write memoranda in three parts or two parts.' The teaching methods are very similar to those in American business schools, with plenty of computers, but the content is different because marketing, financial analysis, accounting were omitted: there is more law, economics, administration. 'We learn advanced techniques, but I doubt whether we shall use them, because the junior civil servants do not know how to.' He had spent the practical part of his course working in a prefecture: when he joined, he had no idea what the state administration was like, it is only now that he has discovered, and he has been amazed by what he has seen: he confesses 'I thought it would be very exciting.' Now he is desperate to get all these examinations over, because he is finding the book learning 'very boring. I am not an intellectual, but a civil servant. I want to solve problems, not to write memoranda.' He is not sure that he chose right to come to ENA, for the pleasures of his career will depend on just how fast he is rewarded. He speaks perfect American-English: he belongs to a new generation that could serve in any country, provided there was enough power to attract him.

But he is unusual in saying his goal is power: few of his colleagues would be so blunt, or personal. It is more fashionable to talk about wanting to work for the general interest (as a priest would say he aimed to work for the salvation of souls). Since bureaucrats are as despised and envied as the nobility of the *ancien régime* once was, many shy away from admitting that they have a vocation for bureaucracy; some ENA graduates modestly say they entered the school in order to avoid becoming professors, or to avoid working solely for money. An investigator who has studied them says 'they are arrogant but also adaptable, wanting power but also lacking any passion or ideal, brilliant intellectually, but weak in common sense, widely read but only superficially so, energetic and fluent in speech but cold.' I agree they all wore rather expensive-looking clothes (that does say something about them), but the idea that they all have one predictable character seems to me to exaggerate both the influence the school has on its pupils and the uniformity of their motives. The real test of an *enarque*, or of anyone else, is not how

I only got the second prize at E.N.A. I'm finished.

Mathieu

ambitious he is in his youth, when almost every institution is organized to encourage ambition, but what happens to that ambition when he reaches maturity.

To outsiders, ENA suggests that power is not something ordinary people can expect ever to touch, but only to stare at from a distance like a rare object in a museum. But the *enarque* is no longer a rare object: there are over 3000 of them now, and as they increase in number each year, it is becoming clear that the school is not a sausage machine, and that its graduates are not all carbon copies of Jacques Chirac. As always, it was a few remarkable individuals who gave this institution its reputation. The *enarques* are almost exactly equally divided in their politics, between left and right, and that is not a plot to ensure that they are always in charge of the administration. Originally three-quarters of them had passed through the equally smooth corridors of the School of Political Sciences, but now only a fifth come from there, their origins are increasingly varied, but then they have always been far more versatile than the pure politicians like Chirac suggest. The most savage criticisms of ENA have come from old *enarques*, who hated it as a symbol of all that was most rigid in the folklore of French bureaucracy, the mania for form combined with the whiff of Americanism, the dream of 'ruling France like a department store', by managerial techniques. They tell the story of the *enarque* who was so busy making his career that he asked his father how many hours a day would be needed if he got married, and when told, decided to remain a bachelor; but there are *enarques* who have written books almost in the tradition of Trollope; they are busy men, but some manage to have quite a nice time chasing round the world on 'missions' in the process. In ENA's impressively modern library, with several sets of video-tape recorders on which pupils can learn to spot the people who matter, I noticed one pupil was studiously watching a Fred Astaire film. The 'Sciences-Po style', meaning the art taught at the School of Political Sciences of answering questions by arguing for and against issues, in a perfectly planned, clearly expressed three-part essay, is not really peculiar to them: every English sixth-form schoolboy is taught essay-writing in much the same way. What is special about ENA is that it has given the routine business of training civil servants the aura of an organized conspiracy, and so acquired many of the traditional trappings and myths of a secret society.

What happens when an *enarque* faces the detailed problems of administration may be seen in Josselin, a small town in Brittany. A visit to a town hall is always a useful tranquillizer after a dose of stonewalling in a Paris ministry, or perhaps a useful stimulant, because it often contains a surprise. The surprise in Josselin is that the mayor is the fourteenth Duc de Rohan, whose family once owned a third of Brittany, but which now has little property left besides the moated medieval castle that dominates the town. The duke is a graduate of ENA. But after twelve years in high administrative posts in Paris, he became disillusioned with the way his fellow civil servants were dominated by their personal ambitions, and with their intrigues and disloyalty; he got himself a routine job in a nationalized industry (Elf Oil), and went into local politics (in France you can combine the two, with important results). He was elected mayor of his home town, the youngest mayor in France. He is a totally unpretentious man, who regards his ancestry as a per-

sonal matter that confers no special status; he married a journalist; he gets his satisfaction from being useful to people; he
likes talking to everyone he meets and hearing the local gossip;
there is much less of that clash of accents that distinguishes the
English country gentleman from his neighbours, though the
duke could almost pass for an Englishman, his command of the
English language is excellent, having been brought up by an
English nanny; he has an English nanny for his children, and
even a little dog imported from England who follows him
everywhere.

The duke was certainly not elected because he is a duke, nor
just because he is friendly or even because he is efficient. His
most important qualification is that, as an *enarque*, he has
contacts with the government which give him exceptional
influence. This was quickly revealed after he took office. There
was no money in the municipal coffers to lay down the new
drainage system that was needed. It so happened that the duke
had had Jacques Chirac, the prime minister, as a tutor many
years back when he was cramming to get into ENA; a call
ensured that a state subsidy was granted for the drains. Some
time later, the major issue was where the new regional slaughterhouse should be built: it would bring seventy new jobs and
was of crucial importance to all the farmers. A neighbouring
town was being backed by a local member of parliament. But
the duke had friends from his student days highly placed in the
ministry of agriculture and the slaughterhouse came to Josselin.

This may suggest that all important decisions are made in
Paris, and that personal relations are what are needed to influence them. But that is only half the story. The way issues are
presented to Paris, and the way its decisions are applied, are the
subject of a great deal of local debate; the duke needs every vote
he can get to stay in office, and he has made the personal
satisfaction of each voter his goal. He complains that the powers
in Paris do not know what an important problem is. 'No
problem is a small problem,' he says, 'because to the people who
are involved in it, their own problem is an important problem.'
He recalls one incident that particularly shook him. One Saturday afternoon, the wife of the butcher telephoned him in great
excitement to say that she was unable to find the key to the

slaughterhouse, her whole life seemed to be destroyed by this loss; she asked him to call the fire brigade; she made what seemed to him a trivial incident into such a tragedy that he burst out laughing. That woman no longer speaks to him. 'I didn't take her problem seriously enough. I now think I was wrong.'

The primary schoolmaster, Monsieur Moisan, is the leader of the socialist opposition to the duke: he is a jolly man with a beard, and in his spare moments, president of the football club. He protests that the duke is authoritarian; 'when he takes a decision, either alone or with his council, he refuses to go back on it or to reopen the discussion, on the pretext that if there are choices to be made, someone has got to make them and take the responsibility for them.' The duke retorts that he is not authoritarian; he only uses the authority the law gives him as mayor and Moisan would doubtless use that authority if he had the chance. In fact he gets on very well with Moisan, because though they argue vigorously, they do so courteously and impersonally. 'He is as objective as a party man can be,' says the duke. To please everyone is, of course, impossible. 'In a small town you sometimes dislike your neighbour or have personal squabbles with people for reasons which you don't always exactly know, or because it was your father who was not on speaking terms with your neighbour, and you carry on this quarrel to the next generation . . . Local fights are sometimes civil wars.'

The duke has been hurt by the animosity that local politics has kindled. 'When there is hatred, I think there is something wrong.' Disagreement is natural, but 'the man who hates another has something rotten inside him'; he cannot help being upset, because the alternative is to become insensitive, and that is even worse, it diminishes one's ability to understand. Here, private lives are scrutinized as much as political programmes: when the town clerk was discovered to be carrying on an affair with an employee in the town hall, he was forced to resign, and he now lives like a hermit, a broken man, in a shed behind his house, speaking to no one. Everyone comments on everyone else's comings and goings, on what they wear and to whom they speak; everyone observes the gradations of snobbery, the hidden resentments, the hypocrisy behind the friendliness.

Some of the duke's opponents are the children of former

employees at the chateau, who want to eliminate the memory of their former subordination. Madame Martin is an example: the daughter of the old duke's gardener, she has no children and is bursting with energy; she has married a workaholic wood sculptor who produced furniture that was too expensive to find buyers, so they have together created a furniture factory, mass-producing machine-made parodies of tables, cupboards and chairs in pseudo-classical styles, and a flourishing souvenir shop too; they like to have their opinions listened to. The large and hearty director of the agricultural co-operative, Monsieur Fablez, whom the duke only narrowly defeated in the elections, is, says the duke, 'a popular character who likes to speak his mind very openly, even in front of the mayor and especially in front of the mayor, but I think this is more theatrical than anything.'

Monsieur Le Net, the largest employer in the town, with 300 people working for him in his sausage and ham factory, complains that the duke does not consult the employers sufficiently. Monsieur Le Net has built a miniature estate on the hill opposite the chateau; he has not a drawbridge, but massive electronically controlled gates, through which he drives in his Mercedes, down a long drive to his swimming pool and his two Alsatian guard dogs. The duke says he does not feel comfortable with moneyed people, but the relations between the two men do not fit the classic confrontation of the capitalist resisting the demo-cratically elected representative of the people. Monsieur Le Net's father had been the town's butcher, with a small shop at the foot of the chateau; the duke's father, being a director of a bank, had got him a loan to start a factory; Monsieur Le Net has expanded that so that it is now, as he proudly says, the thirtieth most important sausage factory in the country. There is no job in the firm that he has not done himself ('I get a certain satisfaction from touching raw meat; you have got to like it, otherwise it's impossible to work in this trade; but I cannot bear to touch a dead chicken, the feel of the feathers irritates me'). He knows all his workers personally, and does not want to expand much more; he wants above all to have a firm where there is no aggravation, which is a pleasant place to work in. He has no political ambitions because he is tired of having to get up at six every morning, having to work at weekends, having virtually no private life: 'I should like to be able to accompany my wife on her shopping trips sometimes, to go for walks, to take off a day in Paris. I have been to China, and I should like to go back; I don't know South America at all. It is with the greatest difficulty that I have been able to take holidays.' His gossiping neighbours relish repeating that he spends them in the Seychelles and Guadeloupe. Monsieur Le Net has been elected vice-president of the National Federation of Salted Meats, which involves him in negotiations with the government and trade unions; 'that gives me a new attitude: it makes me realize one must discuss: it prevents one saying "no".'

It is this combination of a desire for a more leisured life, absorption in making their fortunes or their livings and distaste for confrontation that leads many others besides Monsieur Le Net to leave the actual running of the town to those who want to busy themselves with it; for the rich, it is more fun to go up to Paris for social life than to get involved in local intrigues. That limits the acerbity of personal rivalries. It is possible, therefore, for the town's super-friendly, lame policeman, Francis, decorated with a medal for his forty years service in the same job, to be, as he says, 'a friend to everybody'; he has never given anyone a parking fine. The duke approves that, because he sees himself as an intermediary between the townsfolk and the Paris technocrats. The elite of *enarques* and their like to which he belongs survives in a democracy because so many of its members go over to the other side, to teach the private individual and private business to protect themselves against the state. It is roughly the same principle which makes people employ former tax inspectors to advise them on their tax problems. So the traditional view of France as a bureaucrat's nightmare, with real power very narrowly concentrated, is true only if it is combined with major reservations.

Once upon a time France used to be the most centralized despotism in Europe. Independent provincial and urban institutions were destroyed by kings with an insatiable appetite for power; local notables and aristocrats were ensnared into obedience by the concentration of rewards and prestige in Paris. France used to stand in clear contrast to England, with its amateur, unpaid justices of the peace, and to America's elected frontier sheriff, both of them symbols of local independence. In the United States democracy was based on the principle of the division of power; the legitimacy of group interests was accepted; there were legal guarantees for individuals, and a system of checks and balances to control the government. The French Revolution, by contrast, in the end strengthened centralization by preferring a democracy that was supposed to produce a general will incarnated in the government, which therefore sought to eliminate sectional pressures and impose uniform rights and duties. The legacy of this history has been the French habit of accepting government interference in almost every aspect of life, and of seeing the solution to problems in the granting of state subsidies and the creation of new state institutions. Bureaucrats, therefore, multiplied, each with his little parcel of power. The ordinary citizen who bearded them came to feel that he was like a lone football player faced by a rival team of a thousand skilful opponents, constantly passing the ball one to the other, and shouting Foul if he ever approached the goal. The really determined man could appeal to a referee (the Council of State) to have bureaucratic decisions annulled as 'abuse of power', but that is a long process taking many years. The bureaucrats have united themselves in well-organized trade unions, and they have built a shield around themselves in the form of the most elaborate collection of safeguards against dismissal devised since the collapse of the old aristocracy. There are now 3000 laws and regulations to defend them, contained in a bible of twenty volumes. Since you cannot fight them, it is best to join them. A civil service career has for centuries been among the most prestigious and attractive open to anyone, at all social levels. So the bureaucracy is not seen just as a source of oppression; it is also a means by which people can rise in the social scale with security, influence and dignity.

Bureaucracy has been defended on the ground that it establishes fixed and impersonal rules, and so protects the French from something they hate even more, namely favouritism; when decisions are taken by anonymous Parisian masters who are never seen, that at least eliminates face to face humiliation. But liberals have protested that the system is too rationalist; the idea

that there is only one best way of solving any particular problem, and that one solution should be universally applicable
results in inflexibility; ministries and departments become so
rigid and isolated from each other, that the right hand does not
know what the left hand is doing; that leads to periodic crises,
and the whole system seizes up. Everybody then repeats that
France is a 'stalemate society', and that deep down Frenchmen
hate reforms but love revolutions; crises are the only way to get
change. A few years ago Alain Peyrefitte published a best seller
pursuing this argument, which dates back to Tocqueville: he
argued that the French disease, *Le Mal Français* (as the book was
entitled) could be traced to a single germ, bureaucracy. Peyrefitte thought Britain had avoided this disease (even though
Britain suffered from the British disease, but that was due to the
collapse of the ethos of hard work, or to the trade unions). He
claimed that in Britain people were much more public-spirited,
and that was why they had succeeded in retaining control of
their own affairs. He could never forget how when he was a
student paying-guest in England just after the war, his host
regularly turned off the heating at exactly 9 a.m. because the
government had 'advised' this as a measure of economy. He
contrasts this with Frenchmen overwhelmed by compulsory

Piem

regulations which they spend their time trying to avoid. His book catalogues all the difficulties he had himself as a minister in getting things done: bureaucrats, he says, are dedicated, honest, intelligent and competent as individuals but, en masse, they turn into irresponsible, uncontrollable, mistrustful tyrants.

But this view of French administration can no longer be accepted. First of all, bureaucracy and a large public sector have now spread with consistent uniformity through most western countries. In Britain, 30% of all employees are in some way working for the public sector, almost seven million people in all; though only three-quarters of a million are civil servants in the narrowest sense, another 1·7 million are local authority employees. In France the civil service seems more overwhelming because more people are called by that name, 3·7 million in all, but that includes a million teachers, almost half a million post office workers, and the same number of hospital workers. But only one-fifth (20·7%) of people in employment, i.e. 4·5 million, work for the public sector in one way or another, and the new nationalizations will increase that figure only marginally. France is not all that different from the Federal Republic of Germany, which also has four-and-a-half million public employees. The United States is the exception, with only 2·7 million federal employees (for a population five times larger) but another 13 million local government employees mean that altogether 16% of the labour force are civil servants.

Secondly, French government may once have been more centralized than that in Britain, but that is no longer true. The growth of the welfare state has imperceptibly and gradually brought British local government under the orders of Whitehall, which controls nearly two-thirds of the income spent locally, and insists that the money is spent according to central directives; local authorities are stuck with an outdated taxation system of rates which further restricts their freedom. By contrast, central subsidies are distributed in France on a basis that is much closer to that in the United States, through a large variety of sources, so that there is more room for bargaining; French local authorities raise twice as much in local taxation as do British ones, and they have been more effective in getting tax reforms to increase their independence. France has 468,000 municipal councillors, i.e. 2% of its total electorate, almost twenty times as numerous as the local councillors in Britain (24,000). Participation in local elections in France is twice as high as in Britain. Only one-third of British members of parliament have experience in local government; few remain local councillors when they get into parliament, but four-fifths of French deputies and 93% of French senators also hold local elected office. The consequence is that local grievances get much more attention in Paris, and the French central government has a lot of difficulty in applying its policies at the local level; it is considerably nearer than the officials of Whitehall, who have no links with and no personal experience of local government. Local dissent is more vigorous in France, because there is less party discipline; French mayors have protected their citizens more effectively against Paris than British local councils against London. The British reforms of local government have repeatedly strengthened the central government; in France the opposite has happened, and the socialist government is now promising even more decentralization.

The old view of French bureaucracy was never based on detailed knowledge of what really went on in government offices. It is now emerging that the rigidity of centralization was partly a facade. Bureaucrats are not all of one type. Each ministry has its own recruiting programme and its own quite distinct relationships with the public. Bureaucrats do not just obey orders; they have their pride as experts; they have their aspirations to social approval in their local community. The smaller these communities, the more they make themselves defenders of the inhabitants against Paris and show them how to get round the rules. In towns of under 10,000 inhabitants, people say they are very satisfied with their bureaucrats, whereas in those of over 20,000 they say they are very dissatisfied. Government policy is implemented by a series of compromises between bureaucrats and the representatives of local bodies of different kinds – mayors, presidents of general councils, chambers of commerce, etc. There are altogether 4500 consultative committees to which the government has to pay some attention. So policy emerges in diverse ways in different regions, to the point that it is sometimes even turned against the government. Previous governments have tried to 'rationalize' this chaos by dividing France into twenty-five regions, but that only increased the number of compromises that were made. The same decision is still not always applied in the same way in Alsace and Languedoc. Sociologists have discovered the 'peripheral power' of local notables, acting as a counterpoise to the government, and they have 'identified' five different forms of municipal government: 'hereditary monarchy' in the Vendée, the 'elective' type in Lorraine, 'egalitarian democracy' in the Jura, 'oligarchy' on the Mediterranean coast, and 'federalism' in the Limousin. Centralization survives because the notables who apply it know how to manoeuvre their way round it; since they derive importance from the skill, they have little wish to overthrow it. The civil servants, for their part, are able to manipulate the rules which govern them to their own advantage through their trade unions, and they have made themselves into a pressure group able to defy the government. They have been likened to clergymen who preach the general interest, but flatter the local notables and make deals with them, so that they end up essentially as mediators between forces they cannot control.

The administrative system has moreover been modified several times since the war in an attempt to make it more effective, and democratic, borrowing from what was considered best in British and American examples; and several styles of management therefore co-exist to confront the municipalities. The traditional Jacobin, authoritarian style was supplemented by 'planification', which relied not on the legalistic implementation of rules but on an exchange of information between state experts and business leaders, to concert policies for mutual public and private advantage. The old system of making deals was raised to a new level in this way, basing state policy on wider consultations. But many civil servants did not like this; a division arose between the economists and the lawyers in the administration, and the lawyers often sabotaged the economists' plans. More recently, the growth in the power of the mayors of large cities, who have developed into something like their American or German counterparts, has broken the supremacy of the prefects appointed by the central government. The techno-crats in each ministry began negotiating directly with the mayors, so that new baronial fiefs grew up. Now decentraliza-tion by the socialists will introduce still more new relationships.

A remarkable, detailed investigation of the way government decisions are made and carried out by Catherine Gremion con-cludes that France is not suffering from constipation (which was the view held by Tocqueville and his followers) but from a kind of multiple schizophrenia. That is to say, its problem is that it is divided. The administration contains lots of highly intelligent people; it is a 'meeting place for ideas': and since civil servants soak up ideas from the different sections of the fragmented society that France is, there is 'organized anarchy' when it comes to doing anything. It is not just that bureaucrats dig in their heels to preserve their customs and privileges: that is normal enough everywhere. Nor is it just a question of young turks struggling against old fogeys. The crucial factor which is now said to determine the line a senior administrator takes is the amount of time he has spent outside the normal career pattern, particularly in missions abroad. So, when a government announces a new project, it is presented as a consistent, logical whole, which is a carefully arranged front to conceal all the ambiguities that the different people involved in drawing it up have included in it to satisfy their varying hesitations. Rival ministers agree to disagree with hidden compromises of which the public is seldom made aware. The last regional reform in 1964 turned out very different from what it was supposed to be: what socialist decentralization will produce will only be revealed many years hence.

There are prefects who openly say that since promotion comes only to those who do not get into scrapes, they 'have decided to decide nothing': but there are others who are bursting with energy, love taking risks and ruling their departments like old-style governors. There are those who try to follow public opinion, and those who are bitten by technocratic idealism. It used to be fashionable to copy foreign models, notably American ones, though five years after they had ceased to be fashionable in America and just beginning to fail there. Cath-erine Gremion ends by saying that 'the history of individuals must be taken into account' by anyone wanting to know how reforms will work out. That marks a really important step in the expert's view of administration. France is at last being seen as composed of individuals, no two of whom act in quite the same way. The rigidity of bureaucracy is, of course, largely a defence with which rigid individuals shield themselves because they are scared of their superiors, of others, and of themselves.

'Home is the last refuge of liberty,' says the architect Alain Sarfati. Home, in theory, is where you can be yourself, do what you like and surround yourself with the objects that please you. But how many French people are in fact able to reveal their true character in their homes; and is their character expressed more accurately by the ornate homes of old France or by the stark modern tower blocks that could have been transplanted from almost any other country? No less than one-half of French homes have been built since 1945. Do French people get the kinds of home they want, and how much choice do they have in determining where the major part of their lives is spent? The answers to these questions tell one a lot about how power is wielded; town planners and architects have more power than they are generally credited with. Housing expresses the atmosphere a government creates, as well as being an intimate point of contact between rulers and ruled, for it contributes as much as anything else to people's boredom or sense of well-being. And yet government after government has ignored the people's wishes in the matter of housing. In 1945 the National Institute of Demographic Studies found that three-quarters of the French population wanted to live in single family houses. Nevertheless, fifteen years later, only one-third of the new houses built were for single families. France was the country where far fewer single family houses were being built than anywhere else, even though it had plenty of land. [1] That has now been recognized as a mistake. But architects still have difficulty in giving people what they want, because they have their own artistic goals. The dedication to 'architectural truth' means that the materials and techniques used in building are emphasized, so that they should

[1] 32% in France, compared to 78% in Britain, 76% in USA, 70% in Belgium, 56% in Holland, 49% in West Germany.

be appreciated for what they are (the Beaubourg centre, with all its mechanics exposed, is the symbol of that point of view); their search for architectural purity means that they abandon unnecessary ornament. So there is no longer any 'French' style.

The most famous French architect of this century, and the only one of whom foreigners have heard, is Le Corbusier. He was quite clear that people should no longer live in the kinds of houses they were used to and that French cities, loved though they might be, were organized on the wrong principles. He developed a plan for the demolition of the centre of Paris and for its replacement by eighteen tower blocks: in that way, he believed, light, air and greenery could be introduced into the capital's heart and the 'corridor streets' he abhorred could be done away with. He was not allowed to do that, and the irony of his life was that he was not allowed to build a very great deal in France: he became a hero only after his death. On a humbler level, however, he did build 'machines for living' near Bordeaux, in what was called the Quartiers Modernes Fruges, after the eccentric industrialist who financed this experiment as a 'laboratory' to test Le Corbusier's theories. Le Corbusier mass-produced a series of identical houses. The estate agents, for once, ran out of panegyrics to describe their charms. 'The new look of this villa,' said their prospectus, 'may perhaps raise doubts in your mind . . . The external appearance is not always pleasing at first sight.' The people who bought them obviously agreed with that, for within ten years they had completely transformed the estate: Le Corbusier's uniformity has been turned into chaos: the patios have been enclosed, many of the terraces have been roofed over, the empty spaces beneath the stilts have been blocked off, the wide windows have been narrowed, and the bright colours have disappeared: a great crop of sheds has sprung up, and the general impression is one of dilapidation. Alain Sarfati, who regards Le Corbusier as 'the most dogmatic, disciplinarian of architects', 'a terrorist', asked the question: Why does modern architecture impose itself on the inhabitants of its buildings, so that if the least change is made, if one window is altered, the whole aesthetic scheme is ruined? The complete regularity may have been right when landlords decided how their tenants should live, but is it right in an age of individual self-expression? The obstacle, he believes, is that architects cannot get away from their longing to create monuments that will commemorate their genius: an example is Emile Aillaud.

Aillaud masterminded the spectacular office and housing complex of La Défense, west of Paris, and the suburb of La Grande Borne, which has been called the only interesting achievement of French architecture since the war; he very narrowly missed being commissioned to design the Pompidou Centre: he was Pompidou's favourite architect. Sarfati says Aillaud illustrates the gap between what architects say and what they do, the irresistible temptation of architectural megalomania. Aillaud is certainly as interested in the social as in the technical side of his art: he wants his buildings to encourage people to participate in communal life, while also leaving them free to withdraw if they wish. He puts up enormous portraits of Rimbaud, Kafka and Baudelaire on the outside walls, because he wants to introduce imagination: if the youngsters mistake these for Alain Delon, that is all right with him. He seeks to make the view from each spot different and surprising, rather than conceiving an estate as a whole: 'only God can see it that way'. Being forced by the public authorities to use only approved mass-produced materials, he avoids uniformity by painting these in forty different tints; he has tried to give each front door a different decoration, each staircase a different wallpaper, each block a different colour, so that people can recognize where they live.

However, he does not like those who are going to inhabit his houses to tell him what to do. He is not interested by interiors. He resignedly laments that the public's taste is perverted and that it is best therefore to let it keep its habits. There is certainly some contempt in him for his public; he does not even deny it, saying he is really building not for adults, but for the children. 'The adult', he says, 'is of no interest to me. He is already done for, he is already set up to be "underdeveloped". But a child can still be a free individual.' He imagines that his architecture can lead the child to maturity by creating 'a series of places that have an occult power'. He offers not comfort, but a new kind of urban life, 'whose order is so hidden that it is imperceptible'; there is more than a little in him of the enlightened despot, even if he claims that he is really a poet in concrete, and that his work is essentially psychological rather than just architectural; that makes it all the more insidious. He is furious that he has often been defeated by public opinion and forced to cram fewer people into his estates than he had planned; he gets round regulations on density of population by leaving large empty spaces and putting the houses near each other on one corner; he castigates the nostalgic supporters of '*villages à la Française*'; he has been able to do what he has by getting special dispensations to ignore building regulations. His critics say that La Grande Borne is fascinating but that unfortunately it leaks, because he is more interested in grand conceptions and simply subcontracts all the detail, that the inhabitants do not find their lives have been changed into poetry; on the contrary, they feel imprisoned and complain that they are too surrounded by concrete (even though there is, in fact, more greenery than usual). The small individual home is still the dream.

The trouble about the modern individual home is that it seems to have difficulty in flowering with the same exuberance as its predecessors. First, large scale promoters have moved in and are mass-producing homes of standard design, like motor cars, even if they leave the customer to choose between a dozen equally standard variations, like the bogus *mas provençal* or 'Normandy farmette' with the inevitable authentic beams. Secondly, the architects have not generally been able to turn the vast increase in building, unparalleled in history, into a renaissance of taste. It may be that the profession of architect remains too hidebound by its past: it is an unusually small corporation – not that large numbers guarantee more imagination (Britain has twice as many, to no obvious avail)[1] – but it has never won the prestige of pictorial artists, because it has not broken away from its academic rut. The traditional way to a successful career has been not to strike out in new directions but to pass the examinations, win the top prize (the *prix de Rome*), get a job in the state department of civil buildings, and so join the group that has a dominant share of the major public contracts. The *prix*

---

[1] France has 12,000 architects, Britain 24,000, Germany 40,000, USA 60,000, Italy probably has most of all.

de Rome has now been abolished but not the influence of these academically successful architects. They naturally help along those who share their own tastes. They are accused of being nepotistic (because two-thirds of French architects are from families from the same or related professions). Their image has not been improved by the fact that architects have made a lot of money out of the speculation in real estate that surrounds them; nor that the establishment should allow one of the ugliest buildings in the world to be put up on one of the best sites in the world – the Paris Faculty of Sciences at the Halles aux Vins, on the left bank of the Seine – nor that it has been possible to build public schools out of highly combustible materials, and without fire precautions: in the space of five years, seventeen went up in flames, because the Ministry of Education prefers to repeat its mistakes rather than risk novelty.

But to make architects the scapegoats of the numerous aesthetic and practical disasters is not entirely fair, and the French system of education in architecture cannot be regarded as worse than any other, since architects have made just as much mess in many other countries. It is not surprising that original architects should have a tough time in getting their ideas accepted: the extraordinary homes built by Lovag, Grataloup, Chaneac and Hanserman, who reject the box as the basic shape and substitute houses that look like giant shells, molluscs, caves or birds, have not been copied: Lovag's work was roundly condemned by *Le Monde* as 'perfectly exasperating folly'. That is the fate of most innovations. The real problem is that a consensus about questions of style is no longer possible: there cannot be another French style, immobile for a whole generation. A new relationship between architect, planner and resident is now seen as necessary. Urbanists, sociologists, engineers and politicians and other representatives of the community are now being made to work together with architects and all of them will have their say. But the danger is that they may simply reduce everything to a colourless compromise, and to the lowest common denominator.

Alain Sarfati does not expect such compromise between all possible interests to give satisfaction once the buildings are finished. He takes as his premise that people change in their tastes, and that they enjoy modifying and improving. It is very rare to find an architect who is pleased that a house he has put up should have bits removed or added, but Sarfati genuinely is, and he builds in order to facilitate such changes. Normally, the aesthetic purity of a block of flats is thought to be ruined when the tenants hang out their washing on the balconies, or put up cheap curtains in a discordant variety of colours. Sarfati paints his blocks in many different colours, with half a dozen different types of window, and as many types of frame for them, painted differently, (his windows usually have at least two colours), and several kinds of tiles on adjoining roofs. The result is that a brand new estate almost looks, apart from its cleanliness, like one that has existed since medieval times, and is covered with accretions that the eccentricities of successive inhabitants and builders have put on. 'I am against grand ideas,' he says, 'but am for a profusion of ideas.'

The beauty of a building for him is made up from its details: he likes to see each one as a separate picture, taking photographs of them – a strangely ornate balcony on a completely plain facade, an incongruously added porch, a pot of flowers – as though they are abstract paintings. The magic of his constructions is that he has given the inventiveness of his tenants a start: he has, for example, given each house in one terrace a slightly different wrought-iron balcony; there is virtually nowhere one can look and find repetition. There are no windswept empty wastelands between blocks, nor incomprehensible statues, but ingenious toys and structures for the children to play on, lines on the tarmac to provide the basis for games but also to distract the eye, balconies covered with large glass awnings for the old to enjoy the sun on, plants, gates, an ornate lamp post. He uses the cheapest materials of decent quality, and so is able to set aside 7% of his budget for luxuries which would not normally be found on an estate for poor people, 'in the same way as people wearing jeans and tennis shoes might add a Dior cravat to give themselves a lift'. He includes a variety of materials – for example a little timber, a few tiles – so that when the occupants want to change, they can have a choice of materials for their additions, which will not clash, and if wood which is expensive today becomes cheaper, then the wooden addition will be doubly justified. The variety is increased still further because he lets the builders contribute to it, leaving them the maximum of initiative; he does not like to stick to a rigid plan; if a mistake is made, he exploits it to create something original out of it, whenever he can. He tries to find new and unexpected uses for cheap mass-produced materials, which are ingeniously arranged and painted, so everybody involved in the building is able to contribute some creative idea to the result, and the occupant can continue the process.

Sarfati remembers meeting a monk in a monastery built by Le Corbusier: the monk said it was obvious the architect must have been a Protestant, because he provided no space where anything could be left about untidily, the perfect symmetry demanded that you should instantly pick it up and put it away. Sarfati has not invented architecture that allows rubbish or litter to look pretty, but he has come very near it: the odd lost toy or shoe does not look out of place. His favourite street in Paris is not any of the great perfectly symmetrical ones, but the rue de Babylone, in which no two houses are the same, where virtually everything can be found, from a police barracks to an Oriental pagoda; you could complain that this is as bad a mess as Las Vegas, but he finds that Las Vegas represents a certain American character: there is a harmony of sorts, because there is so much stimulation to the imagination. That is not architecture, say Sarfati's critics, but do-it-yourself *bricolage*. He has tried to raise do-it-yourself to the status of an art, believing that it is more satisfying than trying to build houses by committee, with the future inhabitants being asked what they want and then not getting quite what they asked or hoped for. He has found that participation results in conservative architecture, and the reproduction of the familiar. The successful British builder Barrett says people are conservative and that is why he builds houses that are absolutely predictable. Sarfati replies that such an attitude takes too static a view of humanity. Sometimes, he admits, he goes too far; some people have complained, for example, that the walls of their back gardens are not all the same. He has no hesitation in satisfying them, because he has no desire to impose anything on them.

One of the most striking features of his behaviour is the

Puppet: From *Le Rire* 26 August 1896

The House with Uncombed Hair

The Coquette

The Weeping House

The Hungry House

The Artist

The Military House

The Bearded House

attention he pays to what other people say, and his sense of each person's individuality. That is probably the result of his always having been something of an outsider himself, never fitting neatly into any slot. He sees his function to be, above all, the defence of individual liberty; now that it is increasingly difficult to find liberty in work, or even in packaged leisure, he sees the architect as having a crucial role to play in providing opportunities for self-expression. He recalls his teacher at school saying to him: you will always speak the way your parents speak – there is no escape from your social class; he is determined that home should not be a prison too. The first architectural work he ever did was to knock down the walls in his own three-roomed flat and create the fashionable open plan of the 1960s. That proved disastrous; it helped to break up his marriage, by destroying privacy within his family. Now he tries to do the opposite; his problem is to find enough places where he can introduce variety. His style is not as much at variance with the massive uniform architecture of eighteenth-century France as it may appear; he has studied how Versailles was built, and found that far from being a grandly conceived single whole, it is, in fact, a complex combination of details, put together to give the impression of order; he particularly likes the contrast of the front and rear facades, which may offend the purists, but for him is an essential source of enrichment. He has the same contrast in his much humbler houses. The name Sarfati, he tells those who wonder what he is up to, means 'French' in Hebrew.

He thought of emigrating to the United States in his youth, because it seemed to offer wider scope for innovation, but he no longer feels that. It is true there are not as many openings in France for doing exotic homes for the rich, with no expense spared; Marcel Dassault built himself a replica of the Trianon, almost in the same spirit as Randolph Hearst raised up his castle in California, but most rich people are keen not to show off their wealth. However, in public housing there is so much activity, and the authorities who control it are now so keen not to commit themselves to any one style, for fear of backing a loser once again, that they allow a vast range of experiment; since they are not interested in architecture as such, but only as a tool for solving social problems, they interfere less in aesthetic matters.

Sarfati is himself interested more in the human side of architecture than in technical innovation; others have been free to build estates heated geothermically or by solar power; others still not to build at all, but simply to restore old houses. It is only rarely that a mayor says, as Jacques Chirac said in Paris, 'The chief architect is me.'

11

How to distinguish a manager from an aristocrat

The duc de Brissac is everyman's idea of the typical old aristocrat. He owns a magnificent castle in Anjou (as well as three
other homes); he is heir to a dynasty going back many centuries,
which has produced four marshals of France. But he is also a
gifted graduate of the Polytechnique, an engineer who rose to be
managing director of Schneider-Westinghouse, an amalgam-
ation of French and American technological power. It is true he
married his boss's daughter, May Schneider, heiress to one of
France's major industrial firms, but that was almost a family
tradition. His ancestors married the heiresses to Veuve Clic-
quot's champagne company and Say's sugar refineries. He is
president of the most aristocratic club in France, The Jockey,
where all that matters is who one's father was, but he has also
shown talent of his own as the author of half-a-dozen books, and
competitiveness as a versatile sportsman. He could be regarded
as one of the country's leading experts on privilege, because
there is virtually no privilege he has not enjoyed; and he is not
ashamed of it. His view of himself is that though he has only one
vote, he is not just anybody. Authority, he says, comes easily to
him: 'rarely in my long life have I had to raise my voice to make
myself heard.' He concedes that it may be unfair that it has
fallen to his lot always 'to command', but that is the way the
world is; 'some girls are pretty, and some are ugly: each of us
must make the best of his gifts.' It is a mere accident that a gift
for mathematics made him an engineer. 'No one gets what he
deserves, we know that,' He does not discourage the less lucky
from being ambitious, and from trying to climb; ambition is a
good thing; but there is little point in overreaching oneself: the
modern world is based on the stimulation of desire rather than

on the satisfaction of needs; people imagine they will be twice as happy if they own two cars, but they are mistaken. His own property he regards simply as a 'responsibility'. If all this sounds very old-fashioned and paternalistic, well, he says, paternalism is no worse than the cold anonymity of modern capitalism. But he denies that his outlook is a static one. He prides himself on having adapted to his times, unlike his father, who found democracy absolutely too much, and referred to everyone connected with it as a pig: *les cochons* the ministers, *les cochons* the tax collectors. The duc de Brissac's daughter married a famous technocrat, Simon Nora. That marriage eventually ended in divorce: 'our villages are too far apart,' commented the duke, because Nora's father was an ordinary bourgeois doctor. But he was wrong. Nora is a genuine member of the new aristocracy, even if he does not have a title.

It may seem strange to talk of aristocracy in the post-revolutionary Republic. What of liberty, equality and fraternity? The words are on coins, on public buildings, but their meaning in real life is less obvious. Liberty does mean you can say and do what you like within reason, but provided you know how to get round the rules and regulations of the bureaucrats. For example, the most publicized of all French laws (that of 29 July 1881) allows the government and property owners to put up notices on walls, saying it is forbidden to put up notices on walls (*défense d'afficher*); people discovered that the law had forgotten to mention drainpipes, so these have become free advertising hoardings. Equality does mean you are as good as anybody else, but even socialist and communist ministers earn six times as much as labourers, and the amount of income tax you pay still depends partly on your wits and your honesty, since avoiding tax remains a national pastime. Fraternity does mean that there is state help for the old, sick and unemployed, but a school somehow managed to have three dining rooms for its teachers, so that those with higher degrees, ordinary degrees and no degrees at all could eat separately.

The French invented their motto 200 years ago, but they have given their energies as much to getting round it as to implementing it. Their alternative code of conduct, the Système D (D for *Débrouillard*, which means the art of getting by, of finding one's way through obstacles) often turns into the art of doing better than one's neighbour. So the claim that since World War II the French have turned over a new leaf and have modernized themselves, that there are now just two kinds of Frenchmen, the modern ones and the old sort who are vanishing, is not very helpful, because it glosses over the question of what the modernizers are really working for, and how different they are from their parents. The distinction between old-style and new-style Frenchmen is just as ambiguous as the previously fashionable distinction, between bourgeois and people, which is now even more hopeless than the old division of Englishmen into gentlemen and the rest, for at least the gentleman was supposed not to be a cad. What is more important to me than the vague distinctions of social class is how people behave and treat each other, how they conceive human relationships, what they try to get out of life. If I apply that criterion to people at work, I see a separation of French people into three groups: those who like to lead others, or to give orders, and who believe in hierarchy, though they may do so for widely differing reasons; those who hate or resent their boss, who fight him, but without replacing the hierarchical relationship by any other; and finally those who opt out of the hierarchical system and concern themselves with creating a life for themselves that imposes no constraining demands on others. The duc de Brissac obviously illustrates the first category; far from being the last of a dying breed, he is part of a greatly expanding mass of ambitious people, anxious to command, who have formed a new kind of aristocracy.

The old nobility is the least important part of the present aristocracy; a title of nobility carries weight for few except those who have one themselves. However, it is more than the mark of membership of a genealogical society, for the nobles have the largest family network in the country, having devoted endless attention to advantageous intermarriages. So they have still more than their fair share of top jobs in industry (in which about a quarter of the survivors of old families are employed; about a fifth of them are in the army and another fifth farm; about a tenth are bankers). For example, General Alain de Boissieu Dean de Luigné, some time Chief of the Army Staff, married

General de Gaulle's daughter: three of his relations hold about twenty business directorships among them. Of course, nobles have always been opponents as well as parts of the establishment, so it is not surprising that one of the Maoist militant workers arrested at the Renault factory some years ago was the Comte de Choiseul-Praslin or that one of the leaders of the Breton Communist Party should be the Comte Meriadec de Gouyon-Matignon; it was after all the nobility that started the Revolution of 1789; but whereas the English peerage divided itself pretty equally between Whigs and Tories, so that it was never in danger of being completely discredited, the French nobles lost their nerve and did not know how to make large enough sacrifices to keep their position of leadership.

The Comte de Paris, the pretender to the throne, used to have hopes of a restoration of the monarchy; he believed that General de Gaulle was creating a charismatic current that would have permanent consequences. The General encouraged him in these hopes and treated him with great politeness, assuring him that the attention of the gossip writers, who wrote endlessly about every royal family but the French one, would eventually reach him. But the Count still counts for nothing, because he has not understood that a royal family, or indeed a noble class, cannot be popular if it embodies only a single principle e.g. national unity or authority. De Gaulle was more successful, because he won votes from the left as well as the right. The British royal family survives because it is so many-sided, each of its members having a distinct outlook; it personifies outspokenness as well as tradition, competitiveness as well as decorum, humour, horses, technology, glamour and even frustrated love; there is at least one element that anyone can find to identify with; the British monarchy is not really an essentially inherited institution, because it constantly changes; it used to be unpopular in the eighteenth century and it has repeatedly found new ways of winning popularity. By contrast, the Comte de Paris refused to attend two of his children's weddings, on the grounds that his prospective in-laws were beneath him. The different fates of the British and French royal families is due not to fundamentally different popular mentalities in the two countries, but to the skill of one family and the incompetence of another. The Comte de Paris' snobbery might have been tolerated if he had shown more varied prejudices. To judge a person by who his parents are is not just a traditional mark of the old nobility, it has existed and exists in other classes too, and the well-to-do bourgeoisie still have their own *almanachs*, just like the nobles, in which they catalogue their marriage alliances like a horse's stud book, with an infinite sensitivity to gradations of status. People who have noble titles are not necessarily aristocrats in the full sense today, and not only because so many titled people are bogus aristocrats. One of the surprises of French history is that in the revolution the nobles had their heads chopped off, but somehow there are now more of them than ever before: the explanation is that in addition to the 4000 genuinely noble families surviving from the 12,000 who existed in 1789, perhaps ten times that number now pretend to be noble, having assumed titles to which they have no right. But aristocracy implies power and prestige and many titled people now have very little of either.

Thus the Marquis de Brissac could be said to belong to a different social class from his father the duke. He has no important influence over other people, which his father, as a tycoon, did. He is more a *rentier*, a man who lives off inherited wealth, with all the problems of the bourgeois *rentier* whose wealth is not adequate. He is a quiet man, with a gentle manner and no urge to compete. He is happiest when he is with his horses and his dogs. Indeed he spends much of his time either hunting or looking after his forty stag hounds, whom he knows individually by name (Conquérant, Protocol, Francophone, Impudent, Ingénu, etc.); he has known them from birth; 'I know their fathers and grandfathers; they are like a second family to me.' A huntsman who plays no part in local affairs is a sportsman, not an aristocrat. The Marquis has in effect found a new role for his class, as hereditary museum-keepers. He loves his home, which is a magnificent fifteenth-century chateau, and he and his wife have devoted themselves since their marriage to restoring it and to living off the proceeds of opening it to the public: he organizes 'prestige dinners' for business executives with money to spare and a taste for antique grandeur. His young son thinks life on the chateau is 'paradise' and intends to follow the same career, looking after it. The family regard this as a form of business: the marquise talks of making the chateau *une affaire* (a business), and she has worked at it with great commercial as well as artistic skill. She has now, in her forties, enrolled as a student of theology at the nearby Catholic Faculty of Angers; that has helped her understand her purpose in life, which is to worship God and get to heaven. Christianity for her does not require one to give up one's worldly goods in order to be saved: she does not think a rich man has more difficulty in getting into heaven than a poor man: 'it is not one's own merits that take one to heaven, but the merits of Jesus Christ.' So she studies divinity while he hunts. Each has created a world of their own, in which they have found, more or less, contentment, he probably more than she, for he has a more easy-going temperament. When I asked him what he thought of meritocracy, he genuinely did not know what the word meant.

By contrast, there are people in the working class who believe they have the capacity to boss their fellows around, and who hope to ensure that their children get to the top too. Monsieur Perrin is production manager at the Rossignol ski factory at Voiron in the Isère, one of France's most dynamic companies, and one of the world's largest manufacturers of skis and tennis rackets, with factories in several countries. He began life as an ordinary worker, having been trained as a turner, but he always dreamt of 'being in command'. 'To command' is his 'vocation', he says. After eight years he got himself promoted to foreman; six years later he was chosen for his present post, in charge of several hundred men and women. He sees his rise as 'logical', because 'one cannot change one's character', and he is demonstrably tough, driving himself as hard as he drives others. He does not mind being called hard. The workers do not like him, but he accepts that. He has all his life worked at least eleven hours a day, sometimes thirteen. His philosophy is that one should 'extract as much as possible' from oneself. He is very demanding of others too: he walks about his factory with an evident sense of authority, giving orders firmly though politely, and no one argues with him. He believes that it is right that he should get paid more than his subordinates because he has worked hard for his reward and it is open (he claims) for others to do the same. In France, he insists, anyone can rise if he wants to.

He laments, uncomprehendingly, that French workers do not work hard enough, talking almost like a British manager, to the point of adding that only a war will put the spirit back into them – otherwise France will go to the dogs. Perhaps the war will be a civil war, he adds darkly. For him, a good salary is the necessary basis of a good life, which means two things; to live comfortably, and to educate one's children. It is 'absolutely necessary' to make good money. He pushes his children in the

Lauzier

same direction, and hopes they too will draw the maximum from their abilities. He gets up at five in the morning to help his daughter of seventeen do her homework. A close family life is his joy; his weekends are given to hunting, fishing and gardening, in which his wife and four children all join in. He talks contemptuously of his neighbour (also a manager) who has been seduced by success into leading such a busy social life that he hardly ever sees his children: he shudders at the consequences he foresees from children being left to their own devices. Though contented with his job, he is ready for further promotion, and is willing to undertake whatever training might be needed. Ambition is a way of life for him.

The French like to imagine themselves as an independent sort of people, who will not be bossed about. But many of them obviously also like telling others what to do. For in the thirty years after the war, the ambition to be a manager became so pervasive that they doubled the number of their managers and trebled the number of their foremen. So on top of every two people doing a job, there is a third telling them how to do it. The myth that the French are more egalitarian than the Germans has become clearly false, since they now have twice as many foremen as the Germans. The enormous expansion of the managerial class gave many people the feeling that they could rise in the world. But the recession having put an end to that, managers are now complaining that the bureaucratic institutions they have raised up have become obstacles to their personal creativity: that opens up the prospect of a new 'revolt of the nobles'. For the remarkable characteristic of French managers is that they are much more a hereditary class than in comparable countries. A German journalist has calculated that whereas only a quarter of the managers of the 200 larger firms in Germany are the sons of rich families, in France three-quarters are; and in the United States less than a tenth are. It certainly is still possible to become a capitalist boss (a quarter of a million people have that status), though France is nothing like the land of opportunity for businessmen that the United States is: ten times more new firms are started each year there. Still three-fifths of the bosses of small and medium-sized firms in France do come from modest origins. That means that the rags to riches story is not uncommon. But the heads of the large firms come very largely from well-to-do backgrounds.

France failed to abolish aristocracy in 1789, because meritocracy, which it put in its place, has not eliminated the inheritance of power and privilege. The most original French tax is that on 'signs of wealth': you are taxed if you keep a yacht, horses, a castle. The effect is that on the whole the rich in France are far more discreet than they are in most countries. The uniform facades of Paris streets are designed to keep individual wealth a private matter; the ostentation of the old nobility has been eliminated. But the rich have not been eliminated. Some years ago, experts produced figures to argue that France had greater extremes of wealth and poverty than any other western nation, even than the United States and Britain. Other experts have disproved this, but no one really knows just how rich the rich are: it is impossible to be certain that France has fewer or more millionaires than Britain, partly because the secretiveness of the rich has meant that they do not give ostentatious benefactions, and there are comparatively few philanthropic foundations on the American model. Only 8000 people have admitted to annual incomes of over a million francs (£100,000 or $200,000); but billions of francs have apparently vanished into foreign banks as a result of the socialists' very moderate wealth tax. The result of all this is that the French have a very poor idea of their inequalities: when asked to estimate other people's earnings, they know pretty well what those of roughly the same social level as themselves earn, but they underestimate the salaries of managing directors by an enormous margin. Aristocracy survives also because though the state has waged war on the rich, the top civil servants of the state have themselves become a hereditary elite. In the fifth republic top civil servants have increasingly gone on to become ministers and members of parliament; there are far fewer members of parliament of working-class origin than in Britain or the United States, and the proportion who come from the upper classes increased steadily since the war, until the last election. It is still the same kind of civil servant who will manage the nationalized industries. So the idea that because France is a republic with egalitarian principles, every French soldier carries a Marshal's baton in his knapsack and every labourer can hope to rise to become a director is both true and false, but more false than true. The majority of the French ruling class owe as much to their daddies as to their own merits.

The desire to be a boss, says Yvon Gattaz, head of the Federation of Employers' Unions, is 'congenital', you either have it or you do not; it is in your chromosomes. He feels that the tragedy for France is that many people who have it are put off from trying by the hostility that bosses encounter from their

workers, by the idea that a boss is a member of an elite which
exploits the masses. A boss, he says without worrying about the
paradox, is first of all a nonconformist. He explains his own
'non-conformism' as being inherited: his father was a teacher
who abandoned his safe job to become a painter. To have his
own business was Gattaz's way of 'expressing myself, of discovering my identity, as the psychologists say'. At twenty-
seven, he gave up his own safe managerial job in charge of the
metal-buying at Citroën to start a firm of his own. 'I asked
dozens and dozens of people for their advice – all of them agreed:
"No, don't do it." There is a very important factor in such
decisions, that of one's family, and especially one's wife. Too
often non-conformists are held back by wives who say to them "I
was the wife of a chief engineer, I shall become the wife of an
artisan – it is not honourable for me." A man needs courage to
resist that.' Gattaz sees the boss as one who loves taking risks.
'The taste for risk-taking decreases inexorably with time; it is
bound to diminish with age, with comfort, with security, with
family obligations, and with unsuccessful experiences.'

He has doubtless been encouraged by the fact that he is a born
winner. 'I got through school with ease and rapidity; I had the
good fortune to enter the Ecole Centrale for engineers very
quickly.' He was promoted at record speed at Citroën, being
made chief engineer despite his youth; he had the prospect of
reaching the very top of that firm. 'But I preferred to fall
socially, to become an artisan with two employees. I had always
dreamed of founding a business, to be independent, to be able to
give free rein to a creative imagination. I had luck on my side,
because I had a brother of almost the same age, who is also an
engineer, and we happened to get on well and complement each
other both in character and professionally. We had the feeling,
without too much modesty, that we could become very good
heads of firms, which has more or less come about. It was the
wish to fly by our own wings, more than the rather childish
desire, which we all have in us, to make a fortune. It was rather
the ambition to take our decisions ourselves. Many believe we
are influenced by the myth propagated by American films,
which show people in sumptuous villas and magnificent motor
cars: I do not say that did not play a little part, but I think the

principal reason was our wish to fulfil ourselves, our desire for independence, and taste for risk, perhaps our taste for command, or what some call the taste for power. I do not want great power, but power that comes from independence.'

Gattaz made his name by preaching the virtues of the middle-sized firm, the firm 'of human dimensions'. He knows everyone in his factory by name (even if they still call him Monsieur). Gattaz says large firms do not make the largest profits; and profit needs to be interpreted in a wide sense. A firm must not only succeed economically, it must also give wide satisfaction to its shareholders, clients and employees, by pursuing the general interest, by making things of which all can be proud. The employees must be satisfied not only by good wages but also by attractive conditions of work, by interesting work and a share in responsibility and profit. This is only possible, he argues, in firms of below 2000 employees, in which the human scale is preserved. In fact a quarter of French wage earners work for firms with under fifty employees, a quarter for firms over 2000 and one-half in medium-sized firms. At present, however, France's exports are the work almost entirely of the large firms; only when the medium-sized ones learn to export will they be fully justified, for at the moment they are dependent on the large ones, for whom they are often subcontractors.

Gattaz wants to make his employees happy, but not equal; the boss must remain the boss; the socialist ideal of autogestion is inspired, he says, by political ideology, not business realities. He favours decentralization of firms into groups of 200 or 300 workers, and small 'task force' teams within this; and giving workers more information, which a law of 1977, to come into force in 1982, makes compulsory. He advocates part-time work both as an enrichment of life and as an answer to unemployment, and points out that a law of 1975 compensated employees for any loss they incur by setting up two part-time jobs instead of one full-time one – but this has been largely ignored. Finally, he gives his workers one-tenth of their time off for 'public service'.

Gattaz has calculated that only 0·3% of the engineering graduates of the *grandes écoles* establish their own firms. He wishes to create a new fashion, to revive the inspiration of the success stories of the American millionaires, and of Renault, Citroën and Michelin. Success for him, however, has meant not luxurious living (he has reinvested all his profits in his firm and draws only a salary); it is partly social success, to 'join the establishment', partly the taste 'to lead a team'. Independence he has found to be a bit of an illusion, for 'a business is like a mistress' and it is the client who rules him: he works a six-and-a-half-day week; he has only recently allowed himself to take an annual holiday − of two weeks. His firm has continued to grow despite the world recession because he has specialized in one particular item of electronic equipment (professional coaxial connectors), in which he has become the world's second largest manufacturer employing about 800 people: the American leaders produce standard types, he caters for special needs. His second-in-command is a Frenchman trained at the Stanford Business School. He has not decided what should happen to small businesses when their founders die. He is convinced that his children must not simply inherit his firm; if they are interested by business, they should start their own. But it remains to be seen just how much help they will get from him, apart from the privilege of having had an exceptional education. He is less keen on offering his employees promotion than the chance to start another firm. He has helped five of them to set up on their own, as well as creating an advice centre, 'Allo Création', to encourage others to do the same. But he gives that help only 'to those who deserve it, because one must beware of urging on those who do not have the force of character'. And he declares himself helpless before the rival attraction of a civil service job: 'it has never been possible to alter the prestige of that, it's the summit of the summit. A reputation, in my view, somewhat exaggerated, because many enter the civil service for a quiet life, to snooze with total job security.' He admits nonconformism is not for everybody: 'people have a tendency to do what is expected of them, and it is a pity, because those who succeed are those who are slightly mad, who do the opposite of what is normal.' Now that he has the job of representing the employers, he dreams of making them speak with one voice, but that obviously contradicts his view of them as nonconformists. The Employers' Union is formed of over 800 federations, which have long jealously guarded their independence. The federations of gold-topped walking stick manufacturers, of Basque beret producers, of tanners of reptile skins, of angora wool weavers, of makers of boxes for cheeses, are more eccentric examples of the individual pride and internal rivalries of bosses. Just as the old nobility was bitterly divided between a court nobility and provincial country gentlemen, so the nationalized, the multi-nationals and the small business man remain at loggerheads.

An important part of the aristocracy in the old regime was the abbots of wealthy monasteries, whose property increased steadily with time. Their modern equivalent is the multi-national firm, ever growing in the same way. Today foreign multinationals (European and American in roughly equal proportions) own about one-fifth of French industry: that is the overall figure but it is in modern dynamic industries that they have invested most – they own four-fifths of the business machines industry, 68% of oil, 60% of agricultural machines, 51% of chemicals, 41% of mines and iron, 39% of pharmaceuticals, 36% of precision instruments, 28% of electrical domestic appliances. So French businessmen must not always be expected to behave in what are traditionally supposed to be French ways. IBM France insists that it is French, all its directors are French, even if they have been trained in the United States as well as in France. But Jacques Maisonrouge, the head of IBM Europe, says he is inspired by the idea that you must succeed by your own efforts, which he significantly sees as an American rather than a French idea, that you sink if you fail, that it is no use hoping for a providential state to reform society. In the cafeterias at the Motorola factory at Toulouse, social distinctions are theoretically abolished: managers and juniors all eat together and they use first names; everyone is superficially friendly, but when there is disagreement 'knives come out'; the neighbouring Dassault airplane factory claims to have a more genuinely relaxed atmosphere. When IBM France borrowed money from an old-fashioned French bank, the arrangement was made in a letter of a single page. When it borrowed from the Paris branch of the Chemical Bank of New York, the contract ran to ten pages; when it borrowed from Morgan Guarantee

Bank, which has been in France for a long time, a contract of five pages sufficed. Americanization does not necessarily mean greater informality, it also means greater influence by cautious lawyers.

The modern feudal barons are the business tycoons. With time, they will doubtless increasingly be lawyers and accountants. But there are still many adventurers among them, like Maurice Bidermann. Abandoned at the age of five by a wayward Bohemian father, he works 'like a dynamo' to do all that his father failed to do. It is not the desire for money that pushes him, he says, but love of authority, the taste for 'commanding men'. At first he dreamt of having a thousand employees; he imagined he would simply press buttons in a plush office and all would revolve around him. He wanted money only as a means to adventure, to enable him to take risks. He used to want to be loved by his workers, but no longer. The boss, he says, cannot be loved, at best he can be respected. He has won no love by taking over firms in distress, some of them highly respected old firms, run by proud old families, which were horrified to have to kneel before such an upstart. He replies: 'Don't forget it is I who saved you from the worse dishonour of bankruptcy.' He has expanded into America, and it is the American tycoon he admires most. What he likes about the American mentality is that when you drive in your chauffeured Cadillac, the workers do not shout insults at you but say, 'In the US I hope to rise to have a Cadillac too.' What he believes he shares with the Americans is the religion of hard work, rather than the French obsession with political argument. These are rather facile generalizations; there are always some Frenchmen who denigrate their own country at the expense of an idealized foreigner. Bidermann is in fact the universal businessman: his success started with a contract to supply the Russians with 300,000 garments, and then with others to provide uniforms for the police and the Paris bus and metro men.

The art of commanding is, however, also in the process of refurbishment and 'modernization'. The Auguste Comte Institute for the Study of the Sciences of Action was established by President Giscard d'Estaing as a super business school, where managers and civil servants with ten years of successful experi-

Lauzier

ence, reliably destined for the highest echelons of power, should spend a year's sabbatical leave rethinking their methods. The socialists did not like the pretentiousness and elitism of this idea and one of the first things they did on coming to power was to close it down. It had been installed in the old buildings of the Polytechnique, in the rue Descartes, which have now been handed over to a new ministry of research and technology. But this institute revealed the intentions of the believers in a liberal capitalism, men who continue to hold key positions in the country. The head of the institute was a physicist, Michel Lafon, a graduate of the Polytechnique and of the School of Telecommunications, who as Regional Director of Telecommunications in Orleans had 'discovered that my problems were not technical but ones of human relations; if I could not win over the mayors, I could not do my job'. He discovered that some mayors spent the middle of the day, from 12 to 5, having lunch, and that was where issues were decided; his problem was how to get invited to their lunches. His technical training had left him completely unprepared: he had been taught quantum mechanics, but had never used it. Mathematics was supposed to have instilled rigour into him, but he thinks that was a mistake, rigour comes from hard work as much as mathematics, and more philosophy would have been preferable, since that would have taught him how to interpret and participate in discussion. The main thing he had been taught was how to learn up a subject quickly in one week before an examination, that is, how to work fast; seeing now how his daughter was doing very advanced mathematics just for her *baccalauréat*, he thinks the craze for more and more knowledge has gone too far.

He wanted the Institute to offer something like the Yale Organization and Management course, mixing people from different parts of the business world, studying future trends, but he thought that though Yale's objective was sound, its methods were too much in the French tradition, because the courses were taught by specialists. It is true American executives had a lot of practical experience, and what they felt the lack of was more theory, but the French ones were in the opposite situation. The engineers of France lacked a social, cultural and historical background. 'The old system of command cannot be maintained and is likely to change'. It was not just the managers who had to learn new attitudes; trade unionists had no habit of participation in management; workers were seldom keen to share in responsibility, he claimed. 'Scientific method is inadequate to resolve the new situation'. His aim was to take into account the element of the irrational that is to be found everywhere, and that the technicians had spurned. He would be more American than the Americans.

His institute offered no lectures. They had seminars in which they discussed labour relations with bosses and trade unionists who had had strikes; they spent a quarter of their time on problems of 'communication and behaviour, negotiation, expression, media and language, with the intention of changing the boss's personality, ending his theoretical approach, making him more 'relaxed'. Another quarter of their time was spent on international economics, decision-making and the environment, and they talked to people like Maisonrouge of IBM Europe. But their main efforts were devoted to solving practical problems in groups of three, and problems completely outside their usual experience. For example, there was the problem of French timber: it was more expensive than Swedish timber, vast quantities of the latter were imported, and French carpenters were convinced Swedish timber was better; the result was that French furniture was built with imported timber. The three executives who looked into this and who knew nothing about the subject discovered first of all that five different ministries claimed to be in charge of the timber problem, and there was nothing to be got out of them. They approached the Vosges timber producers, who however were unorganized, did not know each other, and were not interested in these interfering investigators when they proposed collaboration among all the different stages of production. So the three men organized a voyage to Sweden by the civil servants concerned and the foresters. The result was that they were convinced that the low reputation of Vosges timber was unjustified and could be remedied; and the civil servants handed over all the subsidies necessary to change this: 'they found the irrational factor'.

An additional purpose of these teams of three was to iron out their rough edges. One dynamic woman manager from near Bordeaux put everybody's back up by her bossy and intolerant manner (it was guessed that she was probably taking a year off because her husband also could bear her no longer). She was a self-made woman, with no diplomas, head of the Young Employers' organization of her city; and with a good business record. But when she tried to impose her will on her two team-mates, who were graduates of the Polytechnique, they would have none of it. According to them she was 'transformed' by the experience, and 'realized that her intransigence was a handicap'. Of course, this is a one-sided report, and Michel Lafon, when talking of his own keenness to be 'flexible' with his employees, added that sometimes 'you are forced to be tough', because they might try to take advantage of you: 'you must not allow them to think you are weak.'

Lafon admitted that his concern for a broadening of the culture of managers did not mean that he had succeeded in broadening his own: he hardly ever read books, except on holiday – 'a Polytechnic education does not encourage reading.' But he was in favour of reorganizing French education so that everybody should be able to speak English. He claimed the teachers' unions had too many vested interests to allow that. He likened the need to know English to the need to be able to swim, which was a compulsory entrance requirement of the Polytechnique. Though the Auguste Comte Institute has vanished, the search for models of 'leadership' other than the traditional ones of France continues in the numerous schools of business administration. The Paris Chamber of Commerce, for example, has founded an Ecole des Affaires de Paris which has three branches, in Paris, Oxford and Düsseldorf, and the students not only spend time studying in England and Germany, but also go and work in British and German firms as part of their training; this is a school, moreover, which is keen to admit foreign students and which in effect is training a European businessman.

It is because managers have, as it were, put on new suits, that the aristocracy system is surviving. It is surviving also for the same reason that there was no expropriation of all landowners in 1789: too many of the peasants were already landowners themselves, in a small way. The landless labourers, therefore, gained very little from the revolution and were unable to get fairer shares. Today, likewise, so many people have obtained a small share of power over their fellows that they do not see themselves as likely to benefit from equality. It is not only the madly ambitious yearning to get to the top who accept aristocracy.

Monsieur Cazeau is an engineer who has never sought to be his own boss. 'You've got to be realistic: there are people better than you, and others who are more unfortunate.' He is content to have got where he has. He has always wanted to build aeroplanes, since childhood. Now, aged thirty, having graduated from the country's leading aeronautical college, *Sup. Aéro.*, he is proud of his achievement that he is an engineer in Dassault's aeroplane factory at Toulouse. All the more so since his father is an ordinary policeman, his sister a nurse, his brother-in-law a worker. He feels he has made a big sacrifice to become an engineer, he had to give up 'part of his youth' to study, and he thinks that is the justification for graduates being paid more than workers, who have been free to have a good time. It is acceptable to him that the wages of some should be five times that of others; he is not worried by inequality. In practice, in any case, he is not richer than his brother-in-law the worker, since the latter's wife also works; his luxury is that his own wife does not have to take a job. He is also not an individualist in the way that Gattaz believes bright young people ought to be. 'To be constantly searching for something is the way to become frustrated, to ruin one's life. To be free one must not go against the current of evolution, the way mankind is moving, it is too powerful. Liberty means not to do what one wants, but to do what one is almost forced to do. Not to want to integrate oneself is to commit suicide. One must find one's liberty in an understanding of the direction in which things are moving.' Besides, his kind of work is done in teams; his training always involved team work, exercises with at least one other person. 'Scientific creation is by teams, not individuals; we need computers, so many people are involved. There is no longer one father of new ideas: Nobel prizes go to several people.' He is not attracted by the 'supercilious' Americans. 'We are planning an airplane for the American navy: they were surprised we could make planes.' Cazeau does not believe in making difficulties for himself. He is quite happy to go to work every day, a man can get used to that, provided he does not think he is being forced. He must derive pleasure from his work, from his leisure, and from his family. He is fully occupied with these, and has no time for worrying, for reading, or for idle dreams.

No one would think of calling Monsieur Cazeau a bourgeois, despite his job. He may seem too unpretentious to be called a new aristocrat either, but he has joined those who order and judge their fellow humans in a style that still, not infrequently, involves authoritarian relationships reminiscent of a previous age. The 'bourgeois' certainly has not vanished, either in his 'upper' or 'petty' variety, but that designation represents nostalgia more than reality. It is possible to subscribe to the bourgeois ideal of a measured, thrifty life, to feel that one is not 'common', to be proud that one comes from a 'respectable' family, to dress to show that one is not a manual worker, to cultivate social aspirations and contempt for one's 'inferiors', to pay lip service to the ennobling results of education and culture. But the bourgeois connection with power is gone; few who value bourgeois ideals can afford to employ domestic servants; skilled manual workers can earn more than people with such pretensions, and often do have a style of life that is virtually indistinguishable; education is universal, and the ability to speak standard French correctly and fluently is not limited to any class; 'workers' no longer necessarily work with their hands, and the dividing line between them and the petty bourgeois clerk has virtually vanished; family life is not an exclusively bourgeois virtue. A professor and a shopkeeper, who might once have both been called bourgeois, now seem to have little in common. Eighty-five per cent of the French are now wage earners, and most of those who might once have been called bourgeois are wage earners too; wages have become 'salaries' for most people, paid monthly. There is much less contrast between bourgeois and proletariat. The proletarian used to be one who had no wealth but the ownership of his children: children have ceased to be a source of income for parents; and one-third of 'workers' are now property owners. To be a member of the proletariat meant that one was insecure, liable to be thrown on to the streets at one's employer's say-so, with no dole to keep one from starvation. Today the dividing lines are different. There are those who have secure jobs, with pensions beyond them (civil servants and unionized workers) and those who do not. There are those who do interesting work and those who are virtually beasts of burden, whose job gives neither dignity nor satisfaction. The underprivileged, from the point of view of employment, are immigrants, women, the young, and non-unionized, temporary workers. Aside from them, privileges may differ in degree, but are fundamentally of the same kind. There are certainly snobbish and financial distinctions between the holidays taken by factory workers and their bosses, but they do both enjoy holidays, and free weekends, and that is not everyone's privilege.

The system of aristocracy is maintained because privilege is still sought after by many who hope that they can do better than their fellows. Vanity is still encouraged. French institutions have not progressed much beyond the Napoleonic stage in this respect. The present Prince Napoleon, who is a banker in Switzerland (he is in fact the descendant of the emperor's nephew Jerome, and like him physically a giant) is very cautious and anxious not to say anything controversial, and the least controversial belief he can express, in his view, is that 'every

French person wants and hopes to be decorated with the Legion of Honour, and to be promoted in it.' France is indeed one of the most bemedalled countries in the world, perhaps it even outdoes Russia. There are over a quarter of a million who wear a ribbon or a rosette in their buttonhole to show their fellows their precise rank in the legion, and to warn policemen that they are not just anybody. There are over 100,000 who have been decorated with the National Order of Merit. To placate those whose merits were less conspicuous, virtually every profession was given its medals: schoolteachers got the Order of Academic Palms, travel agents the Order of Touristic Merit, postmen the Order of Postal Merit and footballers the Order of Sporting Merit. This mutual self-congratulation eventually got out of hand, and a halt was called to the award of many of the more bizarre medals. Today a man cannot be certain whether his medal will earn him respect or a sneer. That these decorations are awarded for life only does not alter the fact that Napoleon had intended to create, as the head of his family reaffirms with pride, 'a new nobility'. But Napoleon never found a new solution for the problem of what to do with the children of the men he decorated and ennobled: so they continue to inherit privilege indirectly.

The mark of an aristocrat in the old regime used to be the possession of a grand country house or chateau. About a thousand of these, dating from before 1800, still exist, but ten times as many have been built since then, representing the endless search for distinction in the old manner. The stately homes, however, attract only one-fifth of the number of visitors that the stately homes of Britain do. One of the reasons is that the French prefer to buy themselves their own country homes rather than ogle at those of the rich. Almost one in every six families has access to a secondary residence; about a third of managers and members of the liberal professions have one, and even a tenth of clerks own country cottages, however humble. A Frenchman's second home is his castle. Style of life is not determined just by birth, or by occupation, or by wealth. As with the noblemen of the past, who graded themselves by the number of quarters in their coat of arms, so people today acquire status through a number of different sources of prestige, which they try to accumulate. A sociologist has suggested that the French should be divided not into three social classes, but into sixty-three, to do full justice to all the nuances of culture, experience, possessions, and forms of esteem that they can acquire. That is why the notion of *them and us* is blurred, though it survives.

The old French bourgeoisie represented yearning for respect on an essentially local scale: the successful bourgeois was a local notable. The new French aristocrats sustain themselves in a more impersonal, international technical culture: the successful ones are directors of multinational companies and tax-free officials of international organizations. Should they get the credit for the economic boom that took place after the last war and gave France twenty years of growth at a rate higher than the United States and Germany, exceeded only by Japan? That boom has been depicted as representing a sudden change of heart, transforming France from an archaic, backward country into one that stands in the vanguard of modern progress; everyone would like to pinpoint the magic formula that could account for this. None of the explanations offered by the economists, however, is wholly satisfactory, and that by their own admission. The unique French Plan which maps out targets of growth and investment and co-ordinates the efforts of the private and public sector by agreement rather than by constraint, certainly helped create a favourable climate for expansion, and encouraged modernization, but it would have done nothing if individual firms had not been successful by their own efforts, with a dynamism that no government could create by decree. The sudden growth of population after 1940 is not a general explanation, even if it did rejuvenate the country, for Japan prospered with a minimum of population growth. The shock of defeat in 1940 doubtless was a stimulus, but victory in 1919 had also produced an enormous upsurge in production. Massive public investment helped, but it was not as massive as all that. If economists knew the answer, they would have had an answer also to the depression that came in the 1970s. The mistake is to imagine that modern France is a totally new France, and to forget that France has for centuries been one of the richest countries in the world, and often the richest in

Europe. There have been periods in the past when its prosperity has sagged as in the 1930s, but others when it has spurted ahead of its rivals, as in the eighteenth century, the mid-nineteenth century, the early twentieth century. It has often been in the forefront of technical advance before: until the First World War, it was ahead even of the United States as a car-producer, and it should be no surprise that it is now the world's fourth largest car-manufacturer.

France's strength comes from the variety of the ambitions of its citizens, which are more or less active at different times. The ambitious business executive cannot regard himself as the proto-type of a new French race: a psychologist has found that there is paradoxically much more ambition among the children of schoolteachers and soldiers than among those of businessmen. What keeps France economically go-ahead is that the majority are firmly attached to the belief that by hard work it is possible to succeed in life. Even those at the very bottom of the social scale are almost exactly equally divided on the subject of whether it is work or nepotism that brings success. Hope and despair are equally balanced. That is one reason why, despite the great inequalities, France is not a revolutionary country. What revolutionaries get out of their lives is a separate subject.

No group can feel that it has an independent existence until it has its own jokes and its own jesters, and until it is confident enough to laugh at itself without feeling endangered. The bourgeoisie used to have as one of its main supporting pillars the boulevard theatre, which made fun of its obsession with prop-erty, marriage and respectability, which consoled it for the difficulties it had in keeping up appearances, but which finally reinforced it in these preoccupations. The strip-cartoonist, film-maker and playwright Gérard Lauzier shows the new aristocracy has found its identity too. His *Rat Race* portrayed how awful its life can be, what ghastly people have to be flattered and fought to reach the top, what shams and neuroses lie barely hidden behind the jet-set facade, what merry-go-rounds of promiscuity have to be suffered in the search for an ever-elusive happiness, but why, nevertheless, the struggle is addictive and inescap-able. Lauzier knows this world − he has been a successful advertising executive in his time – but he also knows the world that abhors the rich, for he has been a communist too. What is more, he has bolstered his beliefs by wide reading in the human sciences, so that he can present a case that takes account of other people's thinking. He gets some of his attitudes by inheritance: his father was a businessman and a member of Action Française, on the extreme right of inter-war politics. He was brought up with a heroically nationalist vision of life as an adventure to be experienced to the accompaniment of waving flags, watched over by the spirit of Napoleon; he can still feel the pain he suffered as a schoolboy from seeing the British empire occupying a larger area on the map than the French one, and the grief that still persisted at the knowledge that Canada had been lost to England by the French. He wanted to become an army or naval officer, so as to seek revenge for the humiliating defeat of Fashoda, or to become perhaps a great painter, to perpetuate France's national heritage. But then in the top form (the philosophy class) he read Sartre, who fascinated him, offering what seemed an even more wonderful form of heroism: his hero now became the revolutionary, the suffering intellectual devoting his life to save the oppressed people; capitalism was his new villain; his ambition changed to becoming a tormented novelist giving expression to the anguish of the masses.

'I am by nature superficial and quite jolly,' he says, so instead of throwing bombs, he wrote novels, bad novels which no one wanted to publish. He decided to go off to Brazil to seek his adventure among the poor of the Third World; he got a job in one of the communist party's strongholds, where he became a director of publicity; he wrote for the communist papers; but then all his hopes collapsed when the army seized power and he realized he was helpless: 'that was the first break in my convictions.' He went home to do his military service: he expected to be martyred as a communist and because he had infringed some regulations regarding call-up. He was indeed punished by being sent to a paratroop regiment. 'I thought they would be brutes, like the SS, but they were charming.' Being still left-wing and an anti-militarist, he argued with the regular soldiers, but he was made an officer nevertheless, and ended up aide-de-camp to the general. 'I spoke up in favour of Algeria for the Algerians, even at the general's table, and no one forbade me to speak.' His military service turned out to be 'one of the best times in my life'. He became convinced that the army had been maligned; there were certainly swine and torturers among them; there was one lieutenant he knew who liked carrying out executions, and was regularly given that task; but the majority were not sadists; many loved the Algerian people, some gave part of their pay to help a village school; 'the tradition of the army is an ethical one, of service.' The army was 'only obeying government orders' when it used torture; 'torture is the inevitable answer to terrorism, the two go together.' He hated torture, but he came to share the army's bitter resentment of the insults to which they were subjected: it drove long-serving officers mad to find themselves despised, even by their own children, to return to France like cuckolds. The collapse of the French empire was thus made even more of a tragedy. It moved Lauzier back to the right in politics. The break with his communist past was completed by a lawsuit. He earned his living as a caricaturist, working on papers where most of his colleagues were certainly not right-wing, and he was friends with them despite his political views. Then, in one of those malicious tit-bits that humorous papers publish, he was accused of plagiarizing one of his fellow cartoonists, Cabu. He demanded a withdrawal, he threatened to sue; the row blew up; feeling unable to withdraw, he went to court, even though he realized it was 'grotesque' that he should do so, even though he conceded that Cabu drew much better than himself; they were both inspired by the cartoonists of the *New Yorker*. Now he is no longer on speaking terms with his former colleagues.

He has indeed very little in common with them, and even less now that he is so successful, living in a luxurious penthouse on the Boulevard Exelmans, sustained by a substantial income from a play that has been on in Paris for over two years, from films and from a dozen volumes of comic strip cartoons. Success in theory enables people to lead the life they like, and perhaps only success reveals what they value most. Lauzier knows now what his priorities are. First of all, he says, comes his daughter. Second, equal, are his job and women. Then power and money. His dreams of adventure take concrete shape in a recreation of a colonial magnate's harem. His ideal is 'to have many women and many children', distributed in many little houses around his own, a wife in each house: he claims this is a Mediterranean ideal, an atavistic survival (Louis Funes, who was of Spanish origin, apparently had the same dream); but it is also something he found in Brazil, where the French consul at Bahia had his French wife, and his Brazilian wife, and moved between the two houses. Lauzier in fact lives with his daughter, while his separated wife lives a few blocks away, and the two other women in his life also have homes nearby; he is waited on by a Brazilian servant, whose family is an additional part of his clientele. He needs women not just for sexual purposes, but because 'they are agreeable': they have to be controlled, because they have a taste for power, but it is possible to reach agreement with them. The friendship and conviviality of men is something to be enjoyed separately. These ambitions he regards as 'the healthiest thing in the world; ambition means love of life, being healthy.' He argues that it is a fact of nature that some people come out on top and are boss. 'Domination is not exploitation, but an exchange: progress is to make that relationship as sophisticated as possible, so that the poor can develop their personalities also to the fullest extent. But to abolish domination completely is impossible': left-wing regimes merely replace it by another form, like military rule. 'I like power,' he says. 'It is life, and I accept power over me. My gurus are Bertrand de Jouvenel and Raymond Aron' (both of whom have written conservative sociological treatises on power). The power he is most aware of himself is that of the civil service – who in his view holds the reins in France – and especially its financial branch: 'the tax man could assassinate me.'

But he is also worried by success: it too could easily destroy him if he believed the flattery that it brings with it. Already two research students have written theses about him (one attacking him for being reactionary, the other is so sociological he cannot understand it). He is pleased to receive such attention, 'everybody is a megalomaniac.' His solution is to 'control one's ego', to avoid being pretentious: 'I don't want to take myself seriously, though I take seriously what I do.' He plays down his work as being superficial, having no message; his purpose is only to amuse; he does his work just for fun; he resents being labelled as an author specializing in commenting on managers ('I have nothing against managers'), for he has written about many other things: but in fact, it is normally the middle class that he concerns himself with, and the sexual side of life figures prominently in his work. So his humour performs almost the same function for him personally as for those who admire him. He observes the faults in mankind: 'I cannot be funny about someone who is happy: there must be a worm in the fruit.' He accepts those faults as part of human nature, and he tries to make sure that similar faults do not obstruct his own success. Since he is very ingenious at portraying faults and foibles, his work is almost a guide to success in the business world, which includes the sexual world too. He is willing to fight for his principles; he used to support Giscard and has now also joined the Gaullist party. He thinks it is part of the order of nature that people fight each other and try to be different from each other. He once joined a sailing team, which was divided into two groups: within a week each had developed totally different characteristics, one being earnest and disciplined, the other easy going and devoted to the good life. This, he believes, is why France and England are different. He is going to stick to being a Frenchman: France has a civilization as good as any other: why not accept it? It has traditions, culture, beauty. 'I am completely French.' That is yet another definition of what it means to be French.

12

How angry workers
deal with tough bosses

A man who spent forty years as a labourer in the same factory; who raised thirteen children and felt disappointed with all of them; whose normal attitude was helplessness and resignation; and whose only consolation was drink: that is how Georges Navel remembered his father. Georges became a labourer too, but he reacted by protesting; as a child he spent most of his time at school being punished and made to stand outside the classroom in disgrace; as an adult he was constantly changing his job, often the only protest that a worker could make; he bitterly resented being a mere wage earner; he considered it undignified, akin to slavery, to be so dependent on others. He knew virtually nothing about his employers, who seemed to live in another world, which he occasionally glimpsed when he went to the cinema; they seemed to belong to a 'superior race' that spoke and dressed differently and had reserves of knowledge that he envied. His sense of degradation was impossible to bear without a faith in progress and in revolution: political activity, he said, was the only cure for the worker's sadness. Georges Navel represents a previous generation: he published his remarkable autobiography in 1945. But he is memorable because the protests of the revolutionary worker determined to destroy the capitalist system still continue to resound even after the political victory of the left, with a bitterness that is sometimes almost identically reproduced in the present generation. There are young people today whose memories of their parents are just as harrowing, despite the general increase in prosperity.

Gaby, the welder of St Nazaire, still in his thirties, hates to remember his mother, who had children by three different fathers; she was a bar-maid, a prostitute, and a cook in the canteen at Sud-Aviation. He has broken off relations with her, and also with his sister who married an American from the local army camp; he despises her husband as a social climber. His brother has taken to drink, neglecting four children who have all spent time in hospital suffering from malnutrition. Gaby was brought up in the *bidonville* slums of St Nazaire, where he became a gang leader; he spent a year in prison for making a young girl pregnant. He started work at fifteen as a labourer, rose to become a welder; joined the communist trade union. During military service, a friend gave him a book by Emile Zola that made him develop a taste for reading; when he returned to civilian life he joined the Communist Party. He belonged to the 'tough' section of it, but then he resented the superior airs of its militants, who constantly fed him with Marxist works. 'But what have they got that I haven't?' he asked himself. A professor of philosophy who came to work in his factory converted him to Maoism; he developed a new self-confidence when the professor found everything he said marvellous. He is now regarded as an

Pablo

intellectual by his mates, because he reads books, but he refuses to be made a foreman, or to buy a house, because he does not want to be better off than them. This breeds tension with his wife, who dreams of the bourgeois comfort and the car he refuses to buy. But Gaby dreams that one day she will see the light also, and bring the revolution into the home.

He is, of course, not the typical French worker, which is why there has never been a serious threat to the capitalist system. Only a fifth of working people are unionized, the lowest proportion in Europe, lower even than the United States. And even these trade unionists have not sought to expropriate the rich. About half of them belong to the CGT[1], nominally pro-communist, standing for the abolition of capitalism by daily conflict with it and by constant stimulation of the class struggle, but with an atmosphere like that of a large family with authoritarian parents, offering warmth and security, calling itself a 'fraternal society of mates', in principle rejecting compromise, but in practice concentrating not on revolution but on winning higher wages. It keeps a firm control on its members and discourages unplanned emotional crises. The pro-socialist CFDT[2] union, which started as a Christian union seeking the co-operation of classes, and rejecting ideological confrontation, dropped its religious character and adopted autogestion as its main plank; but only a quarter of its members are labourers or craftsmen; its expansion has reflected the growth in the number of clerks, technicians and junior managers. It worries employers even more than do the communists, because it undermines their authority and seeks to interfere more. The third main union, the FO[3], disagrees with both these rivals: it is anti-communist; it opposes links between unions and political parties, and it is against autogestion which it condemns as chaos; it values unions as the best form of worker organization, which ought to play an important role in industry, but without either managing business or being identified with the state. Because of these divisions, the workers have obtained less power than their British or German counterparts.

[1] Confédération générale du travail.
[2] Confédération française et democratique du travail.
[3] Force ouvrière.

The difference between French and British unions – that the former are divided ideologically, while the latter are by profession – is not decisive. Temperament has been given freer rein in France: the mass of workers do not join the unions, but support them when they wish to: the unions are accepted as being the representatives of the workers' interests by a large majority even if their methods are criticized. So only rarely are there full national or regional stoppages of work: 90% of strikes are disputes concerning individual firms. Negotiating procedures are more disorganized, or rather neither employers nor unions are willing to abide by a set of rules. To compare the number of strikes in France with strikes in other countries is not to compare like with like. From time to time the French have massive protests that border on revolution, as in 1936 and in 1968, which have a profound effect on all aspects of life, and shake the country as a whole to its very roots. The rest of the time the French strike only half as often as the Americans or the British.

The revolutionaries are not typical because most workers are far from being obsessed by politics or agitation. There are innumerable factories where politics are never discussed, or very rarely. Conversation is more often about pop singers, sport, betting. There is plenty of childish horseplay, flirting, dancing and singing, fighting imaginary boxing matches. These games do not succeed in drowning the profound boredom that often reigns supreme. There are plenty of factories where the atmosphere is as drab as it was fifty years ago, where monotonous and repetitive work without any interest, discomfort, dirt and exhaustion continue. It is not surprising, therefore, that underneath the routine there should often lurk a tension that signifies a kind of cold war between workers and employers, a longing for revenge that resembles that of prisoners who feel they are innocent and protest against unjust conviction. The factory is not infrequently referred to as a prison. Petty theft, sabotage, cheekiness may be the only practical ways of showing anger. 'Nothing has changed,' says one revolutionary worker. 'The factory is what it has always been. The boss is the lord. He does what he wants.' When visitors parade through the workshop, the labourers ignore them, because they bitterly resent it that the visitors are more interested in the machines than in themselves.

There are two more particular grievances that stimulate discontent. Discipline can sometimes be archaically severe. Bad marks are given and added up, fines are imposed and misconduct is reported along the whole chain of command. The power of the foreman is probably greater, or more arbitrary, than in some other countries. Promotion is an endless source of dispute. A scale known after its inventor Parodi once aimed to place everybody on one of the 1000 rungs of its ladder, the labourer on the minimum wage starting at 100, the craftsman, typist and laboratory assistant at 155: managers go from 350 to 660, the chief engineer is worth 880; a system of points provided for special qualifications, diplomas and seniority. This was less complex, in fact, than the British Civil Service's 1400 grades; a new, much simpler, scale is gradually being introduced. But the weakness of this hierarchical system is that it leaves too many people with no hope of climbing on it. Very few labourers or clerks go on courses in order to better themselves; they are so defeated in spirit that they do not bother to join the rat race. Almost half of those who do have a go derive no benefit from their courses, whereas only a quarter of foremen and technicians and only a tenth of engineers and managers obtain no positive result from attending courses. Labourers thus have good reason for feeling that they are outside the pale. Technicians also worry about the difficulty of making their way in the world. But it is easiest for those who are near the top to feel that they live in an open society. A sample survey of firms shows that people believe that two-fifths of promotions are made on merit, a quarter through personal influence, less than a sixth on the basis of courses or diplomas and less than a tenth on seniority.

The agitation in industry would be greater but for the fact that such a large proportion of the lowest paid do not complain, for different reasons. One-tenth of manual workers are foreigners, who are worried by racism, and over one-fifth are women, who have few chances of promotion but also fewer traditions of protest. The militants, who create the sense of unity to make these diverse workers feel that they have a common cause against the employers, find that each segment has different attitudes towards unity. The unskilled labourer has no way of protesting unless supported by his colleagues, either informally, or by a concerted refusal to work. The skilled worker wants recognition of his independence, so for him the union is a means to this end, but its constraints are not necessarily enjoyed. The young worker who has come in with his diplomas, with the intention of doing better than his fellows, is forced to accept equality when he bitterly realizes that his paper qualifications are getting him nowhere. It is the unskilled who are most willing to fall in behind the organizer who can talk well: the admiration for verbal fluency increases as you go down the hierarchical scale, because those at the bottom feel tongue-tied. Even when more democratic ways of awarding promotion are introduced, as has been done in some firms, the tensions are not eliminated, because there are always winners and losers. The women on the clerical side see that the best pickings from the new technology go to the men in production.

A British scholar, Duncan Gallie, who has compared two factories doing exactly the same thing on either side of the Channel, the BP works in Dunkerque and in Kent, argues that the French managers are more aloof and cold, uninterested in the workers as human beings. French workers complain about this twice as often as English ones who feel they suffer the same problem. The French BP workers demand workers' control over all aspects of management, whereas the English ones accept the system as it is, and criticize only the managers' efficiency in performing their tasks, which they are content to leave to them. The French refinery worker earns 85% above the national average wage, and the English one only 14%, but the French man is far more dissatisfied with his wages. There is more argument in Dunkerque also because the wage system here involves more severe disciplinary sanctions for breach of the rules and for poor performance, each individual worker being penalized for his faults. But productivity is far higher in France: the same task of overhauling a crude oil unit is carried out in France in two weeks and in England in six weeks. The English management base their approach on consent, they make concessions, they help the unions build up their strength in return for the union giving the managers a certain amount of assistance in controlling the workers; agreements are reached on a local level; the cost of this bargaining is thought to outweigh the cost of conflict. In France, however, there is ideological warfare between management and unions, which enhances the workers' sense of being exploited and alienated, and so, though they are among the best paid in their region, they feel dissatisfied with their standard of living. By contrast, the English workers, who earn little more than the average, are almost unanimous in believing that they are quite well off. The main reason for this is that the French managers reply to the antagonism of the workers by refusing to link pay in a simple way with skill, and insisting on paying 'on merit', based on reports by supervisors, which allows foremen scope for arbitrary decisions and an abuse of their power. The French managers partly succeed in their strategy of dividing the workers, because workers do become more suspicious of each other when they are each paid differently and they think that they are being spied on by their fellows and being reported for their mistakes to the foreman. There are universal wage scales negotiated at national level (whereas in England they are at plant level) but these are so complicated they have little relation to reality; these national negotiations are done three times a year (but only annually in England), so that there is no respite from disagreeing and preparing to disagree.

When the CGT militants in Michelin's tyre factory in Clermont Ferrand distribute propaganda leaflets as the workers come running out at the end of their shift, they are almost completely ignored; they have very little support in this bastion of old fashioned paternalism. But they are very far from downhearted. They compare themselves to the men of the Resistance in the last war: the fact that there are few of them only increases their determination. 'the more we are battered, the more we fight back . . . And we must go on fighting, or we will be returned to the condition of the days of Emile Zola.' They say the management treat them like naughty children, not allowed to do this or that, 'don't talk, just work.' Each year every worker is summoned before a management tribunal, like a child before his teachers, and told what he has done wrong – how he is too often late, for example: everything has been noted. Being a unionist makes things much harder; their children cannot get jobs in the factory; they are spied on. They seldom win concessions from management. The law requires the management to receive a workers' delegation twice a year, who may present their grievances; these delegates showed me how the management had answered their two pages of questions, which had been returned unanswered, the place left for a reply was blank, with only a brief note saying there was nothing worth discussing. The management view is that these men are troublemakers. The militants say they simply want a decent standard

Piem

of living, to be treated with respect and dignity, and they cannot see why 30,000 of them should sweat in foul conditions all day just to make one man rich. They admit they are communist sympathizers, but that is because the communists stand for the rights of the workers. If the Party or for that matter the union no longer advocated the workers' interests, they would have no hesitation in abandoning them. The central officials might express reservations about the Polish Free

Unions, but these workers had none, they applauded them. 'We fight not for an ideology, but to have a better life. But no one listens.' Monsieur Michelin replies to them as he replies to journalists, he does not give interviews. No wonder the revolutionaries can say nothing in favour of their employers, whom they never see.

Stalemates of this kind can go on for decades, and one reason is that the revolutionaries are caught up in a web of family ambitions that accentuates their sense of helplessness. Bernard and Noelle Mortagne, in their mid-thirties, have still not quite stopped struggling with the problem of having somewhere to live. Born in the north, in Dunkerque and Valenciennes respectively, they could not find work there. In 1973 they moved south to Fos, which was being started up as a new industrial city; but there they could find no house. They set up their first home in a tent; then for a year they lived in a caravan with no running water. Fos, says Bernard, was at that time like a town of the American Far West, a messy conglomeration of immigrants from all over France. The people of each region tended to keep to themselves. Noelle, however, had never liked it in the north, and so has tried to break out of that convention to make friends from other provinces. 'It is better to integrate, to participate in local life.' She does not want to feel an exile. 'It's hell to be always rootless. I now feel I have always lived here, and I wouldn't like to leave. But we're different. There are many Savoyards who came here, who couldn't get used to it and went back. I also know some Lorrainers; they have a different mentality, they keep to themselves, they have their own Association.' Bernard and Noelle have never gone back to the north; instead they have a constant stream of family descending on them, delighted to be able to enjoy the sun. After the caravan, they moved into a rented apartment in a municipally owned tower block. They hated it; it was always noisy, with people going to work on different shifts, the Arabs celebrating Ramadan at night, the gypsies playing their guitars, the children shouting in the street, the cars coming and going at all hours; 'for five years, we never slept properly; we were going mad.' Eventually they were able to raise the money to buy a small house of their own, but only because the builder had gone bankrupt; the house was unfinished and therefore going cheap. Saving up for the deposit, and now paying the mortgage, has meant that they have been unable to afford to go on holiday for the past thirteen years; they spend their time off working on the house, which is still not finished. But this year Noelle for the first time, plans to go on holiday in Corsica with three of her women friends, leaving their husbands behind; they have managed to find a cheap shack to rent.

Noelle at last feels that she has made it. Having a house of her own she considers one of the most important achievements of her life. 'I may not have any diplomas, but with my own hands I've been able to get this. I am proud to have reached this position. I have something of my own and something to leave the children; they'll have a less tough time than we did, it'll be butter on their spinach.' The house has indeed transformed the children's lives. 'In the HLM (tower block) they had a rough time; they had nothing to do except be naughty, spoil the walls and break the windows. My daughter never went out when we lived there, even though there were plenty of children to play with; she just sat at home with her thumb in her mouth; now she is much happier and is always going out into the forest.' Bernard, however, has no particular pride in being a house-owner. He is a member of the Communist Party; he says he is not particularly interested in property, though he does value having a detached house so that he can enjoy some quiet and privacy. But it is significant that he does not denounce mortgages as a capitalist trick to keep the workers in their factories, with the carrot of property ownership twenty-five years hence dangled in front of them.

The effect of the mortgage is that they need two wages to make ends meet. Noelle, having no qualifications, could get a job only in a factory, but the experience of it 'traumatized' her; it exhausted her; it meant she hardly ever saw her husband or her children; and it paid very little in the end, since she had to spend half her earnings on someone to look after her children. She now has partly solved the problem by staying at home and looking after other people's children while they work. This way, she feels she can at least bring up her daughter properly, supervise her homework, which is still just within her understanding.

But her son is thirteen and his homework is beyond her; 'he does things I've never done.' The boy says he does not care about getting good results at school; in any case, there are no jobs – 'we can't deny it' – so what's the point of working hard; study hasn't helped Bernard much. Bernard cannot be bothered to help his son in any case, because he has other priorities. Noelle says 'we'd like the children not to have to work as hard as we do.' But she cannot control her boy's independence, 'it's his character; it's hard dealing with children nowadays.'

Neither family life, nor making money, nor winning promotion, are Bernard's preoccupations. He is the son of a miner, one of nine children. 'When I was young, I wanted to be an engineer in "celestial mechanics"; I would have liked a job in research.' He did win himself higher qualifications by correspondence in electricity, and got a job as a supervisor. But he did not enjoy that, first because he earned less than a skilled worker, and secondly because 'I don't like commanding, I couldn't bring myself to shout at the workers. They work the hardest, I had pity on them, why should I shout at them?' His bosses did not like that and wanted him to keep up the pressure on them. So he has preferred to be an ordinary electrician. This again involves a heavy sacrifice. He has to do shift work. When he works at night he has difficulty in getting any sleep in the day. When he works in the mornings, he has to wake up at 4.30 a.m. So it is only in the afternoons that he ever feels right; the rest of the time he is exhausted. He can never sit down at work; he has to concentrate all the time; the factory is exceptionally noisy, with 130 decibels (though only 90 are allowed by law). 'Nevertheless, the job pleases me,' he says. 'It's not the work he likes,' says Noelle, 'but being a workers' delegate. He spends more time on that than actually working.' In fact, he is allowed almost a quarter of his hours at work for his trade union activities, but in addition he devotes about twenty hours a week to the union after work. He is the local treasurer of the CGT and, says his wife, 'he loves arguing with the bosses.' 'I feel equal with the bosses when I argue with them,' he says. 'They think we're imbeciles; they treat us as though we are incapable of thinking. It is the most stupid managers who behave like that; those who are hardest to deal with are those who do not underestimate us.' He is always very calm in his dealings with the bosses. 'That is why he shouts when he is at home', says Noelle. 'The children say: Is papa going to work all day? Good. We won't hear him shout.' She blames shift work for destroying family life. 'It means you cannot go to the cinema, you cannot even watch television together.' She goes to the theatre alone, with two other wives whose husbands also work on shifts. Shift work makes you nervous. 'I got ill from all his shouting, I took all sorts of medicines. To understand each other better, you need time to talk, but he has not got the time. So I explode. We then talk it over, I calm down and all is well again.' For a time.

Noelle does not think their rows are all his fault, though she resents his not finding the time to talk to their boy, quite apart from herself. 'When I was young, I always wanted to have my own way; but I discovered that meant you argue constantly. Love means getting to know each other better, changing with the years, becoming more understanding, learning to live, becoming willing to give way.' He listens to these complaints from her without disagreeing. His friendship for his mates takes precedence: if it is true that conditions of work are such an obstacle to family life, then his concentration on improving them is perfectly logical. He says he cannot influence the way work is organized; but the bosses listen a little more to complaints about safety, because accidents are expensive. They used to have 13% absenteeism. 'The doctors saw workers were completely worn out, but there was nothing else wrong with them: they gave them a week off, that restored them, but three months later they were again exhausted.' They dare not strike to get rid of the asphyxiating dust, because the employers have been talking about closing the factory down. Nationalization, he says, will make him feel more secure. But it is this fundamental insecurity about employment that forces workers to go on with a life in which the convenience of machines is placed above the convenience of humans.

The Mortagnes show how the workers have been, in part, absorbed and dominated by the housing problem, which is almost as important as the employment problem. So in addition to the revolutionary who fights for justice, who resents giving his labour and who sees the factory as a means of rousing the under-privileged to revolt, there is the optimist whose ambitions are concentrated on bettering himself by work, by saving, by buying whatever higher wages are put within his grasp. He bears the imprint of the prosperous 1960s, when a love affair with the consumer society seemed bent on procreating a France that would be pretty much like every other western nation: neither the courtship nor the marriage went quite as planned.

The new goal that dominated the ambitions of the ordinary man became to own his own house. It was to save for this that Frenchmen have, till quite recently, worked longer hours than any other nation in Europe. Actual working hours were still eleven a day in 1975, even though the eight-hour day was theoretically introduced in 1919 and the forty-hour week in 1936. Today, not only do over a third of workers own their homes, but by the time they retire, one-half of them are home-owners. They have achieved this by more than doubling their expenditure on their housing: before the war they spent only 8% of their earnings on it, today 20%. They have not quite caught up with the British (who spend 25% of their incomes on housing), let alone the United States (29%). So French workers are becoming less and less a proletariat. One-fifth of them have inherited property. They have resisted being segregated in tower blocks: in fact only 7% of them live there. One-half of them live in detached cottages, and a third in villages and small towns. It is clerks more than industrial workers who have filled the dreary suburban high-rise estates. As many as 18% of workers have built their own houses. They are keen gardeners; they are obsessive handymen. They have expanded the size of their homes, which are now twice as large as they were before the war. Their wives devote more time than women in other classes to housework, shopping, repairing. They have larger families now; they come home to lunch. They are creating for themselves a cosy family life, a refuge.

These are the successful ones. Over half of workers are still tenants. The foreign immigrants who do the low-paid jobs have stepped into the old shoes, and live as workers used to live a century ago, lonely, crowded, saving to go back home. And the worker's new-won independence is of course partly illusory; he has put himself into debt, deeper than any other class. He has won an illusory equality: it costs him twice as much labour to buy his home than it does a manager. In years of prosperity and full employment the poor could hope to succeed: there is less certainty now that the consumer society will deliver the rewards it promises.

The other new creation of the sixties has been the proliferating foreman. In the years of prosperity, he gave the impression that it was possible to get on in the world; half of foremen started life as workers or clerks. But one cannot go on creating new managerial posts for ever: the process has virtually stopped. Increasingly educated people have to take jobs which are beneath their capacities: already two-fifths of French people say they feel they are not being allowed to use their talents fully. The resulting frustrations have encouraged dropping out more than the desire for revolution.

Why are there so many people who do jobs they hate without grumbling? 'My work is not an essential part of my life,' replies Daniel Bischoff, an unskilled labourer in his early thirties. He and his wife, Marie-France, have toiled at the same machines, performing the most repetitive and boring jobs imaginable, in the same factory for seven years now. But they do not consider they have sacrificed anything, for they have done it deliberately. He does not want responsibility at work: 'I have no professional ambitions.' He has no wish to become a foreman, because he dislikes the idea of bossing others around, just as he dislikes being pushed around himself. He has to remain silent when he is told off at the factory, by foremen he does not respect, but who have the power to fine and punish him if he shows too much independence. As the recession gets more severe, so the pressure on the workers to increase production gets tougher, and he has no wish to go around creating new tensions. After years on the same machine, a worker knows all there is to know about it; he resents the interference of foremen, who know best only in theory. He says the management play off the two shifts against each other to get them to work faster, and have indeed created bitter resentment between them. In the factory, Daniel is taciturn, showing no trace of emotion. But when he gets home he is a different man: his face lights up, his eyes sparkle with curiosity, he has a ready laugh. The great achievement of his life has been the building of his house. They saved hard for several years to find the deposit. They were determined not to live just in an ordinary concrete box. They have bought a prefabricated timber mountain chalet, made of Norwegian logs, imported by a Dutch company, and delivered on a lorry by two English drivers. Putting it up and completing the interior has taken over a year. They have been helped voluntarily by about forty friends and neighbours. At work Daniel hardly speaks to his mates; at home friends are always dropping in, joking, helping each other out. By eliminating labour costs, he has succeeded in creating a cosy home, situated in open country, backing on to forests, with a magnificent view of the Alps beyond. He lives like an independent pioneer here. His aim in life, he says, is freedom, being able to do what he pleases (once he has paid the price of eight hours in the factory). That means going for mountain walks lasting the whole day, carrying sandwiches, marvelling at how agile their two young children are becoming; in winter it means skiing with friends or in a club. They talk lyrically about the beauty of the colours of the trees, the sunsets, the mountain air.

But what are they going to do next, now that the house is at last finished? At the moment, husband and wife work different shifts: he starts at 5.00 a.m. and is back by 1.00 p.m.; she then goes to the factory to do her eight hours. In this way one of them at least is always with the children. 'We do not want to treat our children like dogs, or to give them to childminders.' Daniel thinks that as soon as they can afford it Marie-France should stop working. But she replies that his ideal is to be comfortable, and that is not enough for her. She dreams of finding more agreeable work, with more human contact. 'I am frightened of being too shut in on myself.' He says a woman can flourish at home. She replies that being a housewife cannot satisfy her. He believes it is outside his work that he can find the friendship he delights in. She wants more than that; perhaps she will return to her trade union activities, which she gave up because they harmed the children: she used to keep her little boy for up to three hours under the table when she had to attend meetings. But there is not much alternative employment in the area. So the workers in their factory accept their tasks as a necessary evil, so necessary that they no longer worry much about the pain it causes. They economize by eating sandwiches for lunch, sitting on the bit of lawn in front of the factory: they nearly all have similar outside interests, a little farm, a few cows, or they do odd jobs decorating and building; the factory provides the basic wage, and their enjoyment comes from what they add to it.

People also go on doing jobs they do not enjoy because they can see what happens if a worker without qualifications does not play the game according to the rules. Eluard is out of a job. He went on hunger strike for twenty-nine days to draw attention to his plight, but no one took much notice. A social worker came round, with 300 Fr. (£30) and coupons for two food parcels. 'I refuse to beg and I didn't take it.' He wants to be able to earn his living in a way he considers dignified. That has always eluded him. He comes from the dreary Parisian suburb of Asnières, the son of a labourer who used to work twelve hours a day to keep his family: 'we children ate every day, but my parents did not.' Eluard's brother has got a permanent job at Orly airport, and that has given their parents pleasure. But Eluard himself was, as his mother said 'a duckling in a nest of chicks'. He came bottom in class, but nevertheless dreamt of becoming a teacher. He resisted his parents' efforts to make him take an ordinary worker's job. He became a night porter at the Paris food market (Les Halles), and enrolled as a student of philosophy at the Sorbonne. It was 1968, and he was just eighteen. He was not interested by the demonstrations – 'politics are quite foreign to me' – but he did not seem to be getting far in his studies and gave up after a few months. His intellectual interests have however, remained with him: he has spent all his months of unemployment reading, and has acquired quite a large library, of classics, social science and astrology, of which he is proud: he was just then reading Vuillaume's *Red Notebooks of the Commune.* He talks like a well-read man. But he has no diplomas. He hated his military service; he detested his fellow soldiers' patriotism; he was imprisoned for drunkenness; he ended up being made one of the guards of Rudolf Hess in Spandau Prison. At twenty-one he became a clerk-archivist in an insurance company: 'it was the only job I could get; it was not disagreeable; I stayed two years.' But he fell in love with a girl, who left him after a year of marriage, taking all the furniture with her: 'I came home from the cinema one night and there was nothing at home.' It took him a year to recover from that – 'a divorce is a death' – and all the more so because he was soon sacked for an 'error' at work.

After two months on the dole, he got a job in another insurance company in the nightmarish suburb of La Défense. He liked that because he met interesting people, educated graduates. But he joined the trade union and started a strike, objecting that his job required him to work three floors underground, never seeing the light of day, stifled by the air conditioning. For two-and-a-half months eleven of them staged a sit-in, which prevented any files from leaving the archives; it was 'a marvellous time', but they had to give in when they ran out of money. It was while he was demonstrating in support of another strike that he met his second wife, who was a typist on the eighth floor of his tower block. 'We've had a hard time together.' He decided to become a psychiatric nurse. He took a course, and failed the final examination by half a point. So he was back on the dole.

A friend told him there was plenty of work in Marseille. He went, but found it much harder to find employment, or a flat, than he had expected. Eventually he was taken on as a radiographer in a clinic; they said they were satisfied with him; but suddenly, after four months, they sacked him 'without any explanation at all.' He was pleased by his job, and does not want to learn any other, but no one will take him on. He has written applications to forty-seven clinics 'but I haven't got the stamps to post them.' He tried to set up as a barrow boy selling vegetables in the Marseille market; the authorities first refused him permission and then would not help him to buy a barrow. He has spent months going from office to office seeking official assistance; he is simply shunted around and is declared not to satisfy one or other of the regulations for people in need. His wife works part time, so he is not considered destitute; and indeed he lives in quite a decent flat, in which he has been squatting without paying any rent. The official attitude is that he is a permanent rebel, who will never be satisfied, but who will not go to extremes. Just to show them, the friend with whom he had gone on hunger strike therefore attempted suicide. Eluard says perhaps all that will convince the authorities is if he kills everyone in sight, since no one cared when they threatened to die of hunger, but 'arms are no solution'. Perhaps, he says, he ought to go to prison, where he would be lodged, fed and have his clothes laundered free of charge. He cannot train for a new career, because he would not be eligible for a grant, having already had one. He considers himself a victim of all the regulations the civil service has invented to help the likes of him. What is worse, no one cares about him. The local press will not advertise his problem, because it thinks he has brought it on himself. He talks nostalgically of starting up as an artisan weaver in a village; why are people not allowed to occupy all those ruined hovels?

He hates Marseille now, 'the most rotten city in France; they greet you with open arms when you go to the café, but they are hypocrites, when you leave, they forget who you are.' He would be willing to go anywhere; 'I feel at home in any country'; he liked the Germans he met on military service 'they are clean, very clean . . . I don't care whether someone is French or German.' But the Americans seem to be an exception. Those serving in Berlin, just back from Vietnam, he thought were 'mad . . . always drunk', taking their military manoeuvres very seriously: 'they are imperialists just like the Russians.' It is the whole social organization that Eluard finds 'con'. He grows increasingly nervous as no solution comes in sight. His wife is complaining at him for not finding a job. His son is becoming uncontrollable. His flat is situated just next door to the bar where ten people were killed a few years back, in a notorious mass murder that symbolizes how hopelessness turns to violence.

That despair so seldom turns into violence has been explained by Jacques Fremontier in a harrowing account of the many months he spent talking to a large number of unsuccessful workers. He concludes that part of the art of putting up with being such a worker is to accept the frustration of one's ambitions. Even marriage is a repression of fantasy; girls think of themselves as finished at twenty-five. People who are 'castrated by lack of money', who are imprisoned in their box-like shabby flats, who are forced to work or play at times to suit their masters, who are unable ever to establish a self-respecting identity for themselves because they have to learn to obey, to economize, and to control themselves according to the precepts of others, such people learn to rationalize the inevitable; and in addition they are intimidated into controlling themselves by the fear of what other people will say if they fall out of line. Revolutionaries may believe that the workers of the world will eventually see that they have common interests that transcend national boundaries, but in practice there are too many immediate pressures, too much concern with survival from month to month (an improvement – it used to be from week to week), too many temptations and distractions, for that to happen. So often, but by no means always, workers do not raise their sights above following in the footsteps of those who have made good. Which means that they often bolster up dying values just when the disenchanted bourgeoisie is losing faith.

Chenez

Managers' Sons   Workers' Sons

13

Where to find a Communist's heart

Didier Chatel has no interest in making his fortune. He is twenty years old, a book-keeping clerk in the housing department of the communist municipality of Arceuil. He is very pleased with this job, because he has no qualifications, and the only alternative he can see for himself is as a labourer. His mother is a book-keeper too, and his father a metal worker: 'when you are the son of a proletarian, he says, you are stuck with it.' He used to dream of studying political science and becoming a lawyer, 'to defend the people'. 'I would like to do many things with my life'; but he knows these are just dreams. That is why he joined the Communist Party at the age of seventeen. Politics he sees as an alternative to the education and career he cannot hope for; it is 'one way of broadening my vision of the world, of flowering'. He is not really interested in material possessions: 'I have everything I want; I have my music – records.' But he is worried that if he loses his job, he would have a tough time finding another one. What he wants more than anything else is a feeling that he is not useless: 'If I am of no use, they should eliminate me, throw me into the dustbin . . . Young people are the ones who have been sacrificed in this generation.' The idea of unemployment haunts him as a condemnation, a rejection, rather than as a loss of earnings. What he appreciates in his job is that his bosses are not profiteers, 'in it just for the money': they listen to him when he gives his opinion; he and his mates asked for more variety in their work, and that was granted them; now he does not just fill in forms, but has dealings with tenants also, and he finds that satisfying. His bosses are not just a contrast with the capitalist ones, however: previously he worked for another public organization,

A LA FÊTE DE L'HUMA

Siné
The Happy Photograph Stand at the
Communist Annual Festival

the post office, and there they were very rigid: he used to sort parcels, but they would not even allow him to move the parcels for a change. Nor does he want to challenge the need for hierarchy: that he considers as 'normal'. All he seeks is a sense of his own worth. 'I want to do something, not just for myself, but so that the next generation will say, He did it. Otherwise, what is life for?'

However, communists are not all utopians, willing to work like saints for the common good. When they say they are materialists, they often mean it in a practical way also: they want a larger share of the cake, even if they value other things too: higher wages are a very high priority; they have so many generations of poverty behind them, they do not want to wait any longer. Maurice Roche, a chemistry teacher in Limoges, the son of a railway foreman, has been quite successful, and is besides married to a librarian, but he complains vigorously that he is underpaid; why should chemists in private industry earn more than he? Why should he earn no more than a bus driver? He is not for equal pay for all. Daniel Bourge, a communist activist, who has been a highly skilled welder in the secret prototype department of Renault for over twenty years, is quite clear that he is not going to accept the same pay as his less qualified mates. He thinks the people at the top should reasonably earn five times as much as those at the bottom: they deserve rewards for their studies, their sacrifices. The fact that he loves his job, which is much more interesting and pleasant than that of those who work on the assembly lines, since it involves creating new parts for new cars, does not seem to him to be relevant. 'We will never abolish differentials.' He needs money because he likes to have a wife who does not work; he finds that a 'reasonable arrangement'; he thinks the feminist movement is 'exaggerated, not serious: if women want to join organizations, there are plenty of others they can join, like the political parties.' He is short, bald; he wears a trilby hat and an overcoat that make him look, as his own fellow communists tease him, 'like a bourgeois'. Why not? Some communists feel left out, they want those who have arrived to make room for them, to acknowledge them as equals.

Daniel Bourge can talk with a fluency that many would envy; he is obviously a very tough negotiator; and he is going to help those who put their trust in him up the ladder too. His son has already made the jump, and is enrolled in a technical university. But the way the communists differ from all those who are struggling in the rat race is that they insist that it is no use each man trying to better himself on his own. Individualism is a natural attitude, particularly in a period of unemployment and intense competition for jobs: 'We cannot blame such people,' says the chemistry teacher Roche, 'but they are wrong: they won't get out of their difficulties on their own; collective solutions are the only ones that will work. Besides the very poor people, at the very bottom of the ladder, are in complete despair, and do not even hope for individual solutions.' To be a communist is to wish to pull together and 'to express the generosity that young people have'. Without illusions, however. Roche lives as a tenant in a very dirty public housing block: there have been plans to get the tenants to share the cleaning, but most have refused; at the moment, Arab immigrants are paid a pittance to clean far more than they can manage; the communist answer is not to share the dirty jobs, but to make them very well paid, and so give them a higher status. 'We cannot have meetings all the time; some people want to work as little as possible, and it is inevitable that they must be forced to.' There must always be someone in charge to ensure that every team of rubbish collectors does its fair share of work. This is far less a radical reformation of capitalist society than utopian socialists dream of.

It is the Marxist dogma, of course, which gives the impression that the communists have completely different ideas from the majority of their countrymen. They imbibe their dogma at the party schools, of which there are several dotted around the country, the principal one being the Central School at Choisy-le-Roi, in the house that Maurice Thorez, and then the North Vietnamese delegation to Paris, used to inhabit. Almost half of the militants who attend the party congresses have been through these schools, which provide courses of either one or four months. You enter by an inconspicuous small side door (of the kind medieval monastries have, while their impressive giant portals remain locked): they have been attacked in the past and want no trouble. There are eleven students in the class I join (it is very rare to admit an outsider, but then outsiders very rarely ask to attend). They are all workers or clerks, with little formal education, in their twenties and thirties, militants from different regions, given scholarships to enable them to take time off from work. The lecturer is a young teacher from a local school, pale face, large glasses, short hair, dressed like the ghost of a schoolboy swot from the 1950s in tweed sports jacket, grey trousers, grey tie, black shoes, in complete contrast with the casual attire of his pupils. He delivers his lecture as they used to deliver lectures in the 1950s: very slowly, at dictation speed, a series of abstract pronouncements. His subject is The Formation of Class Consciousness. His pupils begin writing down what he is saying before he has even got half way through the sentence and before they can even guess what he is going to say: e.g. 'The socialization of work . . .' everybody writes that down and waits for him to continue. 'There are many factors to consider. . . .' Yes, the mustachioed young man with the Provençal accent nods very vigorously. The chubby man in the boots has missed a phrase, he copies it off his neighbour.

The lecture lasts, with a thirty-minute break, for three hours.

Towards the end the Provençal starts yawning and gives up making notes, but he is the only one. He is the one who asks the first question, whose purpose is not at all clear, and the lecturer gives an equally confusing answer. Another student wants to know what anarcho-syndicalism is; a third asks for the division between Left and Right to be explained and he is told it dates from the 1890s. The Provençal asks for the phrase *Grande Bourgeoisie* to be explained. One man believes that the MRP (the Christian Democratic Party) is the old name by which the RPR (the Gaullist Party) used to be known. A certain amount of curiosity is shown about the parties of the right in the discussion, but it is clear not much is known about them. The lecturer included a history of the granting of the vote in France, but that history stopped in the 1880s; not a word was said about the women's vote. When I seek an explanation, I am told there is no need to repeat what everyone knows, that the women's vote was granted because of communist pressure in 1944. The girl next to me admitted privately that in fact most of the lecture was familiar to her: but a forestry worker from the Jura found it all new: what he had been taught at school was just a catalogue of facts, 'Joan of Arc and the Commune were all treated in the same way'; but here there was interpretation. Some of the students obviously did not write with perfect ease, and there is a special teacher who helps them to learn to make notes. The lecturer's repetition that 'things are contradictory' does not, however, confuse them, even if that classic Marxist phase is used to gloss over the complexities of the historical facts he is trying to summarize: the students do acquire a way of looking at the world that they find satisfying. They study from nine in the morning to late in the evening and their only complaint is that they are not taught enough; they are always demanding more subjects to be added to the syllabus, never to have anything left out. As it is, their reading period, in the afternoons, is restricted to a very small selection of books, but mainly articles by communist authors.

Henri Martin, the Director of the Central School, remembers that in 1968 there was some pressure to end this formal lecturing, but that it was decided that the old methods were best; he himself is very keen on having a teacher lecturing, 'so that he can see whether the students understand', rather than leaving them to their own devices with books. The lecturer I heard claimed that he could see that his pupils were following him; that did not appear at all obvious to me; I found it difficult to follow him myself, his utterances were so often a disconnected jumble of abstract formulae and miscellaneous facts. Henri Martin, however, is very satisfied with the way the school functions. That does not mean he is dogmatically blind to criticism, but rather that he is guided by a special sort of pragmatism, a determination to accept present policy as the right one, until it becomes untenable, and another one is substituted. What he wants to avoid is doubt. He is a man in a hurry: he has suffered enough. He regards doubt as simply the path to procrastination. 'We always doubt everything,' he says, 'because we know the world changes; but we say that in the present state of knowledge, this is the nearest we can come to the truth, and we shall apply it; and we shall discover in practice when we are right.' So he is not going to waste his time, or that of the students, reading the works of liberal opponents. 'Our professors have read them, and they can refute them.' He is content to leave it to specialists to 'refute' Tocqueville, whom he has never had time to read, because reading men like him contributes nothing to changing society. The purpose of the school is to train people to see things as they are, not as they might be, who can take action in their place of work, and who have an adequate basis of Marxist theory to do that on their own, without waiting for orders. Of course sometimes 'our historians show that the view we took was too narrow, and that events disproved us. So we went back to reading Marx in the original. For me Marx has collected all that is best in all that has ever been thought, he has condensed the heritage of all centuries, he tells people that they need no longer be mere spectators of events, they can do things themselves, they can transform the world, and their daily lives.'

Henri Martin left school at the age of thirteen-and-a-half, the son of a communist father and a Catholic mother: he was a choir boy and went to mass till the age of sixteen. He joined the Party 'from patriotism' during the war, to help get rid of the Germans; he knew nothing about communist theory at that stage. He was puzzled that those Frenchmen who collaborated with the Nazis were treated so gently; the Party explained to him that it was a question of class, the rulers of the liberation were no different from those of Vichy. After the war, Martin worked in a large factory and then joined the army as a volunteer, only to be jailed for three-and-a-half years for spreading communist propaganda. In the army jail, he was given the Bible to read (which he found interesting); but he was later transferred to a public jail, where the wardens did not really care what he did, and there he imbibed the works of Lenin (putting false covers on them) and of Maurice Thorez. Since his release, at the age of twenty-six, he has been a permanent functionary of the Party. His devotion to it has been such that he has never managed to attend the school prize-giving of any of his three children, and even when his third child was born, he was too busy to go to his wife's bedside, because he was at a Party meeting. All three children are Party members now, though they reproach him for his neglect of them: he confesses, 'I would not do the same again.' He knows he has messed up his family life: that was a mistake. He knows he was too optimistic at the time of the Liberation, when he expected the Revolution to occur within a few years, three or four: 'I no longer have these illusions.' He says he and his party made a mistake in not putting up a communist candidate against Mitterrand in 1981, because that suggested that the communists did not provide a real alternative. But, with or without illusions, he remains confident. He views his mistakes not very differently from the way Christians view their sins: mistakes do nothing to shake him in his faith. And he enjoys his life even while he is indignant at the injustices of it. The lunch I had with the students of the Central School – an ordinary one – was the best-cooked institutional meal I have had anywhere.

A communist is often a sociable being, or anxious to be one, 'always ready to discuss', as the young forestry worker said before pouring out his life history to me. The formal setting for their discussions is their Party cells, the 23,000 groups in which the members meet every week or fortnight. Each cell has on average a dozen to twenty members. One-third of the cells are formed by workers in their firms and factories, the rest are based on place of residence. In the communist suburbs of Paris, each tower block might have a cell of its own; in conservative districts there might be only one cell for a whole town. Their meetings usually last under an hour, when they are held in a café outside a factory, and the members have a long way to go home; more often they are held in the house of a member, where they last much longer; the teachers' cells are said to be the most talkative. They discuss contemporary events, local disputes, national and international crises – they tend to see issues in terms of crises; they try to relate these to Marxist doctrine, which gives them a meaning and a solution. Occasionally their discussions sound more like a series of ritual statements, or like group therapy; satisfaction is derived from repeating that 'this is a very important discussion we are having'. Quotations from Lenin or the Party paper, *L'Humanité*, add weight to the proceedings. Usually it is not friendship that one finds but comradeship, a sense of fellowship which transcends background and personal circumstances, a commitment to team work, with a willingness to accept the leadership of the central committee. Distributing Party literature and holding demonstrations expresses this solidarity, and the organization of these activities in practice often takes up more time than political discussion. The communists are, in fact, ambivalent towards political life. On the one hand they believe in political causes and remedies, and they politicize all issues, all their activities; that is why they have their own societies for everything in sport and leisure, their own shops, books, newspapers, holiday resorts, all of which must serve their ultimate anti-capitalist purpose. On the other hand, they are not always really interested by politics in the sense of enjoying debate with those who hold different views, they know what they think, and they prefer to move among like-minded people.

The Communist Party is not just a ghetto that lives separately from the nation. There are perhaps a quarter of a million Party members at any one time (more or less depending on whether one believes its opponents or its supporters) but there is agreement that these members are changing all the time. The Party recruits about 70,000 new members every year, and about as many resign. This makes it one of the most active expressions of political commitment and disillusionment in the country. There are far more lapsed communists than Party members. The

Party may stand on the fringes of power, but it has marked an enormous number of people at some stage in their lives. It continues to attract the young, even though it lost 'the generation of 1968' through its jealousy and fear of the students who seemed intent on usurping its leadership of the revolutionary cause. It avoids the gerontocratic image of the Russian Party by having several young people on its central committee. In Paris, half of new recruits are said to be under twenty-five years old. The Party has a larger proportion of women members (about one-quarter) than any other. Seventeen per cent of its members are teachers. But the majority are workers, and it is very much a working-class party. Its leaders are required to remain workers in their standard of living; all receive the same wage as a skilled worker, and give up their salaries as members of parliament (or other official bodies) to the Party; the expense accounts or other benefits they sometimes have are not so significant as to make a charge of hypocrisy possible, as it is among supposedly altruistic politicians in some other parties. However, though their long-term aims may be different, most communists do not reject the consumer society in their day-to-day lives. They are indistinguishable from other people in the possessions they have or aspire to.

It is often said that the Communist Party resembles the Catholic Church; that is an outdated comparison. Louisette Blancard, who runs the woman's page on *L'Humanité*, was brought up as a Catholic, for whom the communists were the devilish persecutors of Christianity, and during the war she was in charge of the 'Companions of St Francis'. It was her Christian faith that led her to start working in a factory. At thirty-five she was converted to Marxism. She says 'I have always remained faithful to myself . . . I gave things another name, that is all.' Her father used to say that 'if only the Christians were real Christians, there would be no communists'. For her, communism is the more efficacious way to work for the poor. Six per cent of those who vote communist are regularly practising Catholics and 13% occasional churchgoers. The Catholics argue that the Communist Party today resembles the Church as it was thirty years ago. The modern Catholic does not claim to enjoy the same kind of complete assurance that the communists display;

he smiles at their dogmatism when they say that Marxism is 'scientific'; he is suspicious of their fundamentalist reliance on Party texts; he sees them as parodies of the old-style Jesuit who was completely submissive to his superiors, who caricatured his anticlerical opponents and refused to examine their arguments personally. A communist shop girl says: 'It is not up to us Party members to judge. One cannot cast doubt on everything . . . The Party is after all a guide.' The attraction of both creeds is supposed to be that they offer spiritual security, but the Catholics claim that their aim is now less total, there is less certainty that all is leading to eternal bliss. The communists reply that their rituals are less formal, their organization more democratic. There remains a common puritanism (sexual scandal is carefully avoided by party militants), a common stress on humility (ambition for power is never avowed, officials say they are ready to serve in whatever capacity the Party chooses).

There are a large number who have inherited their communism from their parents. The son of one communist deputy even recalls that when he refused to show interest in the party, his parents sent him to a psychiatrist. Rebellion against parents is another frequent cause for joining: François Hincker, the Marxist professor of history at the Sorbonne, says he joined for this reason at sixteen, while still attending a posh Catholic school. Philippe Herzog, the Party's leading economist, a graduate of the Polytechnique who invented the 'New Logic'[1] (matching the anti-communist 'new philosophy'), said he left government service to join the Party because he felt his talents were not being properly used by the state. He had competed madly to reach its top echelons; but that had left him lonely. He was given tasks which seemed to lead nowhere. He was a mathematician, who saw in mathematics a method of mastering the world, but in an abstract way which ignored reality, and he was frightened by reality. The Party appreciated his longing to explain the world with the mathematician's absolute exactness; it valued his superior training; it offered him tasks where he felt

---

[1] His 'New Logic' is designed to replace the old communist reliance on state control of all economic activity by more independence for the workers in running their own factories. That does not mean the Party accepts autogestion, because autogestion in its view is inadequate without nationalization.

he was personally appreciated; it freed him from loneliness. 'Marxism,' he says, 'means first of all to work collectively.' It gave him a sense of really contributing to the public good: 'the way the Party knew how to use my abilities convinced me of its efficiency.' He was conscious that his scientific background had been narrow, there was much that he was ignorant about in history, philosophy and literature. Marxism captivated him because it offered a 'coherent answer' to his questions.

Even before 1981, the Party was not excluded from state jobs: it always encouraged able men to infiltrate into positions of influence in government and industry. Thus many years ago Tony Duché, a graduate of the School of Political Sciences, asked it in what firm he could, most usefully to it, become a manager; he was told it could do with someone on the railways; he got into the Nationalized Railway Company by saying at his interview the opposite of what he believed; knowing what was wanted, he declared with a pretence of enthusiasm that the railways needed managers who knew how to be 'chiefs': though nationalized they must behave more like a commercial firm. They loved it. He kept quiet about his political opinions for a year; as soon as he got his permanent status, he amazed them by becoming a trade union delegate. Later he took four years leave to become a full-time Party worker, even though it meant halving his income. He is the son of a wealthy bourgeois industrialist, but he felt that if he stayed on the bourgeois side, he would one day be condemned as the collaborators of 1940 had been. He is a fighter. He has no patience for the routine tasks that communists spend so much time on, like selling *L'Humanité*. He sees his work in the railways as a political fight. There are many young people who say the same thing. To join the communists is to fight, though each one may be psychologically spurred by a different enemy.

French intellectual life is deeply influenced by Marxism, partly because so many intellectuals passed through the party in their youth, particularly during and after the war. They continue to take Marxism seriously even when they have lost faith, and debate endlessly against the Marxist position. In the human sciences, notably in history, the bias towards the study of economic influences and class attitudes has been dominant. The communists are thus not Frenchmen who represent a totally different way of life and of thinking, but are rather like heretics, whose emphases are challenged more than their fundamental principles. Even the Catholic Church has many members who are as fascinated by them as they are hostile to them.

The Communist Party is the richest political party in France, even though it is the party of the poor. It is the most capitalist of the parties, because it runs a vast conglomerate of companies whose profits provide it with the bulk of its income. Every year, on the outskirts of Paris, it organizes a spectacular festival and carnival at which they all have a marvellous time, but also fill the party's coffers, because they make the most business-like use of advertising: Coca-Cola, Ford, Renault and many other companies pay to have their names exhibited. Some companies do not, because they are on a black list (e.g. Schweppes, Martini, Evian); having refused to advertise in the Communist paper *L'Humanité*, their drinks are banned from the festival. *L'Humanité* is only the apex of the largest press empire in the country: the communists have about 160 newspapers and magazines, twenty-four printing presses and half-a-dozen publishing firms. These are sustained by subsidies from communist municipalities, who have information budgets to buy the propaganda, and by orders from the town libraries for the books and magazines the Party publishes. The most important sources of the Party's income, however, are the 300-odd firms it owns, and which exist above all to provide services for the communist municipalities – they get the contracts for building works, for supplying food for school canteens and office equipment for municipal offices. One advantage these firms have is privileged relations with Russia and the Eastern bloc. It is by trade with them that the richest communist in the world, Jean-Baptiste Doumeng, has built up his fortune, which allows him to live exactly like an American tycoon, with a private jet and a fleet of luxury cars. Doumeng joined the party at sixteen when he was an ordinary peasant boy, horrified at the injustice he saw blocking his path; he married the local *châtelain*'s daughter; he learnt to buy and sell agricultural produce, until he became one of the world's most important figures in this trade. But he is an independent satellite in the communist empire. More normal are its vast co-operatives, of which they run around 265, selling both food and household goods, benefiting from the custom of loyal Party members. The Party has its own travel agents, estate agents, hotels and holiday resorts, mostly modest, but including one three-star on the Côte d'Azur. The profits of all these activities, as well as the substantial income from Party subscriptions, are deposited in a Russian-owned bank, the BCEN (Banque Commerciale pour l'Europe du Nord).

Communism is not just an attitude of mind. It has long been put into practice, at least partially, in local government. Following the 1977 elections, there were 1813 communist mayors, seven of them in charge of large towns. The Paris region had exactly half of its thirty municipalities run by communists; the communists have been growing in this 'red belt' continuously for some decades. Choisy-le-Roi (on the southern outskirts of Paris) has been run by communists since 1947. Fernand Dupuy was its mayor till 1981. He used to be a primary schoolmaster, until the Party leader Maurice Thorez, whose home was in Choisy, chose him as his private secretary and then got him elected mayor. He is affable, friendly, a devoted family man, a lover of trout fishing. He aimed to be the most approachable of mayors: he could be seen by anyone who wanted to consult him any morning, and between forty and fifty people came to ask for help in finding housing and jobs, but also for advice on personal and marital problems: he says people come to see him as they might go to consult a doctor or a priest; he is proud that he knows how to listen sympathetically. 'Life,' he says, 'is above all an individual matter, the fine speeches cannot suffice. One must never forget or neglect individual worries.' A communist municipality must seek 'mass participation': that usually means knowing the private problems of as many individual electors as possible. It means also that Dupuy, as a Party member, kept close contact with the local Party (which is seen as the representative of the masses as much as the municipal council) and the local CGT union; he also attended meetings with the communist mayors of the region to co-ordinate their policies. He claims his constituents do not lose much in the way of government subsidies by voting communist; the civil service has, after all, its communist members and its left-wing sympathizers too. A great advantage to the Party is that people who were once terrified by the mere idea of a communist mayor see that it does not mean instant expropriation or worse.

Dupuy has evolved with the times. He used, by his own admission, to be 'sectarian', which he now defines as someone in blinkers, with a mind that is not open. He regrets this, and believes he is no longer blind: the revelations about Stalin were a terrible blow to him, they threw him into a state of confusion to the very depths of his being. The invasion of Czechoslovakia was 'a terrible drama' for him. He not only knows better now, but he feels he has matured. He used to be violently anticlerical, he inherited that; but he is such a warm man that he established close personal relations with his priest, who led the protests when Dupuy was arrested by the Germans in 1940. When he had a serious accident in 1968, the *curé* of Choisy said prayers for his recovery in the Cathedral. His anticlericalism has completely vanished; and he does not mock his Catholic wife who still believes 'a little' in God. He has no use for *agit-prop* any more as a way of converting people to Marxism: 'example is much better'. He has lived in a humble apartment in a publicly-owned block for twenty years. When he first arrived, many of the tenants refused to speak to him, particularly those working in the privately-owned Rhône-Poulenc firm; but he is now friends with them all, even with the most violently anti-communist one, who asked him to preside personally over his daughter's marriage. He claims that he tries to be friendly to everyone not from political calculation, but simply because that is his nature. With the years, he has been able to express himself with diminishing restraint. Communist municipalities were, once upon a time, different from other ones in pressing for aid for the poor, scholarships and the social benefits, but today he thinks the differences have been largely attenuated. He has no wish to cut himself off from his political enemies; on the contrary, when he was elected a member of parliament, he quickly established good relations with the Gaullists, because they had a common background in the Resistance: 'we always respected each other.' And he repeats with pleasure the compliments of Pompidou who told a meeting of communist mayors that he knew that they ran their municipalities well and honestly.

Dupuy prides himself on his personal honesty; there is no room for personal enrichment or corruption in the Party: what is the point of money, he asks, to buy what pleasures? He is dismayed to find workers gambling their earnings away. Though Marxists are supposed to believe in the changing of society by the changing of institutions, he is very shrewdly pragmatic in his attitude to reforms, and expects little from the grand principles. Decentralization for him means only getting more money for local government; he is worried by the possible increase in bureaucracy, though he values that as a way of giving jobs to the unemployed. He has no faith in regionalism on the cultural level, saying the Corsican demand for autonomy is the work of a minority. But are communists not believers in min-

THERE IS NO LIMIT TO THE NUMBER OF CANDIDATES ALLOWED TO STAND FOR A PARLIAMENTARY SEAT

Pablo

orities leading the struggle? 'Yes, you are quite right', he replies, with a smile, 'sorry, I have not really thought about these problems, they have not arisen here.' Though a teacher, he is not even sure that the world will be changed by education; one of the schools at Choisy has been burgled over a hundred times in the course of ten years; he has no illusions about the children's attitude to education. It is perhaps because he has so few illusions that he has very nearly been thrown out of the Party for ideological heresy.

Everybody agrees that Fernand Dupuy is a quite exceptional politician, whose personality and charm have been decisive in keeping the communists popular in Choisy. He has now retired in favour of a younger man, Louis Luc, whom everybody compares unfavourably with him, even the members of the Party. Luc, they agree, is an able man, but he lacks Dupuy's tact; he is determined to improve the life of his fellow citizens, but he tends to knock some of them over in the process. It is not that he is more 'advanced' than Dupuy; on the contrary, he is even more of a traditionalist. 'I am more interested in the past than in the future,' he admits. 'I am a materialist, but after that the most important thing for me is culture. I am ashamed that when I went to Versailles, there were foreigners there who knew more about it than I.' He has inaugurated a painting exhibition at Choisy; he is in the process of building a splendid new public library, which will have 50,000 volumes, for a population of 40,000; he has expanded the music school to five hundred places; the schools of dance and gymnastics, the discotheque are all flourishing. The municipal theatre is putting on a play about Bertolt Brecht by a Danish experimental drama group run by an Italian born in Greece; followed by Handel's *Mass*, Rossini's *William Tell*, a jazz festival, and contemporary ballet; the cinema is showing films from Germany, Australia, Czechoslovakia as well as Losey's *Criminals*. But personally for Louis Luc culture means the dream of re-reading Zola, whom he has not looked at for twenty-five years, Victor Hugo and Maupassant — a dream because he has no time to read. He is not interested in computers; what he wants is to catch up on the heritage of his own country that he has been unable to assimilate.

His father was an agricultural labourer from the Corrèze who became a railway worker. He himself, without much education, was a postman before becoming a journalist on *L'Humanité*, via the Resistance: he is yet another of those who became a communist during the war because he was a patriot. The accusation that hurts him more than any other is that he is in the pay of Russia. 'I feel myself to be a free man. When I wrote articles for *L'Humanité*, I said what I thought and signed my name. When I wrote articles on behalf of the Party, I did not sign them. I won't say Shit to Marchais just for the fun of it, though I feel free to do so; there is a struggle on, and I won't do anything to upset it.' The struggle matters to him because 'we have been in a ghetto, and that hurts.' This is a constant refrain, the desire to emerge from the ghetto of the poor. There were old people in Choisy who had never been to Paris in their whole lives; he has organized trips for them; he has chartered planes to take the children to Corsica, the Côte d'Azur and the ski resorts. He has been to Russia several times; he admires its social achievements, but not the 'collective life' – the idea of several families sharing a flat he finds too much; and he missed his Beaujolais. He has been once to the USA and what he likes most there was that there were no fences between the houses; that seemed to him the right balance of privacy and communal life; he thought the USA was 'not more disagreeable' than France, though he missed his French cooking and was shocked by the 'profusion of sex'. He regrets that the electorate imagines the communists intend to reproduce Russia in France. He does not own any property himself, being a tenant in a municipal block, but he has no objection to others owning their homes, provided they do not have too many of them, provided they do not squander their wealth in idle gambling while others slave in factories. But he has not convinced everybody. His own deputy's aunt lives in the town but votes Gaullist, because she fears that the communists will one day take away her house from her, or at least part of it. Precisely because the communists are so close-knit, and keep their distance politically, others must be suspicious of them. They have their own heritage too; people cannot be expected to change their minds about them each time they change their tune. The local communist doctor, who lives in some style in an impressive penthouse overlooking the town hall, says that the communists are a young, immature party, they must be allowed to make their mistakes, to grow up, the old dogmatists must be allowed to die; and he himself has no hesitation in practising his medicine privately, charging the highest possible rates, because he insists that unless the patient chooses his doctor freely, and pays him, there is no true equality in the relationship, only a humiliating dependence. His communist patients presumably feel better for having paid him, since they opt to do so.

A communist municipality means jobs for the boys and favouritism of various kinds, but that is hardly original or unique. It has ceased to be a frightening prospect, any more than a black mayor has in the USA. The inclusion of a few communists in the Mitterrand government has shown that they behave much like most other politicians, but it has not made the bulk of the membership feel all that much freer, any more than a few American blacks in office change the handicaps of racial minorities. The socialists hope that the communists will ultimately vanish if they are given a share of power and if the poor cease to feel they are outcasts. The socialists have made some headway, in that the communists' electoral support has fallen from its traditional 20–25% to around 15%. But much will depend on the policy the communists national leaders pursue, and they are a quite separate subject of study. This is not a book about politics. I deal with the communists because they are not just a phenomenon of party politics, but an illustration of particular forms of experience and emotion, and those emotions go very deep. They are responsible, says the historian Le Roy Ladurie (who used to be one), for the 'serious side' in French life.

14

What becomes of the drop-outs

'What do you want to do when you grow up?' asks the harassed father of his little boy with a vacant face. 'I don't know.' 'Don't know! Don't know! That is no answer: Think. At your age, you must know what you want to do.' So the little boy promises to think. He goes and asks his little girlfriend, but she does not know what she wants to do either. He goes and asks his doddering grandfather what he wants to do in the future, but he does not know. He goes to the kitchen and asks the cook. 'If the pigs don't eat me, I'll get my pension and retire,' says she. 'That's not so silly,' thinks the little boy. He goes back to his father, who is sitting at a desk, by a telephone, with graphs on the wall and glum despair on his face, and tells him: 'When I grow up, I shall retire, and raise pigs, but I'll take care not to let them eat me.' This boy could serve as a mascot for the third category of French people: those who are involved neither in the rat race, nor in traditional working-class protest, those who do not want power over others. What will there be to distinguish him, in due course, from the international fraternity of drop-outs?

Jean Cabut, who drew the strip cartoon containing this story, is now forty-four, and he does not know what he will do when he grows up either. The filmmaker Jean-Luc Godard has called him 'the best journalist in France': he is certainly being a faithful reporter when he presents the dilemmas of his country-men in pithy moral tales of this sort. But it is not surprising that he can give no better answer himself than the little boy did. The basis of his view of life is that he does not like people who know the answers. He considers them dangerous: they never ask themselves questions; they never know doubt and Cabu (which is how he signs his cartoons) insists that it is essential to have at least some doubts. He has created a famous character, Mon Beauf (my brother-in-law) who incarnates all the complacency of provincial France. This only half-fictitious person is partly based on Cabu's real brother-in-law, who is an insurance man in the Vosges (Cabu's sister is a gym mistress), though the face has some resemblance to the Mayor of Nice, Médecin, who once sued Cabu for libel and whom Graham Greene is now annoying in a different way. Cabu is a journalist as well as a cartoonist, because he does not deal in imaginary stereotypes, but always bases himself on real people around him; he is an eavesdropper who has no need to resort to fiction. Every time he goes to see his brother-in-law he comes back with a bag of gems. It was while still at school that he came to hate that type: he started a magazine called *Le Petit Fum*, short for *fumiste* (meaning those who do nothing seriously and on whom one cannot count); that was the label the scientists gave the classicists, on the ground that they did not work much. Cabu hated the scientists because they were always fascinated by how things worked, but never asked themselves the questions, What good does it do? What purpose does it serve? He is one of those who always calls into doubt every aspect of civilization, and he does not spare himself.

He is not sure whether he is a utopian with his head in the clouds or a prematurely senile old fogey worshipping nostalgia. He regards adolescence as the best years of life, because everything seems possible then, because the adolescent lives in a world of dreams, imagining all sorts of wonderful situations, and everything he encounters in the real world has the unspoilt taste of novelty. The first girl Cabu took in his arms, the first cartoon he sold to a newspaper, are memories of ecstasy he has not repeated. Le Grand Duduche, Cabu's most famous cartoon character, is about seventeen, but he is not just a representative of the young generation. Duduche provides one of the most accurate histories of the young over the last two decades, because Cabu has observed them very precisely through his own son and the four children of his wife, but Duduche is much more than an heir of Billy Bunter. He is not a greedy, naughty child, but a naive observer of the law of the jungle that school life is, and through his adventures at school, shows life outside school to be a similar kind of jungle. Duduche is in many ways Cabu himself, still marvelling at the inexplicable imbecilities of those who pretend to be adults. The events of 1968 were the great moment in Cabu's life: 'that was my Great War of 1914'; adolescence he describes as a permanent revolution of 1968 that constantly repeats itself. He would like to keep that spirit alive. But of course he has his doubts. Why is it that 1968 did not usher in a new world? Here Cabu shows that both he and Duduche, while having an irrepressible faith in man, are also disappointed with him. The rebels of 1968 made the same mistake as their fathers; they used violence, and that is self-defeating; they became greedy for power, and that corrupts; and above all they did not realize that they were really just like their parents, and they have now in middle age developed all the awful vices of their parents. Duduche is in love with his headmaster's daughter, and she is a silly girl he has nothing in common with: Cabu himself as a young man always fell in love with prim, Catholic girls: 'we are all like that, our ideas and our behaviour don't coincide.' When Duduche goes to the first communion party of his young cousin, he watches all the relatives pile their expensive gifts on a table – radios, walkie-talkies and toy cars; the cousin accepts politely, and then paints his revolutionary slogan of protest on the wall: Down with the Consumer Society. The pleasures of adolescence are, of course, all to be obtained outside the school syllabus: Duduche is a *marginal* who does not like syllabuses or systems and so is Cabu: 'it is very important for me that each one of us can have solitude when he wants it – as Sartre said, hell is other people; solitude is necessary for reflection; but solitude only works if you feel comfortable with yourself.'

The worst experience of Cabu's life was therefore, not surprisingly, his period of military service. He could not bear that the army should tell him what to do and dress him from top to toe. (He has printed a marvellous, deadly serious, long army report on the relative merits of different kinds of underpants for conscripts.) He was given no responsibility: he felt diminished in the army, as though forced to acknowledge his weakness before the powers that be. Such an admission is all the more painful for him, since he is very conscious of man's fragility:

another of his cartoon characters is a mongol boy – he had one for a neighbour – who symbolizes the narrow line that separates success from failure: that is so frightening that he has to laugh. It was the callousness of the army that turned him into an anti-militarist. He was sent to fight in Algeria: he and his mates had been on duty for two weeks, day and night, and were dying of thirst in the boiling heat: a helicopter came to give them water, but it landed half a mile away from them, and they had to bring the water up in jerry cans on their backs. Then they saw another helicopter land on the doorstep of the commander's post: a general emerged from the plane bearing a bottle of champagne in an ice bucket: he presented it to their colonel and flew off. 'That day, I understood that the military really constitute a caste apart.' Cabu has been a relentless champion of non-violence ever since: he believes one solution for the world's ills that has not been tried is passive resistance; he has demonstrated for unilateral disarmament; his book of cartoons, *Down With All Armies*, has sold 75,000 copies. He has not hesitated to descend to vitriolic insult of soldiers and strident caricature, but he has also published conversations with real soldiers who are perfectly decent people, who claim to be left-wing, who can even quote Mao, and who say they are only doing a job like any other, that offers security and a pension. That only makes it worse from his point of view, that they should spend their lives collecting medals 'for having destroyed a battalion of flies on a dung heap with no thought for the danger involved'. Cabu protests also against nuclear power. He protests against the pollution of the environment. He resents modern concrete architecture, and protests that his home town, Châlons-sur-Marne, should have had all its character destroyed by expansion and rebuilding. He sees no need for supermarkets: 'the little old shops were perfectly adequate.' He knows life in the past was awful for most people, but he regrets something in it all the same. He prefers jazz to rock, and Charles Trenet to any modern singer. He prefers cars made in the 1920s. He contradicts everything he says about his love of youth by complaining that France's old civilization should stoop to borrow from America, which is a mere 200 years old.

Of course, he is horrified by what he says; he cannot stand

Arab music, that is one sign of his Frenchness, but he thinks it really is time he learnt to appreciate it. He feels French because he loves the countryside and the architecture, but he is ashamed that he has not travelled more. His friends think of him as quintessentially French, because of his passion for its old houses and its little shops, and because he makes a virtue out of his nostalgia, but it is not difficult to imagine him attending Aldermaston nuclear demonstrations in Britain, and living in a Suffolk village, for he is not only a vegetarian, but seldom drinks either, so the inevitable excuse of the Frenchman, that he cannot be separated from his wine or his mother's cooking, does not apply. Cabu is puzzled by the behaviour of his son, who mocks him for having made no real difference to the world, despite all his endless protesting. He thinks that perhaps history goes in cycles, and that the young will one day return to the idealistic spirit of 1968. But he is well aware that he is not fulfilling his vision of adolescence, of being always open to new ideas. He admits he might be in a rut himself, that he may be guilty of precisely the same obstinacy for which he criticizes his brother-in-law. So what he does with the second half of his life will be the real test of his philosophy. Is it possible, or desirable, to go beyond passive resistance to the rat race and other forms of violence? There might well be interesting developments when Cabu is a grandfather: that will produce for the first time in history a combination of a sizable group of radical pensioners – in good health and with a long expectation of life, with plenty of frustrated energy for more experiment – and a new generation of precocious grandchildren who will have no grudge against them, as they might against their parents: together they might do more than engage in the traditional spoiling of grand-children.

Dissatisfaction both with the consumer society and with tradi-tional forms of protest against capitalism started when pro-sperity was at its peak. In 1968, in a profound revolution that has been played down with the modest title of the Events of May, many young people suddenly called the bluff of those in authority. Students rioted, workers occupied factories, life came to a temporary standstill. It resumed after a few months, but for a while the whole country was led to question its values, and it emerged that quite a few people did not accept them. The graffiti on the walls of Paris proclaimed: Pleasure not Power. I reject the Past. I want Dialogue. The Right to Enjoyment. Revolution is Orgasm. An End to Metro, Boulot, Dodo, i.e. to a life that consisted simply of travel, work and sleep. The search was now not for money, or promotion or material comforts, but for a more elusive sense of fulfilment, for a combination of security and excitement, for the Good Life, or as it was now called, the Quality of Life. This was not specifically French. The Americans had reacted against their greater prosperity even earlier, and the hippies were the predecessors of the new French *marginaux*, the people who opted into the margins of society. The magazine *Actuel* which kept these people in touch and enabled them to do things in common was partly modelled on New York's Greenwich *Village Voice*. Since then the daily newspaper, *Libération*, and the magazine *Autrement* have sustained and co-ordinated the urge to experiment with new ways

LIFE AT SCHOOL by Plantu

of life. But 1968 has cast graduated ripples far beyond the small groups who have actually withdrawn completely into rural or intellectual independence. Many of those who were in their twenties in 1968 have been permanently marked by their experiences; they are less dogmatic, less political, less brutal than they would otherwise have been. And in society at large, even among those who reacted in horror against the revolt, the sense of hierarchy is less pronounced, personal relations are less liable to be contemptuous; even the prefect of police speaks with a gentler voice. The 'right to be different' is respected more than it used to be, at least theoretically.

The generation of 1968, or more precisely the affinity of 1968, since it is less an age group than a tendency, are worried by their inability to fulfil their promise, in the sense of showing more practical, concretely identifiable results from their agitation and experiment. Cabu says there is something of the old schoolmaster in him (his father was one) wanting to make people happy despite themselves. That is the source of the dissatisfaction that gnaws at him and those like him. They cannot accept that they have achieved a lot simply by living their own lives with greater decency; they cannot measure the moral contagion that has introduced more gentleness into human relationships by the presence of people who are not willing to use violence, and are not inspired by greed for money or power. They cannot reconcile themselves to the thought that what distinguishes them from the rest of society is their acknowledgement that the same ideals cannot suit everyone, so that they would be unlikely to 'make everyone happy' if they did have more influence. They represent a temperament, not a solution. Is not Cabu worried by people who know what the solutions are?

That is all very well, but meanwhile people do have to earn their livings, and the pleasures of creativity are to be found not just in a primitive farm in the Ardèche, nor in an arty workshop weaving tapestries, but also in a 'real' world that for the most part is driven by totally different ambitions. That is the dilemma that has confronted the newspaper *Libération*, which has survived as the main standard-bearer of those who dislike competitiveness and hierarchy. It has won a place in society, like a wayward younger brother in a respectable family, who goes off to become a rock musician, and whom his elders grudgingly come to respect, even while being convinced he is silly if not mad and dangerous. *Libération* is unique in that it has no rich magnate behind it (though it has received donations from a few rich eccentrics, who were soon voted out of their jobs on the paper for 'incompetence'). It is not supported by a political party, nor does it support any party. It represents the triumph of do-it-yourself journalism. It was helped by a few nonconformist celebrities – Sartre, Clavel, Foucault – but it has been built up by young people who have learnt their trade while doing it, without any apprenticeships in the capitalist press. Everybody working for the paper originally received the same salary, from the editor to the cleaners: it sought not only to denounce the spirit of hierarchy but to show that it could be eliminated. The printing works were placed in the centre of the offices, so that journalists and manual workers should not be separated into two castes. It was managed by a general assembly of all those who worked for it, voting equally. It was financed by its income from sales, without accepting any commercial advertising; on the contrary, advertisements could be inserted free of charge by readers. These advertisements came to be one of the most entertaining and informative sections; many bought the

THEY'RE LIKE THIS

Sports journalist

Fashion journalist   Cartoonist   Editor-in-chief   Reporter on a
                                            of a political newspaper   folk music
                                                                       magazine

Jean Pierre Aldebert

paper just for them: they were much more than the equivalent of *Le Figaro*'s society page, much more than the frivolous 'personal' advertisements that once filled the front page of *The Times* when the English upper classes could still afford to be frivolous; here fantasy, eccentricity and obscenity ran riot.

Libération rejects all taboos, it is curious about all forms of experiments in the art of living, it is not frightened of being absurd. It deliberately aims 'to astonish, to surprise', not by titillating its readers with the traditional fare of mass-circulation papers, but by shocking them out of their complacency. It has no preconceptions about what is important and what is not; it is run by a team who are worried if they all agree and who value the 'cohabitation of different types of people', it resists attachment to any party because that would inevitably limit the range of its curiosity. Sartre hoped it would use a 'spoken-written', less formal language that would more genuinely express ordinary people's feelings. Philippe Gavi, another of its founders (a graduate of France's leading business school HEC[1] and of the School of Political Sciences) saw it as an instrument for a new kind of sociability: 'I like hearing people tell their life stories, tell them in detail. Slowly, as our discussion progresses, we feel warmer, richer. We feel the barriers breaking down. I should like to put microphones everywhere, in bistros, under beds, in

[1] Ecole des hautes études commerciales.

Comic strip cartoonist

Cookery columnist

Journalist on an interior decorating magazine

Cinema critic

Journalist on a do-it-yourself paper

workshops, in offices, outside factory gates, in the mouths of kissing couples. Real communication is revolutionary because to speak involves condemning, criticizing, evaluating one's own life or that of others, and discovering it too as the conversation becomes heated.' He urged the paper to go beyond the stereotypes that public pronouncements normally create.

Serge July, the editor, believed originally that the way to 'let the people speak' was to get them to form committees all over the country, which would decide what they had to say; but these committees quickly proved unworkable. He now places increasing reliance on slowly researched investigative journalism; he laments that the press is so poor that it normally gives a journalist two hours, or at most three days, to work on a story. His ideal newspaper would have forty-eight pages, four-fifths of which would contain detailed grass-roots reports and enquiries on ever-changing subjects, from explaining why workers support the right wing, to why one football team has beaten another, or what the latest view of evolution is; he wants his pages to be of the same standard as the great books that have taken several years to write and to include photographs that are coherent sets of documents and drawings that express the point of view of artists. He sees journalism as now being much more than a mere tool of politics or entertainment: 'journalism is today the major form of expression; it is at once literature and philosophy, because there can be no readable literature or philosophy today without the sort of investigations journalists carry out'. Journalism is thus both a model and a basis for all reflection. He wishes to keep on pushing the range of its enquiries across all accepted frontiers, to seek new angles, new subjects, new techniques; he sees himself as leading a band of sharp shooters, attacking all forms of authoritarianism, on the left as well as on the right, allowing all forms of dissidence to be heard, offering news that other papers neglect.

Many of the ideals of *Libération* have, however, been modified, one by one, after excruciating, heartsearching and endless debate: equal salaries, and no commercial advertisements have been abandoned as too utopian, in the hope of widening circulation beyond the rather limited fraternity that loves the paper; it has won a readership which has a larger proportion of university graduates than any other daily, even Le Monde. Its search for professional excellence tries to avoid being unfaithful to its basic tradition, which is one of irreverence, heterodoxy and humour; there is often wit and provocation in its stories and priorities. Its mission is to create a new form of maturity, a new art of being middle-aged without pomposity: perhaps it will do it by showing that maturity is a false ideal, for the fruit that is ripe is ready to fall off its tree.

Libération has pioneered autogestion (self-management) which it is the policy of the socialist party to introduce generally into industry. The problem of making it work in large organizations, of dismantling organizations that are too large to allow it, is a herculean challenge. What new problems the transformation will produce have not even been guessed. That there seldom are permanent solutions is seen in the lives of the readers of Libération, even among those who apparently successfully transform themselves in mid-career: for example, Gérard Barthélemy is a diplomat who has become a carpenter. He comes from a well-to-do family; he studied law, medicine and finally economics and politics at the School of Political Sciences in Paris; he taught economic development at a university and then spent ten years abroad in the service of the Ministry of Foreign Affairs, as an attaché dealing with technical co-operation and then with cultural relations ('it is the same thing with us: we consider all the countries of the world to be underdeveloped intellectually, so we think they need assistance both technically and culturally'). He worked in Bolivia, Colombia, Sri Lanka, Morocco. 'Diplomacy is a fascinating, marvellous job, perhaps one of the best of all jobs, socially, and from the point of view of the independence one enjoys, which is considerable. But like all good things, like chocolate, one must not have too much: after ten years I had the feeling that I was living very artificially; I wanted to take part in the cultural life of my country no longer as a representative, but as a participant, not just to try to sell culture, and spread knowledge of it.' So he came back to France, and was appointed director of a Maison de la Culture, a provincial cultural centre. 'Very quickly I realized that I had made a mistake, because I found the very same cultural imperialism, cultural colonization within France as I had been practising outside France; I was in effect diffusing Parisian culture, imposing an urban culture, spreading a system of values that is simply that of a small group. I realized I was repeating in France what I had given up doing abroad. The people of Verberie, the town where I lived, just did not see or feel things the same way as those of Paris, and I did not want to be the representative of Parisian culture.'

So he resigned after three months. He took a year off, during which he rebuilt his house. 'In doing so I discovered another life, which was not dependent on any organization, but in which survival depended on myself, on the skill of my hands, on my own knowledge. Doctors, some members of the liberal professions, are in that position. So too are artisans. I decided to explore in that direction.' He studied carpentry for a year, in a residential school: he was twice as old as the other pupils: it was a bit like the army, but he learnt the trade. 'My aim was not to become a worker, in the political or social sense, that did not interest me, what I wanted was a style of life.' He set up as a carpenter. His friends gave him his first orders. To share costs, he gradually teamed up with six others; they have a communal workshop and lorry but each operates on his account, though they work together when a large job requires it. 'I am a carpenter, but it is not because I love wood, or furniture. I could just as well have been a mason or a plumber. What interests me in my work is the way I live; my trade is not an isolated one, but a way of having relations with others, with our suppliers, our neighbours, our families – all are drawn in. When people know what I used to be and learn that I am a carpenter, they say, 'Ah, you are a cabinet maker.' If they want to be nice they say, 'You are an artist in wood.' I reply, 'No, I am a carpenter.' Not because I want to play myself down, but because through my work I am seeking relationships, friendly and professional ones. A job well done for me is when my clients say at the end of it: "That is what I wanted." It is not what they had asked for, it is not what I worked out for them, but it is what between us we did together, and they say "Yes, you worked out what I wanted." Because often it is not clear at the beginning. People often ask for one thing because they want something else.'

Barthélemy has been a carpenter for seven years. He does not charge high prices, but he is practical, and he earns a decent living. His home is more interestingly decorated and has more curious objects in it than a normal carpenter would have, because he has the relics of his previous existence around him, but he lives as simply as any other artisan. He has made an enormous number of friends from every walk of life; people are constantly coming to see him; there is no division between his private and professional life. And that has become the first of his problems. His wife Mimi, Haitian by birth, is just as sociable and even more lively than he, but her conception of marriage is too modern for this style of life, which on reflection has a medieval side to it. 'It is extremely interesting to live differently,' she says 'but the family is so open to the outside world, that there is practically no family life.' Her elder daughter agrees with her. 'People are constantly coming and going, having meals with us: it is rare for us to eat together alone, just as a family, the six of us.' 'I think that has happened only twice in the last six months,' adds the younger daughter. Barthélemy invites friends, fellow workers and clients; but also friends of friends, and all the artisans of the village just drop in. And the children bring their friends. Mimi found this too much. 'Because in addition to being the wife of Gérard, and the mother of the children, I am Mimi, I have a personality, and it is very difficult in all this continual coming and going to find a chance to be myself.' She wants more 'intimacy'. That is something the craftsmen of the Middle Ages did not know about. Mimi went off for ten months to Central America to do some work of her own, which she enjoyed very much; since her return she has been pressing for a revision of their way of life, with more privacy. Her daughter Clémentine, who left school to look after her younger siblings while Mimi was away, pursuing her studies by correspondence, wants privacy also: 'I have made my own little house, I put up a door and I have taught people to knock, and the members of my family now wait till I say "come in."' It is thus his own family which has threatened to undermine the way of life he has tried to construct.

His second problem is that he himself is getting restless. He became a carpenter in order to escape from the clutches of a safe, pensionable post, with no element of risk or adventure. But now he has come to feel secure in his life as a carpenter; things have become a little routine; and so he is turning over in his mind a plan to 'escape once again from security', because he wants to do something different, because 'I feel the need to explode'. His plan is to 'free the French university from its sense of security'. This side of Barthélemy is not medieval but revolutionary. Is he a jet-driven dinosaur, or a lonely spaceman with a longing for the traditional village sing-song feasts? Ultimately, I think he is something quite rare, a man of ideas with an unusual degree of courage, who has tried to change the world not by writing books about it, as he was trained to do, but by risking himself in an adventure, the risk being an essential part of the adventure. He is perhaps a nineteenth-century utopian except that he has set up a community just for himself. It is not a mark of failure, but of success, that he still feels the need for more adventure.

In 1936 the workers were promised a forty-hour week. That boosted their morale enormously, even if in practice the promise was seldom fulfilled: at least their rights were being acknowledged not to have to work to complete exhaustion. In 1981 the government promised a thirty-five-hour week, but again employers protested that was impossible; a reduction of an hour per week each year was agreed as a compromise, so this real change in people's lives is going to be almost too slow to notice. But there have been some firms who have shown that an immediate reduction from forty to thirty-five hours is perfectly possible. In Cachan, Jean de Cassagnac has a printing works and advertising agency employing forty-five people – printers, photoengravers, bookbinders, commercial artists, secretaries and delivery drivers, men and women. He has built up the firm over twenty years, but two years ago he carried out a transformation equivalent to the political transformation that took place in France's politics in the nineteenth century: he abdicated from his role as divine-right monarch and instituted what is more or less a democracy. He invited his workers to become shareholders, in a scheme by which, over five years, they would own 70% of the firm, while he kept 30%. Profits have been divided equally between the workers and the firm, fifty-fifty. Clocking in and out has been abolished; everyone comes to work when he or she pleases and stays till they have done their stint; they can choose to work four long days or five short days a week. Cassagnac insists that there is nothing reprehensible in being a late riser, nor in oversleeping: no one feels guilty arriving late, and there is no one to apologize to. The workers make arrangements among themselves when they want to take time off for personal business. The advantage to the firm is that people are on the job spread out over a longer period of time, including Saturdays, so that orders can be received and expedited outside normal hours. If a rush job is suddenly offered to the firm, Cassagnac calls the workers together, they discuss whether it is worth their while sacrificing a weekend or a late night and he then refuses or accepts the order. Another advantage is that workers have to fill in for their mates and so find themselves doing a far wider variety of tasks. Nobody sits around waiting for five o'clock; if there is nothing to do, they go home. Mothers do not have to worry if they are absent because their children are ill, and indeed the doctor's certificate for absence has vanished, because absenteeism has vanished: if anyone feels the need for a couple of days rest, they take it by arranging to fill in for someone else at another time.

Discipline in the traditional sense has disappeared. There is no foreman. Cassagnac thinks there is no need for one: he dislikes treating workers like children who should do what they are told, or like a colonel who yells at them. One of the printers says that he used to work in another firm where he was under the orders of a foreman who was himself under the orders of a production manager: 'it was like being in the army, all that was missing was stripes on our blue overalls.' The difference now is 'like day and night. I am on another planet. I feel that I am responsible for what I do, that people have confidence in me, and, as a bonus, the work is relaxed.' The young man who minds the off-set machine says what pleases him most is being able to arrive late without anyone passing any comments. And if he makes a mistake, it is he who swears at himself; to put it right, he asks the help of a mate; there are no punishments. 'I at last have the feeling that I am an adult.' The man in charge of the paper guillotine contrasts his previous job where his conversations with the boss were 'telegraphic: Good morning, Good evening, that was it: if I had to tell him something I had to go to his secretary who passed on the message. Now it is totally different, I knock at the boss's door, I go in, he tells me to sit down and we chat. And believe me, his chair isn't higher than mine.'

Cassagnac does not stand on his dignity: he can be seen sweeping up the rubbish, or carrying loads to the lorry just like everyone else. No one seems to envy him: he works longer hours than anyone else, but as one machinist says, 'if you want to be the leader, you have to work more.' Cassagnac has not abandoned his leadership: he is the boss, and proud of it, and his purpose is to make profits. But not at the expense of the workers; what he values more than anything is 'human warmth'. He has no wish to interfere in people's private lives, but they must be recognized to be individuals, and the idea that they must all obey the same rules is absurd. Elderly women workers, for example, should be treated with special consideration to allow for any physical difficulties they have. When a wife comes to meet her husband as he leaves work 'is it logical to make her wait outside in the cold? is it not nicer to ask her in?' Every employee has a key, so that he can come as early as he likes, or leave late. 'It is the first time I have seen such proof of confidence in workers,' says a middle-aged platemaker. The firm tries to be a kind of village, where everyone can find expression for his personality, and where no task is regarded as nobler than or subordinate to another, since everyone should feel he is contributing to the general welfare by what he does. When a difficult job presents itself, it is by general agreement that it is given to a more experienced person. What surprises new workers coming in is that 'there is no one who commands'. The twenty-three-year-old off-set margin minder says there is a hierarchy, 'but it is established amongst ourselves. If one of the mates is better at a job, without the boss appointing him, he becomes the leader, he is recognized as such, but he has not got any title.' And if someone does not pull his weight, it is the workers themselves who ask him to leave. The different parts of the firm work as autonomous financial units and that increases the sense of responsibility: if there are disagreements, Cassagnac refuses to interfere and tells them to reach agreement among themselves. The art designer says: 'What I like best is the way people are always given responsibilities when they show they are capable of them. And that is important for the dignity of workers.' Of course, they cannot always agree: for example, they might want to take their holidays at the same time; but they agree then to sacrifice their wishes this year, in return for having their way next year. About a fifth of the workers have preferred not to take out shares in the firm: they are mainly women, who prefer a fixed wage. But everyone has agreed to abandon the concept of overtime.

This firm is very much an exception: in terms of work, France is still a multitude of what are in various degrees despotisms, and not all of them are benevolent despotisms. Why is that? Cassagnac, like a good Frenchman, blames the state: he is horrified at the way foreigners are defeating French competition, with Japanese buying up the vineyards of Bordeaux and Germans buying up the pharmaceutical industry: if things go on as they have been 'all that will be left for me to do will be to turn my printing works into a dance hall and my advertising agency into a sex shop.' But he also gives a better answer: employers fear their workers, and vice versa. His own worries about foreign competition show how difficult it is to escape from fear. But he says: 'I trusted in the sense of honour of the workers and I do not hesitate to say it, I won. The contract that unites employer and employee should be like that of a marriage: for better or for worse.'

The marriage does not always work. Several workers have left because they could not stand the system: there were even some who used to stand outside the gates waiting for eight o'clock to strike, even in the bitter cold of winter, because they could not bring themselves to give an employer more than his due. On one occasion, there was a big job to finish, and the workers decided to stay late to finish it; but two left early, without completing their share; the next day, there was a meeting of all, at which it was decided that people unwilling to place the general interest in front of their own had no place in the firm, and the two were asked to resign. When the government labour inspector came to enquire whether there had been an unfair dismissal, it was the workers, not Cassagnac, who saw her; they told her there could be no choice between the jobs of two people and the survival of the firm: 'she went away dazed.' Some may dismiss this as paternalism turned upside down. But the marriage Cassagnac has offered does seem to be one that is an evolving relationship: the workers may conceivably decide to sack him one day.

This little revolution has been inspired by an employer; but individual workers have also occasionally succeeded in reorganizing their lives to suit themselves, to be more in command of how they spend their time. A post office clerk called Claudie Besse has for twenty years, since the age of eighteen, opened letters in the Paris department of postal cheques, from eight to six, until the hours were recently reduced. She was one of 10,000 women in what was the equivalent of a giant factory. The managers were ruthless: none told them they had a right to a twenty-minute break in the mornings, or to one-and-a-half days off every three months. When she found out and complained, the manager insulted her, calling her a 'provincial flea'. Things got much worse when automation was introduced. Previously they worked in groups of four girls, who could chat, even though the managers forced them to stand so that they would work harder. But then the amazing computer abolished the teams and left each one on her own. The hours were reduced, but the work was more boring than ever. Claudie Besse heard about the law of 1971 which allowed those with children under twelve to work part-time. She can now at last get her children off to school herself, have half-an-hour's breakfast with the whole family, go out together in the evening. She does not want three cars, or a hi-fi costing a fortune. 'What I want is the time to really live, to be with my family, to see friends with whom I can talk and do interesting things.' But her husband still works full time, leaving at eight, returning at seven. She took a long time to persuade him to stop working Saturdays; she regrets that men still think it is not quite manly not to do a full day's work. She herself now takes Tuesdays off completely – 'Tuesday is my day' – to see a film, to read a book. The girls in her office say 'But what would I do with a whole day free? I could not go to the cinema all alone.' Work she answers, is an excuse, which saves you from having to find out what you really want to do. The discovery of that is now the most difficult quest of all.

15

How small shopkeepers survive

Those who see a simple solution in the formula Small is Beautiful have particularly interesting French experience to reflect on, since France has traditionally been the refuge of the 'small man'. There used to be a very large number of 'small men' before 1914, when a political party even existed to defend them, and it enjoyed a majority in parliament for many years. A small man, in the sense in which it was once used, was someone with no pretensions, who simply wished to preserve his independence, fragile though he knew this to be, and who hated all governments as threats to his independence; but by organizing, he succeeded in making the government treat him as a protected species. In order to frighten its enemies, his party called itself the Radical Party, but it was only with words that it attacked all those in authority, the Church and the rich. The small shopkeepers and artisans of today are the descendants of this species. Their inheritance is a very ambiguous one. They sacrificed a great deal to remain independent; they sometimes lapsed into selfishness and demagogy. But they do still form a very sizeable group. France's 800,000 little shops have been threatened with extinction for over half a century; supermarkets seem to have brought them face to face with death. But they still control 60% of the food trade and over 70% of retail trade in general (a complete contrast to the United States, where supermarkets have captured three-quarters of the food trade).

The small artisan dismisses the objections of technocrats to his inefficiency, as being a judgement made too narrowly in terms of productivity and statistics. He represents a search for dignity and meaning which he regards as an alternative to their kind of progress. Gaston Lucas, a Paris locksmith born in 1907, is the son of a gardener who refused to allow electricity into his house precisely because he disapproved of progress, for what he feared above all else was that machines would do all the work and there would soon be no jobs: that was before 1914. He urged Gaston, who naturally dreamed about electricity, to be a locksmith, because these would always be needed. Gaston has never regretted it, though he has had a very hard life in material terms. The joy of his trade, which also involves the ironwork in gates, is that it can never be fully learnt, there is always something new to discover, no job is exactly like another, every client has his whims and tastes. The work is difficult, but when he has succeeded in doing what he has tried to achieve, 'it is nice to look at. I am happy.' He has never wanted to escape from manual work; he is scathing about intellectuals who, because they know nothing about it, feel it must be nothing but drudgery and plan for its abolition. He regards himself as a kind of artist without in any way wishing to deny that he is a member of the working class. The people he feels sorry for are workers who no longer have any say in the shaping of their task, who are told by the new army of designers what to do. He works long hours; when war broke out in 1939, he was careful to finish the job he had in hand before going to enlist.

His son fulfilled his ambition and became an electrician with Air France: but though this was from the point of view of prestige, security and finance a marvellous job, he was unhappy, because he was spending all his time mending apparatus; there was no human interest. So they made him a teacher of radio, but that did not satisfy him either, it was pure repetition. Finally, he ended up as air traffic controller; at last what he did really mattered, the lives and safety of people depended on his skill; he had responsibility and he could really care about doing his job well. The son had reached the same conclusion as the father.

What both sought was self-respect and a satisfaction that went far deeper than status or money. Gaston has had no desire to better himself socially. He was made a foreman at twenty-seven, but he always remained on the shop floor. He is not a jealous or a bitter man. Neither is he conservative in his views nor obsequious in his behaviour. He has always voted socialist. But he does not see the answer to inequality and injustice in political terms. He judges the world from his own experience, and for him class divisions are less important in day-to-day relations than human qualities and conflicts in personality. He refuses to join a trade union because he resents their 'dictatorship'. He calls himself left-wing but he judges his employers on their individual merits. The employer who spends his day drinking – and he had one who got through ten litres of wine a day – is worthy of respect if he is a skilled craftsman in his sober moments; the employer who is tyrannized by his mistress is deserving of sympathy. Ambition for power and wealth he looks upon as a disease: 'The more worthless a chap is,' he says, 'the more he tries to push himself forward.' He has no wish to change places with his boss. This is partly because, having closely studied those he has worked for, he is very conscious of the troubles and worries from which each of them suffered; none could rival his own basic happiness. It is partly also because he has never been interested by the profit or business side of his work; he virtually ran the firm he worked for, but never felt the need to have the title as well as the reality of independence. He does not see the answer to the horrors of industrialism, which forces people to do boring jobs, in turning everyone into an artisan. He says people's tastes and skills are too varied for that to be possible.

His moderation and modesty do not mean that he has no strong feelings. Gaston always had to save and scrape to make ends meet, to feed and clothe his children. His savings were lost in the war, and he had to start all over again. The final tragic reward of his labour was to be sacked by an irascible employer, though he was able to use his compensation to buy his flat. His stoicism has been a mixture of realism and a sense of his own dignity, not of a thick skin; he is tolerant because he does not wish to be interfered with himself. He has behaved in the way he has thought was right. He courted his wife for three years without presuming so much as to touch her; when he took her to the theatre he also paid for her sister to go along as a chaperone. His life has been one of propriety, sacrifice and thrift. His sense of decency is such that one day, when he thought he had let a friend down badly, he attempted suicide. That is how his story – of a kind usually lived in obscurity – became public.

CRAFTSMEN by Fred:
THE MIRROR REPAIRER

Good heavens!
What's it doing?

Ah! Someone
at the door.

I've come
about the
mirror.

It worked very
well until this
morning. It's
an old model but
I'm fond of it.

I understand:
we all get
attached to
things.

Ah! Fantastic:
it's working
again!

We'll soon put
that right.

But you
haven't
mended it
at all!

I must have
pushed too
hard: now
it's fast.

A 'small man' in the past has not necessarily been one who submits meekly to the great. Gérard Nicoud, who founded a vigorous shopkeepers' union, has, on the contrary, adopted the image of a creator of physical and verbal violence, and has been to prison several times. He is the sixth son of a Marseille tram driver, who started work at fifteen as a waiter, learning his oratory in front of the juke boxes and pinball machines. The great moment of his life was when he bought the small village café at La Batie-Montgascon, near Lyon: he felt a new man. 'This is mine,' he said repeatedly to himself, 'and I am in charge of it all.' But, he says, he discovered that one has to fight to keep one's property, to resist the tax man − he calls VAT the Voracious Administration Tax − to protest against the government treating the artisan like a gangster. This kind of anarchism, which led him to invade a taxman's offices and throw all his papers into disorder, strikes a chord of ambivalent sympathy in many sections of society.

The baker, it may be thought, will be the last of the small men to vanish, inasmuch as the French cannot envisage life without their delicious baguette of bread; but that baguette is made at heavy cost in human terms. Jean Marq gets up at three in the morning to bake bread till half past one; he eats his lunch, has a siesta till half past four, and then returns to bake again till seven. He takes off only one-and-a-half days a week. Now in his early forties, he expects to retire at fifty-five, because he doubts whether he could work so hard beyond that age. Meanwhile, he earns a good living; he has bought a country cottage, where he indulges his passion for fishing. He likes his job; he has been at it for eighteen years; he values being his own master, saying that he can work when he likes, even though, in fact, the pressure to produce is relentless. He is stimulated by contact with his clients and by the need to satisfy them. It is not just bread that customers ask for, but bread that is 'well baked', or not too hard, or not too soft, just as though it is a steak they are ordering. He is willing to sell even a quarter of a small loaf to those who ask for it. He alters the kinds of cakes he makes as fashions change: no one asks for 'love apples' any more, an almond cake he once produced with pride. His wife, who serves in the shop, is quite addicted to the incessant file of customers and to the clinking of the coins; she is positive that she would be lost without the constant bustle. Marq's father was a baker too, but his children will not follow him. 'Children see the disadvantages of their parent's job, and not those of others,' he explains, but without bitterness: his eldest is a refrigeration technician, perhaps because the father often points out how exhausting it is to work in high temperatures by his basement ovens. There are bakers who still work a six-day week. Marq says it is hard competing against the supermarkets, 'but we can hold our own if we work more than others.'

However, it is not just the ancient trades that keep the small man alive. The number of small shops has increased dramatically in recent years with a new kind of enthusiast. The small man today is no longer represented by the fat man in a beret lamenting a vanished past: he is as likely to be a chic middle-class woman with an interior decorating business, or a furniture shop, or an intellectual with a bookstore that is as much a meeting place for conversation as a shop. Shopkeeping used to be the classic way of escape for those anxious to move out of the working class into the bourgeoisie. Now the advocates of the small shop believe there is no stopping the trend towards large retail chains where a clear price advantage can be offered, but the small shop can survive by doing those things that it can do better than large shops, producing and selling goods where personal attention, service and quality are appreciated, and by establishing a relationship of confidence with the customer that goes beyond traditional profiteering.

It is difficult to find people who have nothing to complain about. Monsieur Lupis, the owner of the newspaper and stationery shop in Colomiers (Haute Garonne), a small, chirpy, birdlike figure, is as near as I got to such a man. He lives in a new suburb where the municipality has avoided property speculation by buying up most of the land; there is free public transport. Monsieur Lupis is a member of the municipal council and is celebrated for always being in a good humour, always willing to crack a joke. Perhaps he could flower only in such a peaceful community; he hates cities; he has been to Paris only twice in his life and would never live there: 'it is too animated.' He rarely goes to Toulouse, preferring little towns like Albi and

Montauban; he has no wish to visit Marseille. His attitude is not based on ignorance of the delights of urban civilization, for he has travelled round the world; he had just returned from a fortnight's visit to America; he has at different times been as far as Australia, Tahiti and Hong Kong; he has travelled in Spain, Switzerland, Germany, Britain.

All this has confirmed Lupis in his pleasure that he is a Frenchman. What struck him about the United States was the size of everything, the number of people, the impression of power, everything being ten times bigger than it was at home. But even more he was struck by American nationalism. Unwittingly he accused Americans of precisely the same defects that Americans attack Frenchmen for. 'There are American flags everywhere. Americans are not like us, they are proud, though I was well received by them. They have a sense of their power, they want to show it off, they are proud that they do not hide their secrets, as at Cape Kennedy; at Disneyworld they constantly say you can find this only in the USA. America comes first for them.' He was not complaining, however: 'I like this, because I would like the French to be the same, to be proud of their country. I personally hate it when the French football team is beaten, particularly when they haven't put up a good fight. I am all for fraternity between peoples, but when I defend something, I defend it unto death. If I had to defend my country by arms, I would.' He has excellent relations with the foreigners who patronize his shop, though he finds the Germans colder than the English. 'I have not forgotten the war: I had no deaths in my family, but the Germans' atrocities I cannot forget. I don't blame the present generation. But I fear that it is not impossible for it to happen again.' Lupis believes you can be proud without being bossy. He rejects sayings like 'a Breton is worth two Gascons.' He draws the line at regional nationalisms. 'France should be a coherent entity. I am a Frenchman above all.' He regards local loyalties only as agreeable settings for folklore and dancing which he enjoys, and for regional dishes such as Cassoulet Toulousain.

Personally, Monsieur Lupis is not proud. He left school at sixteen. He was the son of a butcher, he did not like studying, and preferred to follow in his father's footsteps. He married at twenty. He became a lorry driver, then worked in newspaper distribution for Hachette. At thirty-two he set up his own business. He does not aspire to being a bookseller also, the next step up, because 'you need to study for that. I cannot discuss books with you. I will admit it, I know nothing about them. I do not read books, except for the occasional detective story; I am not ashamed to say it. Nor to ask questions: I am not timid.' But egalitarian socialist though he is, Monsieur Lupis has an old-world modesty. 'I know many people are superior to me; I recognize the limits of my education. I am very respectful of

Chaval

Self-made man

teachers. For example, I cannot call Monsieur Gillard, the headmaster, by his first name, because he is superior to me. Even when talking to my wife, I refer to him as Monsieur Gillard. It is not a question of profession or culture, but the impression I have that a person is superior to me. Thus I could not *tutoyer* Mitterrand: I say the Queen of England, not Elizabeth. I respect those who have reached their position through work.' This is not an acceptance of hierarchy, but a respect for individual dignity. However, he does not respect

Monsieur Giscard. Would he call him Monsieur? 'If I met him in the street I would call him Monsieur if he shook my hand.' Socialism will not produce equality, because intelligence is unequally distributed, but 'the intelligent should not claim that they are better, they should think about those less well endowed. I have never envied the wealth of any man. I am not jealous of the rich. I am pleased when others win the lottery.' If he won the lottery, he would not invest it, but would use it to make as many people as possible happy, his children first of all. 'I am not miserly.' He dislikes rich men who think only of themselves. 'But if a man does not try to squash me, I do not hold it against him that he is rich.' Personally he does not want to buy a nicer car. He does not like the kind of life that film stars live: 'I hate anything taken to extremes.' That does not prevent him from inviting film stars to the town, in his capacity as its organizer of festivities. He collected an enormous sum to pay Julio Iglesias to come and sing there, because that was what people wanted. Monsieur Lupis is interested not in monetary profit, but in doing service to others, in having friends.

'I do not like to be alone.' That is the key to his life. 'I fear solitude. I am lost without others. Alone, I get bored, I need to talk. I have no hobbies; I never watch television. Other people are not like me because they have personal interests to occupy them, but I always like being with people.' He closes his shop only on Sunday afternoon, and he uses that to go to a sporting match. 'I have a strong family feeling which is very important; we take our holidays as a family. I take part in the administration of the town, because I like the human contacts. I am a shopkeeper because I like being of service, I try hard to please.' And in return, he enjoys having the respect of his clients; he has 'hundreds of friends', though only four or six really close ones, with whom he can discuss 'sensitive or serious matters', but he confides in others quite easily. When others 'do harm' to him, he will not do harm back; he just ignores them. 'I try to do no harm to anyone.' Have not the psychologists discovered that angry people are often just trying to conceal their timidity? Monsieur Lupis says he is self-confident, and that is why he is perfectly content that people should crack jokes at his expense. Joking is the permanent accompaniment of his existence. He was a practical joker at school; he has always loved telling stories; and every bit of business he likes to complete with a pleasantry. 'I say: I do things seriously, but I do not take them seriously.' That obviously is only half true. Monsieur Lupis' jokes are the oil in the town's machinery, and he knows pretty clearly how he wants that machinery to turn. When he goes to church (he is a 'non-practising believer') he takes that seriously, though he jokes when he comes out. Monsieur Lupis is not as universally trusting as he likes to make out: 'Normally, I am suspicious when people question me, but since you were presented to me by Monsieur Gillard, the headmaster . . .' Monsieur Lupis may not be the perfectly happy man, and the psychoanalysts would undoubtedly find repressed worries beneath his smiles, and his non-stop talk, but he at any rate creates an impression of gaiety, and his town values him because of that.

16

How to be friends with a peasant

Peasants are searching for new ways to survive also. For René Cadel, who owns fifty acres at Tornac, in the Cevennes, his work is three crusades in one. Since the age of fourteen his absorbing interest has been the improvement of the quality of wine and the invention of new liqueurs from different fruits, 'to make natural drinks which come directly from the earth'. That is his passion, wine is his life, and all the labour he lavishes on his vineyards gives him a deep satisfaction. All the more so, since helping to improve the quality of the local wine has made it possible for young people to stay on the land, to continue in the traditions of their fathers: every recruit represents a victory against the 'imbecile legislation of governments' and the inexorable forces of economics. For twenty-seven years he has been president of the wine cooperative: that has not only enabled small growers to survive, but it also expresses the moral inspiration behind his own life. 'Cooperation is a notion that we have received from the Russians,' he says, but he also adds that it is the practical application of Christianity (he is a devout Protestant). 'To make machines improve the lot of my neighbour' is one side of it; 'to develop a friendly spirit among the cooperators' is the other. Few people would have joined him had he not been able to prove that he could increase their income. But a most important additional reward for him has been the innovation of selling directly to the consumer, cutting out the middle man. If you come to his premises, you can have a bottle for almost one-third of what it costs in the shops. He has built up a clientele of regular customers who have become friends: the delivery of wine is always accompanied by feasting in the recipient's house, an exchange of gifts, a sense of common achievement. He is very proud that his wine is pure, with no falsification. He is an intensely moral man, for whom personal relations are almost a religious rite. He does not seem to know what envy is, nor anger. He admires simplicity.

His wife, who is the daughter of a wine-grower too, has no hesitation in saying she likes the life they have led together for forty years, in the same house: 'I am very content. There are days when I grumble a bit,' she says, 'but that is when I don't have time to do the things that need to be done at home.' She is as conscientious about tidiness, cleanliness and the proper entertainment of guests as he is about attending his never-ending meetings. Their son has become a chemist at a nearby wine research institute, where he has just invented a new method of making non-alcoholic grape juice, with an unprecedented flavour, which means that there is at last a soft drink that is not too sweet, and that can retain the full aroma and taste of the grape. When I spoke to Rémy Pech in Toulouse, he felt that anyone who did not drink wine with his meals was throwing his friends out of work. Here was an attempt to find a market beyond the alcohol drinkers.

By contrast, it is the pleasure of 'fighting' that keeps Philippe Yverneau going on his farm of about a thousand acres of cereals, beet and pulse near Laon (Aisne). 'I have always liked fighting against something, from my earliest days.' He was hopeless at school, and was sent from crammer to crammer in a vain attempt to get him through examinations. Finally his parents gave up the struggle to make something of him, and agreed to his wish to go to an agricultural school. He believed it was his vocation to be a farmer. His ancestors had acquired the farm five generations back, when it was confiscated from the Church at the time of the Revolution; but the land had been gradually divided into numerous small plots as succeeding generations split it up among their heirs. So Yverneau inherited less than twenty acres, which is why his family was so keen for him to succeed in some other career. He was only eighteen at the end of World War II – which left the family in complete disarray, for reasons which he prefers not to explain: his father went into early retirement. He seems to have started adult life with a chip on his shoulder and a load of debt, which have stimulated him to enormous energy. He decided a totally new attitude to agriculture was needed. 'Formerly farmers worked essentially in order to acquire land. Nowadays that is almost impossible, because to be competitive they cannot invest in both land and equipment. I opted for the modernization of equipment, completely changing the way we farmed.' He has rented his thousand acres from his numerous cousins (with whom he has had occasional mighty rows when they have sold off bits to raise capital for themselves). What he owns instead of land is five tractors and two combine harvesters. He paid off his debts by producing peas and beans which he was able to sell for canning to a neighbouring factory.

He is proud of having proved himself, financially, professionally and socially. He works hard to win the good opinion of his community. He has got himself elected mayor, where he 'fights' also to win people jobs and their rights, 'to help those who have not had the luck that I have had'. He repeats that he had 'enormous difficulties in setting myself up, and I had to fight really hard.' His main battle at the moment is to get a new canning factory established locally. The old one was closed down by the large firm that owned it: again, he is too cautious to say why that happened, he does not want to make any accusations. But he now sees that the farmers must have their own factory. He has made agriculture a business, and he regards himself as the head of a business: his labourers say they just do what they are told; there is no 'cooperation' here. He starts work at six every morning, because he has a lot of paper work to do, and he spends Saturday and most of Sunday in his office; he never takes a holiday; his wife takes the children away for a few days in summer. He is content with his dogs, his hunting and riding as his relaxation. He and René Cadel are transforming farm life in diametrically opposed ways.

The peasant has for centuries been an outcast, an underdog, considered to incarnate boorishness, ignorance, greed, brutality and every other vice that contrasts with the charms and graces of urbanity, or civilization, that townsmen were supposed to have. Townsmen imagined he was silent, isolated and resigned; they have pictured him as a relic of a vanished way of life. But an essential part of the peasant's way of life has been rebellion. The peasant was always oppressed and periodically he rose up in revolt against his masters. His recent invasions of the cities, blocking the roads with his tractors, raising barricades with artichokes or potatoes, even crossing to England to protest against our cheap food policy, are all very much in character. He was deeply moved when television dramatized a novel written by a peasant, entitled *Jacquou le Croquant*; the hero is an orphaned agricultural labourer who leads a riot against the nobleman's castle. The story is set in the mid-nineteenth century, but it was not all that different from the attack a group of

Piem

700 peasants from Normandy launched in 1972 on the actor Jean Gabin. Gabin had become a successful farmer with over 600 acres. They broke into his farmhouse at four o'clock in the morning, demanding with threats that he sell off his land: it was unfair, they said, that one man should have so much. In vain did Gabin plead that he had earned his property by hard labour: eventually he agreed to rent out half of it.

The peasants' fight has always been, first of all, for more land. They have never had enough. The average size of a French farm is one-third that of an English one. A century ago peasants constituted over half the French nation: in despair of being able to have a farm of their own big enough to provide a living, generation after generation have left for the cities. Today there are only one-and-a-half million farms left, the peasants form less than a tenth of the population (7%) and yet they still fight with the same voracity for the land and they still feel they do not have enough. In the Low Countries, where the land available is strictly limited, a highly intensive agriculture has been developed. The French do not think in quite the same terms. Land is not only a living, it is also prestige and security, or the illusion of security. The majority are not content to rent it: they demand absolute ownership of it. Even the communists among them believe in private property. Only two-fifths of the land is tenanted. It is so hard to find farms to rent that premiums of up to one-half their purchase price are willingly paid to obtain a tenancy. The peasants bitterly resent the townsmen who compete against them on the land market, for land has always been an investment, its price rises every year; it is like the gold Napoleon coin, which is hoarded so possessively that it costs far more than ordinary gold bars. Land is in fact much cheaper than in other continental countries (roughly half what it costs in Germany), for France is the least crowded of European nations. But only a fifth of French soil is considered to be of high quality; the competition is intense to round off one's farm, with the hope that a little more will make all the difference to one's prosperity. This is an ambition that apparently can never be fully achieved.

The peasants have a second ambition which is theoretically more attainable but has proved distressingly elusive. They wish to catch up with the industrial workers, to earn as much as them. They have accordingly over the last twenty years quad-rupled their productivity. This has had a dramatic effect on their living standards, particularly in previously backward regions like Brittany, where families have jumped in one step from primitive to highly advanced methods. In 1948 the four Nicolas brothers scratched a bare living from their fifty acres in Pluzunet; three of them remained bachelors so as not to jeopar-dize the viability of their inheritance, for the law would have otherwise required them to divide it equally between them into uneconomical units. They farmed as their forebears had always done: they managed to keep only six cows, three calves and three bony horses. But when the son took over, the state offered him a massive loan at low interest, and even a subsidy to modernize. He went into egg production with 1000 hens, a profitable business at the time; he bought a tractor, built new stables, and thanks to the intensive cultivation of feedstuffs, he was able to keep fifty-eight milking cows, which gave him a very decent living.

But all this kind of initiative has remained inadequate. The effect of higher agricultural productivity has been to lower the prices farmers get. The peasants have always been outwitted by the townsmen who have repeatedly devalued the harvest. Though peasant incomes have risen impressively, those of industrial workers have risen in the same proportions, so the peasants still earn about one-third less, as they have for many decades. This is why the peasants are cross even in their triumphs. Their frustration is embittered by the knowledge that the highest profits are made by the industry which trans-forms agricultural produce into prepared foods – cheap wheat into expensive biscuits; an industry with employs half-a-million people and ranks, for value added, as the second indus-try in France (after machines). They feel that the high food prices the consumer complains about should not be blamed on them; but they know that they are blamed. The productivity of farmers in the Paris region and in the North is high, but there are more farmers who are still not efficient. France uses only half the amount of fertiliser used in the Netherlands; its cows on average produce only two-thirds of the milk that Dutch cows do. Its output of potatoes per acre is only about 60% of the

Dutch output. It is in wheat that it does best, being only marginally below the Netherlands but ahead of both Germany and Britain.

So the paradox is that France has become one of the world's largest exporters of food – the third largest producer of milk after Russia and the United States, the fourth largest of meat and of barley, and the seventh of cereals – but its farmers are constantly complaining. Farmers always complain, it is part of the natural order to do so, but in France about a fifth of them have refused or not thought it worth while to modernize. It is they who have perpetuated the image of farmers as being impoverished. The range of incomes among farmers is in reality extremely wide, wider than in industry; some earn forty times as much as others; about a quarter enjoy what are regarded as high incomes by French standards, but a quarter are well below the poverty line. The poor are to be found in most regions, but they are concentrated in a frightening way in the nine departments whose population has been falling steadily since the war; departments like the Creuse, which is becoming desolate through emigration. The sense of being unloved is nurtured by the fact that farmers are overwhelmingly farmers' sons: there are few outsiders who feel this is a job they would like to do. And of farmers' sons, only a quarter stay on the land.

What then keeps a peasant going? Above all else, he likes being his own master. Michel Debatisse, the leading post-war peasant trade unionist (though as you would expect there are, in fact, four different unions and altogether about a hundred organizations representing agriculture, each jealous of its independence), said the new peasant's motto is Efficiency and Liberty. The two, of course, do not always necessarily go together. The great temptation is to obtain security by entering into contracts with the giant food-processing companies, which guarantee to take one's produce, but which also impose stringent controls on one's methods and activities. Mass-producing tomatoes for firms like Barbier-Dauphin, or strawberries for Lenzbourg, transforms the peasant's life; his standard of living goes up and his house is modernized, but he has less time to waste, financial questions become more complex, he is forced to borrow; he worries more. 'One does not become happier . . . It may not be because of the contrast, perhaps it is simply that life has changed. But now one must produce more to earn less for each item.' Those who avoid, or drop out of the contracts system are told, 'You are the last of the free men.'

Women often benefit from the contract system, because it may free them to pursue their own careers. Those who reject it as slavery are often content to accept a lower standard of living as a price worth paying. The supposedly avaricious peasant can also be surprisingly immune to materialism. 'We have the good fortune to live in natural surroundings, which so many people envy us. There are the dawns and the sunsets, the mornings and the evenings, which are not all bad, the smells, the colours, and all the other riches we enjoy each day. Being one's own master means one is willing to work longer hours than others and to be worse paid. The work and the weather are hard constraints, but one does not think of rebelling against them because they are not imposed by men and that is important.'

The peasant has so far been extraordinarily successful in his ambition not only to remain independent of state control but also somehow to milk the state at the same time. He has long paid less taxes than any one else, indeed has often succeeded in paying no taxes at all. On the contrary, he is subsidized by the state to the tune of about £1000 per head per annum. He has become Europe's feudal lord or ancestral spirit, to whom everybody in the Common Market pays a humble tribute. That is no mean revenge. But he does not intend to play the part for ever. He insists that he is not overproducing, for the world's population is growing ceaselessly, and the poor countries will soon be very grateful for the food he grows. He sees France in the role of the world's granary. Looking further ahead, he predicts the salvation of agriculture through the production of energy from plants as well as the introduction of less wasteful crops. He is likely to have allies, for the countryside is being repopulated by people who are tired of the cities. Half of France's townspeople would prefer to live in the country; only 5% of those who live in the country would like to move to a city. The average countryman is already more often than not, not a peasant at all; that is likely to be increasingly the case in the future.

Part Four

How to appreciate their taste

17

How to eat properly

If you want a good French meal, you do not normally think of going to Hollywood for it. But that is where Patrick Terrail has his restaurant and it tells you something that may not immediately occur to you while dining in Paris. Patrick Terrail is descended from a long line of Parisian hoteliers and restaurateurs, who have never hesitated to borrow new ideas wherever they could find them. His grandfather, who bought the Paris Tour d'Argent, transferred it to its rooftop position after a visit to the United States, where he was fascinated by the Rainbow Room on top of the Rockefeller Center; his uncle, who now owns it, married the daughter of the film-maker Jack Warner, and has turned restaurant keeping almost into show business. Patrick Terrail went to America as a youth to escape his family: he attended the Cornell Hotel and Restaurant Management School, which has emphasized the organizational aspects of the arts of hospitality, and has encouraged restaurant keepers to spend vast sums on comfort and on decoration. He put these ideas into practice working for Restaurant Associates, who coined the phrase 'Dining as an Experience'. All this may seem to take one far from the cosy family atmosphere of the French bistro; but to eat at *Ma Maison* in Hollywood, which he then established, you have to know someone who has eaten there before: it is not in the telephone directory. Patrick Terrail gave his restaurant that name because he regards each diner as a guest, and the meal both as a show and a provocation, like attending a party. 'I put on two shows a day, I want people to enjoy the show and participate in it.' He has to be more than a cook: it is a whole feast, a salon of conversation, that he imagines he is creating. But he is also very much an inventive cook: he claims rabbit is going to be the food of the future, and has created a quite remarkable new dish from it; he predicts there will soon be more turkey instead of veal; he has bred a new duck combining the French mallard with the Pekin duck; he has naturalized the French haricot bean in Mexico, and created a new goat cheese factory in northern California, run by a French expatriate; he has a fantasy that American wine will invade Britanny one day. This is not quite the atmosphere of Paris, even if Orson Welles lunches here every day; but it is after all by slightly outrageous amalgams that cooks keep the palate hungry. He started his restaurant when he had only $2000: he gave a dinner party in his house and raised $35,000 to support him, with Gene Kelly as the first investor. Now he proudly drives around in a 1965 Bentley and indulges his family passion for buying antiques. He has opened a croissant counter in Beverley Hills, which easily outdoes the Americanized croissants now offered in Paris. The purists of Paris gastronomy may feel the same discomfort at this story as they did when the Three Provençal Brothers first moved up among them in the eight-eenth century (when Provençal food used to be considered fit only for the poor). But 'to create a new dish is much more important than to discover a new star,' says Terrail. That spirit, rather than the endless reproduction of the old recipes, is the very essence of France's culinary tradition.

Once upon a time, the Swiss produced the best watches, the Germans made the best cameras and every rich man aspired to have a French cook. For most of this century, the most expensive hotels all over the world have felt obliged to offer French food, or a parody of it, and at least a menu in French. But the supremacy of French cooking is threatened. The mistake the French made was to export expensive food, that is, for a minority. The Chinese have countered by appealing to the hungry student. Since every nation has a fundamental hostility to foreign food, the Chinese were able to overcome resistance by giving the masses a good reason for accepting their food: they made it cheap. The result is that today in Britain there are eight times as many Chinese restaurants as there are French ones[1] and

[1] 4000 Chinese restaurants, 2000 Indian and Pakistani, 1500 Italian, 1200 Greek and Turkish and 500 French.

in the United States the Chinese also lead the field (in equality with the Italians). Simple French peasant food has not entered the homes of the masses: Heinz Baked Beans has been preferred to Cassoulet Toulousain and the Americans have mastered the fast food business. The refrain in every French discussion of their attitudes to foreigners is their inability to tolerate foreign cooking. Food isolates the French almost as much as their language. That would not be serious if France were at least certain of remaining a refuge for good food. But that is in doubt.

There are fashions in food as there are in clothes, and no style can be certain of continuing to please for ever. There are certainly those, like the *Figaro*'s food expert, James de Coquet, who claim that the purpose of cooking is to give a sense of security, and that change is the last thing needed; but against him people like Gault and Millau, who popularized the Nouvelle Cuisine, demand surprise and excitement. France has recently renewed its claim to leadership in cooking by carrying out a very subtle marriage with the Japanese, vast numbers of whom have come to study cooking in France, and the Nouvelle Cuisine is in part the result. The largest cookery school in the world is now in Japan, run in partnership with Bocuse, who was fascinated by the Japanese meticulous care in their cooking, their multiplicity of small quantities, their stress on presentation. Bocuse now says that he is tired of the Nouvelle Cuisine, that there is a 'fundamental difference' between Japanese and French cooking, ('the former is obsessed with texture and the latter with the aroma') and he is planning to return to the classics. It is not surprising that the man he admires more than any other is a designer of clothes: 'what would give me most pleasure is that I should be called the Yves Saint-Laurent of the kitchen.' It is no accident that cooks have a star system like the couturiers and that there should be only eighteen who have the supreme accolade of three stars in Michelin's guide. Bocuse is as much a showman as a cook. He compares his meals to opera: 'I like the lights of the opera, the decor, the choirs.' He regards 'magic' as the most important ingredient in a recipe. He therefore refuses to cook by electricity, saying he needs the magic of gas and the spit. He presents eating as a feast, part of the art of enjoying life to the full; he abhors meals conceived as a

Quino

slimming diet; condemning that kind of food as 'an opera without an orchestra'. Cooking is more than a game for him: 'I hate to lose.' He claims that his showmanship conceals a timid nature: 'I never know where to put my hands. Except with women.' To be a male cook means to take risks: he says even the greatest of women cooks, like La Mère Brazier, stuck to simple, well-tried formulae. His theatricality of course is highly expensive: he employs over fifty people in his restaurant, which means that he needs to charge 150 francs[1] to cover his costs, per person, even before he starts serving any food. That is why he travels around the world, cooking occasional dinners in New York or Tokyo. Haute cuisine is a fragile luxury, like haute couture, which can barely survive in a world that wants to economize. Increasingly the organizational part of it is becoming as important as the actual cooking. The French cuisine cannot simply rest on its laurels.

[1] £15.00 or $30.

Just as the French couturier aims to show off fine fabrics to their best advantage, so the French master cook's first principle is to show off the fresh, succulent, perfectly ripe ingredients that he uses, to draw out and enhance the natural taste of food. Good ingredients are the basis of French cooking, which means accepting the variations imposed by the seasons: it is impossible to offer the same thing all the year round. Each major item served must keep its own flavour, but the distinctive skill comes from the ingenious methods used to achieve this. Thus sea bass in pastry stuffed with lobster mousse is not designed to be a complex concoction: the pastry does not have to be eaten, for it is there to keep in the juices, and the stuffing can be ignored too, its purpose being to keep the fish moist. The distinctive mark of French cooking is not that it uses garlic, or snails, or frogs, which are regional specialities, nor that it drowns its meat in heavy sauces, which is how the naive attempt to give an illusion of luxury. The French admire not just ingenuity but also honesty in their food, which means that it is the variety of the produce they use that explains their success as much as their recipes. That is why Lyon remains a capital of gastronomy; it has long had the most varied supply of fresh produce at its doorstep. Paul Bocuse goes to market every day there and wanders about the stalls, as his forebears, all cooks since the seventeenth century, have always done before him; he usually composes his menu only when he sees what the market has to offer. But this tradition is threatened. It is much harder to cook good food in the same way in Paris, now that the Halles have been moved out. In Lyon every Monday morning the chefs of the city meet at the Café du Marché to exchange ideas; it is from such exchange and from competition that new dishes emerge. The French chef's skill involves knowing how foods vary in taste according to the season, assessing the strength of garlic, which depends on where it is grown and on the time of the year, and using condiments in their most characteristic forms, like preferring vanilla pods to essence. But the final result depends on individual inspiration, which is why cooking is more an art than a science.

This conflicts with the much more usual view of French cooking as being the most rigidly codified of all national cuisines. It is probable that more effort has been put into laying down laws and principles in the French kitchen than elsewhere, and foreign ideas of it are inevitably derived from the reading of recipe books. The French themselves give the title of master craftsman to cooks who pass examinations in which strict obedience to classical precepts is expected. There are megalomaniacs and pedagogues of the kitchen who try to lay down the law just as there are couturiers who try to dictate fashions. There are cooks who refuse to put salt-cellars on the tables of their restaurants, as in the famous three-star restaurant of Alain Chapel at Mionnay near Lyon, who says 'if you think you want a dish saltier, you would be wrong.' Escoffier wrote a cook book in 1912 which attempted to summarize in precise detail exactly how to cook several thousand different dishes, so that 'nothing would be left to chance.' His ideas have been slavishly imitated in the belief that they represent the right way of doing things, but, like all imitations, the point behind this precept has been lost. Escoffier was an entrepreneur in the hotel trade (an associate of César Ritz) and in charge of enormous kitchens with up to eighty cooks under him; he had to train people and he lived at a time when it was fashionable to think that science should govern all activity. But the rules were obviously not for himself. He insisted that a chef must not dictate to his customers; that he must respond continuously to changing fashions and moods; he quoted Carême as saying that 'in cooking there are no principles except the need to satisfy the person one is serving.'

The question whether French food is necessarily expensive is only part of the problem. Carême always insisted that the greatest enemy of good cooking was economy (that is why he liked working only for Rothschild). The Troisgros brothers, who run an elite restaurant, say they refuse even to think about money, because that is incompatible with art. However, grand chefs are not just cooks, but authors too. The ability to talk about food, to turn eating into a philosophy, is one of the marks of a great French cook, for French gastronomy has always been a dialogue: to eat alone is to have an incomplete meal, one needs to discuss what one eats. The cuisine of France has been created not just by cooks, but by gastronomes who have produced a whole literature out of their discussion of their meals; they have often been professional men, bankers, lawyers, doctors, priests, for whom eating has been their main hobby; the most dedicated have been bachelors who know no other love. Puritanism and modesty are incompatible with whole-hearted gastronomy, which is unashamedly dedicated to the enjoyment of sensuality, to the subtle analysis of man's appetites and to delight in their satisfaction. The restaurant has played an essential part in the creation of French cooking, because it has stimulated it by constant public discussion and competition. The great chefs are, therefore, 'inspired' not only by the food they find in the market, but also by their relations with their clientele; they come into the dining room after the meal to see the results. Charles Barrier, the three-star chef of Tours, says, 'When I cook, I imagine the pleasure I am going to give to someone – seeking pleasure for oneself is just masturbation.' Alain Chapel insists that he needs a response from his customer; he likes to meet every guest as they arrive so that each dish is perfect for each individual who eats it; cooking for him is 'an act of love'; since monotony is the great threat, he gets most pleasure from cooking dishes that are specially requested. His conclusion is that of an artist: 'What matters is that I should evolve and search for my truth.' He condemns all attempts to turn cooking into snobbery; he refuses to offer 'elaborate food'. The simplicity of the artist, however, is inevitably revealed as elaborate when it is analysed; and it is seldom capable of being imitated. That is why one is so often disappointed in restaurants. Genius cannot be consistent, and routine is its great enemy.

One of the myths the chefs perpetuate is that French food has always been marvellous, and that good cooking is achieved by going back to the old recipes and to traditional regional dishes. In fact, French cooking has altered enormously over the centuries. Two hundred years ago, the majority of French people ate an average of only 1700 calories a day, which puts them on the lowest level of Third World countries today, and animal products accounted for only 15% of these calories. Until 1900 three-quarters of their nourishment came from cereals. Traditionally the French peasant ate mainly bread, soup and porridge. The bread was not the refined baker's baguette of today but a heavy brown loaf made from all sorts of flours, often rancid. The soup was essentially vegetables in water; fat and even salt were a luxury. The porridge was wheat, maize or buckwheat boiled in milk or water. Meat only gradually entered their diet. Long slow simmering in one large pot was the basic method of cooking. Peasant food was thus either insipid, or too spiced, for it adhered to the medieval practice of mixing flavours indiscriminately when any flavour was available. The traditional French breakfast used to be soup, and many members of the working class today can still remember being brought up on it. The rich used to expand this breakfast by adding eggs, sausages, cheese, and wine or cider. The 'continental' breakfast is only a recent invention. Soup has remained a favourite evening meal, and is only gradually being replaced by modern alternatives. Frenchmen distinguish themselves by insisting on having some bread with every meal, but this is a pale relic of old

Dubout

habits, for their consumption of bread has almost halved in the last forty years, and women now eat only half the amount of bread men do. Some items have almost vanished from their tables, like swedes, turnips and pumpkins; they now eat only one-third of the dry pulses their parents used to and which were a staple item in traditional diet; their consumption of potatoes is falling. Today they are approximating more and more to the average rich western diet in the ingredients they consume. They are now the largest consumers of meat in Europe, on the way to catching up the Americans, though they have quite a long way to go still. Twenty years ago sociologists produced fancy theories to explain the significance of Americans and Britons eating far more sugar than the French, but since then the French have almost caught up, so that they now consume well over twice as much sugar as they did at the beginning of the century. The French are still different in that they drink relatively little fresh milk, making up for it with more cheese: two-and-a-half times as much as in Britain, twice as much fresh fruit, twice as much rice, one-third more vegetables than Britons eat: but in most other foods there is not much difference between the two countries. The general totals, however, conceal the fact that each region still retains a certain identity: northerners eat more vegetables than the rest of the population, the Mediterraneans more fruit, the south-west more cereals, while there is much less meat eaten in the centre-east. The west eats only half the amount of cheese that the Paris region does.

The effect of prosperity, the industrialization of food production and the growth of active leisure pursuits is now threatening yet more of their food habits, which are collapsing all the faster because they are quite recent. In 1960 the French spent 42% of their household budgets on food, but at the last census (1975) they were down to 24%. This is slightly more than one would expect, compared to other prospering nations who always spend less on food as they get richer, but there is undoubtedly a new tendency for the French to shift more of their spending from food to housing, following the American pattern. The sociologist Pierre Bourdieu has claimed that there is now a tension between two different attitudes to food. The old working-class and lower-middle-class attitude, he says, is that eating and drinking copiously is part of the art of the good life: when they have guests, they like above all to offer them plentiful helpings; they esteem above all the kind of cooking their mothers produced; they have little taste for experiment, inventiveness or exotic dishes; it is important to them that the meal should be eaten in a relaxed and friendly, jovial atmosphere, because eating is a feast. By contrast, the educated classes are cultivating a taste for light food, delicately and artistically prepared, with 'amusing' or 'interesting' dishes; their concern is not to fill their guests up, but to ensure they are not bored. The workers' priorities are seen in the budgets of those of them who become foremen: these spend as much money on food as managers, devoting a far larger proportion of their budget to pleasures of the table.

The division is not simply one of rich and poor. The commercial and industrial bourgeoisie share with the workers a taste for heavy and rich foods. The liberal professions and technocrats, for their part, use their money to buy rare and expensive vegetables or meats, but teachers, being poorer, seek originality by favouring cheap Italian or Chinese foods, or 'peasant' dishes. The favourite workers' dish is *gigot* (leg of lamb) and *pot au feu* (hotpot), or, as a special treat, *coq au vin*; they do not go in much for fish, which is considered too light − 'more suitable for women'. They maintain the idea that there are some foods for men and some for women. Escoffier said that he was successful because most of his dishes were designed for women and it is their lighter tastes and their concern with slimming that the upper classes have adopted. When Frenchmen were asked how much time and interest they devoted to cooking, 69% of workers said they liked cooking, but only 51% of the upper classes did; 59% of middle managers and 52% of small shopkeepers. How far these class distinctions still hold, how far they are too schematic, is unclear.

The well-to-do are making increasing use not only of food cooked by take-away shops (which, in contrast to America, sell very elaborate dishes, often of a high standard, providing a replacement for what the family cooks of the upper bourgeoisie once produced, and for dehydrated, frozen or prepared foods). Frozen food initially met with considerable resistance, just as tinned food had earlier, but it is making rapid advances, both among the wealthy and in the catering trade. The consumption of tinned and powdered soups more than doubled in the 1960s; and that of tinned vegetables has been rising at an annual rate of 11%. The growth of institutional food has been very marked. The Americans, watching keenly for opportunities to spread their mass-catering methods, found the fragmentation of the restaurant trade – each being an independent family establishment – an obstacle. But since 1960 when the first modern restaurant chain got going, the processed food industry began growing at the rate of 12% a year. Sixty per cent of the working population of the Paris region now eat in canteens. School meals are being 'rationalized', and in one city a central kitchen prepares 18,500 meals a day, which are then distributed among many primary schools. More meals are being eaten in canteens and fewer in restaurants.

In a poll, 44% thought that food was getting worse in France than it was five years ago and 42% thought there was no difference. But 50% thought that it was worse for the health, and that is a new dimension in food attitudes, which is creeping down from the rich to the poorer. There is a new sort of concern with dietetics, which means their foods are chosen for their supposed medical properties as much as for their taste. That need not create any difficulty, for the great chefs have always considered themselves amateur doctors, but industrialized hygiene has undoubtedly diminished the old piquancies and it is probably creating new tastes which will have to change again when plastic is no longer cheap. An enquiry among young people has revealed that they are not really worried by this: they are not generally much interested by food, in the gastronomic sense. In schools and universities, meals are often gobbled up in less than half an hour, or even less than twenty minutes. This should not be seen as decay; it is a revelation of another aspect of French civilization which has always remained unsung. Napoleon prided himself on being able to get through a meal in eighteen minutes, and his favourite dishes were, to the despair of his clever cooks, simple macaroni, vol au vent, fried and roast chicken, without garlic. Complaints about the awful food served by many French restaurants have been made by gourmets since they started writing, and one has no reason for disbelieving their criticism: the profit motive in public catering, lack of time and money at home, have always opposed the gourmet's idealizations.

Eating the French way, or rather in the gastronomic French way, involves honouring the mind and the body at the same time. It is not a question simply of eating certain dishes. The best French gastronomes do not claim that French cooking is superior to that of other nations — they see that there are wonderful dishes elsewhere — but they do claim that France has the most varied cuisine. The chauvinistic disdain that the French traveller likes to exhibit when visiting foreign countries, so that Michelin can find hardly any restaurants in the United States or Britain worthy of three stars, is balanced by a remarkable ability by their best chefs to naturalize foreign dishes, just as their couturiers redesign foreign clothes and give them a new flair in the process. Carême took Russian peasant cabbage soup for example, and raised it to amazing heights by ingenious modifications. It is the extra touches that count; but these extra touches are never quite the same. French onion soup can be prepared in at least a hundred different ways; there is endless discussion as to just how thick or liquid it should be; some bind it with egg yolks; some omit the cognac and add a drop of vinegar, some make it with milk instead of cheese, and no one can lay down that it should be Camembert, or Brie, or Roquefort that is the right cheese to use. The southerner's alternative to onion soup is probably *soupe au pistou*, but you can never be sure what it will taste like, because though it always contains basil and garlic, the choice of vegetables depends on the season and on the whim of the cook. Oxtail soup is common to France and Britain: the French claim to have invented it, and say that the British have allowed it to degenerate into a mere beef stock: the original version shows the French insistence on the subtle combination of tastes: it should include not just oxtail, but good lean beef, leeks, celery hearts, onions, carrots, butter, the white of egg, and sherry.

French food is indeed sometimes rich, when it is presented in its traditional bourgeois form, like *sole normande*, invented in 1837, which has a sauce of oysters, mussels, crayfish, prawns, truffles and champagne. But rich sauces are by no means a necessary characteristic. The Nouvelle Cuisine which is reacting against richness is not a new or eccentric invention: it is the reiteration of repeated efforts by chefs, over at least a century, to offer an alternative to the ostentatious, fantastic meals with which the rich have always liked to dazzle their guests. Bocuse is repeating what many have said before him. The overwhelming heavy sauces that expensive hotels pour over their food is a parody of French cooking: the source of French pride is that there are several hundred different sauces, which can express the cook's skill and individuality and give a meal its originality. One should not think of French cooking as simply consisting of dishes unique to that country; an equally effective criterion is the style with which it presents dishes it shares in common with other nations. Sausages and beans becomes Cassoulet in France, and that is different partly because so many more varieties of sausages have been developed in France. A stew of meat and vegetables becomes more interesting in France because things like smoked sausages and cloves are added to it. The supreme test is perhaps to be found in apple pie or tart, which have virtually the same ingredients in many countries; the difference comes from the skill, the presentation, the quality of the apples, the exact amount of cooking. What one must beware of is the commercialized French dishes, produced only for export, like crêpes suzette, which appears much more frequently on the menus of pretentious restaurants in New York than in Paris; it is supposed to have been invented in Monte Carlo for a Prince of Wales; it is considered too unimaginative to be eaten by a French person. It is this constant imaginative quest that explains the growth in the popularity of regional dishes, in which there is often as much new creation as genuine redis-covery of ancient traditions. The French ideal is thus dia-metrically opposed to that of the American processed food manufacturer, who guarantees that his food will always taste the same, but it is not as opposed to the American way of eating as it pretends. America has a similar richness of national traditions: it has a similar curiosity about combining and developing them: it is a question of degree.

One of the great barriers that stands in the way of the

appreciation of French food by Anglo-Saxon countries is the myth of garlic. To understand the passion for garlic that southern Frenchmen have, one must read the novelist Alphonse Daudet's hymn in praise of aïoli (garlic mayonnaise). It creates, he says, 'a sensation of well being and fullness, a euphoria . . . rather like that produced by opium, but without any danger'; the sensation improves if one lies down and has a siesta; it induces sentimentality provided both parties have eaten it. But there are French gastronomes who are suspicious of garlic and insist that it must be added only as a hint of a taste, that it is a failure if it overwhelms a dish: and in many dishes it is not present at all. Lyonnais cooking prides itself, for example, on rejection of 'Provencal exaggerations'. Garlic is, in fact, a relatively recent introduction into France. In the fourteenth century it was an essential ingredient of English food, and was used here far more frequently than in France or Italy. A French recipe book of the seventeenth century does not mention garlic a single time, whereas an English one of that time advises putting garlic even in ketchup. One is not breaking a French rule, either, if one eats one's cheese after one's pudding. The French used to do that themselves once, before they got to like cheese (which until about a century ago, was often regarded as a coarse peasant's food); at one time, moreover, their 'patisseries' were much more salted than sweet.

It is around the drinking of wine that supposedly unbreakable rules have been developed most, but that is fairly recent too; for those in the know, there are, of course, no hard and fast rules. Wine brings a special dimension to food, not only because it offers a whole additional spectrum of tastes to enrich a meal, but even more because it symbolizes conviviality and participation, bonhomie and joie de vivre. The element of discrimination is steadily increasing: the consumption of vin ordinaire is falling, and that of fine wines rising: the finer the wine, the greater the sense of festivity, as contrasted with the traditional workers' attitude that wine is a source of physical strength and a manual worker needed so much a day to keep him going. The scandals which break out from time to time, when expensive wine labels are shown to conceal all sorts of inferior mixtures, have never made much impression on the mysticism and rhetoric that traditionally accompanies its drinking.

In France one must not just eat and drink, but talk also. Talk stimulates new ideas about food. The survival of the French cuisine demands a constant effort of renewal. Those who practise it have to be inventors, not parodists. There is no knowing what French food will be like a century from now.

18

How to be chic

Loulou de la Falaise, the daughter of a French marquis, is in her mid-thirties: she is not obviously beautiful in the sense of having perfectly proportioned features, but she is undoubtedly elegant, striking, chic. That is the mystery which women of all countries try to penetrate: how do the French succeed in capturing this indefinable *chic*? Which of course raises other questions: since when have the French been chic, what proportion of them really are that, how long can they be expected to keep their reputation? Why has England, which in the 1960s compensated for its economic decadence by a sudden flowering of sartorial inventiveness, which created an aesthetic revolution by destroying the teenager's longing to look like her mother, been unable to wrest the leadership in the design of clothes from France?

The answer has nothing to do with nationality. Loulou's mother is the British designer Maxine de la Falaise; her aunts by marriage include the Hollywood star Gloria Swanson. At eighteen she married a British art historian; her husband now is Polish. She was sent to a finishing school in Switzerland and then to therapy with a New York psychiatrist. She is completely bilingual: 'I feel French in England and English in France, and both or either in New York. If you have no nationality you don't have to conform, you are free to be creative.' She is now one of the most influential clothes designers in Paris, the chief collaborator and inspirer of Yves Saint-Laurent. She has had no training in art. She dropped out of school at fifteen and led a 'gypsy life' for the next ten years working for galleries and fabric designers, in the company of artists and painters. She devoted her energies, even when she had little money. to 'making everything agreeable to the eye, to turning a pigsty into a wonderful house . . . I like to entertain, to enhance, to create comfort, to transform things, to make them gayer.' She was an unashamed exhibitionist: 'exhibitionism is like taking a sort of liberty with life: you announce that you are not going to be

Gourmelin

conservative, that you are going to break the rules. To be an exhibitionist when you are young is as natural as being a socialist.' For Loulou, fashion is a form of theatre: French women, she thinks, are 'all entrance, effect, brilliance'. But *chic* is clearly not just, or even mainly, courage mixed with intuition. It involves also the control of exhibitionism, suggestiveness more than statement, and Loulou condemns extravagant clothes as being the mark of frustrated designers. The English have often been more inventive than the French; they provide excellent ideas for the very young, but they seldom pursue their success into middle-aged clothes. One reason is undoubtedly that dressing up takes time, and making good clothes takes even more time, and it is only those who are willing to devote themselves to clothes with total dedication who can aspire to be stunning. That is easier to do in Paris than anywhere else in the world, because more skilled craftsmen dedicated to the study of luxury have congregated there over the past century than in any other city. It is the same sort of reason that makes Paris an intellectual capital: there are more people there stimulating each other to ever higher flights of fancy, or deeper explorations of profundity. Loulou's pleasure is to talk with 'the greatest artisans of the world', each highly specialized, who started as apprentices at the age of thirteen, who love their work with passion, so that the more difficult the task given them, the more they are excited, whom she does not simply order to create a new style but with whom she discusses her ideas and asks, What do you think? New ideas flow from their conversations, and amazing concoctions emerge in a spirit of great excitement. These artisans – whether they are makers of fake jewellery or skilled in a particular form of sewing – will work late three nights running if they believe they are making something sensational, and they are always talking about the marvellous things they created in the past. 'My role,' says Loulou, 'is to be a fairy.'

Paris remains supreme because there is a world shortage of fairies to wave wands in this way, and even more of people who are willing to listen to them. French leadership in female elegance rests on the reputation of twenty-three men and women, who constitute the Chamber of Parisian Couture, and who have won that reputation because they work in dream-like conditions. They dress, between them, only about 2000 of the world's richest women and most beautiful actresses. Guy Laroche, for example, serves only seventy-five clients a year. It is very personal attention that they are after, for it is an individual work of art that they are commissioned to produce, and they do not have to count the cost; they can use the most expensive materials. But Paris itself has never been rich enough to sustain such an amazing luxury industry. It has never sold more than a third of its clothes to French customers. French supremacy has been built on the appreciation of millionaires first from England, then from America, and now from all the world. French taste was the taste of the rich, of the international super-jet society. Paris was the place where you could buy the best clothes, but it was not necessarily Frenchmen who made these. The founder of the whole game was an Englishman, Worth. Today four of the twenty-three eminences are of Italian origin (Cardin, Carven, Ricci, Schiaparelli), one is Norwegian (Spook); Yves Saint-Laurent comes from Algiers, Hanae Mori from Japan, Paco Rabanne from Spain. In haute couture, Paris has always given expression to France's universalism, its capacity to speak across frontiers, to borrow and codify ideas from all over the world. It is through Paris that Russian boots and peasant smocks, English tweeds, Scottish kilts, Japanese slit skirts, Chinese jackets and American astronaut gear have been launched as international uniforms. Other cities may have dressmakers of equal skill, but none has such a large and demanding clientele.

Even the rich, however, are not rich enough to keep these artists alive. The couturiers have kept going only because they have devoted equal energy to creating international businesses to exploit their names. They sell not only clothes, but the trademark of their names, which they offer as synonyms of taste. They are advertisers as well as dressmakers. It is by a giant advertising campaign that Paris has almost monopolized the notion of elegant luxury. It began with perfume, and there are now couturiers (like Nina Ricci) who derive nine-tenths of their income from the sale of perfume. She at least manufactures her own (only two others do, Lanvin and Patou); her firm's manager is a perfumer, not a clothes designer. Most couturiers license others to use their names. Cardin's perfumes are made or sold by the American firm Shulton, Laroche's by L'Oréal, Christian Dior's by the Moët-Hennessy champagne and cognac conglomerate, Carven's by Scripps-Cochran (USA), Balmain's by Revlon. When Charles of the Ritz puts Yves Saint-Laurent's name on its perfume bottles instead of its own, it pays him 1%

for the privilege. So profitable is this that it has become worth owning a couture house just in order to use its name on a perfume: the idea is that if you cannot afford a Dior dress, the perfume will create the illusion that you have the next best thing. The process has been extended to an ever-increasing range of products, not just stockings and scarves, but even chocolates and sardines. The couturiers claim that they have 'approved' the products, when they have not actually designed them, but they are essentially lending appeal to what are often ordinary products sold at several times the normal price. It is not just 'French' taste that they offer but expensive taste.

To keep going, most of the couturiers have also become mass-producers of clothes, but of a 'luxury' kind. These account for one-fifth of the French market. Clothes sold with their labels are usually made by the same industrial processes as non-luxury clothes and often in the same factories. France's largest clothes manufacturer, Maurice Bidermann, sells his products under various names, which include not only Big Chief, Henry Thiery, Balsan, etc., but also Yves Saint-Laurent. One can never be sure whether French clothes are made in Hong Kong or Latin America, except for the uniforms of the police and Paris bus drivers, who, as a matter of principle, are guaranteed clothes made in France. Cardin was the first to sign up with a mass-producer: Brill makes 100,000 suits to his design a year. His rivals claim Cardin simply hands a model over to the manufacturer who reproduces it as best as he can, whereas someone like Ted Lapidus, who openly admits using mass-production, says he supervises the details of manufacture much more carefully. These luxury ready-made clothes are very different from the handmade originals they purport to copy, but that emerges only if one compares them side by side. The ready-to-wear boutiques were once places where couturiers could get rid of models which were too outrageous, but with mass-production they have come to sell essentially classical styles. The upper middle classes do not want outrageous clothes; to them elegance is synonymous with security; they expect the label on their clothes to guarantee their good taste.

The less well-heeled get their clothes not from couturiers but from stylists, whose heyday was in the 1960s, when they cut

across the old dividing line between rich and poor, and substituted one between young and old. The boutiques that sprang
up in the rue de Sèvres, led by Dorothée Bis and Emmanuelle
Khanh, were the equivalent of Biba and Mary Quant in
England. They were part of an international movement. But
French girls were about a decade behind English girls in their
liberation, and the miniskirt, for example was never as widely
accepted in France as in England. The stylists are as inhibited as
the couturiers by the refusal of their customers to be too
way-out; today the Parisian-Japanese Kenzo (who was financially backed in his early years by the Saudi Arabian Khashoggi)
remains on the fringes despite or because of his inventiveness.
The English could have captured the leadership in this level,
but according to Yves Saint-Laurent, they did not because they
failed to build up an adequate marketing organization. So the
French stylists now hold about one-fifth of the French clothes
market.

What is remarkable about France is that as much as half of the
clothes bought have the name of some more or less well-known
designer attached to them. Whereas England has traditionally
pursued the aim of low prices in clothes, and has allowed the
multiples to control two-thirds of all sales, France remains more
loyal to the little shop, even if it is more expensive: the chain
stores in France account for only one-third of sales. Nevertheless, the small shops often sell perfectly ordinary clothes, with
no real pretensions. Already 50% of French clothes fall into the
category of 'classic' clothes, that avoid all extremes, that are
moderate in price, in quality and in style, and have nothing
special about them. Mediocrity is the mark of half of the clothes
France buys and that must be seen as part of its taste too. These
are the clothes sold in the large department stores, in the chain
stores Prisunic, Monoprix and Inno. They are mass-produced by
firms whose names mean nothing to most people. Mail order is
growing faster than any other branch in the clothes business,
dominated by three large firms, particularly popular for underwear, household goods and the kind of clothes in which fashion
plays little part. There is a growing demand for really cheap
clothes, catered for by the new Tati chain, which once claimed
to dress a boy from head to foot for £10 (or $20). The French elite

has always denigrated the French masses for having no taste, and what is popular is, by some people, regarded as vulgar.

The little dressmakers round the corner have largely vanished: they were sweated labour. They were long seen as the explanation of French chic, in that they allowed ordinary women to have clothes made specially to flatter them. They were the democratic counterpart to haute couture. They showed how fashion has always meant something different in France and abroad; Christian Dior used to complain that American women attached much less importance to the small details of fit and finish than to the general effect; they were more attracted by variety and frequent change. In the eighteenth century, the French tradition was to have only a few types of dresses but 250 ways of garnishing them; in the nineteenth century vast industries grew up producing all sorts of trimmings and accoutrements, some of exquisite craftsmanship, which served to differentiate basically similar dresses. In the twentieth century Poiret caused havoc by making dresses depend on cut and colour rather than accessories, but the cult of the accessory has returned in subtler forms, and the prosperity of the couturiers depends in part on them. French elegance depended also on the love of fine materials, (and on the 'backward' textile industry of France, which used to specialize in producing small runs of unusual and expensive cloths, while England mastered mass-production). The survival of small firms, inefficient by American standards, is essential to the survival of the French idea of chic.

The French conception of taste is not threatened by the popularity of jeans, for they claim to cut jeans better than anyone else. The tradition of simple clothes is as old among them as their tradition of luxurious clothes. Mademoiselle Bertin, dressmaker to Queen Marie Antoinette, created as much stir by launching a new fashion for simplicity as by her expensive grandeur. Worth's two sons gave Poiret his start as a couturier in the 1890s, saying that they had always dressed the courts of Europe, but now their clients demanded not only grand clothes, but ordinary ones, too; they did not like making ordinary clothes personally and they wanted Poiret to take that task on for them. 'We are in the position of a great restaurant, in which we would not want to serve anything but truffles; but we

now need to create a bar offering potato chips.' Poiret showed
they too could be tasteful. The rebellion against the dictatorship
of fashion, which many considered to spell the doom of Paris'
leadership, will do no such thing, for it happens periodically:
under Napoleon III the magazines were saying the same thing,
that there was no longer any fashion, and women could wear
anything. But that is precisely what fashion originally meant,
not the right but the duty to wear anything, so long as it suited
one. Worth achieved his supremacy in fashion in the 1860s by
offering rich women clothes that fitted and suited them to
perfection; his revolution was only to replace the few traditional
'models', which dressmakers used to copy in a variety of cloths
and colours, by a far wider range of possibilities, so that his
clients could look even more unique. There was no intention
that fashions should change every year. Poiret, who dominated
fashion in the first half of the twentieth century (and who was
the first to lend his name to bags, shoes, etc. that he did not
make) was exasperated by the way American women tried to
create 'fashions' out of what he insisted were only 'suggestions',
because he saw his task as helping each person to look her best,
not designing one style which everyone had to squeeze in and
out of in the wild wish to keep up with fashion. He complained
that American women had the mentality of schoolgirls, which
they kept all their lives; their 'fashion sense' made them look
like a mass orphanage in uniform.

It was Christian Dior who created the present misapprehen-
sion of what Paris fashion means. His 'new look' made women
throughout the world suddenly throw away their old clothes,
bow to the supremacy of Paris, and adopt a universal style. But
Dior himself had no wish to carry out any such revolution. He
was a distinctly conservative man, descended from a long line of
fertilizer manufacturers; he had been a well-to-do dilettante
student at the School of Political Sciences, then a picture dealer,
until he and his family all went bankrupt in the great Depression. He entered dressmaking in desperation for any kind of job.
The novelty in his success was that he was backed by Marcel
Boussac, then head of France's largest textile business, and that
he had as his publicity manager an American, Harrison Elliott.
The new look was turned into an edict by an unprecedented

instrumentation of the press; and by Dior, under the pretence of not wishing to be influenced by commercial considerations, refusing to see any of his clients personally: he was simply the abstract designer. This was a real revolution, that a dressmaker should create a single female image and ignore the real people who have to fit into it. It is the consequent misinterpretation of what Paris stands for that has led to the efforts to dislodge it from its pedestal.

The confusion is best illustrated by the rise of Yves Saint-Laurent. He owes his success not only to his brilliant talents but also to the entrepreneurial skills of Pierre Bergé, who had previously promoted the painter Bernard Buffet, making him a rich international celebrity in a few years. Yves Saint-Laurent had come to Paris from Algiers at the age of seventeen; he had so impressed Dior with his drawings that he was at once offered a job, and when Dior died he succeeded to his empire, at the age of twenty-one. He was then called up into the army, where he had a nervous breakdown; let out two months later, he discovered that his place at Dior's had been usurped by Marc Bohan. He now started his own firm with Bergé's help and the financial backing first of J. Mack Robinson, a businessman from Atlanta, Georgia, then with that of the Lanvin-Charles of the Ritz group, which eventually became a subsidiary of the pharmaceutical firm C. R. Squibb. He has become the head of a great industrial enterprise with shops all over the world, with royalties from thirty-five different products sold under his label, and with himself built up into a star, like a film actor, through clever publicity.

Saint-Laurent presents himself as the incarnation of modernity, but there is a complex mixture of the old and the new in him. He offers himself as the representative of the young generation. 'I feel in sympathy with the young people of today,' he says. 'I feel they are right. They are really changing the world.' He claims to 'translate what youth wants'. He says he despises the traditional clients of haute couture; he hates the Jet Set and does not want to design simply for the rich. He sees himself as liberating fashion from the legacy of Dior, who imposed a style. Instead Saint-Laurent says what women today want is to find and assert their individuality, which means that they do not want to change every year (quite apart from the fact that they do not have the money to do so). This, however, is not new; the clients of haute couture always wanted to be different. Saint-Laurent is unwittingly going back to the nineteenth century in rejecting the enervating game of raised and lowered hemlines and in offering women a basic wardrobe of blouse, jacket, skirt or trousers and raincoat, in the basic colours, black, navy, white or beige, to which they can add accessories for variety and colour. He justifies this with a modernistic philosophy, by saying that he is trying to liberate women from their clothes, in the same way that men have been freed from having to think too much about theirs, and that men and women should have more or less the same kind of wardrobe. His hope is to design clothes that could be worn by every woman, and every man, in every walk of life; his one regret is that he did not invent blue jeans. His iconoclasm against haute couture is almost demagogic, but it conceals that he is a perpetuator of one aspect of it; he himself says he is against the tradition of Dior, but for the tradition of Chanel, of the famous little black dress. However, by becoming an industrialist, he is balancing himself dangerously on the knife edge between style and uniform, and eliminating the conspiracy between the individual and his or her tailor, which has always been a source of enrichment. The paradox is that he is perfectly well aware of these contradictions. He himself admits that the multiplication of objects bearing his label is self-destructive. 'A name is like a cigarette, the more one draws on it, the more it burns itself out and nothing remains but a stub.'

It is not enough to explain chic in terms of economics. There is also an element of magic that is part of the great designer's box of tricks. Yves Saint-Laurent admits he is 'ill at ease with people who talk and explain themselves too much', even if he has learnt to produce theories and epigrammatic pronouncements about fashion. When he first arrived in Paris, he was described as a 'precocious mute', and he still has not escaped from his loneliness, his frailty, his over-sensitivity. When he worked for Dior, he spoke little with him; when he works with Loulou de la Falaise, they trigger off ideas in each other by a sort of empathy. He retires from time to time, injured by his fame, and overwhelmed by the pressure to be constantly ingenious, to psychiatric clinics, where, however, he has also produced some of his cleverest creations. He is in the process of writing an autobiography which is a strange poetic incantation; his favourite reading is Proust; his hero in history is the mad king Ludwig of Bavaria; his preferred musician Wagner. His achievement in creating practical trousers for women is balanced by his search for the recreation of mystery in women, at least in their evening wear: 'women become beautiful when artifice begins'. He wants them behind masks of some kind, cosmetics, or clothes, because he loves the theatrical ritual they involve. He is a master not only of structured clothes but also of *flou*, clothes that look as though they are on the point of melting away, clothes that move: '*flou* is seduction'. His modernity is grounded in a curiosity about the past: he has found the perfection of *flou* in the 1926 designs of Viennet. And at the end of it all he says 'Chic is not in the dress but in the spirit.' That means self-confidence. How far does that self-confidence go?

The socialist President of the Republic dresses exactly like his aristocratic predecessor. The final stratagem in his election campaign, getting him a better, classic tailor, is regarded as having helped him win. All the members of his cabinet parade in dark suits; even the communist ones are indistinguishable. The limits of eccentricity, which one younger dandy minister dares display, involved no more than wearing a pullover instead of a waistcoat. Madame Mitterrand did not want to be dressed by a grand couturier, but the slightly less expensive one she found was no less traditional. Why is there not more enthusiasm for sartorial fantasy and invention? Paco Rabanne should know the answer. He made his name in the sixties for amazing dresses in metal and plastic: they are beautiful enough for one to be preserved in the Metropolitan Museum of New York. 'Every civilization needs a fool,' he says 'and I am that fool. I exist because there are too many conservative dress designers. Balmain represents the most traditionalist wing of fashion. Yves Saint-Laurent stands in the centre: he is very French in his moderation, his reasonableness: that is what France likes, the golden mean. My advanced ideas are on the limits of good taste, I stand on the frontier, I am a barrier against bad taste. I make clothes that create a scandal and I have no difficulty in selling them. But these represent only 15% of my output, the rest is more conventional.' The obstacle in his way is that 'we live in an Age of Cowardice; people are afraid to look conspicuous.' Designers have not been sufficiently creative either. The break will come when women start designing for men. Modern women's clothing has, to a considerable extent, been inspired by men's clothing, going back several centuries, but women have had no hand in creating that. The defect of male designers today is that they produce clothes for women in the abstract. The greatness of Coco Chanel was that she designed clothes to suit herself; she could not design for anyone else, and those who wore her fashions simply looked like her. Women, however, are 'narcissists'. Real innovation requires that narcissism should bear a multitude of new and varied fruits; narcissism is being strangled.

Paco Rabanne regards creativity as being instinctive, not the application of theories. 'I design unconsciously: I do not know what I will do: I am a medium.' He means that very seriously. He was trained as an architect and became a dress designer by accident, when his amateur interest in clothes (stimulated by his mother, who worked for Balenciaga) brought him sudden fame; the public assumed that his technical background explained his stunning aluminium dresses. He does indeed see his work as a form of research into materials and technique, but that does not explain what he does. His physical appearance is also a kind of mask for the man behind it. He has a heavy moustache and looks like Joseph Stalin, a resemblance he is proud of, and which he accentuates by wearing clothes which he says are modelled on those of the artisans of 1900, a kind of bush jacket suit with plenty of pockets; he wants to look like a craftsman. He was in fact introduced to Stalin when he was sixteen years old, by his father, an exiled general of the Spanish republican army. The meeting cured him of Marxism. Rabanne is not politically radical: he worships the Middle Ages. He believes in reincarnation: in a previous life he was a priest of Tutankhamun, and he can often tell what other people were in a former existence: he told me I was a reincarnation of the eighteenth-century philosopher Diderot. He considers that he has psychic powers. His vision of the world is not scientific but mystical, full of symbolism, portent and impending doom. 'Just as three knocks are needed in the theatre for the curtain to rise,' so he predicts a third world war as the necessary preliminary for the next phase of man's development, the Age of Leisure. 'Everyone thought science would save the world, but now they realize the Apocalypse is imminent.' Rabanne takes Saint-Laurent's taste for mystery to the point of mysticism.

He is conscious that the function of clothes is to conceal as much as to express a personality. That raises the question of who prefers to conceal and who to reveal herself, and Rabanne has a mystical theory about that. The masses, he says, desire renewal, a better life. 'Abnormal' people, like himself, and like other artists — for there is a profound harmony between the different arts — reply to their aspirations with creations of different kinds, poetry, music or clothes. The masses accept, digest and reject these and call for more. What they choose depends on how they feel about life; what they choose has a 'prophetic' effect, in that it also influences behaviour: the miniskirt, he says, was the sign of prosperity, black fingernails are the sign of complete despair, bouffant hairstyles spell the doom of political regimes. Rabanne is personally a living refutation of the idea that things are what they appear to be. He takes great care to keep his private life private. 'I am someone else, more difficult to know, more human, happier and unhappier than Rabanne. I can look at Rabanne with detachment. That is a form of protection.' The perfect elegance of his creations conceals doubt and insecurity; the key to creativity, he insists, is to question your assumptions all the time, always to doubt and to have the courage to doubt. Twice a year his fashion collections fill him with terror, because everything seems to be called into question. Is there symbolism in that also?

France may be the world's leader in female fashions, but that does not mean that French women are in the majority fashion-conscious, or necessarily elegant. It means first that France has a successful and long-established fashion industry, but also secondly that French women generally think they are above average in beauty. This is a self-confidence that is not the sort that stimulates them to be outrageous; it is related to their social status; only a quarter of the well-to-do, the members of the liberal professions and industrialists' families think they are below average, but still only two-fifths of peasants are unhappy about their looks; a mere tenth of women think they look older than they are. This, of course, does not mean that they are satisfied with their looks; far from it; the majority dream or wish they could 'have a new head', and it is precisely those who have the better opinion of themselves who would like an appearance

Dubout

that is better still. In theory, half of women (and even more among the upper middle class) think that cosmetics are a legitimate way of concealing age, but in practice less than half of working women and less than a third of women who do not work wear make-up every day; a very sizeable minority never (23%) or hardly ever (35%) wear make-up at all. It is true that nearly half of women spend over thirty minutes a day on their 'toilette', but it is only among the more well-to-do that that includes a daily bath or shower (only a tenth of peasants, a little more of workers, a third of clerks and only a quarter of housewives have daily baths). Only a tenth go to the hairdresser at least once a fortnight. The desire to look 'refined' as opposed to 'natural' is felt by only about a fifth of them.

France is surprisingly the country in Europe where people spend the smallest proportion of their incomes on clothes. Twenty years ago French women bought on average only one dress a year and one coat every four years. At the last survey, they were still buying on average only two dresses a year and one coat every two-and-a-half years. These are averages. Only one in ten are fashion-conscious clothes buyers, who buy more than three dresses a year. Wives explain this by saying that they feel they ought to get new clothes for their children rather than themselves. There is a solid minority (about one-third) of women aged thirty-five to fifty who definitely reject fashion and say they want only to appear 'correct and discreet'. In the working class what women value more is clothes that are practical, or reasonably priced, or which please their husbands; they buy their clothes at markets, or by mail, or from cheap department stores, whose links with high fashion are very tenuous. Interest in fashion rises with wealth, but it also diminishes with age, and often rapidly after marriage and the children's arrival. That means that there is a majority, but only just a majority, of women who pay some attention to fashion, but most of these will copy fashion only 'if it pleases them'. In no age group, except the very young, do the edicts of fashion hold any kind of sway New fashions are far more strongly resisted in France than, for example, in Britain. And the worry about fashion has certainly diminished in the last ten years. *Elle*, which in the sixties was the magazine religiously studied by all those who were proud of the way they dressed, even then sold only 650,000 copies: that was perhaps the maximum size the elite ever reached. Today it is down to 360,000 copies; half its readers are over thirty-five; it seems set to die with the generation for which it once did so much. The magazine that was the basis of the old-fashioned middle-class French chic, *Le Petit Echo de la Mode*, which goes back to 1879, vanished in 1977: it used to sell over a million copies and was particularly appreciated for its patterns, of which it sold six million a year (i.e. half of all patterns sold in France), producing 250 models each season. Women's magazines have seen their sales fall by more than half in the 1970s. The popular source for patterns now is the monthly *Modes et Travaux*, selling one and a half million copies; the most popular source of information about fashion is the *Dépêche Mode Professionnel*, selling a quarter of a million copies, which deliberately ignores the high prices and impossible clothes, and keeps itself independent of the pressure of the advertisers. The American-owned *Vogue*, which promotes 'high fashion', sells less than 70,000.

France is important to taste in clothes, because it cultivates dedication to fine workmanship, beautiful materials, originality and harmony. But there is no evidence that the French people as a whole appreciate these ideals more than other people; they have compromised themselves almost as much as other comparable nations in accepting cheaper feeble imitations. There is French taste, and French good taste.

19

How they choose their style of life

The filmmaker Claude Chabrol likes quoting Oscar Wilde's epigram that Nature Imitates Art. He believes that writers and artists do more than hold up 'mirrors in which people can recognize with delight their ideology, their rites and their hidden thoughts; they also provide a model of conduct, they create a way of talking which may at first appear outrageous but is eventually copied almost religiously. He thinks this imitation is particularly practised by the bourgeoisie 'which has no personality of its own'; from time to time its mirror gets broken, and it seeks out a new model. Which raises the question of what influences the French to be what they are, and what is the mechanism by which influence is exerted.

Chabrol provides one answer. He was subjected to a very definite type of upbringing. His grandfather and father were both conscientious and respectable pharmacists; his maternal grandfather was a draper who rose to be a director of the Samaritaine department store; he went regularly to church till manhood. When he visited England at the age of eighteen, and missed the Dover to London train through delay at the customs, he refused to go on the next train, because it had no first-class carriage, and he had a first-class ticket; he persuaded the stationmaster to add a special carriage to the train just for him. He enrolled as a student at the fashionable School of Political Sciences as well as at the Sorbonne and the Faculty of Law. He led the life of a man about town in the company of other idlers, drinking, chasing girls and paying ritual visits to the brothel on Saturdays. He married an heiress, whose grandfather was a director of Rothschild's bank, which enabled him to retire immediately, listen to music and speculate on the meaning of life and on the stock exchange.

But then with his money he chose to rebel against the values his family cherished. He had already shown some signs of independence as a student. He left the School of Political Sciences after only a week: when faced with a mass of young men from a background not all that different from his own, he was nauseated by their 'stink of caste, complacency and pedantry. Their ignorance of life and of people was crass.' They were pretentious, 'hereditary idiots', or 'servile swots' in the process of becoming idiots. From that dates his deep horror of the 'cold, mechanical, paranoic' technocrats who govern France: he laments that 'we are so stupid or cowardly as to let these midgets rule us'. At the Sorbonne he developed a hatred of scholarship based on dull erudition and memorizing, all the more so since he was able to get a degree with a minimum of work. At the Faculty of Law he bombarded one of the professors with projectiles during lectures; the professor abandoned his course and died six months later. Doing his military service in the army, he so disliked the hard-drinking officers that he gave up his own drinking, just to differentiate himself. Instead of bathing himself in the French classics, he devoured virtually every English detective novel that was published; and now he is an addict of American science fiction. When he became a rich man himself, he damned his own class for being obsessed by possessions. He has never been able to live like a true bourgeois; he spends his money as soon as he gets it; he does not buy houses or furniture, but rents them; he has two failed marriages behind him and now lives unmarried with a third woman. Not that he is promiscuous, but he is not moral either; he says that he is 'monogamous' partly through laziness and partly because he is disgusted by the trouble men go to to deceive their wives, to invent hopeless alibis, and he sees no reason to complicate one's existence by infidelity; he is not entirely serious when he repeats old saws like, It is in old pots that one makes the best soup. He left his children to their own devices; he was never more delighted than when one of them, who appalled him by always working very hard, suddenly stopped doing so. He hates doing anything until the last possible moment. He spends days on end just watching television — which for him means work — and reading at least a book a day. His main physical self-indulgence is food: he constantly talks about what he is going to eat at the next meal: 'I adore eating. It is the only thing a normal human being does at least twice a day, and I consider it perfectly normal to give it one's whole attention.' And in his films he seldom loses an opportunity to put his characters round a well-laden table. Why has a bourgeois background produced such eccentric, nonconformist fruit, and why is Chabrol automatically suspicious of all accepted truths? He explains himself by saying he was given freedom in his teens during the war, when he was sent to live in the country with his grandmother. But that means that he does not consider that his theory of nature imitating art applies to himself: somehow he was able to develop freely and to resist the models of behaviour held out to him for admiration.

As a filmmaker, Chabrol takes care not to offer his audience an obvious message, nor to appear to be trying to teach them. This is partly because he hates idealists, people who are always attempting to change things and only mess them up; he hates pretentious intellectuals, modernistic art. In *Les Biches* he ridicules the fashionable and incomprehensible author Robbe-Grillet through two absurd characters, Robeque and Riais, who produce ultra-modern painting and music out of miscellaneous bits and pieces. He rejects 'gymnastic-mental religions which lead nowhere and in any case do not free man from his egoism'. He accepts the vicious element in man, he is fascinated by war; that, he says, is his 'fascist' side. He thinks the world is going to the dogs because of its cult of money, drugs, sex, alcohol. However, in his films he is careful to avoid being didactic because he expects his audience would react to a message in the same way as he would, by indignantly refusing to be told what to believe. So his method is 'socratic', flattering the audience by putting problems before it and enabling it to come out of the cinema with conclusions which it feels to be its own; the audience believes itself to be the philosopher, rather than having to drink in the thoughts of Chabrol the philosopher.

There are two snags with this formula. The first is that it seldom works as he plans it: the audience, and the critics, misunderstand him; he is cross that his subtlety has been underestimated and his irony gone unnoticed. He has been mistaken for an apologist of the bourgeoisie. The second snag is that Chabrol is himself too complex a character to have a clear message, and that the balancing act of his own life is not something that can be taught. You can react to life's problems, he thinks, either by getting angry, or by laughing; you cannot get angry all the time, so you have to laugh. That helps you to avoid fanaticism, to be wary of your own opinions, to steer a middle course, to protect your independence. Independence is, for him, the key to happiness. However, in his own family experience, he found that giving independence to his children did not make them happy: they are worried and groping for stability. He insists nevertheless that man is born to be happy, and that it simply requires a little common sense to win happiness, avoiding situations and behaviour that can obstruct it, avoiding jealousy which ruins it, avoiding obsession with sex, which is a form of neurosis, because it prevents a man remaining master of himself. The thread running throughout his films is that the only real morality is that which comes from the individual himself; morality does not mean conforming to accepted norms, or to the rules of the game adopted by the ruling class. A murderer can have some good in him; no one is wholly black or white. That, however, means that Chabrol is ambivalent about the bourgeoisie also. He says it is decadent; he is pitiless towards the parvenu; all managing directors, he says, are fat pigs, with few exceptions. But this decadence he also finds in some ways comfortable, and quite amusing; it is fun to film and to watch it; most of all, it is interesting to penetrate beneath the materialist veneer that gives the bourgeoisie a superficial uniformity and to see the vulgarity and the humanity which is not effaced. Almost every one of his films about bourgeois life has a nightclub scene in it, which typifies for him the coarseness of city life; he is a city dweller who harbours a nostalgia for rustic simplicity. He has tried to create some sort of equilibrium out of his vision of a world composed of fools, unable to recognize their own folly, and his sense of life as full of possibilities for pleasure. His conclusion is the same as Flaubert's, that folly consists in always wanting to reach conclusions. Flaubert was, of course, appallingly misunderstood in his own day. Chabrol would have been more consistent if he had predicted that his films were bound to be completely misunderstood too.

Far from nature imitating art, therefore, it is just as plausible that nature is thoroughly confused by art. Most often of all art simply imitates other art, parodying and misinterpreting it in the process: filmmakers are obsessed by the techniques that other filmmakers use and are often as busy talking to each other through their films as in conveying their ideas to their audience. Chabrol is one of the many Frenchmen who worship Hitchcock, but what he selects from Hitchcock's genius as being most praiseworthy is that the latter does not film anything with a pretence of objectivity, but always subjectively, showing truth only as seen by him who sees it. That increases still further the element of art in the observation of nature. Chabrol claims that he portrays violence in order to make the public aware of its dangers, but he takes care to 'sweeten' the violence, to make it 'unexaggerated, urbane', almost 'in good taste'. That again is art imitating art, for the cinema has created a new mythology of violence. So to imagine that Chabrol's work yields a 'true' picture of France is naive: what Chabrol offers is a version of his own vision and of his own recreations of reality. The never-ending flow of filmmakers borrowing ideas from each other continued when the British filmmakers who were employed to produce a series of television films on the present-day French took as their model Chabrol's *Le Boucher* (1969), which they admired as giving the true flavour of France. Chabrol is amused that foreigners have taken

Tetsu

so seriously the 'folklore', as he calls it, with which he padded that film. But then the other source of inspiration of this British team was the fifteenth-century *Book of Hours of the Duke of Berry*, which presents a static view of France, changing only with the seasons, a long-vanished agricultural France that remains the foreign holidaymaker's dream. That is how stereotypes are passed on from one picture to another. It is very rare for an artist to convey a message that is understood. The influence of artists has more often been to inspire other people by the originality of their experience and experiments, and so to encourage them to undertake experiments of their own, to assert their individuality in their own way. Nature may be inspired by art, but it never quite repeats itself. The suggestion that the French reveal themselves in their cinema is as superficial as the suggestion that Hollywood reveals the essence of the United States.

There are, of course, filmmakers who claim that they speak for the public they entertain, that they are successful precisely because of that. Thus Claude Lelouch prides himself on his 'sense of the popular', of having an intuition of what the masses feel; he claims to satisfy the public's taste by using the criterion of his own taste. In particular, he has devoted himself to expressing popular fantasies. He is a cameraman who regards boredom as the ordinary man's great enemy. His own main hobby is sport; and indeed he sees life as a sport; he likes the simple pleasures of excitement, competition and success that sport gives; all his films have some sporting element in them. He does not aim to be realistic, for 'nothing is more boring than reality', but to poetize reality, to create myths, to allow people to dream, to enable them to experience excitement through surprise: 'I wish to astonish.' The critics have complained that he indulges his audience by allowing them to dream about fast motor cars and pretty model-girls, beyond their reach in real life, that he is therefore simply a 'salesman of Algerian carpets' who does nothing to question the taste of his customers, 'a salesman of good consciences at ten francs a seat'. They deplore that someone who has been so innovative in his film techniques should turn his back on the intellectual avant-garde, and refuse to comment on life except with popular banalities. Lelouch, however, does not want to put the world to rights. He has come a long way, he has been successful. He is the son of an Algerian cushion-manufacturer brought up in humble circumstances; he has not turned against his father, whom he describes as an uneducated man, but brilliant all the same, imaginative in his job, kind to his friends, and that is the sort of person he is content to be. Lelouch failed all his examinations at school: the establishment never gave him a single prize. He had no qualifications to enter film school. His father gave him a camera and he became a journalist with it, bringing back unusual films from many countries, including Russia, which the Americans instantly bought for ten million old francs, when he was still only eighteen. He then earned his living by making commercials. He is not the pure artist who needs a patron, but a businessman, who is said to have found the money for some of his films by getting firms to pay him for discreet advertising of their products. He is delighted with his success, which came at last with *Un Homme et une Femme* (1966) when he was twenty-nine.

He is grateful to the capitalist system which has enabled him to do what he wants. He does not think French society is perfect, but it is as good as any that has existed. Capitalism may be rotten but it suits man, who is moved by the principle of the carrot, of profit, of the search for success. There is no point in trying to find deep meaning in this, he thinks; man simply loves adventure. The adventure is meaningless. The desire to be rich is an almost universal dream, even if people do not know what to do with the money when they get it. It is a fantasy that keeps them going. One of his favourite themes, therefore, is conquest; the knowledge that once one has conquered the pleasure goes, does not stop man from always wanting to conquer. Lelouch is a sportsman, dreaming of new records, and of always doing better. It does not matter to him that one has to lie to oneself, and to others, to keep going, or to get what one is searching for. To lie is to create fantasies, and they give charm to life. He is fascinated by the seducer whom he sees typified in Jean-Paul Belmondo, with his gift for charming people, by making ordinary events extraordinary simply by the way he presents them. A seducer has power, he is dangerous. He is no less fascinating if he is otherwise despicable, for he knows how to transform life into something exciting and dangerous – which is why women fall for him, despite his faults. A seducer is someone who knows how to sell himself. Lelouch is not ashamed of being a seducer as a filmmaker: he wishes to please, to make a commercial success of his films. His films are nearly always based not on a personal experience of his own, but on a fantasy that he has had resulting from some experience. It is easier to make films about fantasy than about life. It would be very difficult to prove that Lelouch is right in thinking that he knows what everyone's fantasies are, or that his heroes have been much copied in real life.

The filmmaker who regularly gets the largest audiences of all is Claude Zidi. Nine out of the fifty films of the 1970s seen by the largest number of people were directed by him. Not a single one of these has yet been shown in Britain or the United States, which means that at any rate he cannot claim to have influenced foreign opinion about France; but he is quite clear that he has not influenced the French either, despite his popularity. He too used to be a cameraman; he worked on ten films for Chabrol before becoming a producer, but he has not tried to make his films technical works of art; neither has he tried to say anything in particular in them. He believes Chabrol went wrong and lost popularity because he tried to be too clever, cleverer than his public, and the public did not like that. Zidi is principally a writer of gags. His films are about anti-heroes, the Little Man who has neither courage nor brilliance, who is confronted by Authority, in the shape of a barracks, a school, a supermarket, or a police station, who proceeds to do all the most improbably absurd things to get himself out of his mess. The plots are deliberately absurd; they are supposed to be funny because of the gap of credibility between the persons and the situations in which they find themselves. This is a universal and old formula, and Zidi admits that he writes his gags with an audience in mind, based on the memories of himself when he was young: he writes for the public of his youth. 'There was then an innocence in watching films which was less cultivated, less cinephile.'

No wonder the critics abominate Zidi's films, all the more so since he again deliberately avoids what he calls the typical French type of humour, which involves dialogue, and which he cannot do. He makes people laugh with almost a children's humour. He claims that he repeats his successes because he never thinks too hard about his films; he never looks at them once he has made them, and so he avoids, as he believes, the disastrous results of comics becoming intellectuals, and worrying about their humour, so that they cease to be funny, and cease to have fun: Tati, Woody Allen, Chaplin all in the end took themselves too seriously; the most recent case of a comic being carried away by his popularity was Coluche, who for a while almost believed that he really could become President of the Republic: he became furious that people did not take him seriously — which destroyed his charm. Zidi is completely unintellectual; he was 'enormously bored at school', though he did get a *baccalauréat*; he was admitted with the highest marks into the Paris Cinema School because they tested curiosity rather than knowledge, and his culture is essentially one derived from newspapers — he reads them all every day; he loves to compare how they manipulate the reader, how they create events, and his favourite reading is the little extraordinary stories, the *faits divers*, that the more popular papers specialize in. He likes electronic games, poker, sport. He has no wish to try any other way of making money, since he seems to have found a formula for bringing the crowds in. He has no wish to try to conquer the American market, even if he could, because he is suspicious of America, he finds it too tough, 'you can never lower your guard, they never forgive, whereas in France you can always fix things.' He judges his films entirely by the number of people who come to see them. He regards himself as simply providing entertainment that is fun while it lasts and is then forgotten by all concerned.

His most famous characters are the Dim-wits. There are plenty of people who can identify with them. He follows on the tradition of *La Grande Vadrouille* (1966) a comic war film with Louis de Funes, Bourvil and Terry Thomas, which shows how, even in defeat, the French were able to outwit the Germans: that film was the most popular produced in France since the war. The well-worn formulae of cops and robbers, cloak-and-dagger, farces and series designed to give a guaranteed return on investment, go on being produced relentlessly and they are not concerned to portray the French with accuracy or to comment on the problems of their daily life. The mass audiences readily absorb American films of the same kind, which are simply entertainments and which are not essentially different. The great filmmakers of the past like Jean Renoir, who established France's reputation for originality, were always faced by this difficulty, that the masses were not interested in anything too new or disconcerting; and Renoir's films, which are now considered classics, were flops in his own day.

Now, however, the cinema has ceased to be the major venue for popular entertainment, in France as elsewhere (television puts on over twenty times more films than the cinemas show), and the function of the cinema has been transformed, though not quite in the same way as in Britain. Britain used to have the keenest cinema audiences in the world, with twenty-nine attendances a year per head of population, more than the United States (20·5) and three times more than France (8-10); that was the basis of the flowering of its own productions. Now Britons have gone to the other extreme and attend only 2·5 times a year. The French are more active (3·3 attendances, equal with the Swedes). The Americans go about four times a year, and it is the Italians who lead the world. However, the French cinema audience is now split in two. The mass of the population goes seldom, but Parisians go six times more often than the average: that means that Parisians still go to the cinema almost as frequently as Americans used to in the 1950s, i.e. seventeen attendances per head. Paris usually has about 300 different films showing at any one time, and whereas the number of cinemas has declined drastically all over the western world, in Paris it has actually increased. French cinema fans form a compact group, less than one-fifth of the population, who between them buy four-fifths of all the cinema tickets sold in the country. These fans are of two sorts: well-to-do or 'cultured' people, with secondary or higher education, who take a serious interest in films and follow the work of individual filmmakers, and young people who are less selective, but who want to get away from home. Cinema-going has thus ceased to be a family outing for the masses and has become a form of nonconformism, a way of escaping the endless flow of television output and repeats. Seat prices have trebled, while the cost of living has doubled; the cinema owners have been able to meet the crisis by making attendance more elitist. This elitism is all the more marked in that the cinemas in Paris are largely concentrated in six arrondissements, leaving the working-class areas pretty bare, and the suburbs even more so.

It is on this basis that modern French filmmaking has been flourishing and increasing, to reach a figure of about 250 a year. The important characteristic is that hardly any filmmaker tries to please everybody any more. Low budget films are the rule and France has not attempted to rival the super-epics of the Americans. Trade union restrictive practices are regularly ignored. The state, while not offering as much help as the Italian state does to its cinema, has a system of automatic subsidy, which in money terms does not amount to a great deal since it roughly returns to the cinema what the state derives from it in taxation, but it helps to keep the cameras moving. The state also helps cinema owners – half of whose costs it bears if they build new cinemas – and makers of short experimental films. It fails to subsidize only the distribution of films, and distributors are losing money. So France's cinema industry remains sufficiently *artisanal*, undominated by either large companies or by the state, for optimism to triumph over economics. Only one-twentieth of French films are actually box office successes. The state-run television, which has been bitterly attacked for buying old films at the same price as is charged for one minute of advertising time, has become an important partner in commissioning new films. France therefore has a series of specialized film markets (as in books), catering for different tastes. Films can repay their costs in Paris by appealing to different publics; these are not necessarily those which will sell in the provinces, or in all the provinces. Paris, for example, developed a special pornographic genre (which some serious directors have occasionally stooped to under pseudonyms, to recoup their losses). The audience for pornography is small (about 5%, essentially in large cities), but since such films can be made quickly and cheaply, and since the state has excluded foreign competition, there are profits to be made: in the late 1970s almost half of French films were pornographic. However, Paris has also developed films that are obscure, self-indulgent and apparently meaningless, because the cult of the film, like the cult of literature, has become an end in itself for some addicts. The cinema is an autonomous world, or series of worlds. Those who want to discover France through films need to investigate the motives and obsessions of individual directors, and there is no certainty that the films will tell them what the director is trying to say, or what he is like behind his camera.

Talk about the influence of the 'media' on the public needs to be balanced by something that is talked about very much less, the public's capacity for resistance. It knows how to mock what it is offered, as it often makes clear in cinemas. It has more autonomy than those who decry its stupidity or immorality or conservatism allow. Television and radio provide an alternative indication of the public's tastes: the public can resist by switching off. It is true that in its exhaustion it does not always resist, but far more goes straight into one ear and out of the other than the experts are willing to admit. The most popular programmes on television are sport, followed by films, theatre, variety, serials and games in that order. According to one set of statistics, sport has 29·6% of the population watching, but art and cultural programmes come bottom with only 5·4%. The French say they like listening to the news, but in practice they do not listen very carefully; when they are questioned afterwards, they can remember very little of news bulletins (in exactly the same way as Britons or Americans); and news magazine programmes or scientific programmes make many switch off straight away.

Some claim that what the majority want from television is relaxation. Others point out that there is no evidence that the majority want this relaxation to be totally mindless; the failure of boring cultural programmes proves only that they were boring, not that people are bored by programmes that have something intelligent to say; enough alternative and amusing methods for holding the attention of large audiences have still to be evolved, and constantly renewed; experiments cannot be expected to be always successful; the barriers of jargon and specialization are not easily destroyed. Television, moreover, will always be accused of being politically biased until every party and interest group has its own news bulletins on it; there will always be gaps in the news that with hindsight seem appalling (there were virtually no reports on French television of the objections to Concorde); but the public is not so easily influenced by what it does see. A once famous newsreader, Roger Gicquel, used to be popular because he was handsome and because he got indignant at the news he read; 47% of his audience said they liked him, but only 15% thought that he told the truth. The Communist leader Marchais is likewise appreciated as a performer, without converting anybody. Book programmes which give viewers a chance to make up their own minds about authors do result in people going out to buy more books, but there are best-selling authors, like Guy des Cars, who sell regardless, without any public recommendation.

Watching television is not, however, France's favourite leisure activity (it is the Italians and the British who place it first); there are a surprising number of other leisure activities in which the French participate more than the British. Britain imagines itself to be the sporting nation par excellence, but there are more Frenchmen (and Germans) who say sport is their favourite pleasure pursuit. One in ten Frenchmen goes shooting, two in ten fish (as compared with only 4 in 100 Britons), two in ten do gymnastics occasionally and one in ten do it regularly (compared to only 1 or 2 in 100 Britons). Twenty-four per cent of Frenchmen go out to watch sports (more than twice as many as do in Britain). Sport, however, is still a minority interest. The commonest outing in England is for the purpose of drinking: and the French go to the café almost as frequently as the English go to the pub. But more French people go dancing than Britons do (25% compared to 15% in Britain). Gardening is a passion for almost exactly the same proportion in the two countries, but almost twice as many Frenchwomen knit, sew, embroider, etc. (and one in ten men claim to knit too). Pottering, mending and decorating at home occupies about half the male population to virtually the same extent in both countries, but twice as many French people find relaxation in social games (cards, etc.) than do the British. These statistics may be false, but that is what they say. The notion that the French spend a lot of time on politics is untrue: only one in ten men go to political

Cabu

meetings or demonstrations. That is a small minority, like all the other small minorities with specialized hobbies. One in ten go to the theatre, or to folk dances, or to the music hall, or the circus (two or three times a year on average). Only about one in twenty attend classical concerts, pop concerts, ballet, bull-fights, or operettas. Only one in forty go to the opera, though they go on average five times a year.

These minority tastes are indeed subject to the laws of snobbishness. As soon as an activity becomes popular there are people who consider it vulgar and do something else, or seek to draw a different kind of pleasure from it. Thus Rugby football used to be an upper or middle-class game when it was first imported at the beginning of the century: it was foreign and rare; but it is now popular. The middle classes have moved to tennis and skiing and the rich to golf. As the middle classes grow, so tennis has expanded, and two-and-a-half million people are now said to play it, though a distinction has developed between those who play it in private clubs, wearing the regulation white tennis clothes, and the rest. To take up games of this kind in middle age is another way of being unusual, for the poorer classes quickly transform themselves from football players to football watchers after marriage, and middle-aged sport is essentially upper-class. In 1978 President Giscard set the tone by starting to take tennis lessons early in the morning. The next stage among those seeking to be dis-tinguished is to break the rules of their own class, and take up for example football, even though it is 'popular' — but of course keeping it 'savage', i.e. played without competition and with-out special clothes. In the same way to like *vin ordinaire* is 'common'; the well-to-do reply by keeping champagne to offer their guests; the modern executives try to go one better and drink whisky; and now whisky is 'common'. Those who wish to be different often exhibit a taste for things English (furniture, clothes, hobbies) in the same way as pretentious English or American people show their distinction by liking things French. The *Figaro Magazine*, to give an example of good taste, had an article describing the way Isabelle d'Ornano, the Gaul-list minister's sister-in-law, had furnished her bedroom in what she described as *'style samovar et cosy'*; her bed was designed to 'evoke a gondola'.

This is not simply a war between rich and poor, however: the dividing line of culture cuts across that of wealth: there is a genuine element of choice. People were asked, for example, whether it was possible to produce a beautiful photograph of a cabbage. For most ordinary people this was too ordinary an object to make 'beautiful art'; ordinary people hate incomprehensible art; the proportion of people who thought the cabbage could be beautiful rose steadily with the level of their education; there were nevertheless 15% of those with primary education or less who found the idea attractive or interesting. Every social class has its eccentrics and its social climbers. The petty bourgeoisie has both conformist and pretentious wings. Among those who claim to be cultured there is a mutual contempt dividing those who derive their culture simply from the educational system, and those who aspire to tastes which they claim cannot be taught. The liberal professions thus differ from teachers in trying more often to go beyond the traditionally approved classics, and showing a taste for jazz or science fiction. Teachers keep their distance from the masses by watching television less, or not owning a set at all, preferring to go to the theatre (which they visit twice as often as industrial and commercial employers). The theatre they like is avant-garde or classical, but there is the alternative of bourgeois comedy theatre. Businessmen, for whom 'character' is more important than erudition, can often be found in the same lowbrow lobby as their employees. This is reinforced when they are of the same age, since another division that cuts across taste is that of generation. It may be 'common' to enjoy the Blue Danube, and smart to like Bach or Webern, but there is another hierarchy in which the old continue to like the songs they grew up with, like those of Piaf, Leo Ferré or Jacques Brel; the young find new heroes all the time; these survive, as Johnny Halliday has survived, with the generation that first loved them.

Reading is another way in which individuals can create their own worlds. The Germans, the Dutch, the British all put reading as their favourite leisure pursuit more frequently than the French. The British spend almost 50% more on books, and British lending libraries lend about twelve times more books than French ones do, since the French have very few public libraries, and since British women are easily the most addictive readers in Europe. But the French give the impression of being book lovers because they have a literary class for whom books are almost life itself: 12% of French people claim to have read over fifty books a year, and a further 9% between twenty-five and fifty. Unlike the British woman, who concentrates on novels, French book readers have a broader interest in the human sciences, history, art, anthropology, literature. And the French do not choose their newspapers simply according to their social class. Top people may read *The Times* in England, but there is no top people's newspaper in France. *Le Monde* is very far from being read by a majority of senior managers or engineers (only a quarter of whom read it), only 16% of the liberal professions, 8% of industrialists and 5% of merchants; it is easily the favourite paper of secondary and university teachers (43% of whom read it) and of primary teachers (19%), but even 2% of workers take it, 5% of small shopkeepers and 7% of office clerks. No professor or top industrialist reads the *Parisien Libéré*, considered the concierge's paper, but as many junior managers as labourers do and as many engineers as peasants. The nearest thing to a bosses' paper is *Le Figaro* which has hardly any working-class readers. The paper whose circulation is probably most evenly distributed among all classes is *L'Equipe*, the sporting daily.

The government's sociologists, not frightened of being schematic, have divided French people up into five different species. The cultured elite constitute at most one-fifth of the population, though a fair-sized minority in this group simply admire high culture without actually showing much sign of practising it. One-tenth are the sociable people, who love meetings, associations and sport. Another tenth like going out, to enjoy popular shows and leisure activities – these include a lot of young people. The outdoor types, who go hunting, fishing, gardening, and also like home decorating, are almost, but not quite, as numerous as the cultured elite – 17%; they have a lot of middle-aged among them. That leaves 44%, the commonest type of French person, known as Guy Lux's France, those with no pretensions, those who watch television a lot and who include many over-forties and many over-sixties. It would not be difficult to break these categories down into many more. Each goes its own way.

The final form of resistance to influence comes from boredom. Only in Paris do most people not complain of boredom and feel that they have enough to entertain them locally (though a quarter of Parisians obstinately claim to be dissatisfied, and the absence of amusements in some areas partly explains that). In the Paris suburbs, only a third feel they have enough amusements and do not demand more facilities; in the large cities about a half; in towns of under 20,000, a quarter, and in rural areas, only one-tenth. That is why rural areas lost their inhabitants in the past, and why townsmen are now retreating to them, to escape from facilities. It is in the countryside that nature and art perhaps have their happiest relationship, of mutual respect. The return to nature has manifested itself in another curious form, a vast increase in pet ownership. The French are now said to be importing about 400,000 dogs annually, mainly from England; 34% of French homes now have a dog, easily outdistancing England (where only 23% have a dog), and whereas the English dog population is pretty static, that of France is expected to double by the year 2000. In that again, the French are becoming more like the Americans, who have more pets than people, the French not quite. [1]

To decide what French taste is, compare these five classic examples, collected by the sociologist Bourdieu, which show social class as the principal line of division. But as incomes become more equal, people are able to choose their possessions with more independence, and taste may become far less predictable.

There is the foreman who started working on the railways at fourteen and who has just retired. He lives in a block of flats in Grenoble and he also has a small house in the mountains outside

[1] Pets (in millions)

	France (official figures)	France (unofficial figures)	Britain	USA
Dogs	7	9	5½	48
Cats	6	7	4½	27
Caged Birds	6½	–	2 (budgerigars)	25
Fish	5	–	?	250

the city. He has his own ideas on how he wants to live: he has knocked walls down, modernized and reconstructed all on his own, to suit his own needs. He feels he has been exploited all his life; he hates being swindled; shopkeepers have to be watched or they will overcharge; so he buys most of his food and goods in supermarkets. He has no use for fancy furniture or antiques: it is so easy to be sold a fake. His wife is as careful as he: she avoids window shopping; she never buys anything until she knows exactly where it will go in the flat; knickknacks only collect dust. When his wife goes to stay with her sisters, he prefers cooking for himself. He argues with his children, the eldest of whom is a computer programmer, because they feel the family ought to be less austere, to eat what they enjoy. But he replies that life always involves accepting things one does not like and which one has got to get used to. He is devoted to football, to westerns and cloak-and-dagger films, to the variety shows of Guy Lux. He has been to the museums of Paris: he concedes that he likes the pictures 'that represent something'. 'But when you see four pencil scribbles, which people buy for a mad price, personally I'd throw them into the dustbin. And besides, one doesn't like to be fooled.'

The baker's wife nearby controls her taste by the principle that one must never exaggerate. She has bought her furniture from the popular chain-store Levitan, after much searching of many shops; she decided on something 'halfway between traditional and modern' because she thought that a person of her age (fifty) could not live with ultra-modern furniture. She tried to find something that was not too ordinary, but not too fancy; she chose on her own because her husband has neither the time nor the interest to help her; they hardly ever go out, in any case. She is keen on cleanliness, on solid objects which last. If she has money to spare, she likes to buy a carpet or new curtains that will be useful for many years rather than a dress that will go out of fashion. But she is not one of those who always has to be buying things: there is no point in showing off one's wealth; she will not wear her jewels so that people can say, look, she's brought out her jewels. She spends little on clothes; she hesitates to accept invitations to weddings, which involve getting clothes she will wear only once; she was brought up in the country, where it was not done to sit in front of the mirror and cover oneself with cosmetics; she goes to the hairdresser's only rarely, because one has to keep tidy. She does little cooking when there are only the two of them, though when she has visitors she likes to cook classic dishes, *quiches lorraines*, *gratins dauphinois*, all sorts of roasts, stuffed tomatoes. Her husband has a lot of friends, he likes playing cards and boules, but he hates hotels and restaurants, so they go on holiday in a caravan: before they got it they never went away. They get on well with people who have the same tastes, but they cannot abide the spendthrift. She has not been to the cinema 'for at least ten years', and never has the time to read newspapers or magazines. She watches television but 'not too much', never after ten o'clock, and provided the programmes are entertaining, undemanding and do not try to be clever; she likes singers who sing 'normally', and who look 'normal'. She likes to be busy always; she knits because 'that makes time pass more quickly'.

A forty-eight-year-old nurse, the daughter of peasants, long-divorced, lives in a two-roomed flat with her grown-up son. It is very modest, she repeats; she has no washing machine, she insists she does not like them, she does her laundry by hand, she likes to boil it to get it much cleaner than a machine can. But she has a refrigerator and a cooker, both of which she paid for in cash, because she does not like to be in debt. 'I have a horror of people who have pretensions, who do not know how to behave, who do not say good morning, who come in like that, as though they have not seen you, who ignore you, And why? Because you are not of their level. I don't like being crushed by superiors.' She is conscious that she is uneducated: education for her means 'knowing how to spell and the rules of grammar', and she is appalled that her workmates cannot speak properly, cannot tell which words are masculine and which feminine. She is shocked by such mistakes. She likes things to be 'proper', 'correct'. That applies to her clothes too: she buys 'classic' tailored suits. She loves going to the hairdresser every week, she reads her magazines there, for she never buys any. She eats mainly grills, salads and fruit and is careful not to eat too much. She listens to music on the radio, she likes songs whose words have meaning, she listens carefully to the words. She is content with her lot, modest though it is, and she insists, she keeps herself clean. Her attitudes are very different from those of another Paris nurse, aged twenty-five, who lives in a single room with no furniture, neither table nor chairs: all her possessions are on the floor, her mattress, her gramophone, her records and books; her walls are covered in posters, poems, photographs and necklaces. She has travelled all over Europe; she takes part in theatricals, she is a great admirer of Boris Vian, she goes to exhibitions; life to her is always to hope, never to accept anything as inevitable. She is a nurse of the new generation, educated, with a *baccalauréat* in philosophy; she inhabits a totally different cultural world.

The thirty-year-old advertising executive living in a five-roomed modern flat bought his reproduction English eighteenth-century furniture in London at the time of his marriage: he is not certain whether he would buy the same thing now, but he chose that because it 'is certainly from the bourgeois point of view a good investment'. They had looked around antique shops first but everything was too expensive, and much of it was inferior. This man is the son of the managing director of a multinational, his wife is the daughter of a provincial industrialist. (Both were educated at the Ecole des Sciences Politiques; she works on a weekly journal.) They have, therefore, inherited a lot from their grandparents, family portraits, paintings by Léger and Braque, but they are not sure whether they like them. Nor do they always wear the kind of clothes they like. For work, he has suits in expensive English cloths, bought from Barnes in the Avenue Victor Hugo (English for them is smart: his father goes one better and has his tailor in London). It is important, he insists, to look just right in his job, not as dull as a banker, but not flamboyant either – a velvet suit would arouse suspicion that he was trying to compensate. His wife warns him that it is wrong to be too much in fashion: she dresses her children in 'fairly classical style'. She admits some of her clothes are 'snob', but it is not the same kind of snobbery as that of the women who buy clothes for their children at those little boutiques, wildly expensive, to make them look like miniature versions of their smart parents. She has contempt too for the petite bourgeoisie 'who have no taste' and who fill their gardens with gnomes: she is a little ashamed of this contempt, but her parents are even more indignant about the gnomes, saying their manufacture should be forbidden by law: she thinks that is going too far, people have a right to choose. In their cooking they likewise try to steer carefully towards 'distinction', avoiding pretentiousness and exaggeration: when they are alone they eat only a light meal in the evening, cooked vegetable and some cheese; when they have friends they serve *escalopes à la crème*, *sauté de veau*, curry, salmon. They like old-fashioned dishes too, '*la cuisine de bonne femme*', but have little use for foreign, Chinese or Italian food. He prides himself on his knowledge of wine. They used to play tennis and golf before the children absorbed them; they still ski; they go to the opera and often to the cinema; they listen to Beethoven, Mozart, Schubert on their hi-fi. He reads books on psychology and economics, but few novels. They never do any redecorating of their flat themselves.

Near the top of the social scale is a forty-five-year-old barrister, the son of a barrister, with a large country house in Burgundy and an enormous flat in one of the most fashionable parts of Paris. Taste for him is self-indulgence. He buys rare antiques and expensive paintings 'because they please me at that particular moment'; he despises those who buy objects as investments, or who get others to choose for them. His possessions represent ideals he has long searched for and has finally found; price does not come into it; he obviously cannot buy what he cannot afford; he would not buy Chartres Cathedral, but he would love to have a church to transform because he likes old stones, their shape, their vaults. His criterion is whether he will get pleasure for a long time from what he buys: he likes dreamingly, endlessly looking at his curios, like his ancient Greek head, his Tang pottery, his Paul Serusier. He has travelled all over the world looking at museums and antiquities, but seldom goes to the art galleries of Paris. He is not keen on the furniture and silver he has inherited; his flat is smart with comfortable modern furniture, large cushions and armchairs; his country house he has filled with 'real rustic'. He says he could not live without his hi-fi, which is as essential as a gas cooker; men need music as they need food. Food is a form of relaxation and an art too: he is so busy he would like to be able to skip lunch; good cooking needs time to prepare and a relaxed atmosphere to enjoy; good wine needs to be drunk like a 'liturgy'. His law is his own pleasure. He does not care to show it off. He refuses to dress well: people will not value him any more, he affirms, if he wears a better tie or a flower in his buttonhole.

That may be a sign of things to come. Taste is evolving away from conformity and from set patterns decided for everyone by birth or work. Styles of life are ceasing to be homogeneous; each person is increasingly able to select forms of behaviour from many different sources, and create a peculiar concoction of his own. France may be entering the Age of Whim.

Part Five

How to understand what they are trying to say

20

How to make sense of their language

Every three months the French Academy publishes a list of warnings against new mistakes in the use of the French language, which are constantly creeping into common usage and threatening to ensconce themselves permanently. Jean Dutourd is the humorist among the Academicians, but he does not find anything funny in this activity. He is very practical about his concern for his language and its status: 'I need a world that speaks French so that it can read my books. It's as simple as that. I don't care a damn about people who speak English: they don't interest me. I prefer that my books should be read in French rather than in translation.' It matters to him that they should continue to be read, because his main concern is to become immortal through his works. 'To be read by posterity is my kingdom of heaven.' The Academicians are derisively known as the Immortals, and he takes himself seriously enough to believe that his books will survive him. At least he wants them to, because he believes that they are misunderstood by his contemporaries; when he dies, the caricatured view people have of him will fade, and 'they will see me as I really am.' It is difficult for people to like their living neighbours, but when he is dead 'I shall be liked, because I shall no longer be there.'

There is a parallel between Dutourd's concern for the language and for himself. He is the only child of a dentist who spent his life regretting that lack of finance had prevented him from qualifying as a surgeon. His mother died of tuberculosis when he was seven. He grew up defending himself against his father, who constantly pestered him with attention and advice; he became convinced that his father did not understand him, that people in general did not understand each other, and that 'only I understood the world properly, that there was a plot to make me see things the way they were not, and I had to defend myself.' He was convinced that he was unique, in a world where no one resembled him, and that he therefore had to 'guarantee my integrity', not allow himself to be tarnished by common stupidities. He told lies in order to protect himself from others

Daumier

The Academicians

and from the lies people wanted him to believe; he gave the impression of being docile and gentle; when accused of misdeeds, he just laughed; he established a personality that was always jolly. That did not mean he was happy – to want to be that is an 'imbecile ambition' – but that he managed to survive all the difficulties of life with a smile and a joke. He found the years of his youth profoundly boring beneath his laughter. His solution was to cultivate the spirit of contradiction, which was a way of affirming himself. That became the basis of his humour. 'Ideas please me so long as I am the only one to hold them. The minute other people adopt them, I abandon them. The ideas that are everybody's ideas do not interest me. As soon as an idea is shared by the majority, it becomes false . . . because it becomes too simple, and what is simple is always false. So when the world says white, I immediately want to say black.' And when he is alone in thinking something, he is always convinced he is right and the world is wrong. That leads others to think that he is always out to start a quarrel. There is truth in that, he admits; he agrees with Pompidou, who once said to him: 'The trouble with France is that it no longer has enemies.' When one has no enemies, says Dutourd, one is nobody; he has a thick skin, and does not mind being criticized. He likes to be approved and applauded, to be called a great writer, but criticisms do not affect him, nor change him, because he wants to remain 'faithful to himself'; he even gets a certain pleasure from failures in his efforts to receive recognition, for they confirm his belief that the world is an 'insurmountable wall'. He claims that is a French characteristic: 'the French like only war: when they don't fight it abroad, they multiply reasons for hating each other. So one of the constant features of French foreign policy has been to keep the French at war with foreigners in order to avoid, as much as possible, lapsing into civil war.' The real mark of genius is not to mistake oneself for anybody but oneself, and that applies to nations too.

Dutourd is a humorist for those French people who dislike the French people, and whose leader, of course, was General de Gaulle, who loved France but not the French. He resolves the paradox by worshipping the past, which allows him to hate the present. Nations, and cities too, are 'like women: to inspire feelings in men, they must have a past.' He condemns all forms of modernity as the work of 'electricians, and I am not an electrician.' 'I don't care a fig about the voyages to the moon: the smallest drawing by Delacroix, the least sketch by Manet seems to me to be immeasurably more important. My philosophy is that everything is turning out badly, and that everything is going to get worse and worse.' His nationalism does not, therefore, exclude appreciation of some foreign countries. He worked in the BBC French Service after the war, and liked the company of cultured Englishmen, who seemed to him to be the exact equivalent of Frenchmen nourished on comparable classics; there was a common denominator in their respect for the past. But of course all that is gone; England too has not been faithful to itself, and is no longer the real England. 'Perfidious Albion has become sweet England, humane England. It speaks American.' England used to be 'a masterpiece of a nation'; to have spoilt it was sacrilege, 'like drawing a moustache on the Mona Lisa'.

Writing in French is very important to Dutourd because he sees it as 'action'; he transforms the past into art; he 'manufactures life' in his books. 'Each time I write a line, I modify the world.' 'When my writing goes well, I have the feeling that I am dominating everything.' He is quite content to write for a public of only 2000 people, no more than read Diderot and Voltaire, who are the 'true connoisseurs' – though his books sell about 30,000 copies each. He believes God is speaking through him: he once asked God to show him how to finish a novel, and God did: it was a miracle; he has to believe in God now. That is his only modesty: he deserves no credit for what he achieves: it is God's work. He claims to have 'not a trace of pride'. De Gaulle, who is his one contemporary hero and whose death was like the death of a father, was also, he says, a 'humble man'. Dutourd knows he infuriates many people, and he has no intention of doing anything about that. Just how much anger he arouses was shown when someone put a bomb in his Paris flat and blew it to pieces, on a Fourteenth of July.

No foreigner should ever mock the French language, first because he does not understand it properly, and secondly because it has divine status in France. Every foreigner, however, needs to watch the French mocking each other on how they use their language themselves. Two parodists, Burnier and Rambaud, have very helpfully produced a conversation manual to enable the less sophisticated of their countrymen to learn without tears the version of French that the subtlest brains use to

communicate with each other, for not all Frenchmen can understand all forms of the French language either. The highly
esteemed philosopher and critic, Roland Barthes, for example,
expressed himself in a way which seemed brilliant to some, but
quite unfathomable to others. Burnier and Rambaud suggest to
the common herd that they should not make the mistake of
asking too simple a question: 'Is the language of Roland Barthes
difficult even for a Frenchman to learn?' Be braver: say rather: 'Is
RB in its guise as a macrology not a "bristle-array", or a closed
plain (plane) even to gallicist interpellation?'. This sentence
reveals a number of rules: invent new abbreviations and new
words where possible, seek out puns and hidden meanings, say
things twice, or many more times, rather than just once, and
when you have worked as much as you can on the text itself, go
on to the punctuation, and see whether you cannot make it more
enigmatic. You will soon be able to say simple phrases like: 'I
speak the Roland Barthes language fluently: My discourse
finds/reaches its own textuality by passing though RB in a game
(gain?) of mirrors'. Or 'I do not feel well today: In so far as
I-sense-my-own-self, I could be accused of a "difficulty of
habitat".' Once you have learnt to mix incongruous words
together, on the principle that salt and sweet combined are
more suggestive than either separately, to develop skill at
pulling sentences apart as you pull apart the legs of a lobster, or
'telescoping' ideas into a series of less obvious but pregnant
forms, you can move on to more advanced statements like: I
have trouble in getting up in the morning. This should first be
translated into a sort of bogus Japanese haiku: 'The day breaks:
O the torture of leaving bed.' The phrases then need to be
stuffed with additional significance: 'Another (but always the
same) day breaks (me?): O the torture of the bed-leaving process.' Finally, it needs to be made both abstract and concrete:
'Another and always the same (or similar) day, my day but also
your day, in some way faithful to the "ordinary" omoiotic (that
of the *vulgus*?) breaks/brakes (me): (sufficient unto the day): I
used as a child to indulge in a lie — (untruth, fantasy?) in.
Avanti, cretino, the (my?) Mother (Mummy) used to say: O the
torture, hell, terror, pain, sorrow, *angst* of the bed-leaving
process.' It will be no time at all before you will be interviewing

an intellectual in his own language, and learning from him that he uses two pens to write with, the green for composing and the red for crossing out, and it is quite impossible for him to cross out with the green one or compose with the red one, a special kind of pen, of course, no longer made, but he has a remarkable collection of them, and the only person who still sells them in France is the Widow Leblanc's paper shop in Arcachon . . .

If one forced the French to strip-tease, discarding one by one all the outward disguises that give them their national identity, the last thing one would be left with would be their language. In a laboratory on an industrial estate outside Paris, I was introduced to a scientist whose name I did not catch, who would explain to me the significance of the experiments they were doing. I was told he was a Princeton Ph.D., and he spoke perfect American-English. His casual clothes and hippy hair style made him indistinguishable from an American professor who still bore the imprint of a youth lived in the rebellious 1960s. I assumed he was American but I was told he was 'pure French'. I met him later carrying tea mugs: 'We too have our tea breaks,' he said. He spoke the international language of science and while he did so, there was nothing to betray that he was French. Already in the eighteenth century Senac de Meilhan had warned: 'A nation that speaks a language other than its own gradually loses its character.' That no doubt is why the French government cling to their language so desperately as the ultimate safeguard of their individuality and why they spend half their foreign service budget on trying to perpetuate its use in former colonies and foreign countries in general; when forced to economize, this is the expenditure that remains sacrosanct. They are certainly right that their language is the French people's most important common possession. But the question is whether the language does indeed express their character. To know that, one must know what that character is. Various authors have claimed that the character is made by the language. The poet Valéry wrote that French thought is 'nothing but the exploitation of certain properties' of the language. P. H. Simon, who specializes in 'the defence of the French language' has claimed: 'A language is a destiny, the instrument by which a nation's personality is communicated, situates itself in history,

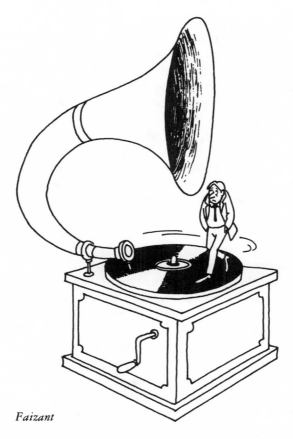

affirms its active and creative uniqueness.' That is a good example of something which can be said only in French. It is impossible to express that kind of thought in English without being accused of woolliness.

There lies the paradox of the French language. It claims that it is uniquely clear, and indeed that ideas are obscure until they are expressed in French, in which everything is necessarily made lucid. That was the argument for having French as the language of diplomacy. But there was confusion in that claim. French was indeed the international language (of the west), as Latin had been before it. It did have the effect of breaking down the barriers that prevented nations understanding each other: to learn French, for a peasant who could only speak patois, was to join an international community of educated men, to escape from the isolation of the village. That escape was completed only in the 1930s, when the last few old people who still clung to patois finally died. The unification of France was achieved in the nineteenth century, at the beginning of which something like a quarter of the inhabitants spoke no French at all and another quarter were virtually incapable of conducting a continuous conversation in it; those who knew the language properly were a small minority. But by the time everyone had learnt the language, its status had altered. English was already becoming the international commercial language in the middle of the nineteenth century, and it now has no rival in any walk of life, from science to leisure. Fifty-six per cent of learned papers published by French biochemists, for example, appear in English. English was even the language that Giscard d'Estaing used to converse with Helmut Schmidt.

So, to learn French means something different now; it involves participation in one particular cultural heritage; if one learns only French, one cuts oneself off from most people; it now stands in the same position that patois once stood. It has all the attractions of maternal familiarity that patois once had. Its lilt is like the melody of a childhood song; the grimaces that are needed to articulate it, the gestures, the intonation have become an accepted ritual, like the ticket one shows to gain admission to a football ground, and the insignia one wears there to prove one's allegiance. But whether the language expresses the French character is quite another matter; it could equally well be said to do just the opposite. For it did not just enable people from different regional traditions to meet on common ground, to find a common set of allusions which added nuance and subtlety to their thought and turned communication into a refined art. The development of the language was presided over by writers, courtiers and administrators, who imposed increasingly strict rules, making classical language a counterpart of classical art, a way of describing or viewing the world with a harmony that people learnt to enjoy; they almost made it a conspiracy, to distinguish those who know the rules from those who do not. This kind of elitism is no longer acceptable. The literary-philosophical mould which was impressed on the language is now seen as not expressing the French character in general, but only the tastes of a minority. Many other kinds of French now claim equality with what is supposed to be 'good French', and no longer acknowledge the superiority of the style adopted by the country's rulers. The schoolboy who says *'Je sèche la philo et pousse en meule jusqu'au troquet incluser un godet et faire un flip'* (I am not going to the philosophy class; I am taking my motor-scooter to the café to have a drink and play on the pinball machines) uses language to assert the particularism of his own small world in exactly the same way as bureaucrats who write letters in pompous prose, *'J'ai l'honneur de vous prier de bien vouloir'* (i.e. please), *'il ne saurait être question d'apporter à cette demande une suite favorable'* (i.e. no), or as businessmen or sportsmen who speak in franglais.

Le Monde now contains an English word in every 166, and it is estimated that 5% of French is now franglais. Professors of language do not object to French borrowing foreign words, which it has always done, but they resent the affront of an invasion that ignores the customs of their country. They want foreign words to be properly naturalized; for them the intolerable aspect of franglais is that it ignores the rules of syntax, semantics, pronunciation and spelling. They cherish foreign importations from Canada or even Senegal, which combine exoticism with a basic respect for their traditional customs. Why, they ask, use the hideous word strip-tease when *effeuillage* or *chatouille-tripes* are available (and these have the merit of distinguishing between a successful and a fake one)? There have been golfers who have voted to stop using English words – their caddies have become *cadets*, their clubs *cannes*; cocktails becomes *coquetèles*. But these kinds of protests are grumbles about changing times; the demands that the government should protect the language as it protects endangered species of animals or birds are unrealistic. People use foreign words because they feel part of an international community, just as they use slang because they are members of groups more restricted than that of their own nation. Frenchmen need more than one language to express the full range of their personalities. The revival of regional pride, the pressure for the teaching of regional dialects, is one expression of the collapse of uniformity as a national ideal. Today,

84% of schoolchildren learn English – to the dismay of some administrators, who advocate more alternative second languages, so that there should not be too great a challenge from English. But in private schools 92% of pupils choose English. In the East of France, where a generation ago 60% studied German as a second language, English is now equal with German, and has often overtaken it. The supporters of English say it is no threat to French: the Dutch and the Danes learn English without obvious harm to their nations. They argue that English has a place between the two French languages – the literary (classical) and the popular, each expressing different experiences. Foreigners who are taught classical French, and who approach the country through the language of professional writers, are handicapped in appreciating the full range of these experiences. Most foreigners in fact learn only about this France through the written word. There is the France whose language is beautiful music, whose richness, ingenuity and atmosphere become more and more delightful and powerful as one learns it better; only a small minority learn it well enough to derive full pleasure from it. But French is not always a lucid language. On the contrary, its second characteristic is its capacity for tolerating verbal gibberish (a quality formerly attributed mainly to German). The explanation is partly that French philosophy has borrowed heavily from Germany. It cannot be assumed that what is written in French necessarily has meaning, any more than an abstract painting must signify something intelligible.

21
How to recognize culture

A teacher who finds reading Balzac hard work: that hardly fits the traditional image of a cultured French schoolmaster, dedicated to the worship of the classics. But Daniel Chateau, head of the Continuing Education Institute situated in the Secondary Technical School of Reuil-Malmaison, shows that education and culture are no longer necessarily the same thing. He has lots of academic diplomas, but they have nothing to do with the classics. Born in the Auvergne, he retains the regional accent in his speech; the son of an artisan plasterer and housepainter, he was educated at a technical school, graduating at eighteen with a certificate (*brevet*) of industrial education, with housepainting as his main subject. The hope was that he would succeed his father in the family business (while his brother went to the equally practical SNCF railway school from the age of fourteen). Between the ages of fourteen and eighteen, he spent two-thirds of his time in the school workshop, learning practical skills, with only ten hours a week divided between mathematics, science, French and building theory. His teachers were former tradesmen; 'culture' was not part of the syllabus; leisure was taken up with rugby and other sports, and a dance every fortnight. At home his father never read anything but newspapers, and he himself hardly opened a book voluntarily till after eighteen. What was worse from his point of view, however, was that his training did not even enable him to run a building firm; it was too narrowly concentrated on technique; he had not even been taught to draw up an estimate. Today, he would advise someone in the same position to do a *baccalauréat* in business administration (G2) and follow that with a six months' practical course.

So he went into the world feeling inadequate, and he has never quite lost the feeling. That may be the true mark of an educated man, that he always realizes there is more to learn, and that he has never found the right answer. Daniel has been a perpetual student ever since, not the old sort who studies because he does not feel ready to work, but the new sort, the worker who is always in search of new qualifications, because change is constantly opening up new opportunities. Doing his military service in Algeria as a chauffeur, he began reading for the first time; and he took correspondence courses in Spanish and book-keeping, to fill up the hours he spent waiting for the commandos to return to base. On his release, his father sent him to a private interior decoration school in Brussels, to extend his repertoire; then he got work as a decorator in a variety of small firms in Paris that restored furniture and pictures as well as doing general decoration. That aroused his interest in art, and he enrolled for a two-year evening course in Applied Art at the National Centre for Arts and Crafts (CNAM) – an institution, he points out, where a worker can rise to become an engineer after about ten years of evening classes. Again, he did not find what he was taught really useful – 'it was too theoretical: the professor lectured about art without illustrations, telling us to go to museums and to see the objects for ourselves.' Daniel did not have much time to spare for that. He left home for work at six in the morning, by a combination of car, bus and metro, travelling over three hours a day in all; he attended his evening classes between 6.00 and 9.00 p.m.; when he got home round 10.00 p.m. he often stayed up till midnight or 1.00 a.m. doing private jobs for customers, to supplement his low wages. 'We worked for the glory of it,' he says. He and his mates had all risen to the status of decorator from that of mere painter, and they were proud of their skill. The trouble was he did not like the bourgeois clients he had to deal with, who were constantly changing their minds, indulging their caprices like spoilt children. 'We knew that without the bourgeoisie, decoration would not exist, but they poisoned our daily lives.' That, combined with the hard-working conditions, incited him to enrol for another course at his evening college, lasting three years, which would qualify him to apply to become a teacher of decoration.

He made his decision in 1968, when decorating work suddenly dried up: the bourgeoisie did not seem keen any more to have workers in their homes. As a teacher, Daniel could hope for the security of a civil service job, and regular holidays; and he could live in the country, he would be able to go back to his native Auvergne. 'I realized I would have a better social status as a teacher, but above all I felt my lack of general culture, because at the CNAM evening school, I met people who had received some higher education, and that gave me a complex. They were at ease when they talked, and in the way they behaved; they had a sense of tolerance towards the problems of daily life that I did not, as for example in my relations with my bourgeois clients.' He was influenced also by the fact that his sister had become a primary school teacher and her husband, a worker, had moved on to be a teacher; his brother-in-law was a journalist; he felt the odd one out. In due course, he was admitted to a full-time one-year course at a teacher training college in Lyon. 'That was glory: I felt I was becoming educated,' because it was no longer just technical education that he was getting. The professor accompanied the students around the city to explain its art and its monuments; he was taught psychology and how to express himself. Most of the course was pedagogy, which gave him a sense of security: he was told exactly what and how to teach; only now, looking back on it, Daniel feels that was a mistake, because in real life teaching was not so simple: 'teaching ability is really innate, you either establish contact or you do not,' and the course did not tell him how to go beyond the rigid recipes it supplied. Still, at thirty, he emerged at last a *professeur*, a teacher in a technical school.

Siné

His dream of returning to the Auvergne was not realized, because his wife promptly got the offer of a job in Paris, too good to refuse (she is an accountant, and earns more than he does). Nor was his dream of a cultured life. The school administration proved too strict for his taste; it told him exactly what to do, and too much so; he felt no respect for the hierarchy; he found the teachers' trade union too preoccupied with its ideological battles, ignoring the children; he became conscious that he was simply giving his pupils the same training he had received, which would send them to work as badly prepared as he himself had been; he could see himself 'ageing prematurely, developing sclerosis of the mind'. So once again he prepared for more examinations and qualified to become a 'director of school workshops'; which freed him from actual teaching. To get even more out of the rut, he arranged to perform that function in a school for sub-normal children. But that was also disappointing: 'I saw we were powerless; the children needed a doctor, not a painter to run their school.' So he moved into Continuing Education. He now organizes classes for working people who wish to improve their qualifications or general education, either in the period of ninety hours a year that the law allows them to take off from their work without loss of pay, or because they are redundant and need to learn new skills.

Once again, however, he is in a series of dilemmas. He believes this kind of education should offer mainly general culture, but he finds that he is personally more at ease with technical instructors than with the teachers of literary subjects. In any case, the technical instructors are seldom capable of teaching the very latest techniques. His job is to find employers willing to release workers for classes during working hours, but the employers know what they want: not education, but immediately relevant training. The Prefecture of the Hauts-de-Seine, for example, needs clerks capable of preparing files of a certain kind; it has thirty jobs to offer at that grade by a competitive examination. One hundred and fifty junior clerks enrol in the course, but most will not get the promotion, and will learn a useless skill. The time has yet to come when the workers rather than the employers can set up courses that really interest them, the threat of unemployment makes that too much of a luxury. Brief specialist courses, which used to be the fashion, are less useful now that the demand changes so quickly. A firm grounding in mathematics is needed to get through a worthwhile electronics course, for example, but few workers have it; a junior qualification in that subject turns out to be a training for a job that does not exist.

Where does Daniel Château, now aged forty-two, living in a very impressively decorated flat in Paris, all done by himself, go from here? Having reached this respectable position he is, true to form, planning ahead. He has gone back to his evening classes at CNAM for yet another certificate, to qualify as an 'economist in psychology' – i.e., industrial psychologist. He enjoys that because it is introducing him to sociology, statistics, psychology. He has read Freud and Adler, though he finds them difficult to follow, and he has not applied any of these theories to himself; he is not introspective by nature. 'I need a guide,' he says, to explain why his search for culture is always done through classes. He hankers after a broader culture, but finds the doors hard to push open. He is giving his son a classical education, so that he will not have to spend his life attending evening classes, or working such long hours. He wants to postpone his specialization as long as possible, or at least give him a chance to choose his speciality freely. And yet 'education,' he says, 'has always disappointed me, both as a teacher and as a pupil.'

He does not discuss his work with his wife – 'it is not her business.' Instead they plan their holidays, which are their main delight. In the last six months they have spent a week touring Austria, five days in the Auvergne, and a week skiing in the Pyrenees. They have rented a country cottage fifty kilometres away, in co-operation with his wife's relatives, so that they can get away for weekends. Daniel does not do anything special there, not even gardening; he 'takes the air'. His son loves the fishing, available nearby, and many other sports, judo, tennis and music. Daniel is chasing endlessly in search of the good life, and is never certain that he has found it. He is a man of the Left ('You can't be a right-wing teacher,' he says), so his main interest is people, not property; comfort is not important to him, though he seems to have got that too. He has a feeling that the 'ability to think, to reflect' can be learnt, that 'our education marks us all the time', that there is some kind of wisdom, or more accurately, serenity, or mastery of the shocks and problems of the world, that eludes him. He cannot console himself with a quotation from Horace or Pascal. That is a sign of a new kind of educated man.

Contrast his intellectual life with that of Françoise Flageolet, who is roughly the same age and who is also the child of an artisan — in her case a worker in marble, from the Champagne. She received a secondary commercial education: her parents did not even ask her what she wanted to do, but sent her to be trained as a secretary, because her mother thought that was a marvellous job. But last year Françoise attended a course in general culture, during working hours, exercising her right to ninety hours of free time a year. It was run by two 'animators'. The first lectured the students on art — Cézanne, Picasso, abstract painting — on literature (she wrote an essay on Dostoevsky's *Idiot*) on music (mainly Mahler), on the American cinema (she read Jean-Luc Godard's *History of the Cinema*), on literature (she read a novel by Balzac, but has forgotten its title), on psychoanalysis (Freud, Jung and Lacan). The second animator offered more discussion than lecture. She got less out of him, complaining there was too much personal opinion instead of facts: they argued about violence, the family, racism; she wrote an essay on the drug problem. The eclecticism of this course suited her, however. She buys at least a hundred books a year: her list for the next three months, which she compiled from newspaper reviews and personal recommendations, included the most recent of Konrad Lorenz's books (she has read several of his already), Naipaul on Islam, Galbraith's memoirs, Anthony Burgess's latest novel, Yvon Gattaz's *La Fin des Patrons* (which she, with wishful thinking, imagined to be about the forthcoming disappearance of the boss), Lesourne on futurology, a book on astronomy, another on *Science and Conscience*, and two about liberty and power. Françoise's intellectual horizons have been widened not by her education, but by her friends and her work. She lives with a mechanical engineer and their five-year-old daughter; they have thought it unnecessary to marry; they are dreaming of starting a firm, on cooperative principles, to build solar power equipment. She has become a socialist because she believes it important to be interested in what goes on around her, but she has no use for active party work, on the ground that the political parties are hierarchical, and she has enough trouble coping with the hierarchy in her own job.

It took her five years before she stumbled into a job to tax her latent intellectual powers: after being a secretary to a series of businessmen ('who always thought they were right and my job was to say amen') and being a salesgirl in an electrical hardware store, she was taken on by an information and press agency: she had to clip newspaper cuttings, and so started reading the newspapers; now her title is 'Information Officer'. Her curiosity is kindled – and she is worried that she might stagnate if she does not go further: 'I don't want to stop, life means doing better, and above all, thinking of other people.' There is too much egoism around her, too much greed for possessions, too much concern for rights as opposed to helping one's fellow man, not enough human warmth (her husband – she calls him that – says the place to find human warmth is Canada). She is planning to take a course now in biology, to prepare herself for the self-sufficient house she intends to build in the south of France, where they already own one hectare of land; but they want to have a group of houses so that the associates in the business can live close to each other, with common sporting and cultural facilities, while retaining their privacy. Happiness, for her, is 'to look in the same direction, to agree, to feel freer, not to be pushed around by a boss.' She believes there will always be a need for a boss, but he should be elected by the workers, and he must not treat them as mere machines: besides, not everyone wants to be a boss. She bitterly resents that her firm is kept going by the employees, but is lorded over by a woman who inherited it from her father. Françoise has not quite the same type of dissatisfactions as Daniel Château: she has more utopian and intellectual consolations for her feeling that she is missing out on something in life, compared to his restless search for jobs and diplomas. Her ability to assimilate ideas may be due to her family background, which perhaps often has a more decisive influence than school. She turns out, on closer questioning, to be more middle class than she made out; her father had his own little business and in retirement has become a cultural organizer for his municipality as well as an artist painter; she is a little shocked when asked whether she ever knew poverty in her youth; she hesitates to give her exact age. Is 'culture' the hobby and the inheritance of the middle class?

The idea that to be French in the fullest sense involves participating in a national culture is no longer generally accepted, because that has been revealed as an unattainable goal. The report of the state committee investigating this subject for the Seventh Plan (1976) admitted that 'French cultural life has not increased in homogeneity at all: on the contrary, each milieu functions in a closed circuit, secreting and consuming its own culture. It is like a series of whirlwinds being created, juxtaposed without communication.' In the previous decade, the French had almost doubled their expenditure on leisure activities, but had increased their expenditure on 'culture' by a mere 10%. The official, national culture was recognized as being the concern of a tiny minority, of a few thousand people, and the planners concluded: 'this club cannot be indefinitely enlarged.' The hope of transforming the masses was abandoned. Subsidies from the state were seen to be simply helping a minority to maintain peculiar activities that accentuated its difference from the masses. Though the number of visitors to museums is rising, neither art nor literature have become central concerns: only 2½% of household expenditure goes on 'cultural' activity, whereas 20% goes on other distractions. Traditional culture is certainly still cherished by those who value respectability, but it is condemned by others as being a superficial veneer, 'the art of producing formulae and making polite conversation', in a way that was basically the same as it had been in the seventeenth century; it was the art of keeping up with good society, going to the right galleries and concerts from time to time, so as to be able to say the right thing. The essence of French people's culture is that they cannot agree what exactly it is.

Those who challenge the old view have tried to give it a new meaning. It used to be a way of escaping barbarism, paganism, boorish provincialism. It used to be preoccupied with books, plays and poetry. But the criteria of good taste are now regarded by some as outdated, and the very notion of a criterion is being jettisoned. Instead it is proposed that culture should become something quite different. First, its function is to be the defence of the individual and of small groups against the increasing homogenization of the media, against passivity before the television screen or the football match: it is to be the stimulation of individuality, the expression of the infinitely varied creativity that is potentially lurking in all people. There should no longer be any attempt to shape this creativity into approved moulds. The state has indeed accepted that it is not functionaries or teachers that are needed, but 'animators', who are a new powerless species, who are not the leaders but the servants of the happenings they witness. Secondly, culture is seen as an instrument for creating new forms of sensibility, bringing individuals from different social groups together in new forms of common enthusiasm, being in effect a modern version of the medieval festival and carnival, except that instead of performing traditional rites, the modern festival invites people to invent their entertainment and express their own ideas. 'Culture,' wrote Jack Lang, when he was the organizer of the Festival of Nancy, 'is a battle for the right to live freely.' It sought to stress innovation, 'to exalt the creative capacity of all', to be a form of revolution, but to avoid lapsing into mere counterculture, in which sectarian rival chapels closed themselves to all but their initiates. This is a very different approach to that of the official of the Ministry of Culture who said that culturally France is a pagan country, in need of missionary conversion, using the same terminology that Christians use about the unbelief that confronts them. Culture now divides France instead of uniting it (at least it was supposed to unite it), because many of its manifestations provoke horror and delight at the same time. That disagreement is itself a source of pleasure to some: the journal *Esprit* expressed this in its manifesto of 1977: 'We do not believe in a society without contradictions, but in a society of diversity and conflict, in which the ability to analyse, to manage, and to criticize — which organizers and intellectuals have appropriated — should be restored to people in ordinary life;'

that instead of having people producing culture for the masses, and telling them what to think, 'the limits of reason, the importance and value of conflict should be recognized.'

The Ministry of Culture was created by General de Gaulle in the hope of reviving France's reputation as mother of the arts. But the grandiose ambitions of the novelist André Malraux, who was put in charge of it, ended in a failure that was symbolic. Malraux maintained that Art was the new religion of men who have ceased to believe in God. The Age of Art was about to follow the Age of Education, which had been instituted with compulsory schooling and had now achieved its objectives. He wanted to bring culture to the masses as Jules Ferry had brought them education. He imagined himself to be the apostle of a modern art which could unite the world once people had learnt to appreciate the masterpieces of all nations. That would happen because the character of modern art was that it did not tell a story, it was visual. 'Our epoch admires what it does not understand.' Art went beyond understanding; and art was what France really stood for. 'I am France,' he used to say, in the same way Picasso used to proclaim, 'I am God.' He implemented an idea of the Popular Front by establishing cultural centres – Maisons de la Culture – in the provinces, which he liked to call the cathedrals of the twentieth century, where all sections of the community could meet to discuss and express their creativity, to worship art. The success of these as experimental theatres has, however, only shown up the opposition between the view of art as tradition and art as innovation. Though Malraux called himself a 'specialist in rebellion', he had a conservative attitude towards art, being obsessed by the idea of the museum as the repository of art; his concern for culture was ultimately a concern for the past.

Pompidou redecorated the Presidential palace in modern style and with contemporary paintings. Giscard ripped them all out and replaced them with French eighteenth-century styles, which he considers perfect. Pompidou was not frightened of foreigners: the Opera was handed over to a Swiss, the Museum of Modern Art to a Swede; the Beaubourg Centre has become so international that it has been accused of being 'the instrument of a formidable Franco-American artistic lobby'. But successive

Ministers of Culture have given priority to saving ancient monuments rather than to encouraging new French styles: ironically, in trying to resist shapeless Americanization, they restored Versailles largely with grants from American philanthropists, organized by the American wife of the curator of that palace. 'It is no longer Versailles,' mourns one of those who think the restoration has been overdone, 'it is Technicolor made in USA.'

This is more than the old quarrel of ancients and moderns that goes through all the history of French literature. When Jack Lang, the present socialist Minister of Culture, was in opposition, he wrote that 'all cultural action must be against power.' But he also thought that television should be made more 'pedagogical'. The present crisis regarding culture revolves around the difficulty of evolving a new form of pedagogy. For culture is now experience, not instruction. The snag with the old culture was that it taught people what was right. The new culture requires each individual to choose for himself what experience he will attempt. Culture can no longer be presented as a single whole, which people either accept as connoisseurs, or reject as philistines; it is an expansion of horizons, just like getting to know another person. No one can predict how two persons will react to each other, nor insist that they should like each other.

22

How to judge the effects of their education

'I hated my education and I despise the instruction I received.' Jean Effel, France's most prolific cartoonist (of whom Malraux once said 'Out of all of us, Effel is the most certain to survive') is now retired. But he talks of his schooldays with passion. 'I never had a good teacher. They were always boring. No one ever told me what a good poem was. They never explained to us why we should study what we did. And when I left school, I realized they had taught me things they could not explain.' He holds it as a grudge that he was always sent to stand in the corner. Because I, too, have taught in my time, he wrote this inscription in one of his books that he gave me: '*A Theodore Zeldin, en toute sympathie, un mauvais élève, Jean Effel.*' That a person should, after fifty years, still feel that he has been branded as a *bad pupil* says something very profound about the place of schools in the lives of the French. It does not signify hate of the schools, but love-hate, for Effel deeply regrets that he never had a good teacher. And he insists that the pleasure he derives from being a Frenchman is due in large measure to the common foundation that his compatriots have got from their primary schools: all of them know the fables of La Fontaine, just as they all like cheese, and bread, and wine; they all share the 'time-honoured custom of fooling around' and 'a certain way of accepting life'.

'I am the only member of my family not to be a teacher,' he says. His brother is a professor of archaeology, his sisters both teach, his mother was a teacher of German who was made to teach English. That was a great achievement, for his father was an illegitimate child who never went beyond primary school, who became a commercial traveller and finally attained comfort and modest wealth in his own haberdashery firm. Education was the way beyond that to full respectability. However, climbing to success involved repression that Jean Effel could not stand. His mother, he thinks, abused her power over him. 'I felt freer in the army than at school or at home.' His father forced him to take his customers to business lunches and to the opera (which he still hates): 'we didn't dare take them to the Folies Bergères.' Eventually, he was allowed out of the business, with a gift of 800 francs, with which he bought the equipment to set up as an artist. He began drawing for newspapers, because only they paid at once: within a year he was earning four times as much as he had done in his father's firm. He signed himself Effel (a play on his initials, his name is François Lejeune) to establish an independent identity. He became a man of the left wing 'if only to be the opposite of my parents'.

A child who is too original nearly always has trouble of one kind or another at school. Effel's originality led him to transform the humour of newspaper cartoons. Newspaper editors used to think up subjects on which they wanted a cartoon, for example some pompous moral about fast girls or seduced servants, and tell the cartoonist to illustrate it, which was done to the accompaniment of a caption several lines long, what Effel calls 'sub-Feydeau'. There is a long tradition of this: in Daumier's day the drawing of cartoons was done by the artist, but the caption by the journalist. Effel turned the cartoonist into a new kind of man of letters, a poet. He took it as his principle that he would not do anything others had done before him. He made this explicit by using not the customary fine pen (such as is favoured by Ronald Searle) but a thick industrial one; and he tried to find subjects untouched by anyone. *The Creation of the World*, his masterpiece, was the result: 'it has nothing to do with God, but is a history of a worker.' God is presented as simply a nice old man with a big job to do. He is assisted by little angels, in a combination which often suggests an idealized version of a witty teacher and happy pupils: He has a blackboard on which He writes announcing the creation: I shall be, You shall be, He shall be. As a cartoonist, Effel reveals that he was a good pupil after all. His work is based on a rereading of his schoolbooks, from which he got the facts which he twists in his drawings; he uses the Larousse Encyclopaedia (1914 edition), which belonged to his grandmother, for his anatomy drawings, (veins in red, nerves in yellow). He loves encyclopaedias and dictionaries, 'and I need them because I cannot spell.' Out of these he has created poetry. He likens his work to a Chinese poem, (though he admits he knows nothing about Chinese), where, apparently, art consists in putting an unexpected adjective to a name, and adding a couple of words to a drawing. His drawings are the expression of a poetic idea, reduced to its simplest form, the caption is the last line of the sonnet and the drawing is the rest of the sonnet. He puts as little as possible in the text, and gives a great deal of attention to punctuation. He cannot do drawings without captions, 'that is a totally different trade, as ballet or mime are to the theatre': he cannot stand ballet; he loves words. He always wanted to be a playwright and a painter. His cartoons are his plays, complete with characters, text and decor: 'So I have found what I sought.'

But he has found what his teachers did not see. His skill is in carrying logic to its absurd conclusions, in taking obvious facts too literally, in connecting subjects that occur in separate syllabuses, and in making boring subjects amusing. God puts the stars into the sky by letting off fireworks, to the delight of His little angels; He hurls the planet Saturn into space like a discus thrower; He manufactures the sand for the beaches by grinding stones up in a coffee grinder; while the ice that makes the angels slip on the streets is spread by the devil, who sprinkles the powder used to smooth dance halls. God is an inventive and charming teacher: when He sees a dog raising its back paw over a boy's leg and peeing onto him, God says: Do you see now why I created the tree before the dog? In such conditions, study becomes worthwhile: Effel went to watch three operations in a hospital before he drew his cartoons showing Eve being created out of Adam's rib. He has found a way of marrying his sense of independence with the acquisition of knowledge. The only advice he will give to young cartoonists is: Make your signature legible.

He bitterly resents any threat to his originality; here perhaps the nationalist indoctrination of his primary school survives still. The Americans are his *bête noir*: 'they are so proud of being powerful, they think they are liked, but we detest them; the best thing de Gaulle did was to tell them to go away; you cannot see them in uniform in France and that is a good thing; they very rarely marry French people, because they are coarse, and their children are badly brought up.' He finds it inexplicable that they come top in so many spheres of life. His father sent him to England for a year, to learn the haberdashery business; he can speak English pretty well and is 'one of the rare Frenchmen to drink tea for breakfast' (not so rare, 19% do that, at least sometimes); he owes it to the British army that he was shipped out of Dunkerque in 1940, in a state of inebriety achieved with stolen Benedictine; but he thinks there is a deep spiritual gulf between England and France, due ultimately to the former's Protestantism. His *Creation of the World* has never been published in the United States, and it has sold only a few thousand copies in England. 'It is because the Protestants take the Old Testament very seriously,' he says. However, the book, which has been translated into seventeen languages, has done best of all in Germany where it has sold one and three quarter million copies (compared to a million in France); it has succeeded also in the Communist world. His chandelier was bought with his Czech royalties. He has lived altogether for a year in Russia, earning his keep by drawing. His enthusiasm for the Russian Revolution has not palled: at least, he says, the Russians do not have unemployment. However, he is a member of no party. He laments that socialism has never changed much anywhere; there is still a need for a new French Revolution, to reorganize industry so that it should suit people, and not vice versa. When American aid came in 1948, he drew a cartoon showing Uncle Sam running France-Marianne over with a cart full of bombs. But when General de Gaulle was elected President for a seven-year term, Marianne cheekily asks him: What about seven years' paid holiday for me too?

Looking back on his life, Effel says what he has enjoyed in it has been 'friends, women, and my marvellous wife: I am happy since I got married: at home I find gentleness, peace and good taste.' But 'my life is like a bistro game, an accident', it has passed without his really thinking about it; 'I am not organized enough to have sought anything in it.' He has spent many hours sitting in cafés, sipping drinks: there is a film about the café du

Cadran, at the corner of the Avenue de l'Opéra, where he and his fellow humorists, and Pierre Benaert, the editor of the *Canard Enchaîné*, who is said to have died of drink, drowned their gloom while thinking up jokes. It is Effel's achievement that his jokes are never personally nasty: he has come through with no malice. His teachers are proud of him now: he was asked to decorate the Lycée Carnot, where they once made him so miserable.

This kind of story about a bad pupil who makes good after all, by breaking the school rules, pinpoints the tragic element in the country's educational system. If large numbers of French people are highly articulate and sometimes exceptionally graceful in their speech, a whole century of intense educational effort has more than a little to do with it. But so much has been expected of education, that few people are fully satisfied with the way it is dispensed. Before one visits a French school or university, it is best, therefore, to know all the worst that can be said about them, so that one can put the frustrations and the complaints side by side with the self-congratulation, and judge for oneself, depending on how one personally feels about the universal experience that schooling now is.

While the bureaucracy has tried to force a sense of common destiny on the French by channeling all decisions affecting them through Paris, teachers have sought to create a deeper unity by giving children the permanent imprint of French culture, elusive though that is. A French education is supposed to be something that one does not easily forget, and that marks one for life. It has the reputation of being particularly tough and demanding, of requiring children to work incredibly long hours, but that is a reputation given to it by just some sections of the system, notably the top forms of the most competitive lycées. The average school day, lasting from 8.30 a.m. to 4.30 p.m., is, in fact, broken up by two hours for lunch; Wednesday is usually free; the French school year is the shortest in the world, and since one month is devoted to examinations, teaching is effectively provided only on 155 days. There are indeed ambitious children, or children with ambitious parents, who stay up very late doing their homework, but these are a minority: the majority devote only one or two hours to homework each evening; only one-tenth of secondary school pupils spend more than twenty hours a week on homework; surprisingly few complain that they find it difficult.[1] French children probably do emerge from school better informed than those of the United States, because Americans work on a different time scale; they catch up in their colleges. Compared to other countries, however, the results of French education are uncertain. International tests in mathematics showed the following order of attainment, but the experts do not agree that the tests were fair:

Thirteen-year-olds:	Israel	mean score	32·3
	Japan	mean score	31·2
	Germany	mean score	25·4
	England	mean score	23·8
	France	mean score	21·0
	USA	mean score	17·8

Mathematics specialists in their final year at school:

Israel	36·4
England	35·2
France	33·4
Japan	31·4
USA	13·8

France did best in the tests on non-specialists studying mathematics as subsidiary subjects in their final secondary year:

Germany	27·7
France	26·2
Japan	25·3
England	21·4
USA	8·3

This last result may suggest that the special quality of the French system is rather that it aims at a more balanced general education, and that its pupils specializing in the humanities have to know a certain amount of mathematics and science also. That certainly distinguishes the French from the English, who

---

[1] Twenty per cent spend 0–5 hours a week on homework; 36% spend 5–10 hours; 33% 10–20 hours; 1·8% over 30 hours. *Les Lycées* (1980), 28.

now encourage specialization at an earlier age than any other country in the world. As opposed to the two or three A levels that are normally taken in England, the French *baccalauréat* requires no less than six subjects, though these are studied with differing degrees of intensity. But it is the Germans who have the most balanced system, requiring their pupils to study languages, humanities and sciences in equal proportions.

The ideal of a proper French education, as it used to be understood, is in fact not dispensed to the majority of French children at all. The most notable characteristic of the traditional syllabus was that it was crowned by the study of philosophy and rhetoric. When done efficiently, this turned out highly polished men of the world, who did not need a university education, unless it was for vocational purposes, for they could write and talk with fluency and eloquence, with that peculiar sense of order that reduced all complexities to three arguments and a conclusion, with that dash of literary refinement that, like a perfume, added charm and sophistication to their argument. However, the philosophers are now under attack. It is no longer believed that they alone can give children a truly critical spirit, an ability to see problems in the widest context in the light of general principles, or that they are responsible for that special kind of urbanity which used to be the mark of the polite educated Frenchman. Many argue on the contrary that philoso-

Mathieu

phers encourage only empty and indeed dangerous verbosity. Philosophers teach what in Oxbridge entrance examinations is more humbly called the general paper: the questions they set in the *baccalauréat* involve mainly reflexion on general problems: Can history teach moral lessons? Is art imitation of nature or creation? What can one hope for from technology? Does the variety of philosophies destroy the claim of philosophy to be true? Philosophy classes enable the best pupils to discuss such matters with surprising maturity and knowledge, but they can also degenerate into cramming sessions of pot-boiled theories and ready-prepared answers. Philosophers have lost their prestige by becoming increasingly incomprehensible to the general public, narrow specialists, without, like the scientists, having practical results to offer as a compensation. Their often remarkable personal adventures of the mind have become lost in a fog of abstractions with no meaning for the common man. The government recently proposed that philosophy should be removed altogether from the schools' compulsory syllabus. The philosophers have managed to stop that, but only just; they survive today in a very limited way. Most schoolchildren never study philosophy. Of those who reach the top form and do, most get away with reading only one or two authors and answering only one question in the *baccalauréat*.

How long, under such conditions, the peculiar French way of arguing will survive is uncertain, since 'rhetoric', which used to bolster philosophy, no longer exists as a school subject. Its methods are preserved in the teaching of the French language and literature, which tries to develop the ability to analyse and summarize texts, to express one's emotional reactions to a piece of prose or verse, and above all to write essays which both express a personal point of view and show one's acquaintance with classical authors. However, teachers who insist on perfection in grammar and spelling, and adulation of traditional models, are fighting a losing battle; they complain indeed that many supposedly educated people can no longer write French correctly, that Racine is probably unintelligible to the majority of Frenchmen. The gap between the spoken and written language is becoming more obvious in the age of the television and the telephone. There are modernists among French language teachers who argue that it is enough to teach people simply to understand newspaper articles and contemporary issues, that the spoken language of the children should be taken as the basis of the syllabus, which should encourage spontaneous expression. This has aroused horrified cries that French civilization is being threatened. The question does indeed arise whether traditional French literary education is compatible with modern aspirations.

In the past, it was only a small elite that received a literary education: it was the vocal part of the nation which won its reputation for fluency. The idea that all the French are inherently marvellous talkers is not supported by the investigations of the Englishman Arthur Young, who toured France at the end of the eighteenth century: he thought that their peculiar characteristic was their remarkable silence, not loquacity. Only 1% of the population obtained the *baccalauréat* in 1900. These were envied because education was seen as the instrument that enabled people to talk interestingly and convincingly, to converse with ease, to argue and to communicate across classes and regions. Today a quarter of children are obtaining the *baccalauréat*. But it is now no longer the same kind of communication that education stimulates. There are now no less than twenty-eight different kinds of *baccalauréats*, most of which are predominantly scientific or technical. Only 65,000 children (under 20%) opt for the literary-philosophical *baccalauréat* (known as Option A) which used to be the mark of a complete education. This was easily the single most popular option until 1968; since then it has rapidly declined and a few years ago it was overtaken by the Natural Sciences (option D). Today, the obsession in French schools is with mathematics. Proficiency in that is the key to a successful career. Whereas in England getting into a university is usually a good pupil's ambition, but there is no pressure for a clever pupil to choose a particular subject, either arts or science (which are chosen in almost equal proportions), in France there is cut-throat competition to get into the classes preparing for the mathematics and physics (C) option. Those who succeed are treated as the elite. Though the technical *baccalauréat* has less prestige and is taken by children from humbler social origins, it nevertheless has a few sections which are tough, sometimes involving fifteen extra classes a week, and these pupils believe that they are getting a better education than the literary pupils, even if they end up only as technicians. So the majority of the ablest children are now trained predominantly as scientists, and are, therefore, being inducted into an international culture, and no longer into a primarily national one. This is a recent trend, and the results will not be fully felt until the new generation comes into power. Maths has replaced Latin as the instrument for selecting the elite; the prestige of this elite can be judged by the fact that an unusually large number of people are called scientists and engineers in France: one-and-a-half million, as compared with only one million in Germany, and two-and-a-half million in the United States.

The change from the ideal of bourgeois rhetoric to technocratic numeracy may seem to be a slight or subtle one, since abstraction continues to be esteemed. The change is also concealed by the literary veneer that the most successful technocrats use to give themselves added cachet. But the vast majority of ordinary scientists and technicians – and even more so of ordinary working people – have no literary aspirations or interests. The schools have failed to make the French literary or bookish. The French as a whole are distinguished by the fact that they do not read a great deal.[1] They do not even like reading newspapers all that much, let alone books. Their newspaper circulation is roughly equal to that of Singapore, Korea or Ireland; they buy only half the number of newspapers the British, Germans, Dutch, Japanese or Swedes do, and 40% less than the Americans.[2]

Why is this so? French children get a head start over those of their neighbours because they go to school earlier. Parents are happiest with the kindergarten schools, or *maternelles*, for two to five-year-olds. These are more numerous in France than anywhere else and are considered one of the glories of the French

[1] Total books published annually (in thousands): France 31 or 21 (depending on whether pamphlets are included), USA 85, USSR 85, West Germany 50, Japan 43, UK 36, Spain 24, Brazil 20, Netherlands 13, Italy 10.
[2] Newspaper circulation per 1000 inhabitants: France 205, USA 287, UK 410, W. Germany 423, Netherlands 430, Sweden 529, Japan 546, Ireland 220, Singapore 215.

Grandville

Man proudly allowing himself to be led by his dog

system. There have been few complaints in the past, and children are being sent to them earlier and earlier because they were the least pretentious schools; the teachers regarded themselves simply as substitutes for the mothers, not superior experts; few demands were made on the children, who were not actually taught in any formal sense. But now the *maternelles* have been given the task of 'spotting handicaps' from the age of four, which is seen as likely to lead to segregation according to ability even of toddlers. More and more experts – doctors, social workers, psychologists as well as teachers – must now contribute to the file everybody must have kept about them from the age of three. Every child is in danger of becoming a pathological problem in need of special attention. In the Paris region, 25% of all children in the *maternelles* were referred to a psychologist as having something wrong with them; in some *maternelles*, as many as 44% were; and it is very rare for the psychologists to say that there is nothing wrong. The schools are trying to pass the buck to the hospitals.

The primary school (where children begin their compulsory education at six) used to be regarded as the main instrument for incorporating the masses into French civilization. It was once the respected outpost of progress, established among ignorant peasants, which taught them how to speak and read French, and instilled the rudiments of morals and civic spirit among them. Today it carries its elaborately regulated traditions like a burden, because it no longer has a pioneering role. It is television and no longer literature that gives children most of their heroes; more time is spent listening to radio and watching television than reading, by children and adults alike. So the teachers are torn between, on the one hand, a desire to ignore these changes, which they deplore, and to improve the minds of their pupils, and, on the other hand, an acceptance that the academic ideas of the past are no longer relevant. Thus the syllabus still aims to give all children an average knowledge of the 3 Rs: it is designed for pupils with an IQ of 100 to 110, which means it is too demanding for a large minority; only 11% of children go to 'remedial' schools, but there are another 20% in primary schools with IQs of between 85 and 95. Unlike most other countries, where children move from class to class according to their age, in France they are promoted only when they reach a certain standard. So a class may have children aged from eight to thirteen, all of supposedly the same educational level. Inability to perform adequately in some parts of the syllabus can hold a child back. This is widely regarded as one of the major faults of the system, but there seems no escape from it, except in the few experimental schools. It does not even ensure that pupils emerge from the primary school properly grounded in the 3 Rs: only one-quarter are judged to be capable of reading with any fluency; one-quarter are still at the stage of reading each syllable separately and mouthing the words to help decipher meaning; the remainder would take about four minutes to read this page. [1]

One cannot attribute these results to any peculiar method of teaching reading, because there is no 'French' method. Every teacher works out his own compromise between his ideals, the rules, the books available and the children's protests. The old 'syllabic' method, denounced in the eighteenth century by Rousseau, (learning in turn letters, sounds, syllables and words) has not vanished: it survives in what is known as the 'mixed' method, which combines it with the 'global' method, in which

---

[1] Twenty-seven per cent read under 550 signs (i.e. letters and spaces) a minute, 46% read 550–820 (much below the speed of normal speech), 26% read 820–1300, and only 1% are fully efficient readers at over 1300 signs a minute.

a story is read and the words then gradually identified: one of the best-selling reading books is still *Daniel and Valerie*, whose modernity can be judged from the fact that it is about two children living in clogs on a farm. There are numerous variations on and recombinations of theories in the large number of reading books that are used: Plocki's 'English' method, Gablier's 'Quebec' method and the new phonetic 'linguistic' method. Some teachers use *Red Riding Hood* and *Robinson Crusoe* as their books; others refuse to use any books at all; some get the children to compose their own reading material by speaking into tape recorders or producing a newspaper (Freinet's 'natural' method). In Fontainebleau, teachers tend to use mainly the 'traditional' method because, they say, they are tired of being criticized; in the twentieth arrondissement of Paris, where the majority of pupils are immigrants, the 'natural' method is most frequent; in Toulouse, books have been almost entirely abandoned. The official view is that the best method is that in which the teacher feels most at ease; so many beginners stick to textbooks as a safeguard against the chaos that confronts them. They complain they do not really understand the fancy new theories or vocabulary of the 'orthophonists' and experts in 'psychomotricity' and 'lateralization'. A journalist who went round primary schools to investigate the working of these various methods found that half of the teachers refused to allow him into their classes. Most teachers approve of the regulation that prohibits parents from visiting. So the primary schools together form a museum in which almost every type of teacher can be found, from the strict disciplinarian to the experimenters and those who simply like children and have fun with them.

The pupils of the primary school on the Ile St Louis have recorded what they think of the system. This is a school where they call the teachers by their first name, where the teachers no longer think of themselves as being in charge of what goes on, and where they allow the pupils to say more or less what they please. 'I do not like school,' writes Anna, aged eleven. 'In the school I used to attend, I was told I was not capable of learning to read.' 'My teacher always used to slap me,' writes Sylvie (ten), 'when I did not understand she sent me out of the room . . . it is nicer here.' 'In arithmetic,' says Alain (nine) 'we were not allowed to ask the others if we had not understood. The teacher used to separate us if we had a friend. Here the teacher is affectionate: he makes me do interesting things. Besides, in my previous school, they used to call me Jew.' 'In my previous school,' adds Patrick (ten), 'they said I had a bad character and always got cross.' At the Ile St Louis, the children are, however, as severe with each other as teachers sometimes are with them. In their democratic elections of class presidents, and in council meetings to discuss their lives, they record the accusation that 'Patrick is a jealous brute,' that 'Sylvie is too much the baby,' that 'Jean-Claude thinks he is always right and pretends to be doing well in class,' that 'Antoine plays all the time and laughs at everything,' and as for their teacher, he is very nasty towards Patrick, Annise, Alain and Stéphane, but sometimes he is nice; he teases everyone; he does his work well; he is right to get angry with Patrick, whom he sometimes kicks in the backside. The teacher has only one vote in the election of the president: he votes for the boy who turns out to be the winner.

One gets another view of school atmospheres in reading about the strike of the teachers at Villeneuve-sur-Lot, in the Ecole Nationale de Perfectionnement. This is a school which far from 'perfecting' anybody, harbours the rejects of the elementary schools, those who have failed to make the grade and who are condemned to remain within the primary system till sixteen, learning to become gardeners, builders, local authority employees and, more likely still, queuers for the dole. The teachers are mostly nearly as unqualified as their pupils. They went on strike because one of them was transferred against his will, having offended the headmaster by his black leather attire, and, as the final straw, by allowing the children to dance '*le slow*': 'even the boys danced together, under softened lights,' complained the headmaster. This is a mixed boarding school, but there is no sexual education, since the primary syllabus does not include that. The rules forbid the children to hold hands, or to sit on each other's laps, though girls are sometimes granted this favour. The explanation is that 'it always begins like this, and they then go and lie on the lawn,' which is also forbidden. The children's nickname for the headmaster is 'the Madman' (*le Fou*). He is a vigorous man in his forties who, say the teachers, lives by the bible of the Minister of Education's book of rules and regulations; he believes a solution to every problem can be found there, and when it baffles him, he telephones the Inspector. A journalist thought the teachers were exaggerating, and went to interview the headmaster. The headmaster very politely held up a thick blue volume: 'Sir, I must be clear, this is the compendium of laws and rules, in which it is written that I am required to be reserved in my dealings with you. I shall, therefore, make no statement to you. And if you do not believe me, we can telephone the Inspector.'

Most of the children who pass through the schools are marked out as failures of some sort. At present about one-third of the adults over thirty-six (born before 1947) have no school diploma of any kind, and another third have only the primary school certificate. That certificate meant something once, but with the expansion of secondary education in the last two decades, it has been devalued into a sign of incapacity. Only 6% of these adults of over thirty-six have the *baccalauréat*, only 4% have a university degree. The raising of the school leaving age to sixteen has not made education much less discriminatory. Success is still

Claude Serre

largely determined by the education and status of a child's parents: the myth that the school would introduce equality has been exploded. Only about a half of children get through elementary school without having to repeat at least one class; 26% of the children of agricultural labourers have to repeat a class, but only 2·2% of those of senior managers. In the 1960s and 1970s attempts were made to help these 'backward' children to catch up in the lower forms of secondary school, but that only led to their being segregated into 'transition' classes taught by junior teachers, and only a tenth of these pupils ever succeeded in getting back into the main stream. Today there is theoretically one comprehensive secondary education for everyone, lasting four years. But in practice some drop out after two years and settle for training for a manual trade.

For those who stick it out, decisions still have to be made as to what kind of diploma each child should seek, and each diploma has a different prestige. The children are supposedly protected by an 'assessment of their personalities' known as 'orientation' or vocational guidance. This is meant to be fairer than a mere examination: their teachers have to produce seven files about their past history; the wishes of pupils and parents are supposed to be taken into account. But after all the discussion the teachers decide on basically academic grounds what their pupils will do in later life. Those children who get the best pickings are those who are good at maths. The less bright children have to settle according to available vacancies: a pupil who asks for a course in cookery might end up with one in carpentry and a girl wanting to be a typist may find herself on a dressmakers' course. Upper-class parents, who are most ambitious, argue with the teachers (30% protest), but the uneducated do not dare; most parents find it impossible to make career decisions for children of fifteen, and say they only want them to be happy. Children who do not know what they would like to do accept the decisions made for them with surprising docility, contenting themselves with making the best of the present. The teachers are, of course, not really able to judge which of the 350 different technical diplomas would suit a child; they know little about industry; the whole process has been called by one of them 'a masquerade that pushes children like cattle to the slaughterhouse'. That means that eventually children are divided up between courses leading to jobs with very unequal salaries: short technical courses lead only to manual work, longer technical courses give scope for more skilled jobs; only the academic lycées open the door to a university education. Girls are prepared for unemployment by being herded into the literary classes (they constitute 74% of these, but only one-third of the C maths classes). The one option with no maths (business studies G1) is regarded as the 'wastepaper basket' class; 40% of those who are in the other business course (G2) with a minimum of maths say they were put down for it against their will, because their maths was not good enough for anything better. Even the musicians complain that admission to the music classes depends more on proficiency in maths and French than in music. The way the schools reinforce acquired privileges is seen in the C maths classes: 40% of the children of managers get into these, 25% of those of middle managers, but less than 5% of those of workers.

The boy who said he would like to study for a diploma in road sweeping was not entirely frivolous. That is perhaps the only job for which a course has not yet been invented. The mania for examinations and paper qualifications grows unceasingly. A child who forms the modest ambition of going to work in a laundry is now made to prepare himself by taking one of four different diplomas in this subject: he must opt between dyeing, preparing, washing and ironing. Is France the only country in the world with a diploma in ironing? No wonder launderers now refer to themselves proudly as 'clothes doctors'. The irony is that many employers do not set much store by diplomas, and that diplomas are very far from being a guarantee of a job. The more complex the educational regulations become, the less contact they have with reality.

It is true that the schools have made concessions to democracy. Discipline is no longer what it was and is officially replaced by 'autodiscipline'. The lycées are no longer a cross between a Jesuit seminary and a military barracks; even though some old school buildings do look a little like prisons, less than a tenth of pupils are boarders now, and only about a half even take their

What has changed in Duduche's school…

Cabu

midday meal at school. [1] There are innumerable councils paying lip service to 'participation': pupils and parents elect delegates to the councils that run each school; each class has a council under the presidency of its principal teacher; the pupils have a council of their own with two delegates from each class. No country has formally carried democracy so far; but that has not made education a matter of personal negotiation rather than an imposed burden. The councils have completely failed to change the spirit of the institution; the parents are often absorbed by internal rivalries or political bickering. What the pupils learn, when and how they do it, is still fixed by the omnipotent Minister, who changes his mind and the syllabus with the same distraught frequency, to the point that the year's set books are sometimes not revealed till the last possible moment. The increased autonomy the Minister announces from time to time is purely illusory, for he holds the purse strings as tightly as ever. In 1973 one Minister allowed schools to dispose of 10% of their time as they pleased, but very few took advantage of this liberalization, partly because little money was made available. The history of education is full of such well-meaning decrees that are quickly forgotten.

Why do parents put up with this system? Because it is like the national lottery, it offers the chance of a prize for the child who succeeds, even if the majority emerge with paper qualifications that are of little use, and 20% get no paper at all. Parents both approve and disapprove of the school. They are often content with the progress of their own child, though they criticize the school for purveying useless knowledge; they admire the 'culture' their child picks up but they also say they do not understand the system, that they wish it paid more attention to parents and imposed more discipline. Well-educated parents are critical of the teachers and want reforms; but the majority are content with the traditional methods that survive. The poor, who have had very little education themselves, are intimidated by the teachers, whom they treat virtually as representatives of the government; they are concerned mainly to avoid getting into trouble with them by not filling in

[1] Boarding is more common in lycées (15%); in short technical schools and in upper sixth form colleges (preparatory classes for the grandes écoles) it is 20%.

the right forms. Some talk of going to school in the same terms as they describe their own day at work: putting in one's eight hours; they make Freudian slips, calling teachers employers. They say they are too busy and tired to see the teachers; only a quarter of a sample of such uneducated parents ever did visit the schools; they often felt humiliated when they did go, conscious that they could not speak properly themselves. 'They despise us because we have no education.' They have no wish to go to be told that their children are good for nothing. Many are unaware of the subtleties of courses which effectively downgrade their children; to fight for one's child needs more resources than they have.

The teachers are perennially dissatisfied, complaining not just of too much work, of over-large classes, of too much violence in the schools, as teachers more or less everywhere do, but also of not enough respect, initiative and freedom. They no longer feel themselves the pioneers of progress as they used to. Men are deserting the profession (61% of secondary and 75% of primary teachers are women). Teaching no longer even offers the consolation that it is a step up in the world: the working and lower middle classes are much less attracted by the profession now; it is increasingly middle-class girls and mothers appreciative of long holidays who are going into it. The competition for the jobs is more intense than ever with the over-supply of graduates, but many teachers are unqualified, on low pay, a relic of the days of rapid expansion. Over half of teachers in one survey admitted they chose the job not from a sense of vocation but as a last resort. That still leaves a very large number who are altruistically and passionately dedicated to their work, and love it, but their affection is not always returned, or at least not quite in the way they would like it returned. Their role is ambiguous because they are both part of the establishment, dispensing compulsory lessons, and (for the most part) rebels against it; they claim to be preparing the young for the future, but they are ill at ease with many aspects of modernity; they see the television as a dangerous, sometimes an evil rival; they represent values which are not those of most of their pupils; their cult of equality is open to the charge of hypocrisy, in that they are a highly hierarchical corporation receiving widely different salaries for very similar work, treating diplomas almost as though they were aristocratic titles. 'In my lycée,' says one teacher, 'the headmaster shakes the hands of the *agrégés*, holds out two fingers to the *certifiés* and merely nods distractedly at all the other teachers.' The teachers allow themselves to be given marks by inspectors, as though they are overgrown children. They are infinitely touchy about the level at which they teach. Though they disapprove of the system, they apply it because they cannot agree on an alternative. No agreement on education is of course possible; but the system works to categorize children, allocating them to classes which usually decide their fate for life.

University teachers are probably the most frustrated of all, even if they are the most privileged. University students in 1968 rocked the whole of society but they failed to change the universities in any profound way. The professors feel powerless to escape from the traditions they have inherited. French universities in the nineteenth century were very humble affairs, little more than examining bodies for the secondary schools and training colleges for teachers, lawyers and doctors; it was the secondary schools which formed the real heart of the educational system. When after the war higher education suddenly became fashionable and student numbers rose eight-fold, it seemed that the universities were at last destined for a new role. But they have remained shackled by their past; they marvel with envy and resignation at their international counterparts, whom they endow with imaginary advantages.

The first reason for this is that most of the best or ambitious students do not go to them, but to the *grandes écoles*, which are run independently on different lines; their grudge is far more serious than anything felt against Oxbridge or the Ivy League. Napoleon created a few *grandes écoles* to train high-level technical specialists for the top echelons of the state administration. As the number of possible specializations has increased, so too has the number of these schools, of which there are now 275, teaching everything from aeronautics to chemistry, telecommunications to agronomy and business, and they draw away 100,000 students. Until these two parallel systems are combined, the universities will remain the inferior partner in higher education. The *grandes écoles* have specialized in practical, scientific training and so it is to them, and not to the universities, that the leaders of industry and business are loyal; it is through their old boy networks that one gets a good job; the competition to enter them dominates the lives of the ablest schoolboys; because they are scientific, only about one-tenth of the students at them are women, and this helps to entrench male predominance in the top posts in business. But the *grandes écoles* give able people such unique privileges that their graduates have succeeded in maintaining them as an impregnable fortress.

Secondly, the universities cannot get used to the kind of students they are forced to cater for, and whom they have no say in choosing. They do not encounter sufficiently often that Chinese relationship of teacher and pupil, sustained by respect, affection and the shared excitement of discovery. At the University of Nancy, for example, there are students who say that for them the most important feature of university is their initiation into sexual life. The booksellers of that city complain that they sell few books to students and that students seldom have books in their rooms. Some students see their university years as essentially an intermediary period between their childhood under parental control and the slog of work that awaits them. It has been calculated that the majority work less than thirty hours a week, including attendance at lectures, scientists about thirty-two hours. They often say provocatively that their main interest is their leisure activities; if pressed for time, it is their work, rather than their leisure that suffers. One-third of them work part-time. They are not quite certain what they want to study, for on the one hand they dream of finding attractive jobs, and so seek diplomas that will help them to do that, but on the other hand they know that there are too many university diplomas, which are of little use on the job market; they are tempted, therefore, to study subjects that are at any rate interesting. But they are not generally willing to give their whole attention to their professors. When the competition is made severe, as in the Nancy medical school, where three-quarters of freshmen are thrown out after the first year, they work frantically for the last two months before the examinations, with the only aim of beating their fellows: no one enjoys the nasty atmosphere that is engendered. Professors always do find some keen students to compensate, but they look on the mass instruction as a chore, and they bitterly resent being so often treated as part-time entertainers. Their own dedication to their subjects has so dominated their own lives, that they cannot get used to their pupils treating study as a hobby, in an easy-going way. French students, in fact, are adopting the approach that was quite normal among the young aristocrats who went to Oxford in the eighteenth century, a forgotten precursor of the age of leisure.

Thirdly, most government-supported research is separated from the universities into special research institutes. Though it is not uncommon for a professor to hold a dual appointment in these, their existence does detract from the universities' prestige, and limits the opportunities for industry to make the universities feel partners in the development of new technology. In the 1960s some universities (particularly Grenoble) did do research for outside firms, but the enthusiasm for this kind of activity has waned; the new multinationals have set up their own research establishments and prefer to negotiate research contracts with the National Centre for Scientific Research and similar institutions, rather than swell local universities. An enquiry, a few years ago, among businessmen in Aquitaine, revealed that two-thirds of firms could not think of any way the universities could be useful to them, and only 3% had research contracts with them. Occasionally professors do play an important part in the transformation of the environment, as when one at Lille planned the local metro, and others at Pau university helped with the exploitation of the Lacq gas reserves. But what differentiates them from foreign and especially American counterparts is the wall that separates them from the business world. Michelin's factories dominate Clermont-Ferrand but he has done virtually nothing for his local university. There are old ideological reasons for this: the faculties used to be outposts of left-wing animosity against the rich. That is no longer true, but there is a new reason now for hesitating to build bridges with business: the universities, never having had much to do with private benefactors, imagine that such financial support will obstruct their independence.

Fourthly, the universities are all state institutions, dependent on changing governments for their budgets. That by itself makes it difficult for them to win the autonomy they long for, but their cult of national uniformity has led them to refuse to issue anything but national diplomas: until each university has the courage to award its own degrees, and stake its reputation on them, it will be unable to develop a truly independent character. But since professors are civil servants, they do not have the traditions of managing their own affairs; it is the ordinary professor's unwillingness to participate in the running of his own university that has ultimately defeated the hopes for autonomy. The committees that have been established have been dominated by divided, politicized trade unions, which have been incapable of wresting real power. If they knew more about the constraints on self-government that exist in foreign universities, even supposedly democratic ones, they would be less gloomy about their own achievements but, as it is, they are bitterly conscious only of the inadequate resources placed at their disposal to meet demands that are quite beyond them to satisfy.

For, fifthly, no one is clear what these universities are supposed to do, apart from harbouring nearly a million restless adolescents. The universities have traditionally specialized in self-reproduction, training for teaching jobs, but they are confronted with an over-population of teachers. Most of their diplomas have little immediate practical value. If they offered students a guarantee of 'general culture' at least they would be valued for that; but they are apparently inescapably dominated by the cramming and examination system, which does not encourage purely disinterested enquiry or reading. Their adoption of an inter-disciplinary syllabus has been disappointing, because this has often simply meant an invasion of mathematics into the humanities, without any compensatory study of poetry by scientists, but above all because it has increased the number of examinations. The attempt to break radically with tradition by the establishment of the University of Vincennes has ended in tragedy, and in its exile to the suburbs. French education has always supported limited innovative experiments, despite the superficially asphyxiating uniformity; that is why French pedagogy retains its intellectual vitality. But the destruction of old formalities at Vincennes, even though it did not go much beyond what many American universities were doing at the same time, did not have as widespread an influence as the reformers had hoped; the great ferment of enthusiasm around the early Vincennes, when almost anything seemed possible, has turned sour.

The hope that the universities may find a new spirit as pioneers in 'life-long education' and in the 'universities of the third age' for the elderly remain unfulfilled; only a tiny proportion of their budget is being devoted to this; only a tiny minority of the public has shown itself to be interested. The universities are not really equipped, as they stand, to teach the practical skills most adults demand from them. All these frustrations make professors forget that there are plenty of nooks and crannies in their system to allow them a great deal of freedom, so that as individuals they are able to perform in teaching, writing and researching at a level that is frequently unsurpassed abroad; they have ample scope for good relationships and interesting work when they have the talent for this. The *grandes écoles* have made themselves into mutual admiration societies: the universities could do so too, if they wanted.

The practical results that follow from this system of higher education are not as eccentric as is often supposed. The institutions may have a very different appearance from what is found abroad, but their graduates cannot be categorized as forming a completely peculiar breed. In the training of engineers, for example, the commonsensical British have the reputation of producing commonsensical and practical engineers and the French high-flown theorists. That may perhaps have been partly true once. British engineers used to be trained by apprenticeships, but they are now largely taught in universities, where engineering is a branch of science and therefore considerably more theoretical than it is in many countries. By contrast, the rather general and abstract mathematical training that used to be given to French engineers is now supplemented by far more concern for practical applications. A French engineering student today follows a syllabus very similar in academic content to that provided by British universities, except that he takes longer over it, and so studies his subject in greater depth and develops a higher level of mathematical ability. In his final year, however, he specializes in a particular branch and, increasingly, practical training in industry is being included in his course. French engineers criticize themselves for being good at solving problems, but less good at discovering what the problems are. British engineers complain for their part that they are being trained by the universities to be scientists rather than potential managers, which is perhaps saying almost the same thing. British engineers therefore often go on being engineers all their lives, whereas an American engineer who is not a manager by thirty-five is considered to have missed the boat. The French are in fact now much nearer the American than the British in this respect. The existence of the *grandes écoles*, with their prized special privileges, encourages bright students to become engineers: so though France and Britain produce an almost identical number of graduate engineers, the French ones emerge from a far more competitive selection: between 30 and 40% of applicants for courses in engineering at British universities are admitted, and two-thirds of applicants for mathematics courses, but in France the proportion of applicants to admissions can be as high as 100 to one (in aeronautics) and is generally around ten to one. The disadvantage of that is that engineering has not become a general degree taken by run of the mill students, as it has in the United States and Japan, both of which produce 80,000 graduates a year compared to France's 12,000. France, however, partly makes up for this by a strong non-university training for technicians.

It does not, of course, follow that a country is more successful industrially because it has a lot of engineers. An inventor is, after all, usually a person who does not take his education too seriously. What is probably more decisive today is not just the ability to invent, but the willingness to borrow other people's inventions. British engineers, perhaps because they were once the world's inventors, are less good at this poaching. Judged by the balance of trade in income and expenditure on patent rights, Britain borrows very little from abroad, whereas France buys up foreign patent rights almost as avidly as the Japanese though the Americans are easily the world's most willing buyers).[1] One should not deduce from this that French engineers are open-minded in all aspects of their lives. Engineering students are certainly politically more conservative, more religious and more conformist in their social opinions and behaviour than university students; they are not generally high-flying intellectuals and read surprisingly little (one-third do not even read a daily newspaper); having crammed themselves silly to get into the *grandes écoles*, they take it fairly easy there, most of them not exceeding a forty-hour week of study. That may perhaps pass for a portrait of engineering students in many countries.

Even though there are so many experts on education, they have not managed to produce very much in the way of serious comparisons between what they do to young people in France and what happens elsewhere. They have certainly not managed to destroy the myths that continue to be cherished, and which are not only untrue today, but were never true. Thus, for example, England is supposed to have had its class system bolstered by its public schools, in contrast to France's lycées which were imagined to have opened the path that led every talented boy to the top. In fact, the best French secondary schools of the *ancien régime*, which were run by Jesuits, deliberately sought to produce pupils who would be 'gentlemen', *comme il faut*, distinguishable from the masses by their tastes, manners and knowledge of Latin; and the lycées of Napoleon continued that tradition, openly creating an 'elite'. Until the present generation, far fewer boys received a secondary education in France than in England, whose grammar schools contained twice as many pupils. In England scholarships were far more numerous and it was far commoner for poor children to move up from primary schools to the grammar schools than to the lycées. The English public schools were probably as open to new blood in the nineteenth century as the lycées; the English boarding school system was probably more cruel, but was not in total contrast with the way lycée pupils were treated, for two-thirds of the latter were also boarders. English education

---

[1] Ratios of receipts for patents sold abroad to expenditure for patent rights bought: United States 1:10, Japan 1:4, France 1:3, Germany just under 1:3, Britain 1:2, though other sources give Britain a ratio of 4:3.

was supposed to emphasize character; the lycées set about achieving that in a different way, but the French private schools became increasingly popular precisely because they aimed to shape character too. The cult of examinations engulfed both countries, even if by different routes. And in both countries it soon became obvious that what determined a child's success in life was not necessarily his examination results but more often who his father was. So the sharp distinctions between English and French schooling rest on flimsy evidence, even if there are subtle differences of atmosphere and major differences in detail.

The teachers have so grown in numbers that they now form a kind of new army, with its own ways of thinking, and its own ideals. Everybody has done compulsory service in this army and has emerged more or less influenced, grateful, or resentful. Precisely because the teachers are now such a powerful lobby, they arouse a new kind of anticlericalism against them. Their mission in the past was to civilize the nation and nationalize its citizens; it was in the schools that children were taught that they were French. Uncertainty and scepticism about their mission confronts them now, rather in the way that hostility to the Church threatened religion in the past. It is not just French education that is in crisis (it always has been in crisis) but education itself. It is increasingly obvious that no solution will please everybody.

So a fair judgment of a French person's education must involve not just an assessment of how good his (or her) school and teachers were, nor how much he imbibed from them, but also what he succeeded in rejecting, and, above all, what he has found out on his own. Inside every French education, there is usually concealed a more or less minor French revolution.

23

How not to be intimidated by their intellectuals

Every week, in the *Nouvel Observateur*, Jean Daniel gives his opinions. Every week he is read by people who want to know what they ought to think about what is going on in the world. Jean Daniel has been called one of France's chief 'spiritual directors' and his paper 'the intellectuals' parish magazine'. Intellectuals deal in opinions and that is a trade in which it is easier to make a fool of oneself than in any other: the demand for guidance is larger and the temptation of conformity is strong. Jean Daniel, however, does not know for certain what he thinks. He would like to know: 'I need a faith,' he says. But his greatest antipathy is reserved for the dogmatic and for experts. He calls economists practitioners of science fiction and observes that no two experts ever agree, not even two Marxists. He has his gods, Gide and Camus, whom he greatly admired in his youth, but he does not want to be a slave of a great thinker. His whole life has been 'a slow search for a solitary affirmation of myself, on the side lines of the great thinkers'. He refuses to be a mere follower, but he has also always loved admiring people; he gets pleasure from finding people whom he can admire and he mistrusts those who do not feel a need to, or cannot admire. His taste is for the complex; he wants 'to possess all, without having to choose between alternatives'. He feels happier asking questions than answering them, but he is opposed to scepticism; he values discussion, but he wants it to give rise to solutions, even though these solutions are multiple; he seems happiest when there are several solutions.

He was trained as a philosopher, but at the age of twenty-five was suddenly given the opportunity to become an influential political speech writer. That brief experience put him off both politics and power. So when the socialists were elected to office in 1981, and he was offered a ministry, he refused, deciding that he had no desire to make others bow before him, and partake in a play in which people would treat him as a Superman. To enjoy power is to hope that by wielding it you prove that you are up to the task, that you are not a bundle of weaknesses, but that is to blind yourself. He would prefer to be a Flaubert than a minister. Or at least that is just one of the things he would like to be. 'Everyone wants to be multiple,' in other words, to be lots of other things. Whether that is indeed true of every one, in his case at least this wish expresses a longing to escape from his sense of his own limitations. What he regrets most of all is that he has only a few talents. As a young man he would have liked to be an actor, because an actor is precisely the person who can attempt, or at least pretend, to be what he is not. Alternatively, he would have liked to have been a novelist, who can create a multiple world in fiction, and live through his characters. As a magazine editor, he does the next best thing: he lives through his contributors. In his earlier years, he used to spend a great deal of time with his writers and reporters, working out what they ought to say: he played a role akin to Pygmalion. The journalist is a novelist of sorts: even today, when he sends out a reporter, he feels a pang of jealousy that it is they, and not he, who will have the joy of creating a story.

He won international fame himself in his youth for being one of the first reporters to reveal the use of torture in Algeria; he was severely injured during the fighting there. He feels very strongly involved in what goes on around him; he needs to feel 'engaged', committed; like an actor, he is dependent on other people's reactions to what he does and says; he is unhappy alone and needs the constant stimulation of other people's support and criticism. He therefore refuses to despise people. He knows he writes for an audience which is not a carbon copy of himself; he is careful not to insult it, not to criticize it except through the medium of self-criticism. Though fascinated by Sartre, he could never share or understand Sartre's hate of his background and of the family. Himself the son of a worker, he says he has no guilty conscience about having become a bourgeois. He dreams of a country without classes, without races, without frontiers, without hierarchy; and that means also, a society in which intellectuals do not congregate in a ghetto and form themselves into ideological chapels. He holds the position he does, as one of the major political opinion leaders in the country, because ultimately he is not interested in politics. It is the moral side of politics, not the day-to-day squabbling, that really concerns him. He has an exceptional capacity for empathy, for understanding what people feel. 'I am so interested in people that I agree with them,' but he also says he does not believe much of what people tell him; and good talkers he likes least of all.

His horizons extend beyond France. He can speak English, though he is only really confident in French. He feels personally injured by the decline of Britain, whose civilization he regards as having embodied permanent values, like the fair play of cricket, a sense of proportion (*mens sana*), humour, and above all habeas corpus, which he ranks as the third most important inheritance of mankind, after the sacrifice of Abraham, and Jesus saying that he who has never sinned should throw the first stone. But though he partly modelled his magazine's style on that of America's 'new journalism', and though he feels some kinship for the 'wandering Jew' element in American life, his sympathies do not extend to the United States. He once interviewed John Kennedy, who said to him that he had decided not to bother any more about Franco-American relations, because it was a pure waste of time: Kennedy had found that he and General de Gaulle agreed about absolutely nothing. Daniel claims that the different attitudes of France and the United States to food are a major barrier between the two countries (whereas a Frenchman instantly understands Chinese food). This is not flippant: it points to a visceral discomfort, which no amount of individual personal friendships or of admiration for Americans in particular professions can overcome: ultimately that is explained by the fact that Daniel's focus has always been France. He was brought up in Algeria and used to think that 'France was enough', that everything that came from France was extraordinary. Since the loss of Algeria, and the death of his mother, his attachment to that country has faded. Over the last ten years, he felt France was becoming less lively, but the socialist government has revived his faith in it, because he thinks it may again become what it used to be, a country of generosity, enthusiasm, welcoming and open-minded. He concedes that France is no longer a great power, but he hopes that it may recover its significance by carrying out an original experiment in socialism, which would serve as a model to the world. But he admits that it is old-fashioned to try and give other people lessons. He admits that it used to be easier for France to be welcoming in the past when it could be generous from a position of strength and that is one way to explain the new chauvinism of some Frenchmen: they feel on the defensive; but they are just large enough as a country to go on as though theirs is a separate, self-sufficient world.

Jean Effel

The Creation of the World

Why did you create all this?
If people ask you, say you know nothing.

Ultimately, what has interested Daniel is human relations, how people treat each other in the different spheres of their activity: he sees these relations as having been radically transformed by the collapse of the belief in hierarchy, and by the new attitudes of women. However, now as old age approaches, he is finding human caprice a little trivial, and he is trying to sort out what he should think about God. Daniel writes with a seemingly authoritative voice, which conceals the hesitation behind it. It is because outsiders do not see that layer of uncertainty beneath the convictions, and beneath the forceful, polished prose, that they are intimidated by French intellectuals, as the backbone of the country's obstinacy. But it is wrong to see them as a distinct class.

Far fewer French people have read the books of Lévi-Strauss than have worn the jeans of his American namesake: why then does this author, and intellectuals in general, enjoy such high status among his fellow countrymen? Why is the Latin Quarter in Paris the object of pilgrimage for so many foreigners long past their student days? Why is it that, nevertheless, even these pilgrims have so much difficulty in understanding what French intellectuals are talking about? What kind of opium or laughing gas impregnates the atmosphere of the Left Bank cafés to make those who sit in them feel so intelligent and exhilarated? The answers to these questions take one into the realms of magic. Any exploration of the French must include a visit to a Parisian intellectual, because he belongs to a small group that have cast a magic spell on the way the French are perceived by themselves and by foreigners. One needs to learn how this magic works, or one will continue to repeat parrot-like the old platitudes about France and persist in believing the myths that have been created about it. Intellectuals are specialists in the interpretation of the meaning of life; they are professional manufacturers and salesmen of opinions; the opinions that are held about France were invented by intellectuals. So France has in a way been created as much by intellectuals as by kings and armies conquering territory. On a superficial level, the French derive their identity from more or less believing the myths which the intellectuals have taught them. The intellectuals have made France not just a place, but an idea, a dream, and they have given that dream its special flavour, like cooks who transform a dish with an exotic sauce. One must distinguish the sauce from the basic ingredients. One must, therefore, meet the cooks to understand what goes on in their kitchen.

It is they who explain why the American dream appears to be so different from the French dream. The American dream is incarnated in the experience of Americans themselves: the Founding Fathers, the frontiersman, the migrant, the tycoon served as models everyone could hope to imitate. But there are no exact French equivalents of these: instead the French dream is a nightmare discussion of principles and ideologies. It is wrong to conclude that the Americans are practical and the French are abstract. The Americans can also be abstract. (Thornton Wilder has indeed argued that Americans are essentially abstract, in their physical mobility, their superiority to place and environment, their attraction not to the present but to the future; though Vann Woodward has replied that it is the Northern States that are abstract, while Southerners fear abstraction.) However, in France it is the intellectuals who have claimed to play the role of the frontiersman, and it is their language that has coloured the debate as to what France is about. They have formulated the national goals and have given Frenchmen a sense of being the Chosen People. (There is as much in common between a Dutchman and a Frenchman, said Voltaire, as between a tortoise and a lively monkey. 'When I was a child,' said Cocteau, 'I believed that foreigners spoke no language, and only pretended among themselves to speak one.')

But whose kitchen should one visit? In 1981 an enquiry to discover France's most influential intellectuals revealed little agreement. The ethnologist Claude Lévi-Strauss came top of the poll, but with only 24% voting for him. The political theorist Raymond Aron was second, and the historian of ideas Michel Foucault third, each with about 20%. Another forty names received between 10 and 20% of the votes and beyond that votes were cast for a further 164 supposedly highly influential people, most of whom have probably never been heard of by the majority of the French people.[1] It was said that had Jean-Paul

---

[1] Jacques Lacan came fourth, Simone de Beauvoir fifth and Marguerite Yourcenar sixth. *Lire*, April 1981.

Jean Effel

The School for Flies

'It's as simple as that'

Sartre still been alive, he would have been overwhelmingly declared the winner, but that ignores the fact that Sartre had always stood at the very extreme of the left wing, disagreeing with most people most of the time. What this uncertainty does reveal is that intellectuals are themselves divided into groups and cliques which often abominate, or ignore, each other. That may appear to make their peculiar essence all the more elusive, until one realizes that their power of attraction comes from the application of the same principles that give French cooking its glory. French intellectuals are not modern specialists but heirs to a tradition that demanded that thinking should, like a subtly flavoured dish, be a concoction that leavens science with poetry and philosophy. An intellectual is not just a scholar, but an artist also. How he says things is as important as what he says, in the same way as how a piece of meat is cooked and seasoned is as decisive as the quality of the meat itself. He makes life more interesting and intense.

Claude Lévi-Strauss is a professor, such as are to be found everywhere, but he has more courage and wider horizons than most. He goes beyond knowledge, describing his theories as 'an act of faith'. He has indeed formulated a faith: it is both consoling and exciting: it is a way of looking at the world. His approach is all the more potent because it is not too eccentrically original: it is in fact a reiteration in new language and with new proofs of two ancient principles – the unity of human nature and the presence of order and system in an apparently chaotic world. It suggests to many that it is possible to find meaning where none seems to exist, and that there is a wealth of symbolic significance even in the most trivial details of life; it is a reaffirmation of the value of abstract thought. It is this promise of wisdom that makes it attractive as a master-key to knowledge, in much the same way as, a century ago, the 'positivism' of Auguste Comte, now out of fashion, was heralded as the open sesame to progress. Intellectual fashions give people the hope or illusion that they possess tools that can perform magic; they stimulate new discoveries by altering people's angle of vision; they create new common bonds among people in different professions; and they sprout a new jargon which ends up by becoming conformism and banality. Lévi-Strauss himself denies that he has any real disciples and he rejects the title of *maître à penser* (tr. guru) to his generation. He insists that his work is technical and can provide no guidance to others as to how they should behave. He abandoned all interest in politics in early youth. The purpose of life, he says, is 'not to get too bored'. He is, in other words, not the herald of an ideology, but a magician, and one who is not fooled by his own skill. His magic is in many ways a game for him. He has written his books as though he were composing operas, feeling that he was writing now a tune, now a recitatif, now a choral ensemble. He has always been a dedicated music-lover, who writes with music playing all the time 'as a stimulus to thought'; had he not been an ethnologist he would have liked to have been a composer. Music enables him to be carried away beyond himself, and that sensation is the nearest thing he knows to happiness. He does not claim to have found happiness, any more than certainty or truth.

He became an ethnologist because he felt ill at ease in France. He is not the archetypical Frenchman in whom his countrymen can recognize themselves. When asked what country he belongs to, whether he feels most attached to Alsace where his family originated, or to Paris where he lives, or to Brazil where he worked as a young man to escape from what he considered as the stifling atmosphere of France, he replies not that he is a Frenchman, but that he is first of all a Jew. He is an outsider. Though his grandfather was Rabbi of Versailles, he has never practised as a Jew, or had any use for Jewish theology; for him, to be a Jew means to be devoted to art, to the cultivated life. He regards himself as being a man of the nineteenth century, deriving his identity from the artistic world of the Second Empire, and owing more to his parents than his teachers. His father and two uncles were painters; he himself grew up with a passion for art; as a boy, he used to spend his pocket money collecting Japanese prints and African sculptures, exotic curiosities and old musical instruments. And Lévi-Strauss has become a guru, despite himself, because he is poet in prose, a writer of great skill who can charm, but also because he is an explorer, always bent on new adventures, who can carry his readers beyond themselves and give them the feeling that they are about to make contact with deeper truths and a broader life than they are used to. He is not just an armchair scribbler. When he was seventeen, his parents bought a peasant's cottage in the Cevennes, which led to his 'discovering nature', and finding physical effort as important as intellectual curiosity. He has always insisted that it is impossible to understand the world unless one enjoys manual contact with it: he is skilled also as a handyman. He has been three times married. He is, in other words, very much an individual who has sought to create his own kind of life and to transform his world into a more interesting place.

Lévi-Strauss is regarded by foreigners as incarnating qualities that are immediately recognizable as being French. But his combination of abstract reasoning, systematization and flowery language is very much his own: he has brought together common ingredients and concocted them into a very special intoxicating brew. This brew is probably as popular outside France as within it, because Lévi-Strauss reflects and appeals to a certain temperament that delights in systematization and theoretical speculation. Outside France this temperament is eccentric and is found mainly among academics. Inside France it is less odd, because it is manifested, even if only as a veneer and in certain situations, by educated people in general, and particularly by the ruling class. To talk in abstractions has become a sign of good breeding, a new version of the old aristocratic formulae of politeness. People like Lévi-Strauss are admired because they are not only clever at this game, but play it beautifully: his literary style has been as decisive in his success as his exceptionally powerful mind. He is the equivalent of the popular singer whose tunes everybody whistles; but it is foolish to imagine that the words of the songs represent the credo of a whole nation, or are even thought about much. Whereas the popular singer or film star is an exception, one in a million, trying to pass himself off as an ordinary person with the same feelings as anyone else, the intellectual is conscious of his abnormality and makes a virtue of it. His purpose is to discover an independent identity for himself; he is a pioneer of introspection. The most important influence intellectuals have had has been to cultivate individualism. They do not, therefore, reproduce themselves immutably, but encourage even greater variation between individuals; the influence of individual intellectuals is thus constantly eroded. Of course, since finding one's identity is no easy matter, there are plenty of intellectuals who masquerade at being original: the adoption of Lévi-Strauss' vocabulary is not a sign of his influence but of the extent to which he is misunderstood, because he worked it out to suit his own personality. Just as politeness or gallantry can conceal hypocrisy or a thousand other emotions, so the intellectuals' style of speech is the expression of a search for escape from doubt; its apparent dogmatism is a polished brilliant surface that hides as much as it reveals. There are few calling themselves intellectuals who will admit to being happy.

Polemic is therefore usually another aspect of the

intellectual's daily sustenance, because he is someone who likes to exert his critical faculties. That is why Sartre is, or was, another hero. Sartre represents another tradition, in that he told people what was wrong with the world. He defined who were contemptible, (*salauds*), in the same way as his own hero Flaubert had castigated the philistine 'bourgeois'. But Sartre raised this condemnation to a new plane, because whereas previous objects of the intellectuals' opprobrium had been specific classes of people, the *salaud* is a universal person, every one of us is a *salaud* to somebody. Sartre was suspicious of everyone with prestige or importance of any kind, whoever believed he had done his duty, as a son, a father, a spouse, or a leader; it was impossible to have any power at all, or any wealth, without being guilty, without being in some way contemptible. The only way out was to be committed (*engagé*) in the struggle for the liberation of mankind, fighting side by side with others. It was not just by subscribing to support insurrection of guerrillas in Africa or Latin America that one became free, but by making one's commitment one's dominant passion – a passion in the Christian sense also, in that it involved sacrifice. (It is no accident that a synonym for intellectual is cleric: both try to be witnesses to truth; if necessary they are martyrs.) That is why Sartre long continued to accept the insults of the Communist Party but supported it all the same. That is why Stalin's Russia, Mao's China, Castro's Cuba, Ben Bella's Algeria, were idealized one after the other; the struggle is never over. Sartre offered a stronger medicine than Lévi-Strauss, not a theoretical discovery of meaning in the world, but a passionate experience of it, creating the meaning by one's own actions. That forged deeply satisfying bonds of friendship, even if it sometimes involved creating myths.

Today the 'new philosophers' polemicize against these myths, and the new fashion is to attack all the old dogmas, and all dogma. Intellectuals are thus not necessarily 'left-wing'. They appeared to be so after the war, because the right wing had discredited itself by collaboration, but the right wing has now taken up arms again. Both left and right find the common man in the middle inadequate. The myth that French people are either left-wing or right-wing is another of the influential ideas the intellectuals have produced. It has meant that the French cannot work harmoniously together, and that old quarrels are perpetuated like family feuds long after their meaning is forgotten. Its logical simplicity is an example of the taste for dichotomy which follows from the reluctance to accept the contradictions of human behaviour. There are many intellectuals who believe they can master the world by explaining it, by reducing its apparent chaos to an order that can be expressed in words. To find the right word is half the battle. When the French play this verbal game, they appear to be a nation of intellectuals, but it is only one of many games they play, and they go on being contradictory despite their principles.

Paris lives by controversy, even if the shouting has made everyone hard of hearing. The excitement is never dimmed, because no one needs admit defeat. Paris is no longer obviously the intellectual capital of the world, as it could once claim to be, but it is probably the city that has the most intense intellectual life. The reason is that it is a capital at the same time of government, finance and of artistic activity. New York's intellectuals may be as active, but no one claims that all the best minds, let alone all the most powerful figures in politics, business and education, are concentrated here. More ideas may

Desclozeaux

be bursting like fireworks in California, but they are dispersed over a coast of a thousand miles. London's supremacy is challenged by Oxford and Cambridge. But though there are French cities with rich cultural heritages, none claims equality with Paris. It is the concentration in Paris of all those concerned with power, influence and entertainment, with decision and administration, that gives it its peculiar megalomaniac atmosphere. It is possible for people to know each other at much closer quarters, and to argue as unceasingly as a family does. The intellectuals of France do not feel they are prisoners in an ivory tower.

Moreover, they have behind them a glorious tradition; they walk the same streets where Voltaire and Rousseau, by a mere scrawl of the pen, were able to topple a whole kingdom. They sometimes, therefore, argue that they are so unique, that foreigners cannot hope to understand them properly. Pierre Nora (a Paris publisher, editor and professor) has warned Americans that French intellectuals are ineradicably 'Gallocentric': that though the young generation is fascinated by America, this feeling does not go deep; there is an 'incommunicability' between the two countries, 'an impossible dialogue'; this is not anti-Americanism, but worse, a basic incompatibility. The French intellectuals, says Nora, are heirs to a traditional role of 'spreading cultural values' which does not have an equivalent in America. 'American intellectuals are invested with a function, not a ministry; they exercise a trade, not a stewardship.' Many non-Frenchmen may indeed find that distinction difficult to understand, but it is a sign of the sense of community that sustains French intellectuals. France is to a certain extent an island, isolated intellectually from foreign countries, because only a tiny number of foreign publications are ever bought by its libraries and a very much smaller number are available for purchase; if one can read only French, it is difficult to know much about what the rest of the world is thinking. That is partly why France retains its character, and its sense of being a self-sustaining unit. But in reality French intellectuals have much more in common with foreign counterparts than they realize. The 'French' kind of intellectual can sprout as successfully abroad. How does Richard Sennett, spinning theories of authority and solitude on the fringes of Greenwich Village, differ from the system builders of the Latin Quarter? His Institute of Humanities is no imitation of the Paris House of the Sciences of Man, but it thrives on the support of a large audience of very intellectual laymen, as devoted to abstract discussion as the habitués of the College de France; the New York press follows these lucubrations with almost as much keenness as the journals of Paris. E. P. Thompson's fulminations against the currents of his time may be in the tradition of British nonconformism that goes back to the preachers of Oliver Cromwell's age, but they are no less in the tradition of Proudhon or Sartre. Carl Sagan is an example of an intellectual who has turned science into poetry for mass consumption, and he has been taken much more seriously, not surprisingly, by the French than the British. His manner is neither French nor American but simply nineteenth-century. There is still a demand for that.

French intellectuals are now being faced by the same problems that are challenging intellectuals everywhere. Their status is now quite different from what it was when the majority of their countrymen were illiterate, when books were virtually the only way to circulate ideas, when universities were no more than examining bodies, when government was carried on by comparatively few people, when the economy was decentralized, and when the church was the major spiritual force. They have lost some of their independence, for they are now part of the establishment. They have lost some of their authority, because they are increasingly specialized, unwilling to make judgements on matters they consider to be outside their competence. Their self-confidence is much diminished.

In the eighteenth century, the model Frenchman was the well-born courtier who had mastered all the rules of politeness. The intellectuals replaced that by a model of one who had mastered language and literature, who could argue logically and sophisticatedly, and above all who could talk about virtually any subject in general as opposed to in specialized terms: their ideal was the man of 'general culture'. They created a view of France which reflected that ideal. But now they have new preoccupations. Their goal of universal education has, more or less, been attained, which means that they have reached their frontier. As knowledge becomes increasingly difficult to synthesize, they are lapsing into the status of mere experts. As they become more numerous, they are more conscious of their diversity. Their international audience is no longer what it once was. Unesco's list of the world's most translated authors is not an adequate indication of their prestige, but it is significant that the French thinker who comes highest, Jean-Paul Sartre, appears in the 125th position. Lenin, Agatha Christie, Walt Disney, and Karl Marx head the list; the only French books in the top thirty are Perrault's seventeenth-century fairy tales, Jules Verne's nineteenth-century fantasies, Goscinny's comic strip Asterix and the crime stories of Simenon (a Belgian).

Finally, technocrats and media men everywhere have formed rival international fraternities; the intellectuals feel as challenged by them as parents do by disrespectful children. The philosopher Michel Serre has said, 'The place left vacant by

Zoran Orlic

Sartre is not available for anyone else to occupy, because it has been filled by the media, and not by a man. A philosopher no longer represents anything; it is the journalist who transmits the messages that matter.' And the journalists are keen to accept their role. The new editor of *L'Express* has made his motto: 'Out with the intellectuals, make room for the professionals.' The intellectuals have, of course, also become professionals, and that has forced them to leave the business of communicating with the public to experts in communication. This has placed the very notion of the intellectual in jeopardy. Intellectuals now feel they are being censored by the media men, and that they are in danger of being swept back almost into the same obscurity as their monkish forebears. They complain that it is no longer enough to write a book to exert influence, that there are so many books that only those which are recommended by the press and television are widely read (which is not entirely true). *Le Monde* receives about 10,000 books for review each year, but discusses only 1600 of these. Mention on the front page of *Le Monde* consecrates a book as important, and there are just a dozen people on that newspaper who decide that. 'A book which *Le Monde* does not mention does not exist', says Professor René Remond. To get an even larger audience, a book needs to be discussed on television, and particularly on the most influential programme, Apostrophes, which is run by one man, Bernard Pivot.

The intellectuals' quarrel with Pivot reflects discomfort in their relations with the public. Pivot is not just a media man, but a representative of the traditional provincial middle-class general reader, who likes reading books, but who has no pretensions to being a profound thinker. He is the son of a Lyon grocer; he never went to university and does not mix with people who have; he plays football; he loves eating as much as he loves reading and he is always seeking out new literary curiosities in the same way as he searches for new gastronomic delights; he is an observer of, but not a participant in, the rivalries that absorb the intellectuals; he is as interested by people as by ideas and likes to know what kind of person an author is. It is this class of general reader which explains why a philosopher can sell 30,000 copies of a book improbably entitled *The I-do-not-know-what and the Almost-nothing*: when Jan-

kelevitch appeared on television, the viewers found him interesting and went out and bought his book. However, there are
intellectuals who criticize Pivot for discussing books on subjects
he knows nothing about. That shows how some intellectuals,
transformed into experts, find it difficult to accept that everyone
has a right to his opinion, and how the tradition of general
culture, which abhorred specialization, has declined. Authors
of course complain just as much that those who do know about
their subject do not do them justice either. The polemic among
specialists is just as painful to them as the failure of the press to
notice their work. If they are absolutely determined to make
their voices heard, they can become television pundits as well as
authors, and part-time publishers and university professors also;
two or three dozen people who wear these four different hats are
regarded as the real powers in the intellectual world; they are
not troubled by censorship; on the contrary, they play some part
in censoring those who do not interest them. Everyone with
power is a censor of sorts, and not just the media men. So long as
authors wish to sell books, they will be faced with the problem
that not everyone wants to buy their books. Popularization
(significantly called vulgarization in French) used to be one of
the strengths of French scholarship, but now that the size of the
academic community has grown, it is possible to publish just
for one's colleagues. The pure researcher who will not or cannot
say anything intelligible to ordinary mortals can get by without
them, and they sometimes resent it.

That is the problem of their external relations. Their internal
relations are dominated by their division into mutually contemptuous cliques and systems for mutual congratulation,
which both console and worry them. French book publishing
provides a good illustration of this. Authors have used it to
build up networks of patronage and clientage which centre
around the 'director of series': publishers employ part-timers to
find books for them, whom they reward with a percentage of the
royalties. Their directors usually seek to build up a series which
reflects their taste, which adds to their prestige and creates little
groups around them. There is nothing unusual in having to
please a particular individual in order to get one's work published, but in France favouritism is openly publicized by this

Sempé

In your last novel, it clearly appears that you are a worried
and nervous man. Can you explain that to us . . . ?

method, and made the basis of ideological or aesthetic wars.
Loyalties are developed to an extent unknown in the Anglo-
Saxon world. For example, many authors who review books
somehow find that they review books from their own publishing
firm, in preference to others; when they award literary prizes,
they give the prizes to authors from their own firms. Three firms

publish 25% of all French novels, but their authors constitute 70% of the judges of the major literary prizes, and they win 82% of those prizes. The judges are given six weeks to read 150 novels; they look at only a tenth of them, selected largely according to who publishes them; they are wooed by presents, flowers, inflated advances. Instead of spending large sums on advertising, publishers concentrate their efforts on prizes, and on personal recommendations: authors are given an almost unlimited number of free copies, sometimes as many as three hundred, to send, suitably inscribed, to influential people in the hope of being talked about. It is not by accident that book dedications have become even more ornate and delicately flattering than the flowery final sentences of letters. Winning a literary prize has become one of the main ways of making a book a best seller. The clannishness is strengthened in the periodical reviews. Pierre Nora, who has a monthly journal as well as editing several book series, sees himself as an 'orchestra conductor' for ideas, 'creating intellectual waves'. That is why it is a stormy and noisy sea. The numerous small publishing firms established, often with no profit motive, to challenge the domination of such conductors, have been only partially successful, because their distribution has never been very effective.

France's leading intellectuals have a role that in Britain is shared by the Church of England and Her Majesty's Opposition. They explain what is wrong with society and lament that people do not heed their wisdom and their precepts. Their complaints are part of the system and they are treated with respect. In France 12% of the population say that the support of intellectuals for a political candidate influences them. That is almost exactly the same proportion as in England regularly go to church or chapel and listen to the preaching of the clergy. In some circles, and in some moods, respect for intellectuals is raised to the point that they are transformed into counterparts of the cherubim and seraphim who in Christian mythology surround the throne of God. (Cherubim represented excellence in knowledge and seraphim fervour in love.) They can play tunes on the trumpets of reason and emotion with such skill that they are sometimes taken to be almost minor gods themselves, with an independent power of their own. The belief in their influence on humanity's destinies constitutes a private sort of astrology in which the educated dabble. This astrology can be stimulating, amusing and sometimes convincing, but it does not rule the whole of people's lives. So the purpose of visiting a Parisian intellectual is not necessarily to meet a leader of opinion, but to get a feeling for the complex aspirations that are concealed behind the French reputation for logic, and an understanding of the approach that makes them such apparently obstinate opponents in international argument.

It will also paradoxically reveal that not only the intellectuals are intellectuals. Régis Debray, formerly adviser to Che Guevara and now adviser to President Mitterrand, has calculated that there are today 130,000 intellectuals in France (which is by a strange coincidence, almost exactly how many clergy there were in France in the eighteenth century). But I think it is out of date to regard them as an elite, in terms of power and influence: that is a legacy of the age of illiteracy. There is no longer any necessary link between how much education a person receives, or what job he does, and his mental life. It is time, perhaps, to stop using the word as a noun, and start using it only as an adjective; and to ask not who is an intellectual, but what portion of people's time is taken up with intellectual concerns; when they are vegetables, when animals and when thinkers. That will require quite different calculations. 'Intellectuals' themselves do not give top priority to things of the mind all or most of the time; a large part of their energies is absorbed in gossip and factional strife, in bargaining for reputation; for those who seek to influence others are often most dependent on the good opinion of their fellows. To be an intellectual is to make oneself vulnerable, and not necessarily powerful. The archetype of the intellectual is one who loves to question everything, but who nevertheless has gods whom he cherishes; each has his own heroes, his own form of self-esteem; he is liable to express himself very strongly about his enemies, even though they may be separated from him only by the subtlest nuances. Which is why, in the cafés of St Germain des Près, one can express any opinion one likes, but with more than a fifty-fifty chance that one will be branded as an idiot.

Part Six

How to sympathize with them

24

How to interpret
the anger of teenagers

The bored teenagers who hang around aimlessly at the street corners of dreary suburbs look dangerous; and if you are lost, they may not be the best people from whom to ask the way. They will not talk to you unless you make a real effort, and they have good reason to be suspicious — they are the children who have never won any prizes. For example, a criminal record is the only qualification that Emmanuel has acquired by the age of eighteen. His suspended prison sentence for burglary and car stealing hangs over him like a third-class diploma. The police have several times suspected him of other crimes, but have been unable to pin any more on him. Emmanuel left school at fifteen, on the ground that he was learning nothing useful: he told his parents that they could summon the police to take him to school every day, but otherwise he would not go. His parents, who are utopian, individualist middle-class people, acquiesced. Emmanuel has made a few attempts to work, but not for long. Since he has no skills, he cannot get any work that interests him. His parents are forced to support him, because he warns them that if they do not, he will resort to theft. He has spent the best part of three years wandering around the country, occasionally dabbling in drugs, trying to start rock music groups, but mainly just seeking out the company of others who share his attitude of rebellion. He seems, on first acquaintance, to be a perfect example of a boy who typifies the conflict of generations and the total rejection of the adult world by the young. But it is only to defend himself against strangers that he adopts his distant look, his curt speech, his provocative attire and the menacing suggestion that he is a dangerous and dim lout. When he wants to, he can talk with a fluency, a lucidity, a sharpness that verge almost on poetry.

There is no rancour in his attitude to his parents. 'My father,' he says, 'is not made to be a father, he does not know what a father should do, which is why he gives me money, to assuage his conscience. I do not blame him.' There is no empty arrogance in his rebellion either: when his father reproaches him for his lack of ambition, for being 'a rat trying to profit from the society he rejects', for wanting money without working, he replies, yes, that's true; and he admits that he has not been able to put forward any real alternative to his father's values. So it is impossible to argue with him, because he does not claim to know better than his elders. He used to have fun with his parents until about the age of fourteen; he enjoyed participating in their adventures and demonstrations as ecologists, but he now thinks that was a superficial happiness, he was merely copying them. The great break came when they went together to protest against nuclear power at Malville: the police threw grenades at the crowd, causing much injury and even death; 'I do not blame my parents for not fighting the police (they are believers in non-violence) but I was disgusted that they simply watched from a distance, instead of going down and putting themselves face to face with the police. I never again believed in their principles, their ecology or their activism.' Emmanuel tells his parents that all their principles and values have got them nowhere, that they have never been able to change anything; they cannot provide a model. He regards his father as being a happy man, who has professionally speaking made a success of his life, but his father cannot give him what he needs most. 'I have never had the approbation of my father because I have always disappointed him. My teachers always said I had potential, unfulfilled potential.' His parents sometimes do praise him, but he cannot accept their praise as being objective. So his life has necessarily involved searching elsewhere.

First he has tried to win approval that he can really believe in. 'I need others to prove that I exist, to enable me to be proud of myself; I need encouragement from others.' He once drew a series of comic strips 'which really came from the very depths of myself, they were a sort of song which I put in pictures, trying to show the boredom of life; it had no words, no beginning and no end; it was sad, lugubrious; no one understood.' His father could not see what it was about. His mother said it was good, 'but that was not enough. I know it was good, that it was not empty. I was very disappointed. I feel alone in my ideas, in my way of seeing life.' Emmanuel has, therefore, secondly, devoted himself to finding soul mates. He deliberately sought out *voyous* (layabouts) in his travels, 'perhaps from romanticism', young people on the fringes of society (*marginaux*) who were trying to construct their lives independently and who were protesting in a different way from their parents. He became a punk. For a time he found in the nihilism and anger of punk music the expression of his own despair, 'I thought we would become a new class, I thought I had found brothers, because I need to feel I belong to a group or class. But I realized punk was not getting me anywhere. All my friends are still punks, but their heads are empty, they simply plug their emptiness with punk, it simply stops them thinking about themselves and their situation; they do not think. I imagined the punks were like me, but they were not. We pretended we were in the shit, but we were not. I was living like a poor boy, but I was really a petty bourgeois supported by my father. We smashed things up because the English punks did, but we were not English.' He enjoyed the fancy clothes, but that was not enough: he thought there was a philosophy behind them. The punks replaced the laws they detested by laws of their own which turned out to be even worse, 'fascist, useless, cheapening violence: that helped me live, but only for a time, not in the long run. I discovered I was still alone.' Punk music now annoys him, because it got him nowhere, and because he was disappointed to discover that he was 'just an imitation of the 1960 rockers, stupid and nasty'. He would very much have liked to have become a good musician, but he decided he did not have enough talent.

'I feel confused,' he keeps on saying. Nevertheless, he can fathom what he is seeking when he tries. Friendship matters a great deal to him. 'I feel happy when I have satisfying relationships with people: to be a friend means to exist for someone else, who exists for you, but going beyond mere mutual aid.' But that is not easy to find: he lives now with a pretty punk-looking

NO FUTURE... QUELLE AVENTURE...

Boredom

girl, formerly a member of the Communist Youth, who laments that he remains deeply pessimistic. However, he has yielded to his parents' pressure and started attending a course in drama. He quite likes it, but 'it does not come from the heart': he is not going to commit himself easily. Acting may prove a way of earning money without too much effort; perhaps, he adds, it may make him happy – which is why he is willing to try it. (He does want to be happy.) The fact that it is unlikely to offer a regular job does not worry him, because he claims he does not want security – he has always had that from his parents. Acting might be something he could do well, it might not be too boring: 'I feel I could do it,' and he certainly has that combination of cocky good looks and sultry contempt that are so often popular. He drew a picture about modern youth at my request; it is the terrifying portrait of anger and despair on page 420. It was clear he could become an artist too, if he wanted. Provided he could find his self-esteem, rather than the esteem of his elders. His is not a story about rebellion, but about an independent effort to find his own individuality. Emmanuel is a true descendant of the several generations who have sought to make the individual think for himself. And the moral of his story is not in his view that his parents ought to have been more strict with him: if they had been, he says, he would have left them, and 'I would have become a real layabout.'

The conflict of generations may appear to represent the most dangerous and powerful form of modern anger, which has most chance of translating itself into change, since the young will sooner or later, inevitably, assume power. The conflict of generations is, however, largely a myth, and that helps to explain why change is so slow and superficial. Adults undoubtedly believe that there is a conflict of generations. They believe, for example, that most young people are left-wing, rebellious or revolutionary. That actually is false. A decade ago, only one-quarter of young people (aged sixteen to twenty-three) were unambiguously left-wing; today, the majority vote left-wing, but so do the majority of the middle aged. However, when asked what the political leanings of their own children are, parents answer either that they mainly have no political opinions, or that they share their parents' opinions. In talking about their own children, they are right. But youth in general is a bogey and they wrongly imagine that it is a threat to them, like some invading horde of barbarians. It seems to be so, because, following the baby boom after the war, youth appeared to be more numerous than ever; and indeed almost half of French people (45%) are now under twenty-five. Will that tilt the balance of power in their favour? But in the past, youth was even more numerous, because the old died off more quickly; in fact there is a smaller proportion of young people today than in the Old Regime. The young seem more numerous partly because the other change of the post-war era has been that they have been kept on at school; their segregation today contrasts with their former rapid absorption into jobs and factories in their early teens or even before; King Louis XIII was told that he was an adult when he celebrated his fifth birthday. The rebellion of youth, in so far as it exists, is directed as much against the school and the constraints imposed upon the young, as against the adult worker. All the more so since today children are being given far longer scholastic sentences than ever before: 80% are already attending kindergarten at the age of three, and 50% of boys and 58% of girls are still at school at eighteen; even after all that training they are not certain of a job, of being able to exist independently. They on the whole accept this because they are less iconoclastic, and more timid, more concerned with security, than their reputation suggests. They absorb more of their parents' values than the parents themselves realize. Only one-third of young people say that their parents live in a mental world so different that there is no point in having discussions with them. One-third sometimes think this, but rarely. The rest consider themselves to be on the same wavelength. It is the same with religious beliefs: 54% of children have the same degree of religiosity as their parents, 14% are more religious and 33% less. So more than half of young people are definitely not at loggerheads with their parents.

It is true that from time to time the young appear to rebel in ways that make adults feel completely alien and rejected. The classic way of doing this is to adopt clothing, hairstyles, slang and music that adults find abominable. It is a classic way, because generation after generation has done it, only to forget just how outrageous they once were. *Epater le bourgeois* (to shock the respectable) is an old French tradition. Before punk, successive generations have distinguished themselves with provocative names: the fashionable young were les Incroyables in the Revolution of 1789, Les Jeunes France under Louis XVIII, the Cocodès under Napoleon III, les Toufous, les Zutistes, les Hirsutes in the Third Republic, les Zazous under the occupation, then les J3 at the liberation, les YéYé in the early 1960s. The cancan, the polka, the waltz were all condemned as immoral by archbishops, only to be followed by the equally disgraceful shimmy, charleston, rock and roll, etc.; all appeared additionally disgusting because they were foreign importations. The revolt of 1968 may seem to be a much more serious attack on adult values. It certainly shook the country's complacency and did force a limited reformation of manners and ideals. But it was not a battle of the young against the old. The young were as divided as the old. Their crime, indeed, was that they momentarily tore off the veil of hypocrisy that enabled adult society to survive; they showed up its guilt, its contradictions and absurdities. But by stimulating the pruning of the old tree, they have enabled it to take on new life. After all this commotion, one-half of unmarried people aged over twenty-six still live with their parents. That does not prove that harmony exists between the generations, but shows that the choice between adventure and security is not a foregone conclusion for the young. The generations take increasing care not to offend each other. Half of young married adults say they abstain from discussing certain subjects with their parents. The subject on which they disagree most, of course, is how to bring up the children. Should adults teach the young what is right and what is wrong? Eighty percent of grandparents say yes; 55% of parents say yes. This does not represent a total breach between generations. The young rebels of 1968, who are now in their thirties and forties, have for the most part followed much the same path as their parents: they have got married, bought a house, and worry about making ends meet. Adults try to dress 'younger'; they pay lip service to the merits of youth. What has youth left to rebel against?

First of all, the difficulty of becoming an adult, of obtaining a job so that they can be like everybody else. They have not revolted against the idea of work: only 5% dislike the thought of working, as repeated polls continue to reveal. It is unemployment that frightens and angers them. Those who hold jobs justify their good fortune on the ground that they have qualifications and experience and refuse to share their privilege with the young, who cannot help having no experience. What is worse is that when the young do obtain qualifications, that does not guarantee them a job. There is now no qualification, even graduation from the top *grandes écoles*, that automatically opens the door to employment. University degrees, the *baccalauréat*, the certificates for skilled tradesmen, no longer count for much in themselves, since more and more people have them. A mechanical engineer graduating from the National Institute of Applied Sciences in Lyon, for example, has spent almost a year looking for a job, and he is becoming desperate, because he knows that his chances will diminish when the next year's lot of graduates comes on to the market. He is rejected because he has no experience, or because employers prefer someone with fewer pretensions from a less prestigious college (like a technical university, IUT), or else for no obvious reason at all: much more humiliating than a simple rejection by return of post is an interview followed by a slip of paper giving no indication of why he failed to please. The young are caught in a vicious circle. Since there are no jobs, they go on studying to make themselves more qualified, but there are even fewer of the specialist jobs they prepare themselves for. As they receive more education, the number of labouring jobs increases; the demand for unskilled workers has increased by between 7 and 10% since 1965, and is expected to increase by 1% per annum for the next decade. The result is that the proportion of young people under twenty who get jobs as unskilled workers has risen from 22% to 35%.

The young see themselves as the most underprivileged in the matter of security. Those in employment are divided into two categories, those who are privileged to have jobs from which they cannot be sacked, most notably civil servants, and those who are at the mercy of their boss. The young are not sacked

quite as often as immigrants, but they do change jobs frequently, partly because they too are paid low wages; they are on
the look out for more money, and for more congenial work; they
resign more easily, unthinkingly, though they are doing this
less now. Since they have to go off for their military service at
eighteen, employers do not want to commit themselves to
them, and the young often do not see much point in trying to
get a permanent job until they have fulfilled that obligation.
Unemployment is looked on in much the same way as military
service: it is a *corvée*, a compulsory inconvenience that they have
to undergo. All this is less intolerable than it might be because
the young and employers have made the best of it. Employers,
anxious to escape the controls imposed on them by legislation
and trade unions, have increasingly made use of temporary
labour, which can be sacked without compensation, and which
suits small businesses paying low wages and having a seasonal
demand. Over 3000 agencies providing temporary workers
have mushroomed in the last few years, and France now stands
second only to the United States in its use of this kind of labour.
A small town like Valenciennes, with a population of 43,000,
has seventy such agencies. Temporary workers are of course
often exploited both by agencies and employers; they cannot
strike, they are the first to be sacked in a crisis; they cannot
think about marrying and getting a mortgage. But the young
accept that status when they see work as filling in gaps between
the accomplishment of other ambitions, like foreign travel or
study, or when they are keen to avoid committing themselves to
a particular trade. Temporary work also fits in well with the
rapidly expanding Black Economy. Unemployment is less of a
threat when one has learnt how to find jobs on the side, which
attract no tax, and which give one more scope for using one's
initiative and individual skills. That is the kind of job many
would like to go on doing.

The anger of the young manifests itself less against unemployment as a general phenomenon, which is often accepted
fatalistically as being a world-wide curse, than against the
individual employer who discriminates against them by not
giving them a chance, by offering them lower wages, by picking
on them when he cuts his labour force − even though they do

their job as well as older people – by treating them like dirt: 'If you are not satisfied, there's the door.' What they want is more respect. Each has his tale of humiliations and frustrations. Even when they reduce their pretensions and agree to be domestic servants, they find five others applying for the same job. This increasing willingness to limit their ambitions shows that even their pride is eroded. Girls dreaming of being models, air hostesses and ethnologists, end up glad to be taken on as clerks, second-class, in the civil service; after a year on a course in pottery or hand-weaving, they resignedly end up working for a bank. The social prestige of jobs counts far less now; prospects of promotion interest only 5% of girls and 10% of boys. What they have turned their hopes to is to leading a better life, despite their job, and if they are lucky enough to be able to choose between jobs, they prefer the one that has the most satisfying social atmosphere.

This has been taken as yet another sign of fundamental youthful rebellion. To be unconcerned by hierarchy and prestige, to lose interest in the problems of the class struggle, in the distribution of wealth and power, and in politics as a whole, implies a greater rejection of adult values than to be left-wing:

Grandville

School

at least those students who are left-wing are willing to play the adults at their own game. Now the young are more concerned by the quality of their lives, that is to say with improving their personal relations, their friendships, marriages, their enjoyment of nature, their serenity. Their goals are more cultural, in the widest sense, than economic or political; they are more individualist, and therefore it is less easy to negotiate with them collectively or even, as some put it, 'rationally'. What they want cannot readily be provided for by state planning. Fewer of them are willing to compete in the rat race. The most dangerous rejection of all seems to be their disillusionment with schooling. Youth, says the sociologist Rousselet, is *malade du savoir*, tired of learning, because the learning that the schools attempt to pass on to them very often does not help them to get on in life, to find a job, to solve the problems they care about; half of children say that the schools' vocational guidance fails to satisfy their tastes. The end result of all the money spent on education is that over half the population is officially condemned as being inadequately educated, for having failed examinations or not even getting a chance to take them.

But to be bored by politics and education is not so revolutionary. Politics was never something that preoccupied the masses, except in occasional periods of crisis; it was most of the time the business of a ruling class. Education likewise was thrust on the masses, made compulsory against considerable resistance, and always seemed to promise more benefits than it delivered. What is new is that scepticism is now more open. Politics, participation and mass education were the new social medicines introduced by the eighteenth and nineteenth centuries. Now that the twentieth century is drawing to its close, they have ceased to be modern medicines, and are being accused of being old wives' tales. People have always been ambivalent towards these cure-alls; today they are less hypocritical.

The quality of life is the slogan of the new generation, but it is far from being a monopoly of the young. It indicates more self-consciousness in the search for happiness, but many young people end up following conformist paths; they momentarily have more choices open to them, but in practice they overwhelmingly reject experimental forms of living for themselves.

The more genuine innovators are the adults who throw up their well-paid careers to seek a more satisfying life in humble but freer avenues. Youth has become the symbol of rebellion, even though it is not all that rebellious. Angry young men end up swallowing their anger, even forgetting it. Youth, in fact, is a state of mind, which all young people do not necessarily have.

That is why there are pop singers, whose task it is to express anger that most of the young cannot do much about, or feel only from time to time; they serve as incomprehensible devils for adults to hate. The majority of French singers, of course, are mild, traditional in their music and their lyrics, and no threat to anyone. But even those who are seen as dangerous and violent are not revolutionaries. Bernard Lavilliers, for example, likes provoking and challenging. He is the son of a factory worker and he started as one also. He grew up, as he says, in the ghetto of St Etienne. He became a gang leader, a *blouson noir*, forming an army of 300 or 400 youths, who entertained themselves going to fight the gangs of Lyon. He learnt to hate the police. He enjoyed provoking them with his uniform of a black leather jacket, which was enough for them to stop and question him, just as today he provokes the bourgeoisie by wearing an earring and weird clothes. 'I detest them and they can feel it.' He tries to express his hate of the country's political institutions and morality in his songs, as well as in his refusal to fight against them, because he despises the Left also. 'Since my adolescence I have fought against the old world. Today, I am trying to think up something different. I am fed up with repeating that the old leftist systems are totally derisory, that politicians are sick and infectious as soon as they get power. This is all so obvious that I want to speak another language, try out new experiences.' When he gave a concert in Toulouse, ten thousand came to hear him, while only two thousand went to listen to Mitterrand, who was holding a public meeting at the same time. 'We both have the same trade,' but 'the old stories the politicians tell interest nobody.' Lavilliers' concerts attracted the young because they were celebrations, 'a fête', an expression of sensuality, fellow feeling: 'the more humble people are, the higher is their sensitivity at the level of vibrations: in the middle classes music becomes intellectual . . . In the ghetto it is *feeling*' (he uses the

English word). His music enables people to 'vibrate', to have 'epidemics, sensual, sexual communication'. The words of his songs convey the misery of life and its violence. But though he needs to express his own violence, he does so only through song, and through his hobby of physical training. His new world moreover is one in which love takes on new meaning: he is fascinated by the women's movement and believes that new relationships with women hold the key to a better future. He lives with a liberated woman, whose hobby is weightlifting. They see themselves as being made dangerous by their physical strength. He likes the idea of being both 'cool' and dangerous, like an animal; he likes relations that are sometimes friendly, but also suddenly violent. Security bores him. That is what he means by saying that he is still a *voyou* at thirty-three. But a layabout who sings, takes exercise and drives a Pontiac has found a way of life.

25

Why Women's Liberation moves slowly

A few years ago, a young woman, Françoise Chandernagor, made the headlines by coming first in the highest of all public examinations: graduation from ENA, the National School of Administration. It was a great triumph for the feminist cause. She was given a senior post in the Ministry of Equipment. She married an inspector of finances. She had all the right antecedents to succeed: her father is a socialist politician and now a minister. How far has she climbed since her famous victory? She is back at home, at her kitchen stove, bringing up her three children. Her explanation goes far to illuminating why women have not been more successful in seizing power. She is quite clear that if she had been a man, she would have been able to have both a satisfying career and a family life. But when she tried to go on working and be a mother at the same time, her male colleagues effectively sabotaged her by sticking unyieldingly to their old habits: they continued to have their leisurely business lunches till three o'clock, and to stay in their offices till nine in the evening. She could not but follow suit, so she used to get home at nine-thirty – with the result that she had no time to see, let alone to get to know her children. She recalls that she herself was brought up with a father who was hardly ever at home: his political engagements meant she saw him about once a fortnight. And now her husband sabotages her just as much. He is a firm feminist, but only in theory. He has encouraged her to develop her personality fully. But when it comes to actually doing 'woman's work', he proves himself totally uncooperative, not through resistance on principle, but by presenting a front of total incapacity: he has been brought up by a mother who never taught him to do any housework. Françoise has tried over and over again to get him to work the dishwasher at least, but he never succeeds even in that. He leaves his things all over the floor; he never closes a cupboard door. She has done her best to teach him, but to no avail. He has never offered to take a sick child to the doctor; he has never done anything about ensuring that there is food in the house; he will not even organize a baby sitter. She has given up: she does not have the energy to fight him. She does not even expect his help on Saturdays; 'On Saturdays, men play tennis.'

And so she is very pessimistic about what the socialists will do for women. Of course they say they are feminists, in theory again, but all her experience convinces her it is just lipservice. When she used to canvass for the party, her male colleagues used to say to her 'We think of you as though you were a man.' They meant it as a compliment: that was equality for them. But she was not a man: she had three children to look after, and they could never understand she had to have somewhere to leave them if she was to go out putting up posters. She would advise her daughter to have a child if she wanted to, but not to get married, and certainly not to have two children. She is attracted by the idea of a kibbutz. Above all, she thinks the answer must lie in mutual help of women among themselves. She is keen to fight for women's rights, but that must include the right to femininity, to be mothers without losing their status in the world of work. As for changing men, that will take several centuries.

Women's liberation has undoubtedly been sabotaged by men, but it has also been sabotaged by women themselves. In the past women sought more roundabout ways of compensating for the disadvantages they suffered. In France their anger has always been more muted than elsewhere, and their victories more subtle. One of the puzzles of history is why French women got the vote so much later than in most western countries, only in 1944, and why their emancipation movement was so much less active or provocative. They had good grounds to be angry, because the Napoleonic civil code had given them a clearly stated legal inferiority, restricting their movements, their property and family rights with definite handicaps. They accepted this in the past partly because they created a private universe for themselves, fortified by the Catholic religion which men had on the whole forsaken; and the roles and duties they fulfilled in this universe did give them many satisfactions, even if they were often painful ones; in the home, they could rise to be matriarchs with formidable influence. 'Though legally women occupy a much inferior status to men,' wrote an English visitor at the beginning of this century, 'in practice they constitute the superior sex. They are the power behind the throne, and both in the family and in business relations undoubtedly enjoy greater consideration than English women.' 'In most French households,' wrote another, 'women reign with unchallenged sway.'

Daumier

A woman like me . . . sew on a button? You must be mad!
She's not satisfied with wearing the trousers,
she even throws them at me.

It is in this tradition that, more recently, there have been women who have deliberately sought to keep the revolt of their sex limited to certain spheres. Probably the leading figure in the popularization of women's new hopes, unknown outside France, but to whom virtually every French woman has listened at some time, is Menie Grégoire. She started the first women's problem radio programme in 1967, which instantly won a mass audience, and which created a new public consciousness of shared worries and animosities. Menie Grégoire has, however, deliberately opposed women's liberation as preached both by Simone de Beauvoir and by the Americans, and she has sought to build a distinctive French form of feminism. Menie Grégoire was inspired to get a job by reading Beauvoir, but she says work is not enough. She had married after finishing her history degree and when she was just embarking on research in Egyptology. 'I sought, met and snatched love in two months.' For ten years she dropped all her intellectual pursuits like a worn-out dress, and had three children. She insists that motherhood has been the most important and best part of her life, more than any career, 'more than happiness and love'; and she predicts that her grandchildren will return to the worship of motherhood. Menie Grégoire says little about her husband, a top civil servant; she is firm that this part of her private life is private; but it is obvious that family life has not been pure bliss. She has had one or more breakdowns; she spent years being psychoanalysed, while apparently fulfilling her role as a high society wife; and she discovered that women's troubles should not be attributed to oppression from outside, but to internal anxieties. Her problem was that her mother hated her, or was jealous of her, and that she felt guilty about all the parental taboos she had broken. She did not feel oppressed by her husband or males in general; on the contrary, she had 'profited' from men, she had known how to use them 'like all bourgeoises'. The French woman is different, she claims; she has 'an exceptional understanding with man, who has always been something else than the master'. She has changed because contraception has enabled her to go beyond motherhood, but she does not resent not being Head of State. Femininity is a 'precious gift' she does not want to abandon.

Menie Grégoire reacted with horror at the arrival of Anglo-

Saxon feminism which was directed against men, which was superficial because it gave too much emphasis to the economic, instead of the psychological aspect. To be free is to enjoy one's sexuality freely: formerly men alone had this freedom, now women do too. The problems involved in gaining that freedom, against the traditional trauma of frigidity, were the really important ones. That is what she emphasized in her radio programmes; and the millions of letters she has received, she claims confirm her diagnosis, that the main difficulty the French suffer from is premature ejaculation ('80% of the difficulties that couples have are related to this'). The Americans, by contrast, she claims, suffer from impotence, which is very rare in France; and occurs mainly in the form of 'panic after fiasco' that expresses the Latin sense of dishonour. Her explanation is that American mothers are 'infinitely more castrating' than French ones; American women are powerful, independent and self-confident, and they are willing to play the role of nurse to male sexuality. The French have far less interest in sexual perversions than the Americans, because sexuality has always been openly accepted. But there is one exception: French women are masochists, who demand that males should be sadistic, though they seldom are: French women 'brought up with the mentality of slaves, demand the executioner and incite men to brutality or contempt by their attitudes'. There is no danger, therefore, that French women should want to copy men, as American ones do; she wants to keep a distinct female form of pleasure; the Americans are wrongly trying to make the clitoris into an instrument to copy and punish the male. Recently, however, she has acknowledged that French women's relations with men are not all that simple: men are reacting against the women's liberation by withdrawing their affection. Menie Grégoire says she can put up with many things, but the one thing that terrifies her is the sense of being abandoned. When Women's Liberation groups want to vent their feelings, they plan to abduct Menie Grégoire, or to burn her in effigy. She replies that Women's Liberation has affected only 5% of the French population.

   The American female, and the American male, are regular bogey figures. Just how much faith should be placed in international comparisons on this subject is shown by two recent polls. France's best-selling 'male' magazine *Lui* recently presented a statistical portrait of the French lover, based on a 'scientific' public opinion poll. An American magazine of the same kind, *Oui* (whose title shows that France's reputation for libertinism survives undimmed), put the same questions to an equal sample of people in the United States, and was surprised to find that its portrait of the American lover turned out to be virtually ident-ical to the French one, even to the extent of often getting exactly the same percentage of men confessing to the same habits, tastes and peculiarities. There was only one difference between the two nations: fifty times more Frenchmen than Americans admitted to occasional impotence – exactly the opposite of what Menie Grégoire believes. The myths will doubtless survive all the same, even if, as *Oui* put it, there is no support for the view either that Frenchmen are 'the world's gold medal superstuds' or that they are more braggart and less frank than the Americans.

The feminists are cross with another of France's most famous women, Françoise Giroud, whom they find too pragmatic, 'reformist', too optimistic about what can be achieved by cooperation with men. She was willing to serve in the same government as Jacques Chirac, who has said, 'For me, the ideal woman is the woman of Corrèze (the part of France he comes from) of the old days, who works hard, serves the men at their meals, never sits at table with them, and does not talk.' But she accepted power precisely because, as she said, 'Women are a category apart, and what we must try to bring about is that they should cease to be that.' She claims that French women do not want to change their role, to stop being valued as lovers, mothers, consolers, educators, and cooks, but that they want something in addition to that; they want a person's full rights, not to be indistinguishable from men, but to be recognized as of equal value, so that each can choose to do what she considers suits her.

Françoise Giroud's own career shows what she means. She left school at fifteen, became a film script girl, working with Renoir, and going on to a successful writing career in films; she was the editor of *Elle* and *L'Express*, helping to make them best-selling and influential magazines; in 1974 she was appointed Secretary of State for Women. She has never been dependent on a man financially, and she has succeeded in a man's world. But she insists that she has no wish to ape men; she cherishes what are considered feminine virtues. Every woman, she says, is in various degrees a courtesan, who knows how to make herself attractive, how to advise and to encourage men, with more or less skill. 'The more perspicacious she is, the more she can pretend, the better she can detect the wounds that her balsam can soothe. The only women who are more intolerable than

Bretécher

Human Contact

It's difficult because of the language barrier, but it's very, very, very interesting

(Advertisement for the travel agency Nouvelles Frontières)

women who cry are women with cold faces.' She does not
identify with the 'new women' who lack the patience or talent to
be courtesans, who refuse to give themselves up to men as an
oblique method of gaining dominance over them, who are tired
of the 'eternal comedy of women', for she admits to enjoying
'the refined satisfaction of imposture' to be derived from that
comedy. What she rejects is the notion that women should not
be allowed to be themselves, should be forced into wearing a
'permanent make-up of body, face and language', to be forbidden to say what they think, to have drooping breasts, shapeless
waists or hair on their legs. But she does not expect women to
emerge very fast from their traditional attitudes; she fears that if
they take more part in politics they will simply develop their
violent and aggressive side; she does not believe that if they had
power, they would necessarily produce peace; she herself has
used a machine gun against Sudanese rebels and she can still feel
the exhilaration and excitement of shooting.

She is a woman who has no illusions about women or about
life, but is not, therefore, a pessimist. On the contrary, she
believes in happiness and insists that it is capable of attainment
– the proof is that when it vanishes, one is immediately aware of
its disappearance. But she is not willing to fight for utopias, to
carry out revolutions which kill or hurt a lot of people so that
Peter can take over from Paul, though one is sometimes forced
to do it: she does not want a new master, but a world without a
master, without men bossing women, bossing each other, or
women bossing men. She can feel no reverence for fathers,
guides, presidents, perhaps because her own father played little
part in her life, was usually absent, leaving her unused to the
notion of authority. That is why after a couple of years as
Minister, she resigned, tiring of 'the comedy of power'. Her
philosophy is that one should draw as much out of oneself as one
can, but respect oneself, be kind to one's body, accept one's
animal side, decide what one values most and not waste effort in
battles about things one does not regard as essential: conform on
superficial issues.

As Minister, she ordered a public opinion poll, which
revealed that only one-fifth of women had an 'aggressive desire
for change', that two-fifths would like change but were not

willing to act to bring it about, and that the rest were content
with things as they were. And yet women hold the worst-paid
jobs in the country, two out of three are on the minimum wage;
only a tiny fraction are managers. This is partly explained by the
older generation having received less education, but even
though now girls are doing better at school than boys, they still
prefer literary studies, and obtain far fewer technical qualifications. Though women are supposed to get equal pay by law, in
practice, for various reasons, they often end up with less.

Gisèle Halimi, the founder and leader of the moderate
women's liberation movement, once said that it is best for
women's organizations not to admit men, however well-inten-
tioned. On the other hand she insists that the only way to
liberate women is to liberate men. It is probably because of this
contradiction, and of the sectarian isolationism of many of the
women's organizations, that they have been able to achieve
relatively little. The main conquests have concerned abortion
and contraception. Gisèle Halimi knows from personal experience how deep-rooted male resistance is: when she was a
nineteen-year-old student seeking a secret abortion, her doctor
deliberately operated without an anaesthetic, causing pain she
likened to torture: he said: 'this way you won't do it again.' But
the efforts to arouse women have only split the movement into
rival groups with rival theories, often mere echoes of men's
rival theories. Simone de Beauvoir, the most widely known
internationally of French feminists, has probably had more
influence in the United States than in France: her *Second Sex*
certainly sold many more copies in the United States. In
France the Catholics put the book on the Index, and the
left-wing denounced it for not emphasizing the importance of
the class struggle. Marx has dominated some sections of the
liberation movement, with all the usual quarrels about how he
should be interpreted: the woman's organization calling itself
Class Struggle borrowed its vocabulary and methods from the
left-wing trade unions: women were not referred to as women
but as comrades, speeches at meetings were organized in
advance; interruptions were ridiculed as 'unorganized' and
therefore undesirable, deviations from the doctrine stig-
matized as reformist. The ideas of Freud and Lacan dominated

the sect known as *Politics and Psychoanalysis* – hardly a rabble-rousing slogan. This became an intense, close-knit community: the psychoanalyst Antoinette Fouqué, its charismatic leader, was accused of making it into almost a messianic sect, in which she was a kind of father-mother, for whose love the members fought jealously. The problems of homosexuality were particularly discussed and attempts made to develop a new woman's language and literature. The rather hermetic professor Hélène Cixious advocated the need for a 'radical convulsion' of male forms by 'overturning syntax', 'suspending teleology, and developing a new science' based on systematic experimentation on the functioning of the body, and 'a precise and passionate interrogation of its erogeneity'. *Po. et Psy.* insisted, moreover, that it was antifeminist, but 'feminitarian', because its prime concern was the discovery of the originality of the female unconscious, independent of male power; its intellectualism led it to devote its main efforts to the creation of bookshops. Other sects, like the Red Homosexuals and the Trotskyists, and bitter disputes about who had the right to call themselves the MLF (the Movement for the Liberation of Women) added further complications and obstacles to capturing a mass audience. That would not have

Bretécher

mattered in the long run if a viable alternative way of life for women had been discovered, but it has not.

Françoise d'Eaubonne, a novelist of very considerable power and originality, who was originally a member of *Po. et Psy.*, has decided that mere protest and revolution are not enough. She wrote a science fiction story in which men are altogether eliminated and women bred by autogenesis. She says that any man who likes a woman's body is a sadist at heart. She is not content with equality. 'Mutation' is necessary. Heterosexual monogamy must cease to be the basis of society, the obligation to marry must cease to be a norm. That will help solve the world's population problem, particularly if feminism unites with the ecologist movement, and seeks to conserve the world's resources. Women will thus stop being just breeders. To be a woman in the present system is a 'misfortune' (37% of women regret that they are not men): it is to be 'flesh made for rape . . . a zombie, a negation, a hole'; if she tries to be creative or active, it is said she imitates men, though no one accuses intuitive or sensitive men of aping women; she is raped every day, morally if not physically. The conclusion is: no compromises are possible.

This is just a prologue. When President Giscard d'Estaing said, 'The world will be changed by women,' he was not perhaps acknowledging that the power of politicians is superficial and that the important decisions are not made by them, nor was he just finding an excuse to explain why he did not do more for the women's cause. The world in the past often has been changed by women, though not always to their own advantage. For example, the lives of some of the women I have described have been deliberately restricted by their mothers. But the real choice that women face is whether simply to win an equal place in a world shaped by men, with the right to struggle to become executives with ulcers, or whether they can get men to change their ways, far beyond the matter of sexual relations, and give greater prominence to the less violent values that women have particularly cherished.

26

How they treat foreigners and Jews

What have France and Australia in common? They have both, in the course of their history, admitted the same number of immigrants – ten million. Before the war France came second only to the United States as the nation receiving the largest amount of immigration, and indeed, on a per capita basis, it was for a time admitting even more than the United States. Since the war the flood has continued and today one-tenth of the residents in France are immigrants, four million of them foreigners and one-and-a-half million naturalized. The first novel on this subject dates from 1907 – Louis Bertrand's *L'Invasion* – when already one-fifth of the population of Marseille were foreigners. Today it is Corsica that has the highest proportion of immigrants, while Paris has almost one-and-a-half million foreigners.

France has something else in common with the America of the nineteenth century, where prosperity was, of course, originally partly built on slavery. The expert on French immigration problems on the newspaper *Le Monde* has written: 'My thesis is that the immigrant workers are a new sort of slaves.' Immigrants do most of the dirty and worst paid jobs; their children, born in France, do not get much chance of obtaining better kinds of employment; so they form an almost hereditary underprivileged caste. Having lost its colonies, France has imported foreigners to work for it at home, and the colonial metaphor is all the more real because frequently these foreigners live in ghettos which accentuate their isolation and poverty. It is true that other European countries have the same problem, notably Germany and Switzerland, which have the same proportion of one in ten: it has been said that foreigners make up the tenth nation in the European Community. But in France the problem seems to be more acute because it is more long-standing – only a quarter of Germany's immigrants have lived there for more than ten years, but two-thirds of France's have been in France for at least that period. And the French are being slower than any of their neighbours about giving their immigrants equal status. Sweden, for example, allows foreigners to vote in local elections after three years; Germany and the Benelux

Wolinski

countries have instituted elected councils for immigrants, with consultative status. But in France there is no such national policy, though some towns with large immigrant populations have invited foreign communities to send delegates to present their case to the municipal authorities; Laval has an ombudsman for foreigners, Mons-en-Baroeul invited foreigners to participate in a referendum on its local budget in 1977; Tourcoing has held an official public debate about immigrants. But four million residents in France have no real political rights. And French public opinion is hostile to giving them any rights. A poll (in 1973) showed 55% against them being allowed to vote in local elections with 34% in favour. Things may change, because 52% of people under twenty-five believe that immigrants should have this right. But as many as 72% of French people are against giving immigrants full political rights, including the right to vote on the Presidency of the Republic. Just 54% are in favour of establishing Consultative Councils. Such attitudes are difficult to maintain, given that there are towns which have whole districts dominated by foreigners, like Belleville and the Goutte d'Or in Paris, the Grande Côte in Lyon, the Très Cloîtres in Grenoble and the Porte d'Aix in Marseille; the Paris suburb of Gennevilliers is 28% foreign. The situation is necessarily more explosive than in Britain, which has only one in twenty of residents who are immigrants (that is half the French proportion) and most of those have full political rights as British citizens.

The reason why so many immigrants have been able to achieve so little is that their ambitions and skills are unusually varied. The half-a-million Italians and half-a-million Spaniards are heirs to a long tradition of immigration, which has taught them how to find their way around France; there are now nearly a million Portuguese, who constitute the largest single national minority and who are following the same path of acclimatization. The one-and-a-half million Algerians, Moroccans and Tunisians, though superficially distinguished by their religion, have different attitudes; two-thirds of the Tunisians are in France without their wives; they and the Moroccans are considered fairly 'docile' employees; but the Algerians have created a separate world for themselves; one-half of them are in the building trade or public works. The 70,000 Turks are a recent arrival as are the 30,000 Yugoslavs, but the 80,000 Poles are the relic of a community which used to be five times that size before the war, and was concentrated in the mining towns of the Nord; so there are many Poles who have become full French citizens and some have held important posts in government and the trade union movement. Black Africans are relatively few

(20,000 Senegalese, 20,000 Malians, 10,000 from the Ivory Coast). However, there are also 1,133,000 French citizens in Martinique, Guadeloupe and Réunion who do not count as foreigners, and who are not included in calculations on immigration; but they have an official minimum wage 20% lower than on mainland France; their industrial productivity is about one-third of that on the mainland, and they have an unemployment rate four times as high; they have many grievances about the way they are treated both at home and when they try to get a job on the mainland.

The anger of immigrants arises first of all from the appalling housing into which they have been squeezed. In the 1960s the cities of France spawned suburbs known as *bidonvilles*, which were almost exactly like the slums of Africa and Latin America — tin shacks without indoor sanitation or water, vastly overcrowded. The destruction of the *bidonvilles* was often carried out with little consideration; bulldozers were sometimes sent in to tear them apart, and the inhabitants forced out. 'Transit cities' were built to replace them, but these have often degenerated into a new kind of slum, the cheap prefabrications quickly deteriorated; the transit city of Gutenberg went up in flames three times before it was admitted that it had been built of inflammable materials, that there was no fire hose, and no usable telephone. Hostels provided by the state were often as disgusting and overcrowded as those of the 'sleep merchants' who packed ten men into a small room in tawdry hotels. Repeatedly the immigrant tenants have gone on strike; for the last four years over a hundred hostels have been on rent strike; from time to time police invade and brutally expel residents.

Secondly, the immigrants resent their low wages. Two-thirds of them are unskilled workers, or rather are classified as such. Occasionally the public is made aware of the extent to which the dirty jobs are done by immigrants, as when the street cleaners of Paris (nearly all of them blacks) go on strike. The way every new wave of immigrants is exploited was recently revealed in the strikes of workers laying down the Paris-Lyon ultra-fast railway: this marvel of French technology was built in conditions which almost reproduced the callousness of the nineteenth century: the plate-layers, mainly North Africans, complained not only of low wages, but of having to sleep in primitive huts with no washing facilities, and to eat out of doors in all weathers, since they had no canteen. If they wanted to make their own sleeping arrangements, they were given an absurdly inadequate allowance of twelve francs (about £1 or $2) a day. When they struck, the employers found destitute Vietnamese, desperate to get out of their refugee camps, to replace them, apparently at even lower wages and, it is said, with the disguised threat that if they did not accept they would be thrown out of France.

Immigrants have to accept what work they can, because they are so insecure in their right to work; there is always the threat of a cancellation of their permit; employers know how to take advantage of the fact that even greater poverty faces them in their home country. Immigrants seldom succeed in getting better qualifications and cannot even console themselves with the hope that their children may do so, because the children have a lot of difficulty in French schools and are generally one year behind their French coevals; one-third of them leave school illiterate, only one-fifth complete their education; only 3000 get into universities (and there are 1,200,000 foreigners under nineteen). Of course, a few have succeeded. In 1974 a special ministry was established to help immigrants, first under Paul Dijoud, of North African origin, a graduate of the School of Political Sciences and of ENA, and then under Lionel Stoleru, of Jewish Rumanian origin, an engineer graduate of the Polytechnic. Both were admired in different ways, but both have been attacked for effectively restricting the rights of immigrants. The growth of unemployment has not only led them to halt immigration, but also to encourage those already in France to go home. Even an Algerian born in France is liable to be expelled if he puts a foot wrong, if he has a minor scrape with the law. Though the French cannot be accused of being more racist than other similar nations, they are not noticeably less so.

A foreigner who comes to work in France needs to have a very thick skin. A Spanish refrigerator fitter, for example, says he had never been treated so badly as when he was applying for a work permit: he was put in a small room with twenty others and they were all told to undress; he could still see the horror on the face of an old man who was forced to take off his clothes in front of his son, doubtless for the first time in his life; and they were packed so tightly their bodies were touching. When the Spaniard complained, the officials replied: have you never been in the army? He had, but this experience resembled an internment camp. The endless queueing was all the more intolerable because no one seemed to appreciate their offer to work; he was told he should be thankful for being allowed to work, whereas it was obvious he was being admitted only because his labour was needed. He was bitterly disappointed to find such hypocrisy and callousness in a country he had admired from afar as the home of liberty and anti-colonialism. He had worked in Argentina too, but he had never encountered such military relationships as existed between foremen and workers; the latter treated the boss like God on earth; he created a scandal by saying good morning to him. He could not live normally like a Frenchman, because he needed to send money home to his family; he could not find lodgings – why were they not offered better hospitality? When he started, his lodgings cost him four-sevenths of his wages; so he was forced to work overtime. As a Spaniard he had more pride, he said, than the Portuguese on whom he looked down as being interested only in earning money. He resented the police urging him to seek naturalization, which they said would end his troubles; he was infuriated by their harassment, their endless inspection of his papers; he did not want to be French; he wished to remain a Spaniard. He was appalled by the hostility he found among his neighbours, who always complained that foreigners made more noise. But the immigrants were just as bad towards each other, each shut up in their own groupings. His conclusion was that they had been imported to be exploited, to be enslaved. That is why he could never abandon the hope of returning to Spain one day. But Spaniards often do quite well, particularly when their wives join them and work also.

A Portuguese who came to France at the age of seventeen admits that his countrymen come only to make money, and that many of them, therefore, refuse to help anyone; but on the other hand their greatest fear is isolation and loneliness, so they accept any job which will enable them to work with other Portuguese; they stick to their national customs, they eat cod and potatoes at

Christmas to give them the illusion of being at home. Some never even unpack their suitcases, send most of their money home and eat only one meal a day. They save up to buy a bit of land in Portugal, though it is usually not enough land to keep a family; they slowly build a house in their native village. But increasingly the young generation who do not have to support a family in Portugal sometimes try to live like the French.

It is not so easy to do this. An Algerian sweeper in the Paris metro has been in France since 1954. He was joined by his family in 1960, and now has ten children living in a prefabricated house in Nanterre. He came to France with the hope of becoming a mechanic, but he had never been to school in Algeria; when he arrived he had been obliged to accept a job as a miner, and had been horrified. His present job is humiliating, but having suffered a year of unemployment, he is grateful for it. Since he had learnt no trade, he dares not go back to Algeria, where he would have even more trouble finding a job. He accepts his lot for the sake of his children, because most of them had been born and brought up in France, though he is sceptical about their attitude to him: 'As soon as they grow up, they go.' His eyesight was failing him. 'I shall end up an old man with a cane', and the children will do nothing for him. Still, 'they are happy: I have never had that kind of happiness – my youth was passed in the dark, without joy, with nothing.' His children, the eldest of whom was now at technical college fulfilling his own ambition to be a mechanic, speak French much better than Arabic; they have French friends; they play in French football teams; they are no longer Algerians, only 'half-half'. They speak Arabic at home, and one of them has to accompany their mother to the shops, since her French is very poor. Neither wife nor husband go out much. He bets on horses, 'the *tiercé*', and hopes that will one day solve his problems. But he refuses to move to a high rise block of flats 'which is a prison, where one is squashed in like sardines.' 'If I had known France was like this, I would not have come.'

Immigrants are consoled because even if they earn less than the French, their wages put them on the same level as teachers and officials at home. But they are angered because their hopes are so often disappointed, to the extent that they feel cheated. A

Reiser

twenty-year-old girl applied in her native Réunion to become a
nurse in Paris. The clerks promised to arrange this, but when
her papers arrived, they turned out to be a contract to work as a
domestic servant for one year. After that, they assured her, she
could do what she liked. She was sent on a five-month course to
learn how to cook, wash and iron in the French style. She had no
school certificates: she was finding it impossible to move into a
profession she could be proud of.

Most foreign women end up being servants. There are still
about a million domestic servants, half of whom are foreigners.
It is in contact with them, in their own homes, when there are
no witnesses, that the rich and educated French, who alone can
afford servants, reveal the nature of their attachment to liberty,
equality and fraternity. One of these servants, Maria Arondo,
has recorded what the employers said to her, and to many other
servants she got to know. Maria, the eldest of eleven children,
came to Paris because there was no work of any sort to be found
in the poor Spanish Basque village where she was born and spent
the first eighteen years of her life. Her uncles and aunts had
preceded her; she was lucky to have their help in looking for a
job, for she had no education, no skills and no knowledge of
French. But she was not insensitive to the haughtiness, or the
courtesy, that prospective employers showed her; she was overwhelmed by the sight of luxury beyond anything she had
known, but she was not impressed by warnings from proud
matrons that if they employed her 'Monsieur would not tolerate
the slightest crease' in the shirts she would have to iron for him.
Eventually she was taken on by an engineer in the suburb of
Aulnay-sous-Bois, who welcomed her with friendliness and
simplicity and gave her a pleasant little room behind his garage.
She was to work from 7.30 a.m. to 8.00 p.m., with two
afternoons off a week, at a wage of 300F a month (£30), a
quarter less than the rich in the sixteenth arrondissement of
Paris offered, but here she was promised better treatment: she
would eat with the family and not in the kitchen, she could use
the telephone or make coffee when she pleased. But almost at
once her pride was hurt by the wife. Maria was told to do all the
washing by hand, because Madame was against washing
machines and would not even allow her to wear rubber gloves,

because that would damage her delicate linen. She was forbidden to smoke 'because it is not nice for a servant to smoke in front of her employer.' She was given so much to do that she just went straight to sleep, absolutely exhausted, as soon as she stopped. When she complained, Madame went into tirades about 'these Spaniards' who 'die of hunger' in their own country and who 'ought to be grateful that they are given work'. Maria would have left sooner but for her pleasure in the children, and for the reconciliations Madame engineered very sweetly.

She eventually moved to a doctor, whose wife seemed less hypocritical and irascible. But the doctor ignored her, as though she did not exist: she finally won an elementary politeness from him by shouting in his ear, at the top of her voice, Bonjour Monsieur: he always said Bonjour after that. Madame confided all her problems to her: 'You are like a sister to me,' she said. But in this household, the servant's bedroom doubled also as the doctor's waiting room; the servant was not allowed to be visited by friends, and was hardly ever given permission to go out. It was the Church which revealed to Maria that she could hope for a better life: she joined its youth section, and that made her decide she needed more free time, so that she could study French. So she went to work for a school run by nuns. The servants here were respectful and uncomplaining. But Maria could not accept that they should have to eat worse food than the students, never being allowed butter, given mainly leftovers and stale bread; that they should be refused a key, whereas the students were not; they had to have special permission to come home after 10.00 p.m. So Maria became a non-resident freelance charwoman, working a few hours for three different families, and in this way being able to have hours that suited her. But her involvement in the radical Church organization, the Jeunesses Ouvrières Chrétiennes, was making her increasingly cynical towards her employers, very nice though some of them were. One was very 'liberal' and they had interesting conversations about the injustices that servants had to submit to; but that was no consolation for the knowledge that she was being paid to do a boring job so that her employer could be free to do a job which she enjoyed. Maria ended up becoming a full-time trade union official. That is how she came to collect a great deal of information about the lives of the domestic servants in Paris.

Many of them, she discovered, were not rebellious like her. They were pleased by being given presents and discarded clothing, even if they were badly paid, and they were not responsive to her protest that they were old enough to buy what they needed for themselves, that it was not kindness to be made to wear unfashionable clothes the mistress would rather not be seen in. Many appreciated being treated like a member of the family, being loved by the children, being allowed to have the radio playing while they worked. 'I do not feel I have a boss,' said one. 'She never says Do this or Do that to me: I know what I have got to do. If I were in my own home, it would be exactly the same.' But others complained of being insulted as inferiors, ignorant and stupid, and being told when they protested, not to argue with 'people who are more intelligent than you!' One was exasperated by a mistress who insisted on calling her Titi: she stopped answering until her real name was used. 'Just because I am a servant, that is no reason why I should not be respected.' Many conceal their job from their acquaintances, considering it more humiliating than being a worker. And they certainly do sometimes receive treatment that no other profession would tolerate. Occasionally they are beaten. Not infrequently they are given worse food than the dogs, let alone the rest of the family; one household had two sets of plates, one beautiful set for their own use, and another for the dog and the servant: the servant finally rebelled saying, 'I am not a dog. You love your dog a lot, but you would not eat from his plate. Well, I won't either.' The more pretentious employers try to teach their servants to speak 'properly', to follow etiquette, to address them as Madame la Comtesse, and some servants resent that. Worst of all are the grand people who treat servants as non-persons, undressing in front of them without noticing them: 'never would my mother have done that in front of her daughters,' said one horrified servant. Bedrooms are left with used contraceptives thrown on the floor, bathrooms with sanitary towels and dirty underwear. The servant is summoned when the dog makes a mess, and cannot always accept that she should have the monopoly of the disgusting tasks. Amorous adventures cannot be kept secret from servants but it is intolerable when the servants are then given moral lectures about how they should not bring their men friends into the house; employers, apparently, have largely stopped trying to sleep with their servants. The only escape for a servant is marriage but in most cases she will marry a poor worker or clerk, and will go on working to make ends meet.

The anger of the immigrants is ultimately the anger of loneliness. Tahar Ben Jelloun, a Moroccan poet and novelist living in France, wrote a doctoral thesis in social psychiatry to try to understand what his fellow North Africans felt. His clinic's case-books reveal the anguish of those who are overwhelmed by their sense of failure, by their inability to master an alien way of life. The sexual frustrations of men who have left their wives at home often turns their professional disappointments into disasters. Virility to some of them is the essence of man, and when they cannot express it, their self-respect goes. The prostitute is no consolation, they go to her from a superstitious belief that unless they 'empty their testicles' once a week, they will become ill. In the worst cases, they lose their sense of identity, they consider themselves like orphans, they turn their aggressive instincts against themselves and they despise themselves. 'Of all men, I am the last,' says an Algerian labourer of twenty-five.

Why should even the Jews of France, or at least some of them, be angry? They have enjoyed more success, influence and power than the Jews of any other nation, possibly even more than those of the United States. They were leaders in two of the most important movements of modern French history, Léon Blum in the Popular Front and Daniel Cohn-Bendit in May 1968. Mendès-France was probably the most esteemed politician of the Fourth Republic. General de Gaulle chose Michel Debré, grandson of a rabbi, to be his prime minister. Simone Veil, now president of the European parliament, was Giscard's most popular minister, repeatedly top of the opinion polls. The anthropologist Lévi-Strauss put his stamp on a whole generation of intellectuals, in the human sciences and in literature; on a different plane, the New Philosophy is led by B. H. Lévy who even makes Judaism a central feature of his theories. France's nuclear defence has been master-minded by Robert Dautray; its aircraft industry has been raised to international importance by Marcel Dassault; Renault was made into a rare model of a successful nationalized industry by Pierre Dreyfus. France now has the second largest Jewish community outside Israel, after the United States, with around 700,000 members. France was the first country to give Jews fully equal rights two centuries ago. But there are an increasing number of Jews who nevertheless feel that they are not treated fully as equals, who feel (like the feminists) that they have to try harder to succeed; but also that they have been 'betrayed'.

The reason is that the Jewish situation has been changing all the time. There are three different groups of Jews. Until the late nineteenth century there were very few Jews in France, who were largely concentrated in Alsace and the Gard, so that some Frenchmen did not even know what a Jew was. After their emancipation they became intensely loyal to the Republic, and increasingly assimilated, regarding themselves as French people who happened to be of the Jewish faith in the same way as others were Protestants. Then came two sets of new immigrants – from Eastern Europe (escaping from Tsarist and Hitler persecution) and from North Africa (driven by Arab nationalism). Antisemitism which had first become important at the turn of the century, when a Jewish officer, Dreyfus, was wrongly convicted and his innocence blindly denied by the prejudices of large sections of the country, exploded in the Second World War, when, under Pétain, French Jews suddenly discovered that they were no longer given the protection of the law, that they were not considered fully French: the government handed Jews over to the Germans to be exterminated. The result of these horrors is that anti-semitism is now boycotted and condemned in a way that it never was before.

Nevertheless, the Jews, and particularly those who went to the concentration camps, or who had relatives tortured or killed by the Germans, cannot forget, and the feeling that it could happen again remains alive, rekindled every time there is an outbreak of anti-Semitism. This does happen from time to time, when rumours spread, like medieval hysteria, that the Jews have perpetrated some imaginary crime. Parents report their children being teased at school, and teachers do not always stop the teasing. The establishment of Israel has led many to reconsider their loyalties, all the more so when the importance to France of Arab oil has brought to an end the government's former enthusiasm for Israel. The rallying cry adopted by the movement of May 1968, We are all German Jews, shows that attitudes to Jews are more favourable than they have ever been, but there are Jews who reply that these attitudes are confined to only some circles. There is a doctor in Strasbourg, for example, who complains that he receives insulting telephone calls, and that when promotions are discussed in his hospital, it is suggested that there should not be too many Jews selected. This kind of discrimination is resented in the same way as women resent having to be outstanding or pretty to get a job: Françoise Giroud says all she wants is that working women should have the right to be as mediocre as men. The prejudice is more difficult to prove in the case of Jews.

For many French Jews, their Jewishness is no more than an almost forgotten memory; their families have been French for generations; they no longer practise the religion; some more recent immigrants may remember the gastronomic eccentricities of their grandparents; but they reject the idea of the stereotype Jew as a relic of the past; not infrequently their colleagues do not even know that they have Jewish origins. They may be sympathetic to Israel, but in principle rather than from sentiment, as Jean Elleinstein says, because they are against persecutions of any kind; which puts them in a difficult position when the Israelis persecute Arabs; it was Alain Geismar who, though a Jew, helped start the French pro-Palestinian movement and protest against Israeli intransigence. Jacques Frémontier said he first heard the word Jew when he was ten years old, in 1940, when his parents told him the Germans were going to cause him trouble; he felt they could equally well have told him he was Chinese. He went into the service of the state (through ENA) in order to get away from the Jewish tradition of private profit through petty commerce. He left it because he was offered the post of financial director of the state's Oil Company (CFP) until someone asked whether he was Jewish, and then withdrew the offer, because he might offend the Arabs. He has since been a journalist and a broadcaster, a lapsed communist, and also a lapsed supporter of Israel. He rejects the label of Jewishness, in the same way as he rejects many other labels and stereotypes. To be a Frenchman, for him, means to be able to make free choices, to construct his own way of life, and not to ape his neighbours. Assimilation does not mean becoming 'the typical Frenchman'. He caused a scandal as a young man by living openly with a fashion model while still a student at ENA, and he has refused to marry; he has thrown his permanent career overboard and preferred to be a freelance. But he does not feel that he has anything in common with the 'typical Jew' either; the type, he says, is vanishing, now that the Jew has emerged from the ghetto.

But that is precisely what has not happened, because the idea of assimilation is now being opposed by a new generation of Jews. Some children of assimilated Jews are learning Yiddish and attempting to recreate a separate Jewish cultural community, with its own magazines, books and clubs, and with a return to Jewish religious practice. They have been reinforced by the recent influx of Algerian, Tunisian and Moroccan Jews, who stand ambiguously between Arab and French civilization. The old ghettos are not being revived, but there are areas where these Jews have congregated, as for example in Sarcelles, a suburb of Paris, where the communist-controlled municipality has given them special favours in return for their vote. The Jewish school founded by Baron Hirsch a century ago to turn Jewish immigrants into good Frenchmen has done an about turn: it is now putting the emphasis on preserving their Jewishness. The headmistress explains that by the unforgettable shock she received in 1941, when her father, a fervent patriot, whose only link with Jewishness was that he went to the synagogue twice a year, but on the 14th July and the 11th November, rather than on the Jewish feast days, suddenly found himself given an identity card in which his nationality was put as Jewish rather than French. She shows that card to her pupils. She feels the Republic betrayed her. She used to glory in the exploits of the Crusaders; now she teaches her pupils that they massacred Jews on their way. Now she admits she considers she is in the service of Israel more than of France: Israel is the 'America' her pupils have before their eyes; they are proud to be Jewish and keen to develop a separate identity as such. The Jews of the old French style are rather appalled by this: a visiting Rothschild suggested that perhaps they were overdoing the Hebrew; they react contemptuously. The Rothschilds are not accepted as heads or representatives of this new community, still less after one of them said publicly, 'I do not feel at home in Israel.'

The logical step for Jews who consider they have more loyalty to Israel than to France, and who say that they are of French citizenship but Israeli nationality, is to emigrate. But very few French Jews have emigrated. Even the man in charge of urging Jews to emigrate to Israel says he cannot bring himself to go. He explains this by saying that it is not so easy to get over centuries of exile; the imprint of French culture, the attractions of French life are too great. The theory behind the new Jewishness is that education cannot eliminate the ancestral stamp, that no amount of polishing can alter the legacy of Judaism; this is to deny one of the axioms of modernity, that it is possible to create a new kind of civilization, a new way of life, to forget the past. But to forget their French past is something they cannot do either. These conservative Jews have no answer to their dilemma.

27

What illnesses they suffer from, and how they survive them

Dr Gérard Debuigné's job is to stop people worrying, but he worries about himself all the time. He is a general practitioner who takes infinite pains with his patients, but he can find no cure for his own fears and doubts. He comes of working-class origins; his grandfather was a carter, his father an artisan in metal, a foreman, and later a pedlar selling glasses to cafés, who, stopping for a drink too often, finally died of cirrhosis of the liver. Gérard remembers his parents constantly quarrelling, his mother from time to time packing her bags and pretending to move out. There was little warmth at home; he felt unloved and always has done. He has fought very hard to win admiration; but his ambition has always been balanced by self-doubt. No one noticed him much at school, so he took up dancing and became a champion in 'Jiteburg' (that is how he spells it); he haunted the *bals populaires* in search of girls; he took drugs (ortedrine) to brighten his life; he remained a virgin so as to prepare himself for the romantically happy marriage he looked forward to; he masturbated but was deeply depressed at the thought that this practice cut him off from God. He was proud to pass the *baccalauréat* – a rare feat for a worker's son – though he had some trouble doing so, for an unsuccessful love affair made him have to sit the examination twice. He scraped into the Faculty of Medicine at Lille, but found it hard work, both intellectually and socially. In his third year he met a divorced primary schoolteacher who fascinated him; they lived together; they got married; he had to work harder than ever to make himself worthy of her. He tried to become a specialist psychiatrist (this was in 1951); he was admitted into a hospital, but failed the final examination: he had to resign himself to becoming a GP. He set up at Estaires (Nord) in two rooms, sub-let from the widow of a doctor who had recently died of drink, and he eventually managed to buy a second-hand car. His patients gradually grew more numerous, he won admiration for the excellence of his diagnoses, which he achieved by reading medical books every day and studying their descriptions of diseases very carefully; he was constantly worried that he might make a mistake. He was proud of the appreciation his patients showed him; he repeated their compliments, he needed their affection desperately, even more than their fees, which he found it not all that easy to extract from them; he was humiliated by having to clink the coins in his trouser pocket to remind them to pay. But gradually he got rich; he bought a house; he filled it with oriental carpets, Louis XV and Regency furniture, baccarat crystal: his dream was to buy an American car, and he got one. He used it to travel around visiting restaurants; gastronomy became his hobby, he became friends with a master chef and his Sunday visit to his restaurant was the high point of his week. He grew fat. He took up physical training and indeed became so obsessed by this that he wrote two books on the subject. He went to spas to take the waters. He had arrived. He had no money worries any more, at last.

But he was dissatisfied. Having attained the goal he had set himself, he found he had no purpose. He was tired of having to work for money, of being so constantly overworked, of being financially dependent on his patients. Seeing an advertisement for a post as controller of medical expenses in the Social Security, he applied, and got the job, which he thought would, by making him a civil servant with a regular salary, free him from worry. But it was jumping from the frying pan into the fire: he immediately hated the hierarchy and authoritarianism of a government office. He quickly resigned, and yielding to his wife's suggestions, he went to start a new practice near the Côte d'Azur. He loved the beauty of the countryside, but he got more depressed than he had ever been; he went back to drugs, he sought psychotherapy, he became religious. It was loneliness. He knew no one in this part of the world; it took a long time to attract patients, and he needed their affection and loyalty to sustain him. He had been a person of importance in his northern village; here he was a foreigner. It took several years for him to establish himself. Now he is more equable, though not quite content. His depression made him think a lot about the meaning of life; he wondered whether happiness meant to desire nothing. He has tried to forget these insoluble questions by making a new reputation for himself as an author. He put his gastronomic knowledge to good use by writing about it; he felt he had reached the pinnacle when Larousse asked him to write for them: he produced their *Encyclopaedia of Medicinal Plants* (1975). For he has no narrow attitude to medicine. He has become interested by homeopathy and by natural herbal remedies. If he were not a medical man and had to start his career again, he would become, he says, a healer, or, he adds, perhaps a preacher. What he preaches is not revolutionary. He tells his stepdaughter and his nephew, both of whom have become doctors: Do not judge others. Obey your parents. Always give priority to the preparation of your examinations, though without stifling your emotions. Organize your life with academic results as your goal, because, unfortunately, everything has to begin with a parchment diploma. Do not be frightened of exposing yourself to ridicule. Open your heart to others, even to those who do not respond. Give of yourself, and in the end you shall receive. But all the good advice he gives does not do him much good. His relations with his wife have grown more distant: he loves to relive his youth listening to pop music, which she hates. She is addicted to gardening, which he considers himself 'not suited to'. He has no magic formula to cure the itch of self-consciousness or to sweeten the bitter taste of success.

The doctor appears to be France's modern father confessor. The nation seems to have placed its faith in him: more is spent on health than on either education or defence. The present generation has used its new prosperity to quadruple the number of doctors. But it is now well-established that however well doctors do their job, they never eliminate disease: the more of them there are to consult, the more leisure people have to consult them, the more they will be needed. France has an enviable record in health care: its infant mortality rate, for example, has been reduced well below Britain's. Nevertheless, medicine has not made life easy. The most widespread complaint today is tiredness. The first national investigation of this ailment, in 1977, revealed that three-fifths of French women and two-fifths of men suffer from 'fatigue'. Women in their twenties and thirties, and men in their forties are particularly affected. Another investigation, focused on working mothers in the Charente-Maritime, found that though three-quarters of them enjoyed working, only 29% said they felt in good shape: 30% were 'fatigued', 25% 'enervated' and 14% both fatigued and enervated. When tired people go to their doctors, complaining particularly that they feel tired as soon as they get up in the morning, in 57% of cases the doctor tells them to rest. They do not find this particularly helpful, as he is usually aware, so in 78% of cases he prescribes tranquillizers, stimulants and anti-depressant pills of different sorts. Seventy per cent of doctors prescribe between three and seven different medicines per patient; 15% of them prescribe up to ten types of medicines. They get rid of one-third of their patients by sending them on to a psychiatrist. Some doctors think that is avoiding the issue, passing the buck; so a leading 'fatigue' doctor has recently established an Anti-fatigue Centre in the Alps, where patients can recover around a swimming pool in the shape of an Egyptian lotus leaf, and repeat: 'My respiration is healing and calming me.'

Psychiatrists have not yet won the status they have in the United States; France has only about 2500 of them. Most general practitioners have received virtually no training in psychiatry, so though they do most emotional counselling, they use an almost completely different classification of ailments. The lack of uniform diagnosis within the country makes it impossible to say what deeper mental troubles lie behind the complaints; the lack of a uniform international diagnosis makes it impossible to compare the French with other nations. But the French are difficult patients. Dr Olié of Sainte Anne's psychiatric hospital in Paris claims that medicine can 'completely cure' 70% of patients suffering from depression. A famous patient in that hospital, a graduate of the Ecole Normale Supérieure, who has spent many years not being cured, and has used his enforced leisure to collect literary quotations about madness, once told his doctors: 'If we were more numerous, it is you who would be here in our place.' It seems that the abnormal are now firmly in the majority in the country; they shy away from those who offer them too complete a cure. A poll revealed that two-thirds of the population would refuse psychoanalysis even if it were free. Even an expert in neuropharmacology, Dr Jean Thuillier, admits that if his science produced pills that could give people exactly the mood they wanted, they would be very cautious about using them: 'I believe men will always prefer the liberty to balance imagination and reason for themselves . . . and to create both Don Quixote and Sancho Panza in their heads.'

Not that the French disdain drugs. On the contrary, they differ from the British in that they do not concentrate their health expenditure on hospitals, but instead spend their money on drugs. They spend twice as much on drugs as do the British. They even developed an arrangement by which anyone could go and buy medicine without a prescription, and then go to a doctor and obtain from him a retrospective prescription, so that the cost of the medicine would be refunded by the social security. Doctors complain that they are dictated to by their patients, and not only this way. A popular doctor is one who is liberal with his prescriptions, who knows all the latest drugs, and gives large supplies of them. The social security found extraordinary cases of a man aged twenty-three being given a total of sixty-one boxes of five different medicines; another, aged eighty-two, emerged from the chemist's with fifty-four boxes of medicines, all dangerous, which were supposed to last him for six months; another was given ninety-three tubes of anti-coagulant to last him a year; a boy of nine was prescribed twenty-six medicines in one go, in drops, ampoules, pills, gels, to be swallowed, sniffed and rubbed on the skin, and five suppositories of three different medicines to be inserted in his anus. The ampoule is a uniquely French favourite; and is also the most expensive way of packing medicine. There are other pecularities about French prescriptions. Librium, for example, used to be prescribed for severe nervous anxiety in the United States and valium for mild cases. In France it was the other way round. The reason was that in the United States librium was normally available as an injection, whereas in France valium was, and an injection seemed more appropriate for a serious case. But these are superficial differences, because 60% of French medicines are now American: there has been a complete transformation of the pharmaceutical world in France.

Before the war, there were about a thousand laboratories producing an endless variety of traditional remedies. These have nearly all been swallowed up by giant international firms. Competition between them means they have to put 250 new medicines on the market each year; medicines have a short life; nearly three-quarters of medicines prescribed today are less than ten years old. The pharmacist, who used to be a minor scientist in the nineteenth century, has been almost reduced to the status of a grocer, but a wealthy grocer, for he receives 28% of the price of the medicine for handing it over the counter; he has no need to maintain an enormous stock, let alone to make up medicines, because there are now three major wholesalers who provide him with a very efficient computerized source. The pharmacists are keen to revive their status, and to become a new kind of social worker, organizers of local environment and sanitary policies, and educators on drugs, sex and medicine; but they forget that the public is no longer as illiterate as in the nineteenth century. The general practitioners are even more worried that they themselves are becoming mere technicians, writing out prescriptions, helpless instruments of the drug firms. They, of course, are quite unable to remember the names of more than a few out of the 8500 in existence; surveys show this memory varies between eighty and 200. In all their seven years of study, they have received only seventy hours of instruction in pharmacology. So they are at the mercy of the advertising of the drug firms, who indeed spend twice as much on advertising as on research. Once a drug is available only on prescription, it cannot be advertised publicly, but only to the medical profession; and these firms, therefore, subsidize 550 medical journals. They keep card indexes of fashionable doctors willing to try new medicines; they pay handsome fees to those who are willing to experiment with them; they send out armies of travellers to hawk their wares and offer samples.

It has been found that doctors tend to stick by older medicines which seem to have worked, but also to be attracted by the very latest thing; it is the slightly outdated one which gets abandoned. The mechanism of pharmaceutical renewal closely resembles that of fashions in clothes. Of course buying fancy new clothes does not mean you wear them, and 40% of medicines are thrown into the waste paper basket by those to whom they are prescribed. The demand for medical attention may also be compared to the demand for culture, which is insatiable. Getting hold of the latest and most powerful medi-

Claude Serre

cine (however dangerous that may be, and so much disease is being caused by medicines that a new specialization to study it is growing up) is flattering to both the patient and the doctor. General practitioners say that they do not really know precisely what is wrong with three-quarters of their patients, but they have to prescribe them something, to show that they have something to say to them, to meet the patient's belief in his right to a cure. He is a feeble doctor who can do no better than to prescribe aspirin: fortunately for him, the drug firms have produced more varieties of it which have the appearance of being more 'serious'. The choice of medicine is no longer made by the doctor, but is the result of a subtle negotiation. Often the patient demands a particular medicine. More often still, it is not the doctor's university training, but the drug firms which are behind the prescriptions.

It can almost be said that even being ill is, to a certain extent, a matter of individual choice. A particularly keen municipality which started a programme of checkups found that two-fifths of the population were ill without knowing it. The Minister of Health stopped any further investigations of this sort saying it reminded her of Nazi enquiries. Absenteeism from work certainly reflects factors which are not just medical. France has a higher rate of absenteeism than Britain or the United States, but that conceals the fact that some British car factories have double the national rate, which makes them equal to some regions of northern France; absenteeism in the Nord is almost three times as high as in Aquitaine; male clerks are absent from work twice as much as female clerks; but the highest rate of all is among female factory workers. Insomnia, described by one psychiatrist, Dr Yves Pelicier, as 'the language of distress', affects a quarter of the population, and one-third of those over thirty. But sufferers bear this with differing degrees of resignation, as was revealed by doctors investigating the Breton village of Plozevet ten years ago; they found that it had fifty times more mental disease than Parisians of equivalent social status, eight times more sexual diseases, three times more digestive troubles and twice as many bone and muscular defects. The Bretons, however, did not all respond in the same way to their troubles: 20% of the women took sleeping pills, but only 8% of the men; it was the women shopkeepers who had most trouble sleeping (35% took pills) but male shopkeepers seemed to find life somewhat easier (only 5% took pills). Likewise peasant women took sleeping pills almost twice as often as peasant men (18 and 10%).

With a cigarette drooping from his mouth, and a glass of wine in his hand, the typical Frenchman, as he is seen in caricatures, habitually complains about the government and about his liver. In real life, the addiction to cigarettes is both more and less typical than it is supposed to be. Tobacco consumption has trebled in the last twenty years; but it has lost ground among the well-to-do, managers, liberal professions and people with higher education; over a fifth of these have never smoked, and another fifth have given up smoking – so that 45% in all do not smoke. The figure for non-smokers is 35% for the working class and 37% for clerks. So it is only in the last generation that the French have caught up with the caricature. By contrast, only 39% of Britons and 36% of Americans are smokers.

The Frenchman's concern with the state of his liver is likewise only sometimes justified. France does indeed hold the world record for consuming more alcohol than any other country – twice as much as Britain or the United States – and for having more deaths from cirrhosis of the liver. Alcohol kills more people than motor accidents, and is the third major cause of death after heart disease and cancer. The addiction is not so ancient; in the eighteenth century, wine was still largely a rich man's pleasure; and during the Second World War it was so difficult to obtain that the illnesses associated with it became scarce and hospital teachers had trouble in teaching their students to recognize delirium tremens or cirrhosis. Since the war, the consumption of alcohol has fallen significantly; less wine is being drunk (though more beer and whisky). It is now officially estimated that France has two million alcoholics and three million 'excessive drinkers', who will turn into fully-fledged alcoholics in a few years. Alcoholics are particularly numerous in Brittany, Normandy, Picardy and the Nord. There are other regions, too, like the Haut-Rhin, where parents still give their children 'a good fill of eau-de-vie' every morning before sending them off to school; in the Auvergne, village football matches played by fifteen-year-olds are preceded by each player drinking a litre of wine; it is not unknown for toddlers of two to be given wine so that they can get used to it. Governments have not dared to interfere, even though they complain that the cost to the country in hospital bills, crime and lost work, is greater than the budgets of the ministries of education and justice put together (40% of hospital patients have alcoholic symptoms). So wine pays no more VAT than non-alcoholic drinks; indeed, it is non-alcoholic drinks and mineral waters which are subject to additional taxation.

The young have their own varied reasons for adopting the traditions they have inherited. At eighteen, nearly 40% of schoolchildren neither drink, smoke nor take drugs. It is true that 50% of them have 'had the opportunity' to take marijuana, but only one-sixth of boys and one-eighth of girls did actually make use of the opportunity and took the drug; at most 7% of schoolchildren smoke it with any regularity. Tobacco smoking has fallen very sharply among the young in the 1970s: only a quarter smoke regularly and only one-tenth smoke more than ten cigarettes a day. The consumption of alcohol among the young has more than halved in this decade. What has increased is the taking of pills for nervousness or insomnia, and now it is the girls who are setting the pace: by the age of eighteen, a quarter of girls are consuming such pills (and a tenth of boys); in the Paris region, a fifth of girls are already taking them at the age of sixteen. When questioned as to why they abstain, drink, smoke, or take drugs, the children relate their behaviour only marginally to the degree of their unhappiness. Group A in the table that follows are children aged sixteen to eighteen who neither drink, smoke nor take drugs (they form 38% of the sample). Group B are children of the same age who consume one or more of these products in significant quantities (they are 24% of the sample). This is how they describe themselves.

	A	B
Easily irritable	46	71
Anxious	46	61
Pessimistic	21	33
Spendthrift	40	66
Often depressed	21	55
Often thinking of suicide	3	13
Wanting everything immediately	26	40
Not very ambitious	25	30
Silent	57	42
Having a strained family life	18	35

But as soon as they start working, things change. Twice as many working young men of eighteen smoke, compared to their coevals at school; almost three times as many drink (34% instead of 12%); and girls at work are 50% more likely to take medical drugs than school girls.

Perhaps one discovers more about what the French really want out of life and what they really worry about most from their dreams, rather than from what they say to pollsters. The people who speak most freely about their dreams are the peasants, who treat them as they treat folk stories: dreams are part of their lives, and they arouse little anxiety: peasants dream a lot about the dead members of their family, but not with distress: at night they seem to re-establish the continuity of the generations. Music and play have an important part in their dreams also; dreaming is a feast. By contrast, shopkeepers are often unwilling to talk about their dreams. 'I dream about my tax collector,' says one, 'if you really want to know, I find it painful and I prefer not to dream.' Many say they deliberately eat a lot at night so as not to dream. That is because they dream frequently about their shops, and about people attacking or robbing their shops; there is a butcher who dreams all night about preparing meat; there are shop owners who dream that their assistants serve their clients all wrongly: 'I am at my till and I cannot intervene.' 'I tidy my boutique and I go on tidying it as though a wind is blowing through it and is constantly putting it into disorder.' Artisans have this trouble too: an apprentice cobbler hears criticisms of his work all night, and dreams that he has become deaf. An assistant in a shoe shop dreams that all the shoes fall out of their boxes and she cannot stop them. The cosy little shop, which symbolizes friendly service, is thus clouded by nightmares which are very often about the problems of daily life, exacerbated by logic and routine suddenly disappearing. Clerks have a particularly common, characteristic dream, about flying, or about driving fast sports cars, imagining themselves to be escaping from their life of routine and the persecution inflicted on them by their bosses. They dream of being able to buy everything they see in the shops, but there is seldom much imagination in their alternative life, which is not all that different from their real life. They are held back by haunting fears that they may lose their jobs, their motorcycles, their hi-fis, their electrical appliances, that they will not be able to maintain the style of life they are aspiring to.

It is only in degree that their dreams differ from those of managers. Managers sometimes say they are too busy to dream – 'my responsibilities do not allow me to dream' – or they pretend that dreaming is simply a relaxation like one of their hobbies. It is true that they do dream a great deal about holidays, about sea, sun and doing nothing, often to the accompaniment of music – the women favouring classical music, the men reviving the pop songs of the 1960s; they imagine that they are able to play musical instruments. But at least half their dreams are about losing their privileges; doctors lose their diplomas and are forced to become nurses, engineers lose theirs and are forced to spend the night in a hostel for vagabonds, managers find their qualifications cancelled by a revolution, but are unable to obtain new ones; others are arrested for driving without an insurance policy, or are kidnapped. The wives of managers lose their property and their status, but unlike shopkeepers, they do not refuse to talk about this, but seek to interpret their dreams, a surprisingly large minority having studied psychology in some way. The dreams of the social order being overturned are not necessarily unpleasant. One manager dances with his female workers, all of whom seem pretty, and he promises to appoint them shorthand typists so that they will no longer need to dirty their hands 'and so everybody is happy and I become very rich.' The wife of a manager gives a ball in the prefecture, the prefect becomes very small, begging for food like a baby, 'and I take him in my arms and cuddle him.' The children of the rich dream more often of committing suicide than do those of any other class, but most of the time they are less anxious or frightened in their dreams than the poor. Young workers become revolutionary chiefs in their beds; they become dynamic and aggressive, physically stronger, supermen. 'I am an engine-driver, and I succeed in saving the train from an accident and people applaud,' or 'I climb onto a table and make a speech and everybody claps.' Workers do not dream about their work or their factories (unlike peasants). A plumber says 'My dreams are separate from what I am.' Many dream that they can wander around freely, sleep in the open, travel endlessly in a car: 'no one bothers us, we are free'. Older men dream of meals in the country with their family, of doing nothing. Many dream of the Second World War, or the Algerian war, and other collective experiences. The television and cinema introduces numerous themes: pop music, happy times with the boys or the girls, love, libertinage, liberty, the sun, happiness . . . Some women dream of being attacked or raped, but on the whole dreams enrich people's lives as though with interesting experiences.

It is perhaps significant that in all classes dreams about food are much more often about conviviality than about gastronomy: there are few dreams about not being able to eat the kind of food one likes. Hunger may have a sexual significance for Freud, but dreams of hunger seem to be frequently associated with memories of hunger during the last war, and with a fear of having to suffer from it again: 'We are lots of children on a main road; the Americans drive past in large lorries and throw roast chickens at us, and we devour them because we are hungry.' Dreams about death are most frequently about one's own death or about universal destruction, rather than about Freudian patricide or fratricide. The sexual act is surprisingly rare in dreams except among the young and the old; perhaps those in between hesitate more to mention them. Those under thirty, at any rate, do not complicate their sexual dreams with guilt or fear; many of them dream of a retreat where they can establish calm and profound emotional understanding with another person, but many also see participation in a group as an essential aspect of this relationship; they do a lot of talking, it is not just lovemaking. But there are still plenty whose loves are theatrical and romantic. There is a whole class of persons, drawn from all social classes, who turn their dreams into a theatre, and who become poets at night, creating a different world rather resembling a fairy tale, occasionally drawing inspiration from past literature, placing themselves in unusual situations, with magic, hypnosis, metamorphosis and strange ceremonies. The most important influence of all, more than radio or television, seems to be the comic strip: people dream in little isolated scenes, as though in vignettes taken from Superman or Asterix, with chateaux, caves and pursuits, good and bad men. In the dreams of the young of all classes, the happy family, the group of friends untroubled by demands, the home set in a rural paradise, are much repeated. The old do relive the violence of television; they return frequently to childhood, they dream a lot about sex and are worried by this; but they dream little about death and rarely about God or religion.

Psychiatrists like to discover frustration, desire and suffering in dreams. Sociologists suggest that there is a recurrent obsession with consumer goods and a hedonistic attitude to life. Jean Duvignaud, who made this collection and analysis of French dreams, argues that there is a third possibility, that dreams are just a game with no special significance, a game in which people juggle the world and throw accepted institutions and customs into a whirl. He has arranged them by social class and age-group, because those are the categories most familiar today. But it would be interesting to create new categories among the population, according to the kinds of dreams they have: that would need a much larger sample, but it may contribute to a better understanding of emotions that are not easily expressed, and of the private battles each individual fights.

A psychiatrist, Madeleine Laïk, went around the grim suburb of Bobigny to question people on what it was they feared most. She had her own reasons for being interested. 'I am blonde,' she says, 'I walk with my stomach drawn well in, my head held high, my eyes are blue and very honest. I am warm. Never, seeing me walking down the street, would anyone think I make secret bargains with life all the time, like a little old woman, ladling out my gestures in doses, rationing my energy. I do not want to lose my body and I hardly ever make love.' She got people to confess likewise and collected 3000 pages about their fears. She started with a girl of fourteen, who says she is frightened nine-tenths of the time: she fears her mother ('she'll strangle me'), she fears men (when they look at her going out alone), she fears eating too much; when she is very frightened indeed she laughs like a lunatic; but she tries to look pretty, and that reduces her fear, for people smile at her then. Mr Chica, a retired goldsmith, has many fears, all of which he refers to as 'my greatest fear'. One is not to be quite up to what is expected of him and not to produce work of a sufficiently high standard. Another is loneliness: he was absolutely terrified when his wife

WHAT ILLNESSES THEY SUFFER FROM 471

died after forty-six years of marriage; the one year he spent on his own after that was terrible, and that was why he moved into the old people's home of Bobigny. Here, he noted, everybody was frightened of death; they tried to distract themselves playing cards, but he found that boring; he preferred playing with women; his greatest fear now was to become impotent sexually, and helpless physically.

By contrast, a group of six adolescents lounging in the streets say they are afraid of falling in love. 'If I fall in love with a girl, she must love me too, otherwise I shall look a fool.' They did not get on with girls. 'I cannot say I love you to a girl. It would be shaming. Once a girl said it to me. I fell on the floor laughing.' The old fear they will be attacked by the young. The young are frightened of being attacked by other gangs. Parents conjure fears in their children by threats to induce good behaviour; if you lie, your face will split open. If you bite your nails, your hand will fall off. If you read too late at night, you'll go blind. If you suck your thumb, you'll make a hole in your palate. If you pick your nose, it will grow so big, it will have to be carried in a wheel-barrow. If you do not wash your *zizi*, all the dogs will follow you in the street. If you go on touching yourself, you will go black. Children of nine to twelve fear that their high-rise blocks of flats will fall down. Everyone complains they are not solid, that they are made of cardboard, and are likely to explode from burst gas pipes, and burn easily. People do not feel safe in their flats; there is no sense of privacy when they can hear every WC being flushed, every radio playing music. Quite a few keep guns, or whistles, or alarms; an old lady takes a revolver with her every time she goes to Bobigny post office to collect her money. Housewives fight their fears by eating, praying, keeping busy with cooking, doing housework (the constant battle against another fear, that of dirt), watching love stories on television and reading detective stories. They pass round tranquillizers and homeopathic remedies amongst themselves. But none would like to be freed from their fears entirely. 'To have no more fears is a little like entering the ante-chamber to the cemetery; fear is life.'

Fear of the future is of course a constant worry, and there are little industries to offer help with that. Graphology has been

officially recognized as a science of public utility, and Air
France, for example, regularly uses it to predict how candidates
for employment will behave: it is convinced that it is accurate.
Fortune-tellers have a regular slot on public radio. The most
famous astrologer in France, Madame Soleil, who used to tell
fortunes at country fairs, and who now has prosperous consult-
ing rooms in Paris, was given a radio programme of her own on
Radio Europe I by one of her clients, who happened to run this
station: the station at once received 17,000 telephone calls a day
for her, and soon her backlog of letters was said to have reached
300,000. Madame Soleil did so well that in 1977 she was given
a suspended prison sentence for tax evasion. A scientist, Jean-
Claude Corbineau, a graduate of the Ecole Centrale, tried to put
this interest in astrology on a modern basis by computerizing
the requests for advice and the astrological replies, but that was
not quite what people wanted; and he has withdrawn to make
his fortune producing pop records. Today's clairvoyants are
individuals, whose success is due to the skill with which they
give their individual clients what they are looking for. Some
still use bogus exotic names, while some look like efficient
young executives. The astrologer 'Charles', in the seventeenth
arrondissement of Paris, claims 'to have inherited his divinatory
gifts from his family over several generations'. Frère Michael
Potay, white-robed and with a long beard, wearing both a
Christian cross and various other insignia, calls himself an
'ethnologist specializing in Arian Magic, a master of the
Institute of Chinese Philosophy and Acupuncture of Kharbine',
a scientist, Christian Kabbalist and magician, and claims he is
known as 'the saint, the miracle man and the good sorcerer of
Bourges'. Madame Vivier, who divides her time between Biar-
ritz and the east end of Paris, describes herself as a graduate
psychologist astrologer. Belinda of Montpellier promises
'immediate action at a distance in love and luck, magic in the
service of those who suffer'. 'Forget your troubles with the
magic secrets of Jesus' says the Institut Osiris. Madame Ste-
phanou, practising under the name of Flora Stephane, 'author of
the famous Astrologer's Tango', offers her secret processes,
inherited from her Turkish and Tibetan ancestors, at Robes-
pierre's house in the rue Saint Honoré. It has been estimated

that around a million copies are sold each year of books dealing with astrology and related arts. Horoscopes are regularly read by over half the French population, and by two-thirds of clerks.

It is not surprising that what the French lack in psychiatrists, they make up for in massagists: the growth of the profession of kinotherapeutics has been very rapid since the war; they mainly go into private practice, unlike those in Britain, who are largely incorporated into the hospital service. So the French now have as many massagists as they have dentists. The Americans keep up appearances in a different way: they have twice as many dentists

Claude Serre

as the French (per head of population): at least they can keep smiling in public. It is not surprising either, that since doctors with official diplomas are far from always succeeding in curing their patients, and since patients do not always share their doctor's idea of what it means to be cured (like the old lady who on her hundredth birthday told journalists that though she was glad to be alive, she regretted that the doctors had not cured her old age), fringe medicine flourishes. Faith healers are apparently the most numerous, followed by plant-remedy healers, *radiesthésistes*, chiropractors, amateur homeopaths and hypnotists. Old peasant remedies are still handed down from generation to generation in the poorer rural areas, with prayers to cure bee stings and snake bites, to expel thorns from the skin and to encourage fertility in animals. There are still a few people who believe in and practise sorcery. Publishers can still make money reprinting old books giving formulae for casting spells. Healers have got a faithful following, though they are treated in much the same way as unbelievers treat the Church: just as people resort to a priest for baptism, marriage and burial, so they resort to a healer when official medicine fails; there are only two professions who are generally hostile to healers, the clergy and teachers; many doctors are open-minded about them. The difference between the modern and the old style of healer is that today they are to be found in every social class; they are people who follow ordinary occupations, and are treated like everybody else, until there is a call for their services. In the Berry, an anthropologist found some two hundred of them, half men and half women. In Corsica, three-quarters of them are women; in the Aubrac, two-thirds are men. So if people do not choose their illnesses, they can at least choose their healers.

That is perhaps the most characteristic feature of French medicine, that the patient can choose his own doctor, and go from one to another as he pleases, even to specialists, and still have the state reimburse most of the fees. France is a country that practises the cult of the second opinion. The variety of diagnoses is increased by the fact that France has a great variety in the types of doctors offering their services.

A French doctor is the victor and victim of a particularly competitive rat race. Admission as a student of medicine does not mean that one is likely to emerge eventually as a doctor. At the end of the first year, two-thirds will be thrown out – there is no room for them. The old and the new generation are separated by the medical reforms of 1958 and the political revolution of 1968, which respectively changed the organization of medical education and democratized access to it. In the old days a French doctor was essentially a clinician more than a scientist; the emphasis was as much on diagnosing as curing; the rule was to give medicines which did no harm. Medical education involved memorizing and, if one was lucky, serving an apprenticeship. An ordinary student who had the right to listen to lectures and follow professors round the wards at a distance got a very hazy notion of the subject. There was a considerable difference between him and the more privileged students who were admitted to a fuller apprenticeship, for there were two grades of apprenticeships. A doctor with the title of 'former hospital extern' was one better than one who simply had a 'diploma of the faculty of medicine'. The extern had passed a competitive examination which allowed him to participate in the running of a hospital. It is true the examination was not very demanding; to pass it he normally went to a crammer's, where young doctors stuffed the candidates' heads with facts, in an atmosphere of conspiracy, because the aim was to predict the questions and memorize the right answers; every old doctor can still recite without thinking the standard definitions of every disease and every symptom: 'pleurisy is recognizable by a hard, dry, parchment-like crackle in auscultation, resembling two bits of leather rubbing against each other.' It was normal to fail in one's first attempt to become an extern, but one was allowed to sit the examination five times. That meant that on average the old doctor would have spent two years learning about symptoms: today only six months are devoted to this. Once appointed an extern, a student was put in charge of about a dozen beds in a hospital.

Democratization has changed all this. Every student now has the right to be an extern, and the title means very little today. And there are now so many externs, that they can only hope for about half a bed each. The doctors of the present generation have not been taught by the same method of clinical apprenticeship. The new craze is for a more thorough grounding in science, so there are now two kinds of professors of medicine: those who teach the 'fundamental' sciences, and those who teach medicine; a student has to devote a great deal of time to chemistry and biology in the abstract. The old memorizing of textbooks remains, but it is now balanced by fewer practical responsibilities in a hospital ward. The separation between faculty and hospital has been ended: there are no longer any pariahs who get a second-class education; and it is the university-hospital which is the teaching unit. But things have not turned out quite as planned. Few university hospitals are, in fact, able to teach the whole range of subjects; only one new university hospital has been built in the Paris region, at Créteil, to implement the new ideal. What the student learns depends on which university hospital he goes to. There are an increasing number of medical subjects to study, so many have to be relegated to the status of 'optional'. The particular facts with which a doctor emerges vary considerably; they vary also depending on how much time he was able to give to his studies: some lectures are given in the evening because so many students earn their living elsewhere during the day. The modern student's practical experience comes only in his final seventh year, but here again the pressure of numbers is such that most cannot find a hospital willing to employ them: a hospital would often have 300 students but only twenty-four posts for their practical training as interns. So students search for clinics wherever they can find them, often offering their services free, to enable them to qualify. Fortunately for them, if they have got this far, the final examination is a formality. They have to write a thesis to be called 'doctor of medicine': this can be on any subject remotely connected with medicine and is normally examined in three minutes.

The top grade of doctor of the old vintage was one who has done better than this: about 40% of medical students became externs; about 15% of them, after another examination, became interns. 'Ancien interne des hôpitaux de Paris' used to be the really smart title on the brass plate. The intern lived in the hospital and was in effect a junior doctor even before he qualified. But unfortunately one cannot judge a doctor's quality quite so simply, by his titles, because passing these examinations was not necessarily a sign of intelligence. The Hippocratic oath which the newly-fledged doctor has to take includes not only a promise to succour the sick and keep their secrets, but also to aid the sons of his patron. His patron is his professor, and this oath is no formality. French medicine is ruled by patrons. They were notorious for their nepotism in the old days, and the nepotism has not entirely disappeared. To become an intern required obtaining the patronage of a professor and becoming his obsequious, loyal follower. Interns used to be mainly the sons of patrons and of the famous doctors, though students who worked extremely hard could force their way into the charmed circle. This system of patronage has today moved to the post-graduate level. An intern today is a doctor doing a four-year course of post-graduate work in a hospital unit with a view to obtaining a qualification as a specialist, or to attempting the long climb to the exalted status of professor. Today a patron is still indispensable. A doctor cannot have more than one patron: if his patron dies, the whole clan is done for. It is the patron who decides, after these four years, who will be selected for a further seven-year stint as an *assistant des hôpitaux, chef de clinique* – which is the next rank in the hospital's establishment. By the end of these seven years, the assistant will know whether he has got a permanent post as *agrégé*, which involves teaching as well as treating the sick. There is an examination for this promotion, but it is the power of the patrons, more than the merits of the candidates, that decides who is successful. The final choice of all, in which full professors are chosen from among them, has been described as the most politicized election of any held in France. There is little movement between the different cities of France, because each is subject to the rule of a different set of clans; so the medical establishments in Lyon and Montpellier, for example, maintain their separate eccentricities. The power of patrons extends well beyond his hospital. It is an illusion that the patient who goes to a hospital can expect to receive advice from the best doctors in the country. The great men in the hospital are unlikely to see him: the professor, the *agrégé*, even the *chef de clinique* have only one or two sessions for consultation each week. Most people are seen by the *attaché*, who is an ordinary doctor from outside the hospital, on the outer fringes of the patron's clientele. He is employed for fees far lower than those he would receive in private practice, on a part-time basis, but he is honoured by the accolade.

The general practitioner may therefore sometimes be a slightly confusing personality. On the one hand he is a doctor who may have done badly in the rat race and failed to win the coveted prizes of medicine. He may emerge from his training with an inferiority complex, which is swollen into terror when he realizes that in his seven years of study he has had time for only three months of therapeutics. There are general practitioners who complain about 'the crushing pride' of the hospital doctors who 'treat them as contemptible'. On the other hand, for the mass of the public, a doctor is a respected figure, traditionally a 'notable', particularly in rural areas. A general practitioner has to act the part if he can. The role is not learnt quickly, because he has to acquire patients. He is paid for each consultation by the patient (who recovers most of the fee from the government, and if he is a member of a mutual insurance society, he recovers the whole fee). The GP has to begin his career by entering into competition with his fellow doctors like a grocer setting up shop. To earn a decent living he must see at least four patients an hour; it is in his financial interest to see his patients as often as possible, to maximize the number of tests and investigations. A socialist doctor has written that since most doctors need to be supported by their families to qualify, they are 'selected by the criterion of money, and they are most often motivated by money: to make their fortune is their vocation.' That is an unjustified accusation, even if many doctors do admit that only accident led them to choose their profession (as with most people): that does not mean that they do not become dedicated and engrossed, and do their best. As a whole doctors have steadfastly rejected a medical system in which they would all simply receive a regular salary. The reason is not their greed, but that they are as individualist as their patients. There is of course a tiny minority that is mercenary: one doctor systematically revisits all his patients at least once a month, just to increase his income; another raises it further by distributing aerosols, ionisations, infra-red, ultraviolet and high frequency treatments. One-tenth refuse to accept the government's fixed fee and bargain individually with each patient.

The variety of treatments is increased by the GP's relations with the specialists. The more specialists he sends his patients to, say his enemies, the richer all of them become. But the pressure to be sent to a specialist comes equally from the patient, who is as frightened as the GP that the wrong diagnosis may be made. A good GP from the patients' point of view is one who knows his way around the world of the specialists, who will not send them automatically to the specialists with whom he plays bridge, or to those who give him a cut in the fees they charge. The GP complains that the media publicize every fancy new remedy, that his patients demand more and more tests and exotic forms of treatment. He sees himself as a cog in an inflationary machine, whose function is to sign endless prescriptions, order endless X-rays. In fact since patients are free to choose their doctor and change when they like, they end up with a doctor whose values they share or with whom they are happy to be accomplices in the magician's game the doctor is expected to play.

France has comparatively few GPs – not many more than there were before the war. The new influx of doctors are the specialists. A specialist is paid at twice the rate that a GP is paid for each consultation, in theory so that he can devote twice as much time and buy expensive equipment. A famous specialist can charge even more, with government authorization, but the extra difference above the ordinary specialist's fee has to be paid by the patient, and will not be reimbursed by the social security. The trend has been for a good student to aim at becoming a specialist in private practice, but only 25–40% of those who embark on the four-year postgraduate course are given the title of specialist. A patient needs to be skilful to be able to spot who is a genuinely qualified specialist, and who simply puts up a brass plate saying he treats 'Women's diseases'. The busiest specialists at present are the rheumatologists; they are said to make large profits. Cardiologists by contrast have multiplied almost too much for the demand; they are reputed to set up too many tests unnecessarily as a result. It is likely that there will be a further increase in specialists, notably can-cerologists, paediatricians and gerontologists. British GPs remain much more powerful, with their permanent lists of patients and their monopoly as intermediaries between patients and specialists. There is plenty of cynicism in France about medicine, even if there is also plenty of credulity. There is even an association to defend the patient against the doctor, which publishes a journal to warn people against their misdeeds.

These quarrels reflect the different demands made on doctors. One of the main peculiarities of the French health budget is that less is spent on hospitals than in any comparable country, even less than in Italy, and only half what is spent in Sweden, where medicine is concentrated around the hospital. The typical French doctor is an individualist. As in its love relationships, so in its pursuit of health, the public can never decide what it wants from its doctor, and is never quite satisfied. Dr Christian Bourrel, who with a partner looks after four thousand people spread over six villages in the Aude, illustrates what the traditional style of doctor, with modernized methods, can offer. He has a radiotelephone, so that any patient can be reached in ten minutes. But he does not see his role as curing difficult diseases: he readily calls on the specialists; for serious diseases, his role is to support the patient in hospital, visiting him two or three times a week. That is because he sees his main function as psychological: he says he is the equivalent of the American psychoanalyst; he has replaced the lawyer and the priest as the universal counsellor. People come for advice as much on problems of divorce as of health, just as his grandmother used to spend many hours at confession talking about all sorts of things that had nothing to do with religion. But because he is a doctor, the patients hesitate a little to bring up the subjects that are really worrying them: he is used to them raising them only just when they are leaving, saying I'll come and see you some time about . . . Dr Bourrel received no teaching at all in psychiatry as a student; he then served in the army's psychiatric service and 'discovered a fabulous world'. He thinks that psychiatric treatment is appropriate for only very few people: 'it can be dangerous, it can reveal volcanoes which are better left untouched. There is anxiety in everybody, and four-fifths of the time this is of sexual origin, but patients wait for me to ask them about this.' He hesitates to ask: 'it is best not to stir up trouble.' Most patients are not ill at all; they need reassurance and he gives them some minor treatment just to confirm the reassurance.

That is quite different from the kind of behaviour he experienced when he practised in a suburb of Paris, Rosny-sur-Bois, which was a combination of village and tower-block city. The inhabitants of the tower blocks summon the doctor only for medical problems: the doctor treats them and goes away; the patients do their own diagnoses and call the doctor to cure a particular disease; teachers in particular all have the *Larousse Médical* and study their symptoms. Patients sometimes call more than one doctor: he remembers arriving at an apartment in an HLM (high-rise block) and meeting two other doctors on the point of ringing the bell too. In Paris, patients happily summon a doctor for insomnia at 4.00 a.m., or if they vomit after too much drink, or if they quarrel with their spouse: money is no problem. But in the country, now that the price of night visits has gone up, there is much less call on doctors at night, usually only for children's ailments. Dr Bourrel regrets that what is happening in the towns, where doctors are treated like grocers, will almost inevitably happen in the country too, sooner or later: the personal tie with the patient will vanish, and medical centres with salaried doctors will replace the likes of him. He regrets it because he believes that attention at home is best; an old person will be cured twice as fast at home as in hospital. He has to work twelve to fourteen hours a day to satisfy his patients, never less than ten; he takes off only one weekend a fortnight, and every Wednesday. That is because he wants to keep the personal contacts alive: he stops at people's houses just to shake hands. He still goes on delivering babies, though others find it fashionable to go to hospital, because 'I work on life.' He says, 'I believe in friendship.' He inspires confidence by his honesty, his modesty and his warmth. He has no illusions about his erudition: he says his training was quite inadequate, though he has tried to improve it by reading and going to lectures and hospitals. But he has no illusions about the benefits of erudition either; he was willing to recommend a herbal remedy that an English doctor dismissed derisively as an old wives' tale. Far from being the archetypal Frenchman who believes in theories, he represented solid common sense, that the English imagine is their peculiar strength. The alternative to Dr Bourrel is a series of hospital specialists, and psychiatrists, and social workers. That gives people more choices, but not always more friendship. Perhaps new forms of friendship will have to be invented.

28

How not to be bored in old age

'I have led a life in which nothing special has happened.' That is how Marie Selandouse looks back on her eighty-seven years. She has devoted herself to her family: she has seen her grandchildren become dentists, architects and pharmacists, which is quite a source of pride for one who began as a nurse, who married a baker and spent forty years at the till of a small baker's shop. Her husband has died, and she has broken her hip. She has had to move into the old people's wing of a hospital. 'That is not much fun.' Her only pleasures are the visits she gets from the children, who take it in turns to visit, so there are only two days of the week when she has no one to see her. She reads a little, but has not much taste for that, having always been too busy to read; 'I have no preferences in books, it is the children who bring them.' She watches television a little, but there is nothing much that is interesting, she dislikes violent films; she once used to have preferences among actors – Gabin, Bourvil – but no longer. She is rather lost without a house to look after. Her advice to the young is to remain at home as long as they can. Now that she is incapacitated, she has no choice; she does not want to live with her children, because she would be a nuisance, particularly when she was ill; they would be out all day, and she is frightened of being alone, she would not dare open the door, since the old are an easy target for robbery and violence. She and her husband had saved relentlessly – 'that was our aim, to save for our old age' – and so she has been able to get a room of her own in the hospital; but the food is not to her liking, there is neither a private bath nor a kitchen. 'We are w⌐' looked after; it is warm; but you have to take what you are given.' Her mind is perfectly lucid, and she speaks with grace and precision; but time hangs heavily, and she can only lament that things are not what they used to be, that bread today is nowhere near as tasty as it was when she baked it (the baguette was invented only between the wars, it used to be greyish, and only became white after 1940; it began as a *bâtard*, or half a loaf, and was gradually lengthened). She regrets the disappearance of small shops, which used to deliver: the supermarkets are not 'human', and they do not tell you whether the pork they sell comes from Brittany, which is good, or the Auvergne, which is bad. Life, in other words, is not organized to suit her.

Or perhaps it is that she has not organized her life to enable her to enjoy old age more and that her saving money has not been enough. That kind of accusation cannot be lightly made, but it is one that Raymond Jegaden sometimes levels against himself. He is a bachelor, still only in his seventies, and for forty years he was secretary-general of the Chamber of Notaries (almost the equivalent of the Law Society). He found his work very interesting and very absorbing; he was proud to be treated as an equal, even as a friend, by the notaries, who were often cultured and interesting people. Perhaps, on reflection, he should have got married, but he was too busy: 'I was keen to give satisfaction.' He had little hobbies; he helped run an evening educational institute; he used to write articles for an obscure Catholic newspaper; he even wrote a book about the secretaries of the French Academy, but the publishers wanted a substantial sum from him to publish it. He spent his leisure hours in libraries collecting information. He lived in a two-roomed flat and never travelled abroad. His best friend was the local priest. He found his life interesting. But then he began going deaf, and that has made him less sociable. He fainted, hurt himself falling, so he decided he could not live alone any more, and he moved into an old people's home too. Here his life is dominated by the fact that meals are at fixed times, and he feels he must always be back for supper at six. That makes it very difficult to go up to Paris, except for a mere hour or two; he no longer goes to the theatre or exhibitions. A cataract has made reading difficult. He is very bored. 'My inactivity weighs heavily on me. I regret not working, but I suppose one must give the young a chance, and in any case, there are new ways of working now, computers, I would understand nothing.' He looks on the future gloomily: his life is completely empty. He goes to church, but he is uncertain about whether he thinks there is life after death.

Only a third of the French believe in an afterlife, only a third think about death. But the latest view is that they should all think about old age, and make life almost a preparation for it. For old age has taken on a new role; the old are the new class that promises to exert a dominant influence on the next century, as the young were supposed to in this. After racism and sexism, agism is the latest preoccupation, in France as elsewhere. France thinks of itself as a particularly old country, though its proportion of over 65s is absolutely average for Europe:

Per cent of old people over 65 (1976)

West Germany	14·6
Britain	14·1
France	13·5
Italy	12·3
USA	10·6
Spain	10·1
Europe	13·5

These figures are nearly treble what they were a century ago, but to survive into one's seventies is still a privilege: only 30% of people born in 1900 succeeded in doing so; the expectation of life for a French person born today is sixty-nine for a boy and seventy-seven for a girl. Old age is increasingly a female privilege: the gap between the male and female expectations of life has doubled in the course of this century; women now live eight instead of four years longer than men. Two-thirds of those in the seventy-five to eighty-four age group are women, and three-quarters of those over eighty-five. There is still social inequality in survival, in that managers and above all primary-school teachers and clergymen can expect to survive longer than labourers, who lead a tough life, but the sexual inequality is far greater. The question that arises, therefore, is, are women going to blossom anew in old age?

Jossot

I dreamed I was alive

The old and the young have this new characteristic in common, that they have stopped working; they can devote themselves to other interests. The old have the added advantage that they have seven million votes (over sixty-five) and so have the political power to decide their own fate. For most of this century the old have battled for the right to early retirement and to pensions they can live on. They have almost attained this goal. The question is what to strive for next. Retirement is going to come earlier and earlier. The old now realize that their social conquests have been won at the expense of their acquiring an image as useless and unable to work, as well as poor. Improved living standards have now made this image false. Financially, the old have done better than any other class in society in the last decade. The average retired person now has an income which is almost equal (94%) to the national average. There are still enormous inequalities among pensions, and much poverty, but old age no longer necessarily means poverty. Nor does it mean incapacity. The French already stop working earlier than most other people: the United States has twice as large a population of old people still at work as the French, and the Japanese have four times as many. [1] That means that most French people retire with the prospect of many years of life ahead of them during which they are perfectly fit, particularly during the first decade of retirement. They now have two different categories of old people: the Third Age has been followed by a Fourth Age, of those who are *really* old, the octogenarians. Retirement, that is, usually comes before old age, particularly as unemployment makes it harder for the redundant to get new jobs after fifty.

It is the more educated classes who are trying to invent a new style of life for retirement. Whereas 53% of workers withdraw from life almost completely on retirement, going out very little and concentrating on sleeping, eating, and looking after their health, by contrast 63% of managers have adopted a way of life dedicated to the cultivation of leisure activities, to going out and to maintaining social contacts. A large number of clubs and activities for old people have been started, but there is a feeling that this is perpetuating an ideal that the new generation will reject, because it implies segregating the old, and because it makes old age a mere parody of what other age groups do. The old are escaping from their past resignation; they have abandoned the longing for gerontocracy, but they have not found a new role. The traditional solution was to provide them with plenty of medicine, but now it is argued that they need love and attention more than that. The same is said of the young, of course. At the moment the old get only 10% of the gross

---

[1] Working population over 65 (in 1975)

Japan	30·7%
USA	14
UK	10·6
West Germany	9·9
France	7·1
Italy	7·0
Belgium	6·3

national product (double what they got a generation ago), which almost equals what is spent on education. As they become more numerous, there may well be a struggle over money as well as for love. To avoid this, the proposals of the latest government commission are that the retired should be prevented from becoming the inhabitants of a ghetto: the retirement age should be abolished, employers should no longer be able to get rid of their workers simply on the ground of age, pensions should be paid not for retirement but as a reward for working a certain number of years and their payment should not be dependent on whether one stops working or not. It is the sick rather than the old who should be helped. Consciousness of the changing possibilities that life has to offer over the years should be encouraged, so that people should learn, as Montaigne said, to manage their lives, to plan the time they are allowed. This utopian plan is to be crowned by an Institute of Old Age, which will disseminate the new wisdom. This wisdom is, of course, the negation of the prevailing ideal, that youth and maturity are the best years of life and that one should aim to look young.

At present, only two million old people live alone, a smaller proportion than in England, where virtually half of those over seventy live alone. Old age is not necessarily loneliness, or dissatisfaction, but it is undoubtedly the most wasted period of life. This is perhaps where the most changes are likely to occur in the future.

The old have not yet found anything much to laugh about in their condition, but just in case this topic inspires nothing but gloom, it is worth knowing that death at any rate has found its humorist. Dr André Ruellan practised medicine for a dozen years before becoming a science fiction writer: he frequented the Surrealists; he participated in what was nicely called the Panic Movement; and he wrote the scenario for one of the most popular of all comic films, Pierre Richard's *The Absent-Minded Man*. He has produced for his own old age *The Guide on How to Die*. Sarah Bernhardt apparently used to lie in a coffin every day, just for practice. He advises people to go jogging in cemeteries to familiarize themselves with the terrain: the point of his sick jokes is that modern death is frightening because people nowadays refuse to think about it. But he also suggests that some living people are already dead: they should make arrangements so that when they do finally expire, no one will notice the difference, by having themselves enbalmed and left permanently in front of their television sets.

Topor

29

How they pray

'I no longer agree with what I taught twenty years ago,' says the
Benedictine monk Father Luc, 'and indeed I would be ashamed
to repeat what I said twenty years ago.' The Catholic Church in
France is no longer what it was. It is not just that Father Luc
does not look like a monk, in his rather smart, casual civilian
clothes, with no dog collar, no tie, only an inconspicuous small
cross attached to a chain round his neck. More important is the
fact that he no longer has the same status or functions that a
priest used to have. His job, he says, is no longer 'to sell
religious merchandise'. He seldom holds services or preaches.
He does not even teach religion to children any more, since that
has been taken over by professional lay teachers. He lives a
communal life with four or five other monks, but he has become
a parish priest, because he found the monastic life not enough by
itself. He has spent all his twenty years in the same working-
class suburb with a communist municipality, and he has seen
his congregation fall by half in that time: 'a quarter left us
because we moved too fast and a quarter because we did not
move fast enough.' He does not try to be a missionary among the
unfaithful. Fewer than five people a week come to him seeking
the traditional confession. Religion has ceased to mean primarily taking the sacraments or attending church. Instead,
Father Luc spends most of his time helping people to reflect on
their faith. He helps to form little groups, by district, or of just
a few friends, who meet with priests to discuss the way they live,
and the way they experience their faith. He takes part in the
discussion with no superior authority: 'we are converted as well
as they;' he has been as much influenced by the changing
attitudes of the laity as they have by him. Instead of confession

in the old style, these groups meet to discuss their lives in 'penitentials': the participants question each other: what did you do wrong this week? What do you pay your workers? And then they give absolution. Instead of giving baptism to all who ask for it, he insists on discussing the parents' motives with them. He has much less scope for organizing clubs for the young, because the communists have given so many subsidies to the public clubs, that the Church cannot compete. So the emphasis is on discussion. He was for long the local school chaplain: children too go to Church less and instead meet and talk things over; it often makes no difference if they are Protestants: that division he regards as a relic of a past quarrel, like having divorced parents. He offers not instruction, but 'friendship and cooperation with others in seeking the truth'. He is willing to talk with anyone who comes to see him, and he does not look at his watch when the conversation goes on for several hours; he seems willing to talk indefinitely. He interprets Christianity in his own personal way.

Born Jean-Claude Foucher, the son of a cabinetmaker and a mother who came of a family of small shopkeepers, he has renounced his petty bourgeois origins as he has his name. He says he feels ill at ease in the company of the middle classes; he finds the contrast between their wealth and the poverty of their thinking too painful. He has hardly any wish to convert them. He is convinced that Christianity today is a religion for the poor, as it was in Christ's time, for people on the fringes, the *marginaux*, those who do not aspire to becoming bosses: Jesus' announcement that he came to succour the ill and those who had no hope is the message that matters now. He sees his role as that of an intermediary between the establishment or the well-to-do and the poor: he tries to be a 'witness to the poor' to tell them that those who are not hungry have not forgotten them, and a 'witness to the comfortable', to tell them that if they do not look after the poor, 'society will catch fire.' A Christian he defines as one who feels most acutely the wounds and the pain of others; he hopes he can transmit that feeling to the middle classes, because he is certain that they realize there is something missing in their lives. He agrees that he does have things in common with the communists, though his methods and motivations are different, and he is also their rival; he does not like a world in which people are oppressed, suffer ill health, and are exploited by the rich; so he has worked particularly among criminals, drug addicts, and racial minorities. He would not dream of joining a political party, because he considers that priests still have great moral power. Power is what he feels very much in need of, to be able to influence others, to 'help people speak up for themselves', something different from the political power that bishops once loved to wield. The local right-wing leader of the political opposition does not come to Father Luc's church, but prefers to worship some miles away, in a church that retains more traditional habits. Father Luc, far from despairing of his parish, is very much attached to it. He has visited many African and Asian countries, and lived for a while in Ceylon, but that made him ill: he could not bear to be separated from his French food, which he says is very important to him. Now forty-six, the only extraordinary eventuality he can imagine which might induce him to go elsewhere would be 'falling in love with a woman'. Even that once unthinkable taboo is something he is willing to reconsider.

He is not just a radical priest out on a limb: the weakness of Christianity in France has made the majority of Church members rethink their attitudes. That probably means that Christian piety is more profound today in France than it has ever been, in the sense that much that passed for religiosity in the past was simply conformism. So to assume that France is a fundamentally irreligious country, just because it has had a stormy history of anticlericalism, is erroneous. The British, who pay lipservice to the view that they live in a Christian country, go to church less than the French do (only 11% are regular worshippers, compared to 16% of the French). Still, that seems a complete contrast to the United States, where 40% are regular worshippers. But, without denying the greater strength of religion in America, it should be remembered that religion there means many different things: only a quarter of American Protestants, for example, believe in original sin, only half in life after death, or that doing good to others is necessary for salvation; less than half can name even four of the Ten Commandments; a Southern Baptist and a Congregationalist probably have more to separate them than the traditional division of Protestant and Catholic. The institutional vigour of American churches conceals the fact that only one-third of Protestants can be classified as orthodox in their doctrine. France is going the same way, or is discovering that it is more heterogeneous in its beliefs than it imagined. Just as American religion is now much less a matter of community membership than it used to be, so French religion is becoming increasingly a personal rather than a community matter too. And French Catholicism is becoming more like Protestantism.

The proportion of people attending mass in Marseille is half that in Nantes, and one-third that in Strasbourg; it is four times greater in the diocese of Lille than in the diocese of Meaux. Public opinion generally takes the view that it is industrialization, or urbanization, or political propaganda, or educational influences, or communist infiltration that explains the decline of religion, but it is wrong. The USA shows clearly that 'modernization' does not necessarily reduce church attendance. In France, the Catholic Church's own researchers have only recently discovered the explanation of the patchwork that covers their country. Religion, like a fruit or a form of vegetation, has survived where it was most firmly planted during the Counter-Reformation and after. The proselytizing of the country was carried out with very different energy and success in different dioceses. Today the boundaries of these old dioceses still form boundaries between religious and irreligious areas, cutting across areas which may now appear homogeneous, like the city of Lyon or the Vendée, but which contain strikingly contrasted religious behaviour because they were once divided between bishoprics which pursued different policies. There are modern industrialized cities that have grown up in formerly religious areas which still bear the mark of the region's religious traditions, even though the old landscape has vanished beneath factories and skyscrapers. The Paris region is pagan because it was never properly converted, whereas in Brittany Christianity espoused the old pagan rites, creating a unique kind of Catholicism, which has survived because it is deeply rooted in immemorial customs and local activities. Where the Church was most puritan and demanding, it sometimes succeeded, but sometimes caused resentment. So France is covered by a multitude of religious and anticlerical fervours, like a mass of small republics, with neighbouring villages often having opposing attitudes. The average that comes from adding this up gives a false idea of the reality.

The French are not quite as irreligious as they are made out to be: in addition to the regular churchgoers, another 25% claim to go to church occasionally. Over 70% go through a religious marriage; over 80% are baptized; only 54% say they never go to confession. The people who definitely say they have no religion are very much in a minority (15%). The highest proportion of these is to be found among the managers and liberal professions, of whom 28% are atheists, but exactly the same amount of these declare themselves to practise a religion occasionally or regularly, the rest being 'non-practising', but somehow vaguely connected with a religion. The next most atheistic class are middle managers (21%) but 25% of them are regular or occasional churchgoers. Clerks, shopkeepers and workers include between 12 and 17% atheists, but between 18 and 22% are churchgoers. Young people (aged eighteen to thirty-four) are exactly balanced between 21% atheists and 21% churchgoers. The over-sixty-fives include 39% churchgoers (only 12% atheists) and it is, of course, the peasants who have fewest atheists (7%) and most churchgoers (51%). The occasional churchgoers included in these figures cover a whole spectrum of hypocrisy, indifference and piety but they show that religious feeling of some kind capable of being expressed in established churches is far from dead. No one, however, can predict just how many people would get down on their knees and pray in a time of life-and-death crisis.

Hostility to religion used to be strongest among teachers, but that is diminishing as their profession is increasingly taken over by women. It used to be found among men of science rejecting mystery, but increasingly scientists, baffled by the frontiers of their specializations, are willing to accept mystery. The communists now play down their opposition and welcome the stray Marxist-Christians. When a few years ago the Bishops issued a declaration that Marxism and Christianity were incompatible, only 36% of regular churchgoers approved, and only 20% of occasional churchgoers: the general consensus now is that the

Church should not take any official stand on politics. The socialists still have a lingering suspicion of Catholics, partly because of their freemasonry traditions, and partly on the practical ground that the majority of Catholics are clearly conservative; but 23% of regular practitioners nevertheless do vote for the socialists now, and as many as 30% of the clergy. Anticlericalism still has a lot of life left in it, because it expresses scepticism and hostility towards any small group that claims special knowledge, status, or power.

Only one-quarter of practising Catholics are traditionalists, sympathetic to Archbishop Marcel Lefebvre's rebellion against the modernization of the Church. These people are doing more than simply saying that there seems no point in change. Lefebvre, born in 1905, has spent much of his life as a missionary in Africa, and most of the rest of it as a teacher; he does not see

Chenez

Division in the Church

religion as a subtle debate among intellectuals or as a forum for interesting discussions. The priest, for him, represents mystery, ordination does not simply appoint a man to a job but alters his very nature and makes him 'another Christ'; he wishes to maintain a basic distinction between priesthood and laity. So for him there can be no question of altering the traditional liturgy, in which the priest alone says the Lord's Prayer. The priest represents order, he is needed to command the laity, because man is a sinner, and the most important duty of the priest is to ensure obedience to ecclesiastical law. This does not mean that the traditionalists are puritanical: outside the strict enforcement of their religious obligations, they are, in fact, far less austere than the reformers. The Abbé Barbara, one of the leaders of the traditionalist movement, is a noted bon-viveur, who says that if the Pope would only drink more, he would be more relaxed, and more conservative. There are thus several different motivations behind the traditionalists. Their most solid base comes from the working class and petty bourgeoisie, who have no desire to change their inherited customs. Their publicity is organized by anti-intellectual intellectuals, who dislike the new kind of clever priest aping the latest fashions: the journalist and former soldier, Pierre Debray, for example, argues for a return to the 'Judaic origins of Christianity'.

A retired naval officer explains his attitude thus: 'I like tradition.' He comes from a Breton family that has always been religious; he lives in a region which is still largely religious; in the navy, he says, 90% of the senior officers, half of the junior officers (but less than a fifth of the men) were believers; and he is comforted in his faith when he meets converts who have seen the light from outside. He has received his faith as a gift from his parents and he has tried to pass it on to his children. He has ten children, and he held family prayers daily, until they grew up and made it too obvious that this had become 'an intolerable drudgery'. He respects the Church and its priests as representatives of tradition and of Jesus. He has no use for women priests, partly because 'I entirely submit to the decisions of the Pope,' and partly because 'woman and man are not the same, they are not made in the same way, and it seems natural to me that they should not play similar roles in society.' He tried to implement his Christianity in the navy by 'reducing the barriers between officers and men'. He is troubled by the fact that so many others are unbelievers; that makes him re-examine his faith, but he always emerges with his certainty strengthened. His main worry when he was interviewed was where to cut out a new window in his old farmhouse: he did not want to alter the legacy of the past.

But the priesthood is on the point of being abandoned by its own followers. It is aging, it even seems to be vanishing. In the space of ten years, the number of secular priests has fallen by almost as many thousand; there are only 36,000 left. Recruiting has never been so unsuccessful, with only between 100 and 200 new ordinands a year. The forecast is that there will be no more than 12,000 priests by the end of the century. They have failed to find leaders to inspire either the faithful or the masses, for the sort of man who is appointed a bishop tends to be a committee man, skilled in compromise, rather than a saint or a whirlwind preacher: it has been said that de Gaulle would never have been made a bishop. Bishops have become office workers, so busy, says one of them, that he never has time to celebrate mass. Bishops tend to be cautious; they speak out mainly through their Assembly of Bishops, which seeks unanimity for its decisions. Behind this is a bureaucracy run by technocrats, indistinguishable from those in government, intelligent, efficient, cold. The Church is run on a shoe-string; priests are paid the equivalent of the national minimum wage: bishops normally get no more. The Bishop of Le Havre lives in a two-roomed flat and runs a 2 CV; he does not attend civic ceremonies and is not called Monseigneur; the parish clergy have made themselves inconspicuous; they often abandon clerical dress. The collapse of morale is reflected in the figures for church attendance, which are falling relentlessly.

But many religious people are not worried by this, because they think that a new kind of Church is being born, which resembles the primitive Church instead of the medieval one. The political power has gone. There was even a bishop (of Orleans) to say that the Church should cease to worry about itself as an institution and aim only to do precisely what the psychiatrists are doing; help individual people solve their problems. The traditional organization into parishes is being denounced as outmoded in the age of the city, the commuter and the multinational firm, and no longer practical when as many as twelve parishes have to be combined under one priest. The old style Church, empty most of the time, and in which only the priest is allowed to speak, needs to be converted for modern forms of living, for discussion and audience participation. Just as the relations of parents with their children have altered, so the idea of hierarchy must be eliminated from relationships in Church; and religion must not be centred round sacrament, which only increases the power of the priest.

Abbé de Givenchy (the couturier's cousin) organizes not services but meetings of people who feel uneasy in traditional forms of worship, and who believe that the ordinary parish is not sufficiently alive to use their religious energy; he tries to offer them dialogue and an unpredictable spiritual adventure beyond that; he hopes they will soon have the courage to meet outside the Church buildings, because 'breaks' are needed for a new kind of faith to develop. In the ultra-modern Palais des Congrès at the Porte Maillot in Paris, Père Violle has a boutique that sells religion, and that opens from nine to six just like all the others in the gallery: churches, he says, used to be built on the village green because that was where people met; the Church must come to where the people are. Opposite the Beaubourg centre, the church of St Merri has been transformed to offer visitors a place to talk and to sing as they please, and to organize their own kinds of meetings, instead of services which involve one person talking and the rest listening. Whereas the rigorist priest takes the view that 'you do not exist' if you are not baptized, people are now arguing in favour of postponing baptism till a person is able to know what he is doing. Confession is being attacked, at least in its traditional form of a face-to-face private encounter. In Grenoble a group of teachers have, for the past seven years, been meeting weekly, for about four hours, in the house of one or another of them, creating, as they believe, a new form of Church: they have no need for a priest, they take the eucharist without one, they have a meal together; to stress the idea of the Church as hospitality they organize their own feasts to celebrate marriages, Christmas and

Chaval

Easter. They had felt uncomfortable in traditional parish organizations; they say this kind of small and warm unit gives them 'a more balanced life'. The deputy mayor of Saintes, Bernard Thiebaud, who used to work at Peugeot's, and then took up organic farming and converting country cottages to rent to workers on holiday, sees religion as involving above all discussion in small groups of people who can sympathize with each other: he uses the little office in his basement as a substitute for the Church and for the parish, which he sees as a relic of the past.

There are priests who will go along with this, like the one who has taken holy orders because he wants 'not quite to carry out a revolution, but to do something new'; he thinks the Church is dying, but a new one is rising from the ashes: he comes from a wealthy family of engineers; he went to a *grande école* to become an engineer himself, but gave up to become a worker-priest; on doing his military service, the colonel appointed him his chauffeur; he refused and was made to drive the rubbish cart instead; he wants not an ecclesiastical career but a feeling of freedom, to experiment in a new way of living. The French Catholic Church is becoming much less hostile to Protestantism; one professor, Jean Delumeau, even says the Catholics must borrow from the Protestants, must elect their clergy, their bishops, to create a truly democratic organization; the Pope must be like a president elected to serve for only five or seven years: the centralized model must be abandoned. And it is within the Catholic Church that such Protestant movements as the Charismatics are flourishing. Though modelled on the Pentecostalists in the United States, this current has been absorbed into Catholicism because pluralism and tolerance are the new watchwords, for some at least. Catholic trade unionists talk to their bosses in different tones, like Michael Karputa, a miner's leader in Houdain (Nord) who had this conversation with his manager:

'Are you a Christian?' asked Karputa.

'Yes.'

'Then why don't you apply Christian charity?'

'That has nothing to do with the question at issue.'

'Yes it does. To be a Christian means not just going to mass on Sunday, though I know you always arrive late. You have got to be a Christian every day.'

'But these men are revolutionaries,' said the manager.

'Look,' replied Karputa, 'they are Christians.'

That did not solve their dispute, but the manager has used slightly different tones since then. Karputa, for his part, has little use for traditional religion; the son of Polish immigrants, he is particularly scathing about the Polish clergy who minister to his community; he protests that they are greedy, insisting on extracting as much as they can in ecclesiastical fees. There is no way of judging where hypocrisy begins: the Catholic grocer with seven children, who never closes on Sunday, on the grounds that it would be a disservice to his customers, believes he is thus giving expression to his faith; he is certain that faith is stronger than it has ever been: in the old days it simply meant going to church.

Between the 'integrists' at one extreme and the modernizers at the other, there stands the majority, who are, of course, infinitely varied. In bourgeois neighbourhoods, the priest is more well-to-do and the Church exudes an air of wordliness and fashion. In picturesque villages not too far from the cities, the rich who come to their country cottages for weekends are bringing new life to previously empty churches. The majority are not too concerned by principles or anxious for intense mystical experiences.

A widow of sixty-eight, for example, living alone in a basement in Le Havre, suffering from diabetes and heart disease, finds in religion simply the strength to accept her suffering and indeed sometimes to derive satisfaction from her painful existence. The most important thing in life, she believes, is that children should learn to respect their parents and, she adds as an afterthought, their teachers too. The modernization of Church ritual means that people like herself are better respected, because she no longer has to chant Latin formulae which she could never understand; now watching services on television is her joy. She is glad priests have become friendlier and are no longer above coming to have a meal with her. She does not want to say anything against the Church, or the Pope, whom she respects, but her opinion is that there ought not to be so much money in the Church. Religion for her means helping others and increasing her own self-respect, and not least it is an assurance that when she dies she will be reunited with her husband in heaven.

This hope that religion will make children respectful of their elders is tenacious. Far more parents want religion for their children than for themselves. As many as 74% succumb to wishful thinking and claim that their children have received at least some religious education, though this is quite untrue.[1] There is enormous regional variation in their pretence – only 35% make the claim in Paris. But the Catholic schools themselves now minimize religious instruction, and most have completely abandoned school prayers. They are flourishing because they are careful not to frighten children off by forcing religion down their throats, by offering them instead more personal attention and warmer, less competitive conditions than the state schools, more concern for character than for examinations. They are flourishing, of course, only relatively: fewer than two million children go to Church schools (13·6% of primary children and 18% of secondary children), but there are some regions in the west where they are attended by over half of the

[1] Only 15% of primary schoolchildren and 8% of secondary children participate in the activities of school chaplains.

local children; and the numbers of pupils at Church secondary schools is rising slowly. Public opinion now no longer objects to them. The state subsidizes them. They admit Moslems and do not try to convert them. In the School of the Sacred Heart in Ménilmontant, a teacher says: 'I would never dream of talking to the children about God. I would not know how to do it.'

To say that a person is or is not religious in France is, therefore, not to say a great deal. Only his own personal history can explain what such a description means. The Church used to be mainly an expression of community membership, of conformity, of solidarity, of humility before awesome forces. There are now other ways of expressing those feelings too. There used to be a clear conflict between religion and modernity; now the attitude to change is as varied among the religious as among those who are not. Religious people probably disagree as much among themselves as they do with non-believers. Religion used to mean certainty and it means so much less now. It is a breakwater between tension and serenity that is hardly ever fully impervious to the self-doubt that is now the norm of a 'civilized' person.

What this means is that the Christian community is not a minority, but a series of minorities, themselves split into atoms and molecules. Religion is, more than it has ever been, a matter of personal thought and decision, temperament and inheritance. And so the visitor from another country can never be sure what he will find when he enters a French church.

Conclusion:
What it means to be French

The Comte Sanche de Gramont, a member of one of France's oldest noble families, has decided to change his name to Ted Morgan (rearranging the letters of his surname) and become an American citizen. He had felt uncomfortable as a Frenchman, as though he was an actor required to perform a role he disliked, and in which he considered himself miscast. It was not just that there was a certain amount of foreign blood in his family, nor that his father was a diplomat posted to Washington, so that he received much of his schooling in the United States. It was more that he wanted to find an identity of his own, independent of that which his birth gave him. One of the attractions of America for him was that it was a country to which people came to start afresh, and he was fascinated to learn that an enormous number of immigrants had changed their names to mark the break. He discovered that the great American expert on personal identity, Erik H. Erikson, whose psychological theories have been adopted by many people who have never heard of him, had no clear identity of his own, did not know who his father was, and invented his name: he would be his own father, Erik the son of Erik. That was symbolic of the American self-made man. Gramont decided that the Americans were the real existentialists, because Sartre's existentialism basically meant self-reliance. He felt himself to be emotionally a displaced person and America was the obvious homeland for those whose roots caused pain. Besides, he preferred the woolliness of the English language to the restrictive precision of French, rather like Conrad who had said: 'My nationality is the language I write in': Conrad, born a Pole, and fluent in both English and French, considered he had more 'affinity' for English. So, though the

enquiries Gramont had to answer in his application for naturalization included some rather odd questions, like whether he
had ever committed adultery, he became an American in 1977
and he now lives in the mountains near San Francisco. Is this a
betrayal? Could he not have found his identity in France?

South of Paris in the new town of Evry, stands the headquar-
ters of the firm Quantel, situated between Pacific Avenue and
Atlantic Avenue. Half the signboards of neighbouring factories
are those of international companies, but Quantel is a French
firm, producing high technology laser equipment. Its founder,
Georges Bret, was also a misfit, like Gramont. 'I had a turbulent
childhood.' He left school without any certificates at fifteen, to
pursue his hobbies of radio and electronic organs. In due course
he graduated through the Ecole Supérieure d'Electricité, took a
master's degree at Cleveland, Ohio, a doctorate at Harvard, and
became a professor of physics at Paris University. Having convinced himself that he was as good as his teachers, he threw up
his job to start a firm of his own, which now exports 80% of its
products, mainly to the United States and Japan, and he has
established a branch factory in California. He wanted to prove it
was possible to succeed in France without government subsidies, in the way that Americans started firms in a back garage.
Having done that, he has not tried to remain small and independent in the traditional French way, but has amalgamated with a
large firm; he has delegated most of his administrative work, so
that he does not have to think about the firm more than
half-time, and can turn to other interests; he is not concerned to
make a lot of money, because that would simply force him to
devote himself full-time to protecting his capital against inflation. He works because he wants to be free. His wife says he is so
busy with all his schemes, he does not seem free to her; but he
says he has chosen freely to be busy. His wife is the daughter of a
Breton agricultural labourer who, to avoid the traditional career
of teaching that bright girls are led to, decided to become an
engineer: after similar studies in the United States, she is in
charge of the introduction of new computerization into France's
largest bank. They live in a new house that could have been
transplanted from California. One son is already almost a drop-
out; though a medical student, he devotes much time to paint-

ing; he was born in America, which they frequently visit. When she was in Houston last week, she telephoned to express her delight at its architecture. They feel at home in America, though they prefer to live in France. 'I think there is a civilization of technical people,' he says. 'We have Russian friends and Japanese friends and German friends and it is easy to communicate with them because we have a common background and standards, which is mathematics, physics and English.' In his factory, he has a German manager with whom he speaks in English. He attributes his success to his designing products (like the Japanese) for the international market, rather than for the domestic market and then trying to find foreign customers. He asked me to autograph my *History of France*, which he had read in the original English immediately on its publication. He is an international man, but also profoundly French, in the sense that he is interested by all that happens and has happened in France.

Bret has shown that almost anything that can be done in the United States can be done in France; he has not necessarily proved Gramont wrong, but rather that there are very similar energies in both countries. However, many French people are preoccupied by the fear of being Americanized. In the 1950s and 1960s the desire for prosperity was such that American business methods were eagerly copied; 'management' became a French word; business schools were established on the American model for those who did not make the pilgrimage to Harvard; later, when efficiency ceased to be the obvious road to utopia, another American catchword, communication, was adopted in its stead. Foreign investment in France increased so that about one-quarter of French industry is now foreign-owned and half of that quarter belongs to American investors. The media borrowed ideas from the United States freely. *Time* magazine inspired the format of *L'Express*, *Life* was copied by *Paris-Match*, *Fortune* by *L'Expansion*, *Business Week* by *Le Nouvel Economiste*, *Ms.* by *F. Magazine*. The comic strip, which has been an unusually important artistic and intellectual form, owes a great deal to *Mad* (where Goscinny, the inventor of Asterix, once worked). The French popular music business is not only modelled on America's but is now 90% in the hands of US firms, and every

Barbe

child is as familiar with American songs as with French lullabies. At least one-third of the output of French television is American, and one-third of films shown in cinemas. French infants even play with American toys (70% of the toy industry is American-owned). The advertising executives in J. Walter Thompson's Paris office insist that they are completely French, but it is clear that at least half of their ideas come from across the Atlantic.

'Americanization' has caused profound pain to the pride, taste and habits of some; for others, the price of prosperity, implying a 'loss of identity', seems too high. Even among those who have enjoyed drawing inspiration from the United States there is often hesitation. A leading sociologist, Michel Crozier, who has spent his whole life marrying the French and American traditions in the social sciences, has recently announced that America can no longer be a model, 'an elder brother', because it suffers from the 'American Disease', which is even worse than the French Disease. America's essence is to be optimistically confident in the goodness of man, which was a stimulating attitude when the frontier was still open, but which is useless in coping with stagnation: America's disease, he says, is the result of its not having enough sense of the evil in man.

Soon, perhaps, no nation will feel respectable unless it is suffering from its own special disease. But these worries about whether France is losing its identity, and how it relates to other major countries, seem to me to be relics of nineteenth-century attitudes, as well as of habits of speech that go back much further. To describe a nation of 54 million, still less one of 220 million, in a single phrase, to attribute to all its inhabitants identical moral qualities, that in any case are hard enough to be certain about when dealing with one individual or family, is a natural reaction in the face of the complexity of the world, but it is a habit born of despair, which persists because there seems no obvious way of avoiding it. But France can supply an alternative, if one looks at the history of the image it has had in the past. It has gone through three phases. First, its nationalist phase involved trying to unify the country, to make it a coherent whole, where everyone spoke the same language and received the same education; common ideals, like liberty, equality and fraternity, were attributed to it, ideals which were often mistaken for a description of reality by dint of frequent repetition. It is on this foundation that the notion of French people being basically all alike rests. The second phase was internationalist; it represented France as incarnating ideals common to all mankind; a mixture of humanitarianism and imperialism counterbalanced and widened the appeal of French civilization, but it was not always convincing. Third was the pluralist phase, because it became obvious that uniformity represses minority interests, which clamour for recognition and freedom of expression. Pluralism is what the politicians are now trying to institutionalize. Not only in government, but in many walks of life, people are recombining themselves in ethnic, recreational, ideological minority groups: the age of the minority, asserting its right to be different, has arrived. So there is now a whole variety of types of French people.

But pluralism expresses only one aspect of the realignment of loyalties. Minorities are composed of individuals who are no longer content to be the passive recipients of ready-made identities; individuals are becoming increasingly conscious of the multiplicity of their impulses and needs. A fourth, post-pluralist phase is in the process of replacing the 'France of minorities'. It is one in which individuals try to work out their own destinies for themselves, creating a unique identity from a combination of elements drawn from the many different groups and sub-groups to which they feel they have an affinity. This has come not inappropriately at the same time as the computer: before its advent, the mind was accustomed to coping with relatively few simple categories: now individuals are emerging as infinitely varied permutations of qualities and choices. The qualities are no different from the qualities found among all mankind, and the choices are available to most inhabitants of the western world. The traditional categorization of humans into nations, classes, groups and movements is necessarily woolly. Individuals are the basic atom in all of these categories, and a more precise view of them emerges if they are looked at under the microscope. Individuals, like atoms, are made up of masses of particles struggling inside them, and there is more random behaviour and free choice in them than the group stereotypes allow. If France is looked at in this perspective the problem of what exactly its identity is, and whether it is losing its identity, is no longer a real one. No two individual Frenchmen interpret their national identity in the same way, and no two have quite the same combination of background, of culture or aspirations. With time, the French are becoming more and more different from each other. The American intrusion is no different from, and adds itself to, all the other foreign influences that have been absorbed in the past. Anglomania in the eighteenth century, the admiration of scientific Germany in the nineteenth, the attraction, for some, of revolutionary Russia in the twentieth, have been like fruits and nuts thrown into a cake, enriching it, but still giving each bite a multiplicity of contrasting flavours. For those who are able to make the leap out of the nineteenth-century view of nations, into a more microscopic view of man, there is no longer any temptation to interpret French people as mere examples of a mythical national culture, automatically to attribute their powers of rational thought to the fact that they went to a French school, or their success in love to some inherited virtuosity. The French are human beings, who do not obediently lap up everything they are taught, even if they were all taught the same things.

And in distinguishing French people into types or groups within their nation, the only classification that I find satisfactory is between the warm and the cold. Warm people are those with whom I feel I have established human contact and with whom I can share emotions; cold people are those who hide behind masks and whom I do not feel I have really met. The distinction is partly subjective, and partly the result of barriers that humans, for one reason or another, feel it necessary to place between themselves. I like a nation when I have met more warm than cold people. I do not have to agree with them, nor to share their tastes, to find people warm; and a person who appears to be cold sitting across a desk may turn out very different on holiday. These barriers of incomprehension seem to me to be more important than national frontiers or party conflicts. That is why I have abandoned the usual way of writing about France, describing its institutions and saying how different they are from those of other nations. It is more useful that every person should draw his own personal frontiers for himself.

For my part, I include France in my world not just because I admire the French countryside or its monuments, wonderful though they are, but rather because French people have been willing to share their experiences with me, which are even more wonderfully varied, warm and cold, enriching, touching and ridiculous, an inexhaustible commentary on wisdom and folly. A shared experience is more than a bond; it is a joint discovery of unexpected possibilities. That is why no life can be full until it has at least a small French element in it. And no French life is in fact totally closed to foreigners or foreign ways. That popular French singers should think it worthwhile to change their names so that they sound American is not a sign of national degeneration, but an expression of a need constantly to expand the limits of their civilization. The rock star Eddy Mitchell (born Claude Moine, the son of a Paris metro worker) was once a poor French boy: he is no longer poor, but he is very far from being American: he can barely speak English, but he records his French songs in Nashville, Tennessee, because that is where he finds the best record studios. He does not offer his fans an American way of life, but only invites them modestly to keep their options open:

> I set out from nothing, and I have achieved nothing much.
> But I earn a lot of money, it's worth being famous.
> I set out from nothing, but I am always waiting for a
> thousand things to happen.
> If you would like to join me, you are welcome.

The real cause of dissatisfaction with foreigners in France comes not from the French feeling humiliated by borrowing from America or from other countries, but from an annoyance that foreigners are not borrowing much in return. It is the absence of exchange that is galling to the pride. But the more they insist that they are different from others, the more they discourage foreigners from borrowing. In fact, I do not think they are as different as they like to make out. If they stopped believing in their own stereotypes, they would see that they are constructing their lives with a vigour and an ingenuity that are not all that far from those of the American frontiersman. The frontier is still open in France.

The singer Mouloudji, born in Paris in 1932, has given a summary of just a few of the things that make him French:

> Catholic by my mother
> Moslem by my father
> A little Jewish by my son
> Buddhist on principle
>
> Alcoholic by my uncle
> Neurotic by my grandmother
> Classless by long-felt shame
> Depraved by my grandfather

Royalist by my mother
Fatalist by my brother
Communist by my father
Marxist by imitation . . .

Double-dealing like a lawyer
Sensual like a miser
Tough like a soldier
Gentle like a drunkard . . .

Deceived by my better half
Pestered by my concierge
Hated by my neighbours
Detested by dogs

Atheist, O thanks to God
Atheist, O thanks to God.

Each French person inherits and creates a slightly different mixture. But just in case the reader is determined to have a more grandiose definition of the country, I leave him with this one, by one of its most popular comedians, Pierre Dac: 'To the eternal triple question which has always remained unanswered, Who are we? Where do we come from? Where are we going? I reply: As far as I, personally, am concerned, I am me; I come from just down the road; and I am now going home.'

The Cartoonists

Jean Pierre Aldebert (b. 1941), the son of the well-known cartoonist Bernard Aldebert, who taught him, and who, he says, laughed at the same things as he does. He laments that the humorous cartoon is disappearing under the onslaught of the comic strip. He is a commercial artist and painter too; his cartoons are the result of personal experience in the fashion and advertising worlds.

André Barbe (b. 1936) is a self-taught artist who defines his aim as 'to demolish logic with logic itself . . . to show that humour is based on surprise and is a rigorous form of expression, which can speak to everyone without words, and can say what no other form can say.' This is from his album *Vous Cherchez Quelquechose?* (Editions du Fromage 1980); more recently he has published another, *Nous Sommes Trop* (Glenat 1981).

Boredom is the signature adopted by the 18-year-old I meet on pages 417–20.

Claire Bretécher (b. 1940 in Nantes). Convent educated, trained as an art teacher, she worked as a waitress and a babysitter until her drawings were published by the creator of Asterix, René Goscinny. She keeps her distance from her intellectual admirers. About Women's Lib, she says, 'Men should not feel humiliated just because women are tougher, more dynamic and more amusing: it is God who created them that way.'

Jean Cabut: see pages 248–54

Chaval (1914–68, real name Yvan Le Louarn), son of a commercial traveller in pharmaceutics. Trained Ecole des Beaux Arts, Bordeaux, but forced into an office job, he protested: 'I do not see the difference between an office and a prison.' He was launched as a cartoonist by *Paris Match*, where a failed pharmacist, André Frédérique, ruled, 'I never get angry. I have no sense of patriotism, either national or local. Public affairs do not interest me. I astonish myself very rarely, and that alone is what amuses me.' He committed suicide a few months after his wife committed suicide.

Bernard Chenez (b. 1946) worked as a boilermaker in industry till he sent a cartoon to *Le Monde*, for which he has drawn ever since. The cartoon on p. 230, he says, is autobiographical: one of the little boys is himself. 'I try to show that everything one does is unimportant, that one should not take oneself seriously.' He has exhibited in Austria, Bulgaria and Greece, as well as in France: what does that signify for the geography of French humour? From Chenez, *Dessins du Monde* (Balland, 1977).

Honoré Daumier (1808–79). Why, outside France, is he the best known of all French caricaturists? His art is familiar, but very little indeed is known for certain about what he meant by it.

Jean-Pierre Desclozeaux (b. 1938). Son of a winegrower in the Gard, educated by the Jesuits in Avignon, a pupil of the poster artist Paul Colin, founder of the Society for the Protection of Humour, and president of the 'Association des Amis de Ronald Searle'. He feels constrained by the haste and pressure that cartoons for the press involve; he wants 'to avoid always producing the same little people, like Bretécher or Wolinski'; he is now experimenting in cartoon watercolours.

Albert Dubout (1906–76). Born in Marseille, he went to school in Nimes and to the Ecole des Beaux Arts in Montpellier. Famous as a caricaturist of crowds, he explained that he could not help himself from filling the paper with as many people as would fit in. But each person in his crowds was an individual, and an amalgam of grotesque detail. He loved to show incoherence, machinery held together with string, clothes torn and patched, and not least, large fat women bossing their ridiculous little husbands.

Jean Effel: see pages 366–70.

Jacques Faizant (b. 1918 in the Cantal), the son of a carpenter, trained as a hotelier, worked in hotels till 1942 when he took up animated drawing and then cartoons. He has for many years produced a cartoon for the daily *Figaro* with punctual regularity, usually a commentary on contemporary politics.

Fred (b. Paris 1931, Fred Othon Aristides). The inspiration for the Repairer of Mirrors is threefold: Fred's obsession with mirrors as commentators on reality, his mother's superstitiousness about broken mirrors, and the story of Dorian Gray. He regards *Le Petit Cirque* as his most important work because it expresses the problem that he feels most deeply, that of the 'perpetual migrant'. One of the founders of *Hara-Kiri*.

Gad (Claude Gadoud). Born in 1905 at Lyon, where he studied at the Beaux Arts and became a poster artist, eventually founding his own advertising firm. When this work dried up during the 1939–45 war, he took up caricature, and has been a prolific contributor to the popular press ever since. He admires the cartoonists Bellus and Bernard Aldebert above all others.

André Gondot (b. 1930). 'I am not interested in grandiose problems, and I don't want to tell people what to do. We are all small, egoistic, ridiculous. We are all preoccupied by our little habits; the great problem for a middle-aged man, for example, is that he is losing his hair; little details like that, which are not as insignificant as they may appear. Life needs to be treated *avec tendresse*, gently.' This drawing first appeared in *Le Herrisson*, one of the two best-selling humorous weeklies for a mass audience (the other being *Marius L'Epatant*) which continue the traditions of the past with greater commercial success than is obtained by more innovative drawing and more biting satire.

Pierre Gourmelin (b. 1920) trained at the Ecole des Arts Decoratifs. He is a book illustrator and designer of wallpapers and fabrics, who also works in glass. This drawing is taken from his study of Time, *Pour Tuer le Temps* (Balland, 1972); he has published another on Chance.

Grandville (1803–47, Jean Ignace Isidore Gérard), son of a miniaturist painter from Nancy, grandson of an actor. He wrote this epitaph for himself: 'Here rests J. J. Grandville. He gave a soul to everything, made everything live, talk and walk. The only person he was unable to set on his feet was himself.' He came to Paris at the age of 20, published lithographs about the amusements of childhood, the pleasures of youth, the pastimes of old age, etc., then a series on Walking Sticks, Umbrellas, Collars, Pipes, Hats, etc., and most famous of all, The Private Life of Animals and Living Flowers. A devoted family man, he went mad after the deaths of his wife and children, and died in a lunatic asylum.

Gustave-Henri Jossot (1866–1951) came from a well-to-do Dijon family and so was able to devote most of his life to art. He studied painting with J. P. Laurens and Carrière, but took up caricature because he preferred an art that reflected his own whims. Caricature, for him, was designed not to make silly people laugh, but to sow liberating ideas in thinking people's minds. In 1907, following the death of his only son, he fell into a depression, stopped drawing and in 1911 emigrated to Tunis, hoping sunnier weather would cheer him up. There he devoted himself to landscape painting and radical journalism, and became a Moslem to express his protest against 'Western folly'.

Gérard Lauzier: see pages 207–11.

Gérard Mathieu (b. 1949) drew these cartoons for *L'Etudiant,* a series of practical and amusing guides for young people. He has no training in art, began life as a clerk, and a cultural animator, before becoming a professional cartoonist. One of the founders of the magazine *Antirouille* (Anti-Rust), which tried to offer adolescents an alternative to the worship of pop idols, he sees life as a 'patchwork', in which happiness is created out of separate little pieces of joy.

Zoran Orlic (b. 1944 in Yugoslavia) trained at the Paris Ecole des Arts Decoratifs where he now teaches. He is essentially an illustrator, who adapts his style to suit each text; a frequent contributor to *Le Monde.*

Vladimir Pablo. Born 1946 'of a Russian mother and an unknown father', he has been drawing comic strips since the age of twelve, 'a form of expression more direct than the novel'. He is perhaps best known for his parody *Bécassexine.*

Piem (b. 1923 in St Etienne, Pierre de Montvallon). The father of six children, two of whom are also cartoonists (one in Switzerland and another in the USA). François Mitterrand has called him 'a pedagogue disguised as a satirical witness . . . a writer of fables, an inventor of myths to delight and perplex' his readers, who assume the role of children when they gaze at his 'cartoon poems'.

Jean Plantu (b. 1951) was a medical student who abandoned his career to take up drawing: he specializes in cartoons on politics and the third world. The result he values most is that, thanks to the image, his message makes a greater impact on the intelligence and is therefore absorbed and retained. His favourite cartoonist is Reiser, in whom he sees gentleness behind the apparent ferocity.

Puppet: Just one of the many totally forgotten cartoonists of the nineteenth century waiting to be rescued from oblivion.

Quino (b. 1932, Joaquin Salvador Labado) is an example of the international dimensions of French humour. He is an Argentinian who since 1975 has lived in Milan. He has had a lot of success in France, where five volumes of his cartoons have been published and a dozen albums of his Peanuts-style comic strip, *Masalda*, are appearing.

Jean Marc Reiser (b. 1941). The son of a charwoman, he had a tough childhood. Employed by Vins Nicolas, he started offering his drawings to newspapers from the age of 15. 'I like French people who are out of the ordinary, but not the banal kind. It is the same with other nations. I don't feel especially French, and can feel things in common with anyone, Japanese or English . . . I am never bored, which is why I find life tragic: it is awful that it must end.'

Auguste Jean-Baptiste Roubille (b. 1872), painter, decorator, engraver, prolific cartoonist at the turn of the century, appreciated not least because he liked to make caricature not just a 'grimace' but also a form of decoration.

Alain Saint-Ogan (1895–1974). The son of a journalist who used to be editor of *L'Etendard Egyptien* of Cairo, he was a pioneer of the comic strip, creator of *Zig et Puce*, novelist, journalist, essayist, television producer. 'I have a horror of nastiness—to such an extent that I cannot even kill a mosquito. In each mosquito there is a large amount of idealism.'

Jean-Jacques Sempé (b. 1932 in Bordeaux). He claims his ambition as a boy was to become either a musician or a footballer, and since he was incompetent in both of these arts (as well as in his lessons) he took to drawing musicians and footballers. His ideal is to do cartoons in which nothing happens, but magazines insist on him always saying or proving something. He is cross that his message is in any case usually misinterpreted: he is more interested in conveying atmosphere than in making points or drawing morals.

Claude Serre (b. 1938). In turn an apprentice cabinet-maker, porcelain decorator and artist in stained glass (he helped make the cupola of Washington Cathedral), he experiments constantly with new techniques, and also paints miniatures. He prefers to draw people who 'are not too comfortable with themselves', or who are old; beautiful people, he says, are not interesting, or else need too much artistic talent to be drawn well.

Siné (Maurice Sinet). Born 1920 in Belleville, where his mother had a small grocery; his father was a blacksmith. Trained in lithography and typography at the Ecole Estienne, he went off to join a singing group and then spent two-thirds of his military service under arrest. Finally, after discovering Steinberg, he became a caricaturist. He loves mocking the police (against whom he fought in 1968), judges, priests, racists, communists, Zionists . . . in unusually strong language. Married first to a Russian and then to an Italian, he has adopted a Korean son. To those uninterested in politics he is known for his book about cats, for his drawings in the male magazine *Lui*, or for his passion for jazz.

Tetsu (B. 1913, Roger Testu) studied painting with Maurice Denis, but to please his parents he got a 'proper' job, became director of a soap factory and of a kitchen equipment firm, and ran an art gallery. Finally he gave it all up to be a full time artist. He enjoys mocking his own type of family background most, the complacent and rancorous petite bourgeoisie, where he sees women dominating men 'almost as formidably as in the USA'.

Roland Topor (b. 1938) explains his penchant for black humour by saying, 'I do not like the real world, I am frightened by the brevity of life, by governments, by the police, by torture; and I do not eat red meat. But I don't like being an ostrich, so I try to remove the pain from reality by playing with it. I like playing with lies; I like games that mix truth and falsehood; my humour is like a pair of spectacles, to be worn when looking at the sun.' This is one of his illustrations for Dr André Ruellan's *Manuel du Savoir-Mourir* (Horay 1963).

Georges Wolinski: see pages 62–9.

Bibliography

In place of footnotes, I give here a selection of the works to which I am particularly indebted, and which may help readers to pursue in greater detail subjects I have been able to touch on only briefly.

How the French see themselves:
Jean-Daniel Reynaud and Yves Grafmeyer, *Français, qui êtes-vous?* (1981); Gérard Vincent, *Les Jeux français: essai sur la société moderne* (1978); Henri Mendras, *La Sagesse et le désordre: France 1980* (1980); Alain Peyrefitte, *Le Mal français* (1976); Bernard Cathelat, *Les Styles de vie des Français 1978–1998* (1977); Emmanuel Todd, *Le Fou et le prolétaire* (1979); Gérard Marin, *Les Nouveaux français* (1967); Jean-Pierre El Kabbach, *Actuel 2* (1973).

Public opinion surveys and statistics:
R. Muraz, *La Parole aux français: cinq ans de sondages 1972–7* (1977); P. Miler, *Les Français tels qu'ils sont. La fameuse enquête I.F.O.P. France-Soir* (1975); Janick Arbois and Joshka Schidlow, *La Vrai vie des Français* (1978); Gilles Vallet, *Les Français sur le vif* (1979); SOFRES, *L'Opinion française en 1977* (1978); Gérard Vincent, *Les Français 1945–75* (1977) varied statistics; Hervé Le Bras and Emmanuel Todd, *L'Invention de la France* (1981); *Données Sociales* (annual official statistics), and the numerous official publications of the *Documentation française.*

Relations with foreigners:
US Dept of Commerce: *France. A Study of the International Travel Market* (1978); Robert J. Shepherd, *Public Opinion and European Integration* (1975); Robert Mengin, *La France vue par l'étranger* (1971); Jean Plumyene and Raymond Lasierra, *Ces Drôles de voisins . . . ce que les Suisses, les Espagnols, les Allemands pensent des Français . . .* (1979); Sylvaine Marandon, *L'Image de la France dans l'Angleterre Victorienne* (1967).

Humour and insults:
Abraham Roback, *Dictionary of International Slurs (ethnophaulisms)*, (Cambridge, Mass. 1979); Patrick Boumard, *Les Gros mots des enfants* (1979); Nancy Huston, *Dire et interdire. Eléments de jurologie* (1980); Claude Gaignebet, *Le Folklore obscène des enfants* (1974); Robert Escarpit, *L'Humour* (1960); F. Baldensperger, *Etudes d'histoire littéraire* (1907), chapter on les Définitions de l'humour; Fréderic Delanglade, *40 Portraits d'humoristes* (n.d.); Joel Sadeler, *L'Humour en branches* (1979); Antony J. Chapman and H. C. Foot, *It's a Funny Thing, Humour* (Oxford 1977); Robert Benayoun, *Le Nonsense de L. Carroll à W. Allen* (1978); James C. Austin, *American Humor in France* (Ames, Iowa 1978); Walter Blair and Hamlin Hill, *America's Humor* (N.Y. 1978); Joseph Boskin, *Humor and Social Change in 20th century America* (Boston 1979); Jesse Bier, *The Rise and Fall of American Humor* (NY 1968); M. A. Burnier and P. Rambaud, *Parodies* (1977); Jean-Bruno Renard, *La Bande dessinée* (1978); Numa Sadoul, *Portraits à la plume et au pinceau* (Grenoble 1976); Bruno Lecigne, *Avanies et Mascarade: L'Evolution de la Bande Dessinée en France dans les années 70* (1981); Jean Egen, *La Bande à Charlie* (1976); Claude-Jean Philippe, *René Goscinny* (1976); Georges Wolinski, *Les Pensées* (1981); *On ne connait pas notre bonheur* (1980); *A bas l'amour copain* (1980); *Lettre ouverte à ma femme* (1978); *C'est dur d'être patron* (1978), etc.; P. Bouvard, *Un oursin dans le caviar* (1973); *Et si je disais tout* (1977); *Tous des hypocrites* (1979); Guy Bedos, *Je Craque* (1976); *En attendant la bombe* (1980); Roger Pierre, *Raconte, raconte* (1977); Roger Pierre and J. M. Thibault, *C'est pour rire* (1974); Tim, *L'Autocaricature* (1974); Fernand Renaud, *Heureux!* (1975); Mina and André Guillois, *A l'école du rire* (1974); Jean Effel, *La Création du Monde* (4 vols. 1974 paperback); Siné, *Dans Charlie Hebdo* (1982); Coluche, *La France pliée en quatre* (1981); Jean Egen, *Le Canard Enchaîné* (1978); André Stoll, *Astérix* (Koln, 1974, French translation 1976); Maurice Horn, *World Encyclopedia of Comics* (1976); Cabu, *Le Grand Duduche* (1972 ff. in several volumes), *La France des Beaufs* (1979); G. Lauzier, *Les Cadres* (1981), *La Course du Rat* (1978); G. Elgozy, on French humour in *Magazine littéraire* (July-August 1979); *Schtroumpf: les cahiers de la bande dessinée* (periodical); *Carton: les cahiers du dessin d'humour* (periodical); and other comic strip books too numerous to list here.

Some books on regionalism:
Christian Gras and Georges Livet, *Régions et régionalisme en France du 18ᵉ siècle à nos jours* (1977); Alain Greilsammer, *Les Mouvements féderalistes en France de 1945 à 1974* (1975); John Ardagh, *A Tale of Five Cities* (1979); *La Bretagne et les Bretons* (1978); M. Philipponneau,

Debout Bretagne (1970); Pierre-Jakez Helias, *The Horse of Pride, Life in a Breton Village* (New Haven, 1978); Yann Fouère, *Ces Droits que les autres ont (Les Cahiers de l'avenir de la Bretagne,* nos 6 and 7, Quimper 1979); Yves Barelli et al., *L'Espérance occitane* (1980); René Merle, *Culture occitane per avancar* (1977); Mireille Bras, *Petit livre de l'enseignement occitan* (Carcassonne 1980); Rémy Pech, *Entreprise viticole et capitalisme en Languedoc-Roussillon* (Toulouse 1975); Alain Alcouffe et al., *Pour l'Occitanie* (1979); Bernard Cohen and Gilbert Paulat, *Strasbourg entre le musée et l'oubli* (1980); *Etudes Corses* (periodical); Gaston Casanova, *Pour une Corse française* (1980).

On the physical appearance of French people:
Biométrie Humaine (periodical); P. B. Everett and J. M. Tanner, *World-wide Variation in Human Growth* (1976); NASA, *A Handbook of Anthropometric Data* (Yellow Springs, Ohio 1978); A. E. Mourant, *The Distribution of Human Blood Groups* (Oxford 1976); Desmond Morris, *Gestures* (1979); Laurence Wylie, *Beaux Gestes: A Guide to French Body Talk* (Cambridge, Mass 1977) and article in *Psychologie* (Dec. 1976), 9–14; CEHTI, Survey of French Women (1970s); Berlei Anthropometric Survey (1979); P. A. Gloor and J. Houdaille, 'La Couleur des yeux', in *Annales* (July 1976); G. Ignazi, 'Différenciation et corrélation de caractères morphologiques et mentaux dans un groupe de jeunes français', *Biométrie Humaine* (vol. 6, 1971) on the different heights, weights and sizes of heads of students studying different subjects: e.g. literature students are taller, but have smaller heads; Alain Charraud and H. Valdelièvre, 'Le taille et le poids des Français', *Economie et Statistique* (April 1981), 23–38; Prof. A. C. Gimson (personal communication on French phonetics); Pierre Larthomas, *Le langage dramatique* (1972) on gesticulation; J. V. de Boisseson, Président de la Chambre syndical des fabricants de bonneterie et de berets basques du bassin de l'Adour, Statistics on beret production (private communication); Albert Jacquard, *Eloge de la différence* (1978).

Bureaucracy:
P. Gremion, *Le Pouvoir péripherique* (1976); Catherine Gremion, *Profession décideurs: pouvoir des hauts fonctionnaires et réforme de l'Etat* (1979); Douglas E. Ashford, *British Dogmatism and French Pragmatism: Central-Local Policymaking in the Welfare State* (1982); Ezra Suleiman, *Power, Politics and Bureaucracy* (Princeton 1974); G. Thuillier, *Regards sur la haute administration* (1979); Robert Catherine and Guy Thuillier, *Introduction a une philosophie de l'administration* (1969); *La Fonction publique (Les Cahiers français,* 2 vols, 1980); J. Becquart-

Leclerq, *Paradoxes du pouvoir local* (1976); J. Frayssinet, *Administration et justice face aux administrés* (1972); P. A. Gourevitch, *Paris and the Provinces* (California UP 1980); W. R. Schonfield, *Obedience and Revolt: French Behavior towards Authority* (Beverly Hills 1976); Philippe Galy, *Gérer l'Etat: Corriger la déviation bureaucratique* (1977); Jacques A. Koscinsko-Morizet, *La Mafia polytechnicienne* (1973); Pierre Birnbaum, *Les Sommets de l'Etat: essai sur l'élite du pouvoir en France* (1977); Jacques Mandrin, *L'Enarchie ou les mandarins de la société bourgeoise* (new edition 1980); Odon Vallet, *L'E.N.A. toute nue* (1977); Marie Christine Kessler, *La Politique de la haute-fonction* (1978); Hubert Lafont and Philippe Meyer, *Le Nouvel ordre gendarmique* (1980); J. J. Gleizal, *La Police nationale* (Grenoble 1974); Lucien Sfez, *Décision et pouvoir dans la société française* (1979).

Managers:
David Granick, *Managerial Comparisons of Four Developed Countries: France, Britain, US and Russia* (Cambridge, Mass., 1971); Jacques Horowitz, *Top Management Control in Europe* (1980); Serge Dassault, *La Gestion participative: 22 cas d'entreprise* (1978); Les Multinationales (*Les Cahiers français* no. 190, 1979); Dietrich L. Schaupp, *A Cross-cultural study of a Multinational Company* (NY 1978); Jean Boissonnat, *Les Socialistes face aux patrons* (1977); Socialist Party, *Cadres, l'alternative socialiste*, préface de F. Mitterrand (1980); Yvon Gattaz, *La Fin des patrons* (1980); Marcel Caille, *Les Truands du patronat* (1977); Claude Vilefaure, *Neuf leçons sur la condition du cadre moyen, semi-supérieur et supérieur* (1978); André Harris and Alain de Sedouy, *Les Patrons* (1977); Maurice Levy-Leboyer, *Le Patronat et la seconde industrialisation* (1979).

Wealth and inequality:
W. D. Rubinstein, *Wealth and the Wealthy in the Modern World* (1980); *Les Connaissances et opinions des Français dans le domaine des revenus* (July 1973, BN 40 10247); Laurent Fabius, *La France inégale* (1975); Jean Fourastié and Béatrice Bazil, *Le Jardin du voisin, les inégalités en France* (1980); C. de Brie and P. Charpentier, *L'Inégalité par l'impôt* (1973); CERC (Centre d'étude des revenus et des coûts) *Deuxième rapport sur les revenus des Français* (1979); Jean Baumier, *La France riche* (1972); Robert Lattes, *La Fortune des Français* (1977); Pierre Courtois, *Face au fisc, contribuables et contrôleurs* (1976).

Planners and architects:
Raymonde Moulin, *Les Architectes* (1973); Monique Dagnaud, *Le Mythe de la qualité de la vie et la politique urbaine en France* (1978); George G. Wynne, *Survival Strategies: Paris and New York* (1978);

Stephen S. Cohen, in *Le Monde: Cités géantes* (1978); James M. Rubinstein, *The French New Towns* (Baltimore 1978); R. H. Duclaud-Williams, *The Politics of Housing in Britain and France* (1978); François Parfait, *Qui a fait la ville* (1978); Michel Ragon, *L'Architecte, le prince et la démocratie* (1977); Manuel Castells, *Crise du logement et mouvements sociaux urbains* (The Hague 1978); D. Amouroux, *Nouvelles architectures de maisons en France* (1979); M. de Leusse and R. Nicolas, *Dossier A comme architectes* (1980); Philippe Boudon, *Lived in Architecture* (English translation 1972); Norma Evenson, *Paris, A Century of Change* (New Haven 1979); Alain Sarfati, 'L'Architecture comme oeuvre ouverte', in *Urbi* (Sept 1979); Hachette, *Guide de l'Architecture dans les villes nouvelles de la région parisienne* (1979); Denise Basdevant, *Les Villes nouvelles en Ile-de-France* (1979); Chantal Beret, *Architectures en France, modernité, post-modernité* (1981).

Love, marriage and the family:
George Kurian, *Cross-cultural Perspectives on Mate Selection and Marriage* (Westport, Conn. 1979); Louis Roussel, *Le Mariage dans la société française contemporaine* (INED 1975), *La Famille après le mariage des enfants* (1976), 'Cohabitation juvenile', in *Population* (Jan.-Feb. 1978 p. 15 ff.); Louis Roussel and Odile Bourguignon, *Générations nouvelles et mariage traditionnel. Enquête auprès des jeunes de 18–30 ans* (INED 1978); Alain Mounier, *La Naissance d'un enfant* (1977); Jacques Commaille, *Le Divorce en France, de la réforme de 1975 à la sociologie du divorce* (1978); Anne Boigeol et al., *Le Divorce et les Français* (2 vols, INED 1974–5); *Autrement, Couples* (1980); Jeannine Marroucle, *Aujourd'hui les couples* (1980); Françoise Cave, *L'Espoir et la consolation: l'idéologie de la famille dans la presse du coeur* (1981); Daniele Ganancia and Elisabeth Cadot, *Guide de l'union libre* (1980); Michette Ugo, *J.F., bien sous tous rapports, cherche . . .* (1979); Michel Germont, *Gai! Gai! Marions-nous* (1979); *Elle* (11 Aug. 1980, Sofres enquiry on sexual habits); Dr Pierre Solignac and Anne Serrero, *La Vie sexuelle et amoureuse des Françaises* (1980); *F Magazine, La Sexualité des Femmes* (enquête) (1980); Dr Pierre Simon, *Rapport sur le comportement sexuel des Français* (1972); Helène d'Istria and J. J. Breton, *Les Relations parents-enfants* (1978); Geneviève Delaisi de Parseval and Suzanne Lallemand, *L'Art d'accommoder les bébés* (1980); Jean Delais, *Les Enfants majuscules* (1974); Wallace E. Lambert, *Childrearing Values. A Cross-national Study* (NY 1979); Yves Agnes and Frederic Gaussen, *Les Nouveaux parents* (1979); Claude Ullin, *Les Dix Ans: ce qu'ils disent de leur famille* (1975); Etienne Bolo, *Les Enfants de divorcés* (1979); Jean Jousselin, *Enfants perdus ou éclaireurs* (1977) by a scoutmaster; Georges

522   BIBLIOGRAPHY

Snyders. *Il n'est pas facile d'aimer ses enfants* (1980); René Scherer, *L'Emprise: des enfants entre nous* (1979); *Crapouillot* (periodical) *Les Pornocrates* (Feb.-March 1970); Dr Claude Maillard, *Les Prostituées* (1975); George Stambolian and Elaine Marks, *Homosexualities and French Literature* (Ithaca, 1979); M.-F. Haus and G. Lapouge, *Les Femmes, la pornographie, l'érotisme* (1978); Jean-Jacques Lebel, *L'Amour et l'argent* (1979); Régine Deforges, *O m'a dit: entretiens avec Pauline Réage* (1975); Maryat Rollet-Andriane, *The Secrets of Emmanuelle* (English translation 1980); J. J. Pauvert, *Anthologie historique des lectures érotiques: De Félix Gouin à Emmanuelle* (1980); *De Guillaume Apollinaire à Philippe Pétain* (1979); Alain Corbin, *Les Filles de noce* (1978); Claude Jaget, *Prostitutes, our life* (English translation 1980).

Workers:
Jacques Fremontier, *La Vie en bleu: voyage en culture ouvrière* (1980); Danielle Bleitrach et al., *Classe ouvrière et social-democratie: Lille et Marseille* (1981); Michel Verret, *L'Ouvrier français, l'espace ouvrier* (1979); Claude and Michelle Durand, *De l'O.S. à l'ingénieur, carrière ou classe sociale* (1971); Colette Petonnet, *On est tous dans le brouillard: ethnologie des banlieues* (1979); Renaud Sainsaulieu, *L'Identité au travail: les effets culturels de l'organisation* (1977); *Economie et Humanisme* (May-June 1981) issue on Relations professionnelles; Duncan Gallie, *In Search of the New Working Class* (Cambridge 1978); G. Adam et J. D. Reynaud, *Conflits du travail et changement social* (1978); Amisol-Amiante, *Plus jamais ça*, by the CGT workers of Clermont-Ferrand (1977); Alain Geledan, *Les Syndicats* (1978); Christiane Barrier, *Le Combat ouvrier dans une entreprise de pointe* (1975).

Drop-outs and their successors:
Jacques Levy-Stringer, *Les Marginaux, une nouvelle force politique en France* (1977); Dominique Simonnet, *L'Ecologisme* (1979); F. M. Samuelson, *Il était une fois Libé . . .* (1979); Adret [a community], *Travailler deux heures par jour* (1977); Robert Francès, *La Satisfaction dans le travail et l'emploi* (1981); Jean de Cassagnac, *J'ai changé mon entreprise* (Cachan 1982); Yves Renaud, *200,000 emplois pour le qualité de la vie* (1977).

Small men and peasants:
A. Blasquez, *Gaston Lucas, Serrurier* (1976); Gérard Nicoud, *Les Dernières libertés* (1972); Joseph Klatzmann, *L'Agriculture française* (1978); Maryvonne Bodiguel, *Les Paysans face au progrès* (1975).

Communists:
André Harris and Alain de Sedouy, *Voyage à l'intérieur du parti communiste* (1974); Jean Montaldo, *La Mafia des syndicats* (1981); *Les Finances du P.C.F.* (1978); *La France Communiste* (1978); Frederic Bon, *Le Communisme en France* (1969); Fernand Dupuy, *Etre maire communiste* (1975); Roland Passevant, *Les Communistes au quotidien* (1981); J. Elleinstein, *Le P.C.* (1976).

Food:
Annie Fouquet, *Les Grandes tendances de la consommation alimentaire* (1976) (published by INSEE, other interesting issues, M33, M49, M68); L. Giard and P. Mayol, *L'Invention du quotidien, habiter, cuisiner* (1980); Marian Apfelbaum and Raymond Lepoutre, *Les Mangeurs inégaux* (1978); Georges et Jacqueline Bérenger, *Géographie gourmande de la France* (1978); Henri Dupin, *L'Alimentation des Français* (1978); Jacqueline Poelmans, *L'Europe et les consommateurs* (1978); J. C. Toutain, *La Consommation alimentaire en France de 1789–1964* (1971); L. Moulin, *L'Europe à table* (1975); Alan Davidson (ed), *Petit Propos Culinaires* (periodical); James de Coquet, *Lettre aux gourmets . . .* (1977); Robert Courtine, *The Hundred Glories of French Cooking* (1976); Paul Bocuse, *The New Cuisine* (1977); Anthony Blake and Quentin Crewe, *Great Chefs of France* (1978); F. Point, *Ma Gastronomie* (1969).

Clothes:
Pierre Bourdieu, *La Distinction, critique sociale du jugement* (1979), important on taste in general; Olivier Bardolle, *Mode in France: les dessous du prêt-a-porter* (1979); Axel Madsen, *Living for Design: The Yves Saint-Laurent Story* (NY 1979); London College of Fashion Library (press cuttings files); HEC, *L'Homme de la mode* (1967); International Wool Secretariat, *Fashion Marketing – the Next Decade* (1976); Bruno de Roselle, *La Crise de la mode* (1973); Ruth Lynam, *Paris Fashions* (1972); Cathérine Milinaire and Carol Troy, *Cheap Chic* (1975); Ernestine Carter, *The Changing World of Fashion* (1977); *Dior*, by Dior (1957); Ministère de l'Environnement, *Une Evaluation de la qualité de la vie* (Rouen) (3 vols, 1975–7).

Cinema:
Anne Marie Laulan, *Cinéma, presse et public* (1978); Pierre Sorlin, *Sociologie du cinéma* (1977); Jean-Pierre Jeancolas, *Le Cinéma des Français 1958–78* (1979); Gilles Marsolais, *L'Aventure du cinéma direct* (1974); René Bonnell, *Le Cinéma exploité* (1978), on the economics of the film business; Claude Chabrol, *Et Pourtant je tourne* (1976); Jean

Collet, *Le Cinema de François Truffaut* (1977); François Truffaut, *Les Films de ma vie* (1975); James Monaco, *Alain Resnais* (NY 1978); *The New Wave* (1976); Robert Benayoun, *Alain Resnais, arpenteur de l'imaginaire* (1980); Jean-Claude Zana, *Jean-Paul Belmondo* (1981); Richard Cannavo and Henri Quiquere, *Yves Montand* (1981); Simone Signoret, *Nostalgia isn't what it used to be* (English translation 1978); Tony Crawley, *The Films of Brigitte Bardot* (1975); Roger Vadim, *Memoirs of the Devil* (English translation 1976).

Other entertainments and hobbies:
Secrétariat d'Etat à la Culture, *Pratiques culturelles des Français* (1974); Euromonitor, *The Book Readership Survey* (1975); Jacques Brenner, *Histoire de la littérature française de 1940 à nos jours* (1978); Yves Olivier-Martin, *Histoire du roman populaire en France* (1980); J. J. Tourteau, *D'Arsène Lupin à San-Antonio: le roman policier français de 1900 à 1970* (1970); Colette Godard, *Le Théâtre depuis 1968* (1980); G. Enault, *Le Sport en France* (1979); Bernard Caviglioli, *Sports et adolescents* (1976); Michel Hidalgo, *Football en liberté* (1978); Rémy Pigois, *Cyclisme mon amour* (Sancoins, 1977); Pierre Micaux, *L'Homme et l'animal* (1980); François de Closets, *Le Système E.P.M.* (1980); Patrick Renault, *Les Bals en France* (1978); Claude Picaut, *Dossier T comme tiercé* (1975); Frank Lipsik, *Dictionnaire des variétés* (1977); Guy Lux, *Coups francs* (1977); Jacques Charpentreau, *Nouvelles veillées en chansons: des disques et des thèmes* (1970); Sophie Daumier, *Parle à mon coeur, ma tête est malade* (1979); C. Aznavour, *Aznavour par Aznavour* (1970).

Language and culture:
Ethnologie française, special issue on Pluralité des parlers en France, vol. 3, nos 3 and 4 (1973); David C. Gordon, *The French Language and National Identity* (The Hague 1978); Pierre Guiraud, *Patois et dialectes français* (3rd edition 1978); Robert Catherine, *Le Style administratif* (new edition 1979); Paul Ginistier and A. Maillet, *Culture et civilisation françaises* (1972); G. Poujol and R. Labourie, *Les Cultures populaires* (1979); P. H. Chombart de Lauwe, *La Culture et le pouvoir* (1975); Philippe Beneton, *Histoire de mots: culture et civilisation* (1975); J. D. Bredin and Jack Lang, *Eclats* (1978); J. Ben David and T. N. Clark, *Culture and its Creators* (Chicago 1977); Pierre Cabanne, *Le Pouvoir culturel sous la 5e republique* (1981); *Livres Hebdo* (11 Nov. 1980) on cultural reviews, with circulation statistics; Commissariat Générale du Plan, *Culture* (1976); Jacques Rigaud, *La Culture pour vivre* (1975); Sylvie Bouscasse, *Faut-il brûler les nouveaux philosophes?* (1978); *Etats généraux de la philosophie* (1979); *Le Doctrinal de sapience*

(cahiers d'enseignants de philosophie de l'histoire); Edith Kurzweil, *The Age of Structuralism* (NY 1980); C. Biegalski, *Les Intellectuels, la pensée anticipatrice* (1978); Regis Débray, *Le Pouvoir intellectuel en France* (1979); Hervé Hamon and Patrick Rotman, *Les Intellocrates* (1981); Claude Schnerb, *Je pense: manuel du petit intellectuel* (1972); Catherine Clement, *Vies et légendes de Jacques Lacan* (1981); Jean Daniel, *Le Temps qui reste: essai d'autobiographie professionnelle* (1973); C. Lemert, *French Sociology* (NY 1981); *L'Arc* (quarterly review); Stephen R. Graubard, *A New America?* (NY 1978) chapter by Pierre Nora on America and the French Intellectuals 325—337; Michel-Antoine Burnier and Patrick Rambaud, *Le Roland Barthes sans peine* (1978); François Bourricaud, *Le Bricolage idéologique: essai sur les intellectuels et les passions démocratiques* (1980); *Esprit* (periodical) many valuable special issues; Jean Dutourd, *Carnet d'un émigré* (1973); *Le Paradoxe du critique* (1981); *Les Choses sont comme elles sont* (1978).

Education:
W. D. Halls, *Education, Culture and Politics in Modern France* (Oxford 1976); OECD, *Educational Policy and Planning: France* (1972); Joel Bodin, *Vos enfants à l'école, au collège, au lycée* (1979); Torsten Husen, *International Study of Achievement in Mathematics: a comparison of twelve countries* (Stockholm, 2 vols 1967), criticized by W. D. Halls, in *Comparative education review* (NY 1968); Emmy Tedesco, *Des Familles parlent de l'école* (1979); L. Levy-Garbona, *Educational Expenditure in France, Japan and UK* (OECD 1977); Fritz Ringer, *Education and Society in Modern Europe* (Indiana 1977); *Le Monde de l'Education* (periodical, important articles in almost every issue); Max A. Ekstein, *Scientific Investigations in Comparative Education* (1969); Louis Legrand, *Pour une politique démocratique de l'éducation* (1977); J. Terny, *L'Ecole maternelle* (1975); Alice Delaunay, *Pédagogie de l'école maternelle* (1973); Liliane Lurçat, *Une Ecole maternelle* (1976); GEDREM, *Echec et maternelle: avant six ans, déjà la sélection?* (1980); Ph. Baillat, *A la Communale* (1976); John Downing, *Comparative Reading* (NY 1973); Marie-Madeleine Leloup, *Institutrice* (1976); Ida Berger, *Les Instituteurs d'une génération à l'autre* (1979); Comité National de l'Enseignement catholique, *L'Enseignement catholique face à l'avenir* (1977); Gérard Vincent, *Le Peuple lycéen* (1974); Nelcya Delanoe, *La Faute à Voltaire* (1972); Guy Marcy, *Moi, un prof* (1974); Joseph Ben David, *Centers of Learning: Britain, France, Germany, US* (NY 1977); Christopher Saunders, *Engineering in Britain, West Germany and France* (Sussex 1978); M. Fineston, *Engineering our Future* (1980); Italba S. Cohen, *Elusive Reform: The French Universities 1968–1978* (Boulder,

Colo. 1978); Alain Bienaymé, *Systems of Higher Education: France* (1975); *Comment Préparer Sciences-Po* (1979); Catherine Valabregne, *La Condition étudiante* (1970); M. Duffour et al., *L'Université de la crise au changement* (1978); Robert Francès, *L'Idéologie dans l'université: structure et determinants des attitudes sociales des étudiants* (1980); Jacqueline Brunet, Pierre Merlin et al., *Vincennes, ou le désir d'apprendre* (1979); Centre d'Etudes et de Recherches sur les qualifications (Cereq), *Les Universités et le marché du travail* (1977).

Youth:
Jean Rousselet, *La Jeunesse malade du savoir* (1980); Les Dossiers de l'étudiant: *Premier emploi* (1980); *Guide Neret des Carrières* (annual); Alain and Olivier Morel, *Le Drame des enfants martyrs* (1979); Claude Levy-Leboyer, *Etude psychologique de cadre de vie* (1977); Bernard Brizay, *Qu'est-ce qu'un chômeur?* (1979); Annick Percheron et al., *Les 10–16 ans et la politique* (1978); G. Mury and V. de Gaulejac, *Les Jeunes de la rue: ce qu'ils disent de leur vie quotidienne* (1977); François Cerutti, *Les Jeunes au boulot!* (1974); *Autrement, Jeunesse en rupture* (1975); Pierrette Sartin, *Jeunes au travail, jeunes sans travail* (1977); Patrick Huchet, *Guide des jeunes* (1978); Michel Seguier, *Le jeune responsable* (Toulouse 1974); Ida Berger, *Tiendront-ils? Etude sociologique sur les étudiants des deux bords du Rhin* (1970); Otto Klineberg, *Students, Values and Politics. A cross-cultural comparison* (NY 1979).

Immigrants:
INED, *Les Immigrés du Maghreb* (1977); Georges Tapinos, *L'Immigration étrangère en France 1946–73* (1975); *Pluriel* (journal on racial minorities and inter-ethnic relations); Catherine Wihtol de Wenden, Les Immigrés face à l'administration, in *Pluriel* (1980, no. 21); Jean Benoît, *Dossier E comme Esclaves: le dossier noir de l'immigration* (1980); Philippe de Balline, *Les Danseuses de la France* (1979) (on France overseas); Michel Michel, *Billy Francarabe* (1975); Tahar Ben Jelloun, *La plus haute des solitudes: misère affective et sexuelle d'émigrés nord-africains* (1977); François de Negroni, *Les Colonies de vacances* (1977); Maria Arondo, *Moi, la bonne* (1975); *Correspondance municipale*, no. 204, 'Les immigrés dans la commune' (special issue) (Jan. 1980); Don Dignan, Europe's Melting Pot (forthcoming article in *Ethnic Studies*); Juliette Minces, *Les Travailleurs étrangers en France* (1973).

Jews:
Luc Rosenzweig, *La Jeune France juive* (1980); André Harris and Alain de Sedouy, *Juifs et Français* (1979); Paule Darmon, *Baisse les yeux, Sarah* (1980).

Medicines:
Dr Norbert Bensaïd, *La Consultation* (1974); Charles Dayant, *Est-ce normal, docteur?* (1977); *La Santé des Français* (1981); Dr J. P. Escande, *Les Médecins* (1975); *Les Malades* (1977); Jean V. Manevy, *Une Médecine sans malades* (1979); D. J. Ruiz Gijon, 'Comparative study of drug consumption in Mediterranean countries', in *Clinical Pharmacological Evaluation in Drug Control*, Symposium held at Deidesheim, 26–9 October 1976 (Copenhagen 1977), 118–9; Simone Sandier, 'Les Soins médicaux en France et aux USA', *Consommation* (no. 1, Jan.-March 1981); Dr Gérard Debuigne, *Confessions d'un médecin de province* (1976); A. Mizrahi, *Micro-économie de la consommation médicale* (1978); *Autrement, La Santé à bras le corps* (1980); L. Stika, Differences in national drug prescribing patterns, in *Symposium on clinical pharmacological evaluation in Drug Control* (Copenhagen 1976); J. P. Dupuy and S. Karsenty, *L'Invasion pharmaceutique* (1974); J. C. Sournia, *Ces malades qu'on fabrique: médecine gaspillée* (1977); Jacques Dumont and Jean Latouche, *L'Hospitalisation malade du profit* (1977); Centre d'étude des revenus et des coûts, *Le coût de l'hospitalisation: comparaisons internationales* (1979); Henri Pradal, *Le Marché de l'angoisse* (1977); Jean Bernard, *L'Alcoolisme, rapport au président de la république* (1980); M. W. Everett, *Cross-Cultural Approaches to the Study of Alcohol* (The Hague 1976); Dominique Dallayrac, *Dossier alcoolisme* (1971); INSERM, *Les Lycéens et les drogues licites et illicites,* (ed. Françoise Davidson and Marie Choquet) (1980); *Gallup Report* July 1981 for American smoking habits; WHO, *The Epidemiology of Road Traffic Accidents* (Copenhagen 1976); *Archives des maladies professionnelles de médecine du travail* (1978—80) includes articles on tiredness, absenteeism, and speed of eating meals; 1976 on tobacco smoking; P. Pichot, 'Problèmes de mise en application des modèles de formation en psychopharmacologie', in Proceedings of the Tenth Congress of the Collegium Internationale Neuropsychopharmacologicum, Quebec 1976, ed. P. Deniker, under title *Neuro-Psychopharmacology* (Oxford 1978), 1.191 on different diagnoses and nomenclature; Jean Thuillier, *Les Dix ans qui ont changé la folie* (1981); Serge Moscovici, *La Psychanalyse, son image et son public* (new edition 1976); S. J. Rachman and Clare Philips, *Psychology and Medicine* (1978); Henri Baruk, *Des Hommes comme nous, mémoires d'un neuropsychiatre* (1976); Docteur X, préface de Aida Vasquez, *S.O.S. Psychanalyste! Des consultations par les ondes* (1976); Madeleine Laïk, *La Peur qu'on a* (1979); Maurice David Matisson, *Images des psychologues cliniciens* (1971); Françoise Dolto, *Dominique; analysis of an adolescent* (English translation, 1974); Dominique Frischer, *Les Analysés parlent* (1977); Laura

Nosmas, *Les Partages de minuit, histoire de S.O.S. Amitié* (1980); François Laplantine, *La Médecine populaire dans les campagnes françaises aujourd'hui* (1978); Jean-Pierre Desmond and Pierre Goulene, *Enquête chez les voyants* (1978); Jean Duvignaud and J. P. Corbeau, *Les Tabous des Français* (1981); *La Banque des rêves* (1980); Jeanne Favret-Saada, *Les Mots, la mort, les sorts: la sorcellerie dans le Bocage* (1977); Denis Langlois, *Les Dossiers noirs du suicide* (1976); F. Davidson, *Morbidité et mortalité par suicide* (Le Vesinet 1975); Jacqueline Aimé, *La Peur d'aimer* (1978); Elie Grigner and J. C. Faur, *Guide des dangers et des risques quotidiens* (1980), a manual for those who may have omitted to worry as much as they could do.

Women:
Naty Garcia Guadilla, *Libération des Femmes, le M.L.F.* (1981); *F Magazine, Les Nouvelles femmes* (1979); Jean Rabant, *Histoire des féminismes français* (1978); Maite Albistur and Daniel Armogathe, *Histoire du féminisme français* (2 vols, 1977); Evelyne Sullerot, *Le Fait féminin* (1978); Albert Brimo, *Les Femmes françaises face au pouvoir politique* (1975); Jeanne Cressanges, *La Vraie vie des femmes commence à 40 ans* (1979); J. Z. Gicle, *Women, Roles and Status in Eight Countries* (NY 1977); Guillemette de Sairigne, *Les Françaises face au chômage* (1978); Catherine Valabrègue, *Eux, les hommes* (1976); Claude Michel, *Toutes les mêmes?* (1979); Colette Piat, *La République des misogynes* (1981); EEC, *European Men and Women in 1978: A Comparison of their Attitudes to some of the Problems facing Society* (Brussels 1979); Pascal Lainé, *La Femme et ses images* (1974); Menie Grégoire, *Telle que je suis* (1976); Françoise d'Eaubonne, *Le Féminisme ou la mort* (1974); Jean Mauduit, *La Révolte des femmes* (1971); F. Giroud, *Ce que je crois* (1978); *Si Je mens* (1972, English translation 1974), *Cent mesures pour les femmes* (1976); Gisèle Halimi, *La cause des femmes* (1973); *Questions féministes* (review); *Choisir* (review); *Vivre au feminin* (*Les Cahiers français* no. 171, 1975); Anne Pluvinage, *L'Image de la femme dans les magazines féminins, Revue Générale* (Brussels) (Sept. 1975, 21—31); M. and A. Guillois, *Les Femmes marrantes* (1975).

Old age:
P. Chaunu et al., *La France ridée* (1979); Commissariat Générale du Plan, *Vieillir demain* (1980); Bernard Ennuyer and Michele Troude, *Il y a toujours des hospices de vieux* (1977); M. Dacher and M. Weinstein, *Histoire de Louise, Des Vieillards en hospice* (1979); Carmen Bernand, *Les Vieux vont mourir à Nanterre* (1978), on the most awful of all old people's homes; Leon Schwartzenberg and Pierre Viansson-Ponté, *Changer la mort* (1977); P. Ariès, *L'Homme devant la mort* (1977).

Religion:

Jean Puyo and Patrice Van Eersel, *Voyage à l'intérieur de l'église catholique* (1977); *Radioscopie de l'Eglise de France* (1980); G. Michelat and M. Simon, *Classe, religion et comportement politique* (1977); J. Gritte and A. Rousseau, *Trois Enquêtes sur les Catholiques* (1977); Claude Gault and Noel Choux, *Ces Chrétiens du bout du siècle* (1979); Paul Maire, *Des Prêtres parlent* (1979); L. A. Elchinger, Bishop of Strasbourg, *Je plaide pour l'homme* (1976); Janine Garrisson-Estèbe, *L'Homme Protestant* (1980).

Americanization:

Jacques Thibau, *La France Colonisée* (1980); Michael McGiffert, *The Character of Americans* (Homewood, Illinois 1970); Michel Crozier, *Le Mal américain* (1980); Ted Morgan (formerly Sanche de Gramont), *On Becoming American* (Boston 1978). Pierre J. B. Bénichou, *Eddy Mitchell* (1977); S. Hoffman, 'La Nation: pour quoi faire' in *Mélanges en l'honneur de Raymond Aron* (1971) 2. 303–65.

Historical background:

Theodore Zeldin, *France 1848–1945* (Oxford 1973–7), paperback edition in 5 vols (Oxford 1980–81) entitled *Ambition and Love, Intellect and Pride, Taste and Corruption, Politics and Anger, Anxiety and Hypocrisy,* each with guide to further reading.

Finally, I should like to record my deep thanks to all those who have been kind enough to discuss their lives and opinions with me; to all the journalists and investigators whose published histories of individuals have been a most valuable complementary source; to Dr G. Ignazi and Nelly Crété of the Anthropometric Research Group at the Paris faculty of Medicine; to many others, who have assisted me in making contacts; to Gérard Jourd'hui, Jean Estèbe, Jacques and Angharad Pimpaneau, Annette Lugand, Florence Petry and Monique Glasberg, Edith McMorran and Elizabeth Stevens; to the cartoonists who have allowed me to use their works as illustrations; to Christopher Kenyon; to Peter Montagnon, Christopher Ralling, Ron Johnson and Gill Barnes; to Christopher MacLehose, Hilary Davies, Ron Clark and Marian Morris, and, above all, to my wife.

Index

KODANSHA GLOBE

International in scope, this series offers distinguished books that explore the lives, customs, and mindsets of peoples and cultures around the world.

Other Kodansha Globe titles of interest

SCENT: *The Essential and Mysterious Powers of Smell*
by Annick Le Guérer Le Guérer investigates scent and its relationship to myth, psychology, religion, ritual, sex, seduction, and healing practices. "*Scent* is to smelling what *Moby Dick* is to whaling." —Benedict Cosgrove, *San Francisco Chronicle*
($13, 1-56836-024-X)

SEX AND SUITS: *The Evolution of Modern Dress*
by Anne Hollander Nominated for the 1994 National Book Critics Circle Award in Criticism, *Sex and Suits* explores how clothes have been transformed through the centuries. "Entrancing, vivacious . . . [a] dazzling, whirlwind account of Western costume." —John Updike, *The New Yorker*
($13, 1-56836-101-7)

SARAJEVO, EXODUS OF A CITY
by Dzevad Karahasan A Bosnian Muslim intellectual's "biography" of Sarajevo, evoking this cosmopolitan city amid siege and civil war. "A must read for every contemporary person." —*Die Markische Allgemeine*
($10, 1-56836-057-6)

PROPHETS WITHOUT HONOUR: *Freud, Kafka, Einstein, and Their World*
by Frederic V. Grunfeld "There has rarely been . . . so extraordinarily gifted a group as [these] German-Jewish thinkers." —Alfred Kazin
($15, 1-56836-107-6)

Please contact your local bookseller for these and other Kodansha titles, or mail your order with payment to:

KODANSHA
Mail Order Department
c/o The Putnam Publishing Group
P.O. Box 12289
Newark, NJ 07101-5289

All orders must be accompanied by payment in full (*check or money order payable to KODANSHA, in U.S. funds only, no cash or C.O.D.s*), including shipping & handling charges ($3.50 for the first book, $.75 for each additional book). New York State residents please include applicable sales tax. Allow 3–6 weeks for delivery. Prices are subject to change without notice.

When ordering by credit card call **1-800-788-6262**.